Decentering the Regime

WITHDRAWN

Jeffrey W. Rubin

DECENTERING

 the **REGIME**

Ethnicity, Radicalism, and Democracy

in Juchitán, Mexico

Duke University Press Durham and London 1997

© 1997 Duke University Press

All rights reserved   Printed in the United

States of America on acid-free paper ∞

Designed by Cherie Westmoreland

Typeset in Weiss with Franklin Gothic display

by Keystone Typesetting, Inc.

Library of Congress Cataloging-in-Publication Data
Rubin, Jeffrey W.
Decentering the regime : ethnicity, radicalism, and
democracy in Juchitán, Mexico / by Jeffrey W. Rubin.
p.   cm.
Includes bibliographical references.
ISBN 0-8223-2050-9 (cloth : alk. paper). —
ISBN 0-8223-2063-0 (pbk. : alk. paper)
1. Juchitán de Zaragoza (Mexico)—Politics and
government.   2. Central-local government
relations—Mexico.   3. Zapotec Indians—Politics and
government.   4. Coalición Obrera Campesina
Estudiantil del Istmo (Mexico).   I. Title.
JS2120.J84R8 1998
323.1'7274—dc21   97-13515

To my parents

Bernice and Sheldon Rubin

and in memory of my grandparents

Ira and Esther Brand

Contents

Acknowledgments

I would like to thank my wife, Shoshana Sokoloff, for traveling to Juchitán with me. I would also like to thank the many Juchitecas who,
impressed by her stature, patted her forearms admiringly with comments
of "¡Que guapa!," thus welcoming her to her own research on midwifery.
We both owe an enormous debt of gratitude to midwives, market women,
merchants, campesinos, workers, teachers, and their families. In Juchitán
as in the nearby town of La Venta, numerous families accepted us into
their courtyards and their lives, sharing meals and celebrations, recounting political events and reflecting on their significance, teaching us to
speak Zapotec, and asking after our own families and past experiences. It
was these conversations, in their straightforwardness and their complexity, that brought us friendship and pleasure and enabled us to learn about
Juchitán.

Several foundations and research institutions contributed to making
my research possible. The Tinker Foundation, through a grant to the
Committee on Latin American and Iberian Studies at Harvard University,
funded an early summer of research in 1983, including my first trip to
Juchitán. The twelve months I lived in Juchitán during 1985 and 1986, as
well as three additional months in Oaxaca and Mexico City, were funded
by dissertation research grants from the Social Science Research Council,
the Doherty Foundation, and the Inter-American Foundation. The Center for International Studies at MIT, where I was a Visiting Scholar during
1990–91, offered a supportive setting for discussion and writing. The
Center for U.S.–Mexican Studies at the University of California, San
Diego, through a Doctoral Research Fellowship for the spring of 1987
and a Post-Doctoral Research Fellowship for 1993–94, provided a rich
environment for analysis of Mexico, social movements, and social theory.
I am particularly grateful to the Center's then-Director, Wayne Cornelius, for fostering such an exceptional research institution, and to the

Center's skilled and ever-helpful staff for making it run so warmly and smoothly. Finally, an Amherst College Research Grant enabled me to return to Juchitán with translations of parts of my dissertation in 1993.

I leave unnamed, for reasons of political discretion as well as my inability to mention everyone, the many individuals and families in Juchitán who spoke to me about local culture and politics. I owe special thanks, however, to Serafina Luna de Pineda and the late Luis Pineda, who welcomed me into their home during my second summer of research in Juchitán, providing me with something of my own local courtyard and family overflowing with opinions and stories. The late Doña Joaquina Peral, who was then eighty-one years old and just beginning to ease up on her midwifery practice, offered care and conversation that enriched every aspect of our lives in Juchitán. I also owe special thanks to Sabino Jiménez, who responded to my earliest visit to the neighborhood health center in La Venta with an immediate willingness to recount his own and his neighbors' rich history of political activism and to encourage my future visits and research.

In Mexico City and Oaxaca, as in Juchitán, I was aided by numerous individuals who responded to my inquiries, listened to my ideas, and offered their own interpretations and advice. Although some were skeptical, and others cautionary, many of them found value in the notion of a North American seeking to learn from and tell a Mexican story. Their wariness pressed me to question my own project in difficult and creative ways, while their support made possible the commitments, discoveries, and interactions with others on which this work has been based. Among many, I would like especially to thank Adriana López Monjardin for sharing her ideas about Juchitán on numerous occasions, and Lilian Alvarez de Testa for welcoming my family into her own and for her abiding and generous friendship, intellect, and insight.

Two North American colleagues helped me carry out important aspects of this research. Jonathan Fox provided a home in Mexico City when I was beginning my work, and his ongoing generosity of ideas since then has enriched my understanding of grassroots democracy and democratization. Lynn Stephen, along with similarly rich and generous support, offered the quite concrete benefit of doing her anthropological research in the Oaxaca Valley town of Teotitlán del Valle during the same time that I lived in Juchitán. In exchange for the fish that I brought from the coast, she patiently interpreted the process of speaking, listening, being silent, and being met with silence that I was experiencing in Juchitán. And she assured me, with complete accuracy, that the relationships I was building with Juchitecos on the basis of personal conversation and shared daily experience would withstand the distances and distrusts of political leaders. I also owe a special debt to Howard Campbell for the excellent work he has done on Juchitán's cultural past and present and for generously sharing that work with me.

The members of my dissertation committee—Sidney Verba, Terry Karl, and John Womack Jr.—supported, encouraged, and inspired this project in all its stages. I am particularly grateful to John Womack for the many hours he spent talking with me about Mexico. My ongoing interest in the details of Mexican regional history, as well as my hunches about the workings of Mexican politics, took shape in the course of these conversations. The opportunity to present parts of this work to receptive and demanding audiences aided me in the course of writing and revising as well. I am grateful to the participants in the Latin America seminars at Yale, Harvard, Stanford, and Berkeley, the U.S.-Mexico and Ethnic Studies seminars at the University of California, San Diego, and the conferences on Latin American Labor History (SUNY Stony Brook, 1992), Local Politics and Democratization (UNAM, Mexico City, 1996), and Cultures of Politics/Politics of Cultures (State University of Campinas, Brazil, 1996). Parts of chapters 1 and 8 appeared in "Decentering the Regime: Culture and Regional Politics in Mexico," in the *Latin American Research Review* (Volume 31, Number 3, 1996) and are reprinted here by permission of the publishers.

Among the many colleagues and friends who have offered comments, criticism, discussion, and encouragement are Ana Alonso, Arturo Alvarado, Sonia Alvarez, Amrita Basu, Leigh Binford, Barry Carr, David Collier, Barbara Corbett, Ann Craig, Evalina Dagnino, Martin Diskin, Lawrence Douglas, Arturo Escobar, Joe Foweraker, Judy Frank, Deborah Gewertz, Ginny Gordon, Fran Hagopian, Judith Adler Hellman, Ellen Herman, Alan Houston, Jill Irvine, Mimi Keck, Ricardo Márquez, Judith Matloff, David Myhre, Wil Pansters, Miriam Pawel, Eric Poggenpohl, Elena Poniatowska, Mary Roldán, Sara Roy, Benigno Sánchez-Eppler, Karen Sánchez-Eppler, Austin Sarat, Enrique Semo, Helen Shapiro, Ilan Stavans, Wendy Woodson, and Aníbal Yañez. Vivienne Bennett has been a continuing source of friendship, intellectual collaboration, and practical advice. Gil Joseph and Daniel Nugent provided encouragement and editorial guidance that improved both the content of this book and the experience of completing it. Ken Wissoker, Richard Morrison, and Jean Brady at Duke University Press guided me through the publication process with expert care and thoughtfulness. Carlos Armayo produced the index with skill and thoughtfulness. Leslie Salzinger deeply influenced the theoretical course of this book, as well as provided friendship and support. I owe much of whatever is clear and insightful here to our continuing and always animated discussions, as well as to her skillful editing of the entire manuscript, for which I am grateful.

I could not have carried out this long project without several sets of relationships that preceded it and continued throughout its course. Many of the families of Marquefave, France, and the Bellia and Chelle families in particular, welcomed me into their homes in the course of research for my undergraduate senior thesis. Their willingness to talk about their histories and question me about mine began to teach me how to speak and, especially, how to listen in worlds very different from my own. Friends and family members have been generous in their encouragement, as well as their patience in the face of long hours of research and writing. My parents and grandparents made possible all of this work through their ever-present love and support. My brothers offered warmth and wit throughout. My mother-in-law, Miriam Sokoloff, generously provided child care, meals, and friendship during key periods of writing. Jacqueline Osherow's comments pressed me simultaneously to see my work from new perspectives and follow my own hunches and convictions. Laura Rocker and Nathan Levitan have shared meals and discussion, providing comfort and consolation with unfailing warmth whenever I most needed it.

Shoshana Sokoloff has offered encouragement and enthusiasm throughout this project, joining me in field research and pressing me to take my work in the directions that matter to me most. Her advice and insight shaped every aspect of my research and writing. Several years ago our daughter Emma aptly expressed the relationship that she and her sister, Hannah, have had to my work. When Emma was two and I was completing my dissertation, she came upstairs to my study one evening, surprised me with a laughing shriek, and announced, "I'll sit in the chair, Daddy. You work." I look forward to many more such interventions.

Introduction

In the southern Mexican city of Juchitán (hoo-chee-*tahn*), Indian peasants who take legal action to protect their land can speak Zapotec in City Hall. Teenagers from poor neighborhoods write poetry in Zapotec at the Casa de la Cultura, join printmaking workshops, and read plays by Brecht. Women in Juchitán maintain standards of beauty dramatically different from Mexican national standards, reveling in fat bodies and adorning themselves with brightly colored patterns and embroidery that defy Western norms of color and style. Such norms are also challenged by a flourishing alternative male gender role, with males in varying arrangements of women's dress and body forms dancing with one another at fiestas and playing prominent public roles in work and ritual.

In the 1980s, Juchitán's peasant economy of maize production survived government-sponsored agricultural projects and urban commercialization. The sprawling Zapotec market, consisting of hundreds of women vendors, continues to dominate the space and economy of the center of the city and to constitute the most important local network of information. Zapotec midwives deliver the majority of babies born in Juchitán, despite the presence of doctors, and the descendants of Lebanese immigrants wear traditional Zapotec dress and encourage their university-educated children to continue Zapotec traditions. All together, the society forged by Juchitecos provides an example of what postcolonial "development" might have looked like if indigenous and Western cultures had met on more equal terms: not necessarily a rejection of the "Western" or "modern," nor a reinforcing of geographic and cultural borders between local and outside, but rather the creation of multiple modernities by means of non-Western knowledge, language, and style.[1]

A Zapotec political movement, the Coalition of Workers, Peasants, and Students of the Isthmus, or COCEI (ko-*say*), has governed Juchitán since 1989. Virtually without precedent among indigenous and leftist

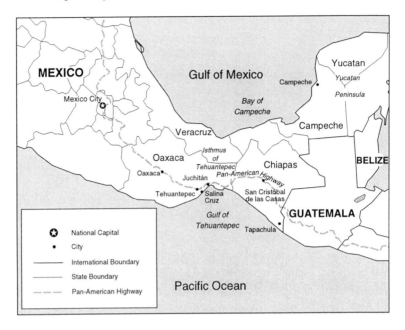

political organizations, COCEI is recognized by the Mexican government as a legitimate and autonomous political force.[2] It administers social-welfare funds for the city of one hundred thousand with widely acknowledged efficiency, promotes Zapotec language and culture, and mobilizes poor people around pressing economic issues. COCEI secured this right to govern through fifteen years of militant grassroots activism, during which it faced regime-sanctioned killings and military occupation. Since 1989, in contrast, Mexican authorities have respected the results of democratic elections in Juchitán, invested in municipal services, and curbed human-rights abuses, outcomes that are particularly noteworthy in light of decades of polarized conflict in nearby Chiapas and Central America. COCEI's current relationship with the Mexican government constitutes a unique model for democratic politics that includes ongoing negotiation over cultural representation and economic justice. Such an empowerment of Indians, including cultural autonomy, relative economic well-being, and political democratization, is without parallel in contemporary Latin America. It is a rare affirmation of an indigenous culture's ability to sustain and reinvent itself and to appropriate the outside from a position of equality and power.

COCEI's success in mounting continuous challenges to local and national authorities in the face of violence occurred in large part because Juchitecos made their neighborhoods, workplaces, and fiestas into sites of intense political discussion, redefining the meanings and alliances of their culture in the course of recurring daily activities. It was this innovative cultural elaboration that enabled COCEI to secure its power even as neoliberal economic restructuring and the demobilization of popular movements dominated policymaking elsewhere in Mexico and Latin America. Like the Zapotec political movements and cultural practices that preceded it in Juchitán, COCEI forged alternatives to the discourses of nationalism and economic development through which outsiders characterized the city and sought to intervene there. By making use of these local capacities for cultural resistance to construct an organized movement and gain formal political power, COCEI brought about an enduring form of regional democratization.

This democracy includes, but is not limited to, free and fair electoral competition and the transfer of municipal power. COCEI's actions in Juchitán also contributed to forms of voice and autonomy in such locations as churches, marketplaces, teachers' unions, municipal offices, and family courtyards. As a result, poor Juchitecos in the 1990s have greater voice, and can hold those with power more accountable, in more arenas of their lives, than they could in the 1960s and 1970s. At the same time, COCEI as a movement has exhibited numerous ambiguities and contradictions concerning such matters as violence, historical representation, internal democracy, and gender relations. COCEI gained its force and its ability to threaten through the capacity of Juchitecos to sustain multiple internal disjunctions in these arenas. In turn, these disjunctions simultaneously strengthened and limited the movement and empowered and harmed Juchitecos themselves.

I went to Juchitán for the first time in August 1983. COCEI's first municipal administration had just been thrown out of office by the state government, and twenty-five thousand peasants and workers gathered in the town square to defend the Ayuntamiento Popular, the People's Government. Juchitecas (women of Juchitán) surrounded City Hall with their fists in the air, dressed in traditional embroidered blouses and gold jewelry, with red confetti streaming over their thickly braided hair. Everything they wore was outlined, ribboned, or bannered in red, the color of COCEI. In raucous, angry voices, they chanted slogans in defense of

COCEI and its mayor, Leopoldo de Gyves, and vilified the official Mexican party, the Institutionalized Revolutionary Party (PRI). On some of the younger women, T-shirts compared Juchitán to London, Paris, and Rome.

At sunset, screeching black birds circled the town square before settling into the trees. Middle-aged and elderly Zapotec women sat in twos and threes on benches poring over the coverage of local events in national newspapers. Slogans painted on sheets covered City Hall with protests against the impeachment of the People's Government and the rapidly increasing cost of living, as well as with defenses of labor unions, peasant grievances, and COCEI itself. Traditional Zapotec songs and revolutionary songs in Zapotec and Spanish flooded the town square from loudspeakers attached to City Hall, much as they had filled the city's courtyards during the preceding months from the radio station of the Ayuntamiento Popular, until it was jammed by private businesspeople and government authorities.

The leaders of COCEI remained in City Hall, refusing to obey the state government's eviction orders. Prominent artists and intellectuals arrived from Mexico City to show support for the radical movement. National and international journalists gathered accounts from local authorities of the PRI and COCEI and took note of the intense heat, the sprawling market, and the striking girth and boldness of the indigenous women. Armed military vans patrolled the streets, watching out over the central plaza and transmitting the palpable threat of violent attack. Local residents glided up and down the newly repaired stairs of City Hall, along fresh concrete floors and walls, avoiding the unfinished portions, explaining to reporters how COCEI, with volunteer labor, had reconstructed the building after years of official neglect. Juchiteco men in simple, store-bought shirts guarded the entrance to City Hall with sticks, while just inside women stirred large vats of coffee and stew. Truckloads of supporters arrived from surrounding neighborhoods and towns for the afternoon and night shifts. Rosario Ibarra, a founder of the national human-rights movement, addressed the local crowd and the national audience with an impassioned speech defending the autonomy of the city. Juchitecas rang the enormous bell on the balcony of City Hall to gather supporters and to respond to the enthusiasm of the demonstrators already there.

Juchitán offered a dramatic example of the possibility of ordinary people challenging domination and exploitation and getting a better deal. Juchitecos were transforming the face of their city and daring the army to throw them out. They were collecting money and signing referenda, as well as securing agricultural credit, payment of minimum wages and benefits, and long-absent municipal services. Juchitecos were literally speaking a language (Isthmus Zapotec) that was foreign to their government, a language rich in puns, evocations of local history, and fidelity to local experiences and needs. In so doing, they were continuing what had by then been ten years of innovative, multifaceted challenges to the state and federal governments, to regional business elites, and to those Juchitecos and outsiders who sought to subordinate Zapotec culture to a national, Mexican one.

Juchitecos' ability to organize and sustain a radical political movement, along with the successes and limits they encountered, grew out of a century-long history of negotiation of political rule, a process itself embedded in the construction and reconfiguration of ethnic identity, gender relations, and economic production. These reconfigurations occurred at the intersection of regional and national political projects, and they linked everyday forms of innovation and resistance to broader and more formal processes of political conflict and transformation. As a result, the process of democratization in Juchitán, as well as the meanings and daily significance of democracy itself, were shaped by such matters as the place of Zapotec culture in Mexican nationalism, reformist critiques of agricultural development projects, and the ability of an Indian movement to manipulate threats of violence.

The chapters that follow will set out the links between present and past, region and nation, and everyday resistance and political mobilization that constitute power relations in Juchitán. By analyzing the internal complexity of what appear from the outside as coherent and homogeneous political phenomena, they will challenge conventional understandings of grassroots movements, regimes, and power. This analysis will show that the Mexican regime is not the holder and exerciser of hegemonic power that has been described in the literature,[3] but rather one partial and changing component in the complex set of power relations within which ordinary Mexicans live. Similarly, a strong and mobilized political movement transforms politics not because it embodies or moves toward a homogeneous class or ethnic consciousness, but because it balances contrasting practices and representations.

In the course of twelve months of field research in Juchitán, I conducted extensive interviews with a wide range of Juchitecos, including politicians, public officials, journalists, midwives, market women, teachers, businesspeople, workers, and peasants.[4] I gathered published accounts of politics, economic development, and cultural activities in the region, much of whose history remains unwritten, as well as government data and studies. In addition, I consulted local newspapers, finding a particularly rich source in the Juchitán weekly newspaper *El Satélite*, published from 1968 to 1979. During an additional two months of fieldwork, I interviewed politicians, officials, and grassroots activists in Oaxaca and Mexico City.

Most of my daily activity in Juchitán consisted of participant observation in family life, work, ritual, and public events, largely among poor peasants and workers, who generally did not relate linear political narratives or present evaluations of political strategies and tactics. In response to my questions about political activism, poor Juchitecos spoke of why or how they believed in COCEI (or why they didn't), who in their family supported the movement, how economic conditions affected their jobs and land, which ritual would be celebrated next, who married whom. My daily fieldwork consisted of discerning and following up on the oblique connections among these details and anecdotes. Often, this involved something as obvious and as complex as being invited to move from the front of a market stall to the personal space behind it, and being told, as a prelude to a detailed personal interview, "People came by here and said you were a spy. Are you a spy?" Alongside this complicated openness to talking with outsiders on the part of most Juchitecos, COCEI leaders refused to discuss their beliefs and strategies with me or with other researchers. However, I found many clues to their views in their actions and in the observations of others, particularly sympathetic leftist critics of COCEI. I also learned about COCEI leaders' views from their public speeches, their published documents and accounts, and occasional private and public airings of disagreement.

Through the incidents and conversations of my fieldwork, as well as through Juchitecos' insistence on the centrality of their culture in their lives, I learned to perceive the connections between daily life and politics that lie at the center of radical political mobilization in Juchitán. From combinations of silence and speech, I learned that the passion and solidarity of COCEI did not grow out of well-defined objectives, strategies, and achievements, but rather were embedded in complex, nonlinear political and cultural experiences. In the chapters that follow, I make use of this insight to develop a variety of different ways of analyzing links between culture and politics, as well as between everyday and broader forms of resistance. In chapter 1, I examine state-centered analyses of Mexican politics, along with conceptions of power as centralized and homogeneous. I indicate ways in which theorizing about Mexico could have incorporated approaches to domination that identify dynamic, cultural dimensions to power and locate power in multiple arenas outside of both formal politics and national regimes. Chapter 2 examines the relationship between ethnicity and power in Juchitán, arguing that recurring tropes of barbarism, confrontation, and rebelliousness have played a series of roles in mediating Juchitán's relationship with outside authorities and structuring class relations within the city since the nineteenth century. Thus, for example, the relative absence of conflict between Juchitán and the outside during mid-twentieth-century years of boss rule, when Zapotec elites claimed cultural and economic predominance, shaped a *pueblo* (people) that could later remember, foster, and come to wield discourses of nineteenth-century violence and barbarism—against the outside *and* against the indigenous elite.

Chapter 3 analyzes this mid-twentieth-century peace, identifying forms of Zapotec culture and Juchiteco politics that were neither radical nor oppositional, but that established capacities for autonomous, locally initiated activity. Subsequently, a combination of national and regional economic and cultural changes played a key role in transforming the alliances of this regional "domain of sovereignty" (Chatterjee 1993). During the 1960s, discussed in chapter 4, Zapotec elites sought to rework regional power relations on their own terms by strengthening their control over land and competing in municipal elections. They wanted to bring more economic and cultural influences from the outside into Juchitán, while maintaining the legitimacy of their own leadership.

Yet they were unable to successfully defend their claim to leadership. By the late 1960s, Zapotec culture had itself become politicized, as Zapotec artists and intellectuals incorporated the critical national and international perspectives of that decade into their own production. Ongoing tropes of barbarism and difference central to Juchiteco identity took on new, explicitly critical political dimensions at the same time that ordinary people's lives were being disrupted by development projects and commercialization. Simultaneously, the meanings and desirability of democracy were publicly debated in Juchitán, with these debates marked by intersections of ethnic identity, economic change, and civic politics. In this context, elite goals of economic enrichment and political leadership were challenged by new articulations of Zapotec identity and by increasingly radical economic and political critiques.

Chapter 5 analyzes the overlapping modalities of violence, negotiation, culture, and electoral politics out of which COCEI constituted itself and engaged in political struggle. It conveys the dynamics of COCEI's activities and its relationships with Juchitecos through partially chronological, partially parallel accounts of the ways people came to join COCEI, the tactics of direct-action mobilizations, local debates about electoral participation, Juchitecos' responses to violence, and the secrecy surrounding negotiations with regime officials. In keeping with my understanding of the place of political activism in Juchitecos' lives and the nature of mobilization itself, I explain this process as the sum of "events that were essentially incomplete, uncertain as to their outcome and unclear in the role played by participants" (Smith 1989, 228).

In contrast, chapter 6 presents a more conventional chronological and analytic narrative of the 1980s, a period of electoral politics, mass mobilization, repression, and reform in Juchitán. Here, because events followed a public political calendar and national prominence brought numerous chroniclers, political and cultural experiences and their representation were markedly different from those of the 1970s. In analyzing this decade, chapter 6 focuses on cultures of politics, where politics is understood largely in its formal sense—elections, parties, and policymaking, along with the actors and processes that undertake these activities. Indeed, in the course of the 1980s, formal political matters were reshaped in significant and enduring ways in Juchitán, as COCEI moved from suffering violent repression to competing in elections and governing as a recognized leftist political force. Chapter 6 shows how the characteristics of the resulting democracy in Juchitán were shaped by the Juchiteco domain of sovereignty and its unraveling, by changing Mexican national politics, and by the fragmented pathways of conflict between regime and opposition since the 1970s.

The character of Juchiteco democracy also reflected the intertwined coherence and fragmentation of both COCEI and the Mexican regime. Chapters 7 and 8 draw on the internal, cultural complexity of COCEI, and on histories of other Mexican regions and towns, respectively, to return to the theoretical arguments about politics and power set out in chapter 1. By applying the extensive historical analysis carried out in the body of the book to two distinct locations of politics—one a regional political movement, the other a national political system—these chapters show how a decentered approach to power illuminates both the origins and meanings of regional democratization and the workings of domination and resistance in Mexico.

1

Theorizing Power and
Regimes

The prevailing state-centered approach to Mexican politics attributes the rise of radical movements in the 1970s to the breakdown of a cohesive and successful form of political control, state corporatism, and explains their subsequent trajectories in terms of regime efforts at negotiation, co-optation, and repression. In contrast, my research in Juchitán revealed enduring regional counterweights to national power in Mexico, circuitous pathways of historical change, and locations of power outside of formal politics, in people's experiences of culture and daily life. Furthermore, while COCEI's strength has generally been attributed to homogeneous class and ethnic consciousness (Gutiérrez 1981; López Monjardin 1983b), my immersion in family courtyards highlighted the coexistence of ambiguous and contradictory beliefs and experiences within the radical movement.

These observations suggest an alternative understanding of power and politics in Mexico. Since the 1970s, accounts of politics in postrevolutionary Mexico have assumed that the ongoing domination has resulted from centralized power that was transmitted outward through corporatist mechanisms, replicating hegemony through a combination of skillful management and efficient coercion. Even as scholars emphasize the breakdown of corporatism and the complexity of current Mexican politics, they continue to codify the past according to this state-centered analysis and to view the present through its lens. Similarly, analyses of regime change throughout Latin America have understood power as something that is amassed and brokered at the center among explicitly political actors. Such approaches, rooted in state theory and political economy, view stability (understood as regime endurance) as resulting from particular, routinized patterns of centralized control over discrete societal forces.[1]

In contrast to state-centered and center-centered conceptions of power, theorists such as Gramsci (1971), Williams (1977), and Foucault (1990 [1976]) argue that continuing domination results from contestation and change in multiple arenas, including numerous locations outside of both center and formal politics. Williams, for example, argues that hegemony "has to be seen as more than the simple transmission of an (unchanging) dominance." Rather, "it has continually to be renewed, recreated, defended, and modified. It is also continually resisted, limited, altered, challenged by pressures not at all its own" (112). Seen in this light, what appears to be ongoing and unchanging domination—the endurance of states based on inequality and coercion in Latin America, for example—is the overall result not of an all-controlling center, or of particular structures of political bargaining and rule, but of numerous, changing forms and locations of domination and resistance. In Foucault's words, " 'Power,' insofar as it is permanent, repetitious, inert, and self-reproducing, is simply the over-all effect that emerges from all these mobilities" (93).

As one of the preeminent enduring regimes in the world today,[2] Mexico provides a compelling case study of the nature and location of power. By examining one Mexican region, its political upheavals and rebellions, and its relationship with the central government, I argue that social scientists in the 1970s were right to characterize the postrevolutionary regime as hegemonic and authoritarian—Mexico is indeed a site of enduring forms of inequality and domination—but wrong about what hegemony is, and thus about what upholds domination and how it may be resisted. In constructing a state-centered understanding of Mexican politics, social scientists have misunderstood both empirical evidence and the nature of power. Through an analysis of the history of Juchitán and the emergence of COCEI, I demonstrate the ways in which politics, culture, and the dynamics of historical change in this region diverge strikingly from their claims. In the final chapter, I extend this analysis to other regions of Mexico, showing that histories of northern, central, and southern parts of the country similarly challenge the state-centered approach.

In contrast to the way Mexican politics has generally been described, the presence of the state has been uneven and incomplete across both geography and political life. Hegemony has taken shape differently in different locations and thus changed or unraveled differently as well, with cultural practices of ethnicity, language, gender, religion, and civic identity playing key roles in its dynamics. Indeed, the founding event of modern Mexican hegemony, the state-building undertaken by President Lázaro Cárdenas in the 1930s, was not a thoroughgoing and homogeneous national transformation, as it has been portrayed (Hamilton 1982). Rather, Cárdenas's political efforts resulted in the simultaneous forging of a multitude of regional arrangements—each a distinct combination of bargains, coercions, and alliances—that together reinforced the power of the center in broadly similar ways. These regional arrangements included, but were not limited to, an institutional presence of the central state. Because the sets of phenomena that were woven together and the ways they were joined varied considerably across the country, different regions experienced distinct processes of development and change. Similarly, different domains of social and cultural life proceeded according to their own dynamics, in interaction with geographically based processes. As a result, while there is an unusually strong and efficient state apparatus in Mexico, it is a mistake to view Mexican politics primarily through the lens of the breakdown and restructuring of national organizational forms. Rather, the Mexican state and regime should be seen as parts of a complex and changing center[3] that coexists with, and is indeed constituted through and embedded in, the diversity of regional and cultural constructions that have evolved throughout Mexico since the 1930s.[4]

Scholars of Mexico, particularly historians and anthropologists, are beginning to rethink politics from this perspective. The authors brought together by Gilbert Joseph and Daniel Nugent in *Everyday Forms of State Formation* (1994) assess the Mexican Revolution and the political arrangements and conflicts it engendered at the level of regions and cultures, arguing that the nature and function of the state itself is established, maintained, and resisted in these multiple locations. Giving concrete form to Foucault's conception of power, they show the ways in which state formation in the 1930s involved particular, localized, and changing forms of resistance and accommodation concerning not only land reform, labor legislation, and party affiliation, but such matters as religious practices (Becker 1994) and Indian identity (Rus 1994) as well. Similarly, Claudio Lomnitz-Adler "specifies and contextualizes the notion of hegemony" (1991, 196) by looking at the geographically specific intertwining

13

of economy, politics, and culture in colonial and twentieth-century Morelos and in the postrevolutionary *cacicazgo*[5] of Gonzalo Santos in San Luis Potosí (1992).

In their attention to the regionally and culturally differentiated construction of regime politics across Mexico, Joseph and Nugent and their coauthors, along with Lomnitz-Adler, illustrate Foucault's claim that power is not to be found in "a group of institutions and mechanisms that ensure the subservience of the citizens of a given state" (Foucault 1990 [1976], 92). Rather, the state apparatus is the "institutional crystallization" (93) of something that happens elsewhere, in multiple local sites of contestation, such as workplaces, families, associational groups, and institutions (94). The apparatuses of the state are thus decentered; they are things which the "dense web" of power relations "passes through . . . without being exactly localized in them" (96).

Through analysis of Juchitán and comparison of Juchitán with other Mexican regions, I argue for broadening concepts of regime and politics, so as to decenter the regime, on the one hand, and place culture and everyday experience squarely within discussions about power, on the other. By decentering, I mean that national politics be understood as something partial and complex that coexists with, but is different from, regional and local politics, and that is only one among several locations and kinds of politics. In addition to affording greater insight than the state-centered approach into the origins and trajectories of political conflict in Mexico, such a framework can also better illuminate the strategies of resistance of leftist grassroots movements. In examining the origins and internal dynamics of COCEI, I show that the movement embodies ongoing ambiguity and contradiction in numerous arenas of its internal functioning and that its successes stem from its ability to manipulate the multiple forms of culture and power in regional politics. Like notions of state and regime as the predominant loci of domination, views of popular movements as instances of coherent and homogeneous class or ethnic consciousness misrepresent the nature of social phenomena and the dynamics of successful resistance and opposition. COCEI derives its identity and strength not from a unified Zapotec or peasant-worker consciousness, but from the coexistence within the movement of ambiguous forms of discourse and practice, as well as contradictory representations of the experiences of leaders and supporters and of men and women.

There is, indeed, a strikingly coherent state and regime in Mexico, compared to other countries, and, in Juchitán, an unusually unified and mobilized popular movement. COCEI, like the Mexican regime and state, can easily be accommodated to theorizing based on a clear divide between state and civil society, on regime as the organizing mechanism of political control, and on discrete, predominantly economic interests. Similarly, both COCEI and the Mexican regime engage in prominent public politics, so that it is tempting to understand power as a public and formally political phenomenon. However, COCEI has successfully transformed relations of power because its internal dynamics and political strategies respond to experiences more varied and subtle than those recognized by the state-centered explanations for Mexican politics. It is not centralized power, in movement or nation, that accounts for the power and endurance of both COCEI and the Mexican regime. Rather, it is the forms of power described by Williams and Foucault—*combinations* of power amassed and power dispersed, of coherence and ambiguity, and of contestation in "political" and "nonpolitical" locations—that shape domination and resistance in Mexico.

The State-Centered Model and Its Origins

In what has become the customary telling of the postrevolutionary past, President Calles maneuvered revolutionary generals into partial subservience to a centralized state and incipient national party in the 1920s. President Cárdenas then thoroughly restructured and institutionalized that state and party between 1934 and 1940, rewarding cooperative generals and ousting others, and creating and fortifying centralized mass organizations. Extensive and unprecedented land reform and labor legislation facilitated this incorporation. The resulting system, according to this state-centered analysis, maintained stability in Mexico for the next thirty years, partly by balancing political constituencies on the left and right and then increasingly by exercising control over those opposed to or harmed by inegalitarian forms of economic development.[6] During this period, regular elections served to ratify what was decided behind closed, centralized doors. The personalist politics of caciquismo coexisted with the new system, forming part of its inner structure.

By the 1960s, in this narrative, the system suffered "petrification" (Pansters 1990, 101); the structures of corporatism and caciquismo on which

15

the edifice was constructed could not respond to diverse challenges brought about by economic differentiation and demands for political participation. This rigidity, which is seen to have led directly to the growth and eventual violent repression of the 1968 student movement, became the central dilemma of Mexican politics thereafter. In the 1970s and 1980s, the regime tried unsuccessfully to recoup, reinvent, or replace corporatist success. Generally, these efforts were seen as failures; policies shifted repeatedly, and they neither revived corporatism nor transcended it. Out of this stalemate, President Carlos Salinas largely completed the process of economic liberalization between 1988 and 1994 in an atmosphere of relative social peace, until the Chiapas rebellion in the final year of his *sexenio* (six-year term in office). In so doing, he strictly limited political liberalization and apparently pacified impoverished Mexicans through a targeted social-welfare program.

Acceptance of the corporatist analysis of the Mexican past as a basis for political analysis abounds in recent scholarly literature. For example, in his introduction to *Popular Movements and Political Change in Mexico*, a prominent collection that addresses multiple instances of grassroots mobilization in Mexico in the 1980s, Joe Foweraker speaks of "the construction of the corporatist state" in postrevolutionary Mexico, as well as the more recent "crisis in local forms of corporatist representation" (1990, 14–16). Alberto Aziz Nassif, in an essay that focuses on a fragmented present of "regions, zones, localities, groups, classes, ethnicities, languages, and organizations," refers to "the shared identity that once existed between the corporatized masses and the state," and to "a PRI-dominated political culture under the rule of the 'unanimous' party front" (1989, 92). These analyses acknowledge the complexity of the Mexican present and the changing nature of recent interactions between popular movements and the state. However, they suggest that the inclusion of ordinary Mexicans in government-sponsored mass organizations was the defining characteristic of postrevolutionary politics from the 1930s to the 1970s. While such state-centered explanations explicitly recognize the centrality of bargaining and exchange to the process of domination, they argue that the nature of the bargaining was circumscribed by the state and that the Mexican system as a whole remained relatively unchanged for at least three decades (Collier and Collier 1991, 574).

This same framework—that of a hegemonic state that can make and carry out policy from the center and circumvent or repress opposition—

was used to explain the apparent success with which President Salinas implemented neoliberal economic reforms (Centeno 1994). While for the moment—since the economic crisis of December 1994—the state's power appears more limited, a comparable focus on the state's ability to recreate centralized control, even in the context of the breakdown of corporatism, is used to analyze the problems of governance facing President Zedillo today: "If the long entrenched corporatist structures and patron-client networks of Mexico's regime are inadequate tools for implementing such [new social] policies and actually obstruct their implementation in many parts of the country, what can replace them?" (Cornelius 1995, 139).

This approach to twentieth-century Mexican politics emphasizes the thoroughness of the transformation achieved by Cárdenas, the stability of the years between the 1930s and 1968, the effective centralization of politics, and the failures of reestablishing stability, even with increasing coercion, in subsequent decades. This model emerged in the 1960s and 1970s as the study of economic and political development took root in the social sciences, and scholars of Mexican politics sought to develop a model for the country's enduring one-party system. In so doing, they first characterized the Mexican system as pluralist and representative, and then as authoritarian and corporatist. Pluralist authors argued that despite the absence of fair elections, the diversity of interests in Mexico was represented through the PRI and its sectors and reflected in government policies, thus making the system as a whole representative. The authoritarian analysis pointed to the ways in which central authorities consistently co-opted, controlled, and repressed political pressures of peasants and workers, while at the same time promoting economic policies that favored a small elite. Corporatism, a variant of authoritarianism, provided a way of making more explicit the connection between the establishment of a state-sponsored system of peasant and labor organizations and the ability of the regime to rule with a relatively low level of overt violence. Corporatism explained how nonmilitary authoritarianism could function.[7]

All of these approaches shared a focus on analysis of regimes, on generalizations meant to apply to politics throughout the nation and over several decades.[8] They sought to understand the ways in which regimes, as singular entities, controlled what were seen as the relatively objective demands expressed by individuals and groups experiencing socioeconomic change. In moving from pluralism to authoritarianism, theorists brought a much-needed critical perspective to the study of Mexican politics, one that was stimulated by empirical work on economic marginalization and political exclusion. At the same time, they left behind useful observations that had been part of the pluralist analysis. What the theorists of authoritarianism lost were notions of actual on-the-ground politics—places where varied forms of contestation occurred without predetermined results—and, in the work that emerged in the late 1970s, of political culture.[9]

The pluralist scholars praised the potential of the Mexican political system and did not see persistent inequalities in the process or results of political bargaining and compromise (Cline 1963; Cumberland 1968; Needler 1971; Padgett 1976 [1966]). Martin Needler described a rough-and-tumble politics in Mexico, where the whole was something that was "held together" by professional politicians, by way of influence, corruption, arbitrariness, and occasional brutality. "[Y]et, despite everything," Needler concluded, "the national party is a force for democracy and progress" (37). Howard Cline argued that the PRI won elections because it "deliver[s] the goods" (166) and "incorporates into its programme any really popular issues that seem to attract votes to minority parties" (167).

An early version of the authoritarian analysis appeared in Pablo González Casanova's *Democracy in Mexico* (1970 [1965]), which documented the economic exploitation and cultural marginalization of the majority of Mexicans. González Casanova's analysis inspired a literature that began in the early 1970s and has endured, in its basic precepts, to the present. At first, however, North American authors who began to discern authoritarianism in Mexico described a relatively noncoercive form of control from above. At this time, what were to become the paradigmatic cases of more brutal authoritarianism in Latin America in the mid-1970s had not yet occurred. Linz's work on authoritarianism in Spain, upon which virtually all theorists of Latin American authoritarianism drew, emphasized limited forms of predominantly elite political interaction and an unmobilized population that "obeys out of a mixture of habit and self-interest" (1970, 255, 270). In a similar fashion, Roger Hansen (1971), who wrote one of the most influential analyses of the national system, as well as Wayne Cornelius (1975) and Richard Fagen and William Tuohy (1972), who studied particular cities and neighborhoods, emphasized management, apathy, and co-optation as the central characteristics of

Mexican politics. These authors understood political culture as something that proceeds in stages from tradition to modernity and concerns explicitly political beliefs and practices. For them, the key to the limited nature of coercion—in a situation where, they believed, objective conditions for class conflict clearly existed—was a political culture characterized by submission to authority and low levels of demand making.[10]

Almost a decade after González Casanova's analysis first appeared, other scholars began to document inequality, marginalization, and coercion in virtually all locations of formal political life in Mexico, such as neighborhood, labor union, rural peasant organization, political party, and election. As they did so, they largely eliminated culture from political analysis and played down the role of contestation and exchange in Mexican politics. They used the word "hegemony" to mean unchallenged control in an authoritarian regime, rather than in the Gramscian sense of the contested and changing configuration of dominant beliefs and practices in any regime. In contrast to Linz's authoritarianism, the control they described was active and all-encompassing, doing violence to ordinary people as they engaged in political activity.

Judith Adler Hellman (1983 [1978]) was one of the first authors to chronicle the ongoing, violent repression of peasant and labor activism in detail. In contrast to claims about the representative character of the Mexican regime made by pluralist researchers, Hellman and other theorists of authoritarianism in the late 1970s and early 1980s demonstrated the ways in which political institutions in Mexico shaped participation so as to preclude effective voice (Baird and McCaughan 1979; Cockcroft 1983; Collier 1982; Eckstein 1977a; Reyna and Weinert 1977). In their accounts, it was the regime's willingness to use force, rather than Mexican culture, that explained the "effectiveness with which the state is able to impose social control over a population of peasants and workers who have every reason to be discontented and rebellious" (Hellman 1983 [1978], 170). These theorists focused on the far-reaching presence of state-sponsored mass organizations and on those organizations' ability, particularly between the late 1930s and 1968, to control potential and actual lower-class demands through co-optation and repression. Furthermore, they identified the origins of such structuring in the state-building reforms of President Lázaro Cárdenas in the 1930s, identifying pathways by which widespread reform and progressive marginalization had become linked (Cornelius 1973; Hamilton 1982; Hellman 1983 [1978]).[11]

Hellman and others focused attention on the historical origins of inequality, the centrality of outright violence, and the discernible structure of coercion in formal political dealings. At the same time, in keeping with political scientists' commitment to characterizing national political models and their tendency to assume that such models were replicated at all levels, those who discerned coercion also claimed virtually unchanging absorption and control, focusing primarily on the ways in which these were achieved by elite policies. In Ruth Collier's words, Mexico was characterized by "a multi-class, integrative, hegemonic, one-party dominant system. In the electoral arena, in the interest group arena, and in the symbolic arena, the PRI has been able to bind and integrate popular sector groups to the state" (1982, 77). Susan Eckstein gave absorption and hegemony an even more active, colonizing configuration, anticipating theories of corporatism: "Mexico's paternalistic system is deliberately recreated in new areas as they emerge" (1977b, 41), "regardless of the intentions of políticos and residents" (25). Such analyses, however, overlooked the possibility of changing configurations, the possibility that mixtures of coercion and resistance, in different geographic and political locations, might indeed create new identities, alliances, and political forces.

Theorists of corporatism in Latin America, much like Eckstein, moved a step beyond the all-encompassing state to discern states that actively structured the very emergence of political activity (Erickson 1977; Malloy 1977b; Stepan 1978; Schmitter 1974). They found in numerous Latin American regimes "interest representation based on non-competing groups that are officially sanctioned, subsidized, and supervised by the state" (Collier and Collier 1979, 967). The edited volume *Authoritarianism in Mexico* (Reyna and Weinert 1977) played a major role in this application of corporatist theorizing to Mexico. Like most observers of Mexico since the 1960s, coeditor Reyna sought to explain the absence of violence in a situation of extreme inequality and suffering. Such an absence of violence would not be surprising in a pluralist regime—ostensibly one of "openly conflictual, multifaceted, uncontrolled interest politics" (Schmitter 1974, 127)—where it was assumed that people had access to political means to challenge domination and freely made use of such means. Without pluralism, however, such thinking goes, oppressed people can be expected to rebel, unless something prevents them from doing so. Corporatism was that something, "an alternative to the indiscriminate use of repressive measures" (Reyna 1977, 161). In Mexico, in Reyna's view, the establishment of a corporatist system was so successful, and power so completely secured within the state, that "there is only one real political center. The state can activate or exclude the masses according to the circumstances" (162).

In *Shaping the Political Arena* (1991), Ruth Collier and David Collier pressed at some of the boundaries of the corporatist analysis of Mexico, emphasizing the diversity of corporatist organizations since the 1930s and the centrality of bargaining and exchange in the functioning of the Mexican political system. In their analysis, the center could not single-handedly impose its policies and had to work hard to maintain legitimacy. However, Collier and Collier, like the theorists of authoritarianism and corporatism described above, looked exclusively at national-level political arrangements and formal political and economic organizations, and they based their conclusions about regime continuity exclusively on the cessation of formal conflict and the maintenance of formal organizational cohesion in labor confederations, to which only a small minority of Mexican workers belonged by the 1980s. As a result, Collier and Collier concluded that "[al]though the Mexican party system experienced some changes in response to these challenges [during the years from 1952 to 1982], it contained them, remained stable, and was characterized primarily by continuity" (574). However, Collier and Collier did not examine the substance of political and social life under the enduring regime and thus gave little meaning, other than formal affiliation, to the words with which they characterized the dynamics of power in Mexico and the political activity of ordinary people—"incorporation" and "containment."

Two directions can be discerned in political analysis of recent Mexican administrations, one finding a continuation of the all-powerful state, albeit without the old corporatism, and one describing complex state-society dynamics, as well as a state made up of diverse actors, on a battleground somewhere between weakened corporatism and emergent pluralism. For Miguel Centeno, the successes of the Salinas administration resulted from the existence of "a well-calibrated authoritarian regime" (1994, 33). This machine enabled Salinas to "dismantl[e] the corporatist structure of the party" (17), while still maintaining firm, centralized control, similar in its overall capacity to the hegemonic state of the past. In partial contrast, Jonathan Fox (1994a), Joe Foweraker (1993), and Diane Davis (1989) emphasize weak points in state power in recent years and corresponding margins for maneuver for groups in civil society. In so doing, they contribute to our understanding of Mexican politics by illuminating key points of innovation in intrastate and state-society relations. For Fox, Davis, and Foweraker alike, however, the battles they describe are played out on the terrain of weakened corporatism (Fox 158–60; Davis 270; Foweraker 162–63, 168). Each reinforces the notion of one system that prevailed for decades, then ossified, and each places nuanced discussion of state-society interaction within a set of narrowly political categories, focusing primarily on formal political organizations, actors, and processes and relatively objective state and societal interests.[12]

If, however, the corporatism described by Eckstein, Reyna, and Collier and Collier is reconceptualized as something that acts covertly to prevent rebellion—that resists resistance—corporatism as a theory of the workings of power begins to seem compatible with forms of analysis, derived from Foucault (1990 [1976]) and Bourdieu (1977; Bourdieu and Wacquant 1992), that find structured forms of power, as well as multiple sites and forms of resistance, in previously unexamined locations. Where theories of pluralism and authoritarianism relied on clearly discernible competition, management, or manipulation among actors with discrete, enduring interests, corporatism suggested that the strategies, if not the identities themselves, of some actors—in this case actors outside the state—were affected by the ways in which other actors—state actors—could shape the very environment in which the outsiders operated. Such an analysis might have been pushed to include the categories of thought, the domain of the imaginable, within which nonstate actors made political choices, and pushed again to recognize the ramifications of actions and beliefs not formally political on such strategies, and again to suggest the permeability of the state, in its numerous forms, to beliefs and practices originating, or adapted, in locations seemingly outside the state. In other words, corporatism's insight into the ability of power to cross apparent boundaries and shape political action and imagination "from the inside" might have led to a rethinking of the all-encompassing state as the explanation for Mexican politics. Instead, however, Reyna's formulation of a state that could "activate or exclude the masses" from the 1930s to the 1970s became codified in scholarly writing about Mexico in the 1980s, and it is being drawn upon once again to explain President Salinas's success in implementing a neoliberal project and to frame the problems of governance facing President Zedillo.

In contrast, analysis of Juchitán demonstrates that situations of contestation do not occur nationally, throughout all of Mexico, but in particular towns, regions, economies, and cultures. And these regions and cultures diverge over time, house new forms of politics, form new configurations with that which might be labeled national, and which is both outside and inside, both shaping and shaped. Negotiation and repression, similarly, occur with particular languages and beliefs, embedded in historical and cultural relationships. This approach to Mexican politics suggests envisioning relationships between regime, region, culture, and daily life in such a way as to keep all of these locations and forms in view, and it shows that a new understanding of politics and power can be grounded in the ongoing contestation and balancing among them. Such an approach, which renders difficult the kind of parsimonious model-building that has characterized political science, has relevance far beyond Mexico. It is uniquely suited to political analysis at a time when the coherence of regimes appears to be giving way to ethnic and cultural conflict with deep local roots and complex historical relationships to nationalism and centralized authority.[13]

2

Continuity and
Disjunction in Zapotec Ethnicity
"Their Own Soul, Now Perfectly Defined"[1]

Ethnicity is the medium through which autonomy and difference, as well as alliance and accommodation, were constructed historically in Juchitán, and it played a central role in the formation of COCEI in the 1970s. In addition, Zapotec ethnicity was itself shaped by the forms of outside intervention and internal mobilization it fostered. This "mutually constitutive" relationship between ethnicity and other social forces (Comaroff 1987, 313) can be seen in Juchitán in enduring capacities for economic self-sufficiency and political rebellion and in the strategic class and gender alliances through which Zapotecs have negotiated inequality and conflict. The interrelationship between ethnic discourse and practice and other phenomena can also be seen in the recurring tropes of savagery and barbarism through which Juchitecos were represented by both foreigners and themselves.

In her analysis of "marginal" geographic and cultural regions in Indonesia, Anna Tsing details the intricate interplay of "outside" and "inside" cultures in the construction of political meaning and action and illustrates the ways in which "the authority of national policies is displaced through distance and the necessity of reenactment at the margins" (1993, 27). Similarly, in analyzing power relations in Mexico, Claudio Lomnitz-Adler emphasizes the rootedness of political authority in the complex deployment of cultural resources on the part of distinct classes and groups within regions (1992). Both Tsing's and Lomnitz-Adler's disaggregations of cultural practice illustrate the ways in which ethnicity can function simultaneously as "a sign of exclusion" and "a tool for destabilizing central authority" (Tsing 1993, 27). Mapping out the history of these functions in Juchitán explains the possibility of enduring ethnic identity and at the same time underscores its contingent nature. This contingency can be seen in the changing ways in which Zapotec ethnicity was deployed historically and in the ways it alternately strengthened and opposed precolonial, colonial, and postcolonial regimes.

The issue of exclusion and destabilization has been particularly urgent in Mexico in the context of the recurring reconstruction of nation and sovereignty in the nineteenth and twentieth centuries, and it has shaped the meaning and possibility of democracy in recent decades. Stuart Hall has underscored the democratizing potential of the tension between ethnicity and nationalism, arguing that "ambivalences and fissures within the discourses of the nation-state" provide opportunities for the establishment of "new, more effectively self-governing arrangements" based in part on reconstructions of ethnic identity (1993, 355). Seen in this light—and the Zapatistas in Chiapas have made the point explicitly—one of the central tasks of democratization involves renegotiating the place of ethnicity and region in the nation and the regime. Both nation and regime, furthermore, exist not only outside of Juchitán and Zapotec culture, pressing at their borders in the form of outside politicians, entrepreneurs, and soldiers, but, as Tsing's and Lomnitz-Adler's works make clear, in the very fabric of local discourses and institutions as well.

This chapter begins by tracing tropes of rebelliousness and barbarism backward from the present, illustrating the range of representations that were applied to Juchitecos and the interplay between characterizations voiced by a variety of Juchitecos and outsiders. The chapter goes on to describe enduring economic and political patterns in Juchitán that fostered and were themselves enabled by the persistence of tropes of barbarism. These included Juchitán's peripheral yet relatively strong economic position and the resistance and rebellion through which Juchitecos maintained their distance from centers of political power. This autonomy from the state—from a position within the state (Tsing 1993)—was further shaped by particular class and gender alliances, such as the consolidation of a multiclass notion of ethnicity in the nineteenth century, and, in the twentieth, women's elaboration of Zapotec identity as a means of securing cultural and economic power and COCEI's appropriation of Zapotec cultural leadership for a class-based political movement.

Thus, in addition to exhibiting compelling historical continuities, ethnicity in Juchitán played different roles in the constitution of social relations and political rule in different periods. The forms assumed by these differences in the late nineteenth and the twentieth century shaped the relations between Juchitán and the Mexican state before and after the Mexican Revolution and influenced the emergence and course of COCEI's radical mobilization. By selectively drawing on this past, COCEI shaped a new, radical politics around images and practices of rebellion and difference, thereby linking particular aspects of Indian identity to the practice of leftist political opposition. Analysis of this process of ethnic continuity and recreation, occurring always in interaction with various "outsides," demonstrates that hegemony is indeed continually "renewed, recreated, defended, and modified" (Williams 1977, 112), that it is characterized not only by antagonisms, but by "the instability of the frontiers which separate them" (Laclau and Mouffe 1985, 136).

A Reverse Chronology

In a 1991 account of COCEI's municipal successes, COCEI leader Oscar Cruz wrote that Juchitecos took up arms repeatedly in the nineteenth and twentieth centuries "in defense of their natural resources and for municipal autonomy" (1991, 77). Anonymous authors of a 1983 pamphlet attacking COCEI also drew on characteristics attributed to Juchitecos in the past. In the pamphlet, they cited the organization's "violent attitude," its "inciting of violence" through local radio broadcasts, the "flowering" of vice and prostitution in the city under COCEI government, and the "sinking [of Juchitán] into an era of terror and anarchy, with blackmail, pressure, and assault the order of the day, [so that] Juchitán became the land of nobody" (Anonymous 1983, 35, 15, 6). In 1983, presiding over the state legislature's successful effort to throw COCEI out of office, Governor Pedro Vásquez Colmenares opened the session by affirming that the situation in Juchitán "threatened to degenerate into a state of chaos and anarchy provoked by COCEI" (Anonymous 1983, 31). In a press conference the same year, a PRI official sent from Mexico City to manage the crisis in Juchitán denounced "threads of violence" in COCEI's Zapotec language.

In 1974, soon after COCEI's formation, supporters of the movement wrote in the local newspaper, *El Satélite*, that "the combative and nonconformist spirit of the Juchitecos has awakened within the Coalition" (27 Oct. 1974),[2] and four years later, after a series of murderous attacks against COCEI, the newspaper proclaimed that "thousands and thousands of revolutionaries are forming in the bosom of the pueblo" (12 Feb. 1978). During one of many violent confrontations, COCEI-supporting fish vendors in the central market, a notoriously sharp-tongued group of women, were rumored to have cornered a young *priísta* (member of the PRI) and, depending on the account, castrated him or stabbed him to death. COCEI leaders themselves "salute the violence of the poor peasant," offering "our warmest welcome" to violent forms of resistance (*ES* 26 Dec. 1976). In response to escalating tensions in the city, political moderates criticized COCEI's use of language that was "out of the ordinary" and characterized the local political arena as "a lagoon in which there are thousands of poisonous animals that can emerge from one moment to the next and you won't know from where" (*ES* 10 Mar. 1974).

The harshness of the Isthmus environment and the strength and tenacity with which Juchitecos conquered this harshness were described in commentaries concerning Juchiteco culture and gender roles during the decades of boss rule, from 1930 to 1960. These writings emphasized the public and political character of local life, and they evoked an underlying savagery through reference to Zapotec sounds and bodies as rugged and barbaric. In 1946, in his accounts of travel in the Isthmus, Mexican writer and painter Miguel Covarrubias claimed that the *son,* the trademark of Isthmus brass bands, resembled nineteenth-century Spanish waltzes, though played "with a colorful, barbaric orchestration that gives [it] a strong and individual character" (1986 [1946], 323, cited in Campbell 1990b, 203). In a 1937 article in the literary magazine *Neza,* Juchiteco Adolfo Gurrión observed that "the Isthmus woman is concerned with the public sphere" (31) and that "the [Juchiteca] political woman is as strong as a lion and as agile as a fox" (30). In 1929, Juchiteco author Andrés Henestrosa characterized Juchitán as a city "for hardworking men who live next to the dead river. To quench their thirst, they have to dig wells seven fathoms deep and have to rip the chest of the earth after scarce rains to obtain its fruits" (1993 [1929], 40). Gurrión located the origins of political activism in just such a physical environment, and he linked the bodies and the desires of women to this public politics: "Women born in Juchitán are not women who will create a world of artifice . . . but rather, beneath the sun and standing on the earth, deal with reality, smiling or laughing out loud, singing or crying, living or dying. And from this harsh contact with reality is born women's desire to intervene in the governing of their pueblo" (31). According to Henestrosa, furthermore, "the bravery, uproar, and misfortune of its first settlers are repeated in all the movements of its current inhabitants" (40).

In 1917, representatives from Juchitán in the national Congreso Constituyente in Querétaro insisted that the bloody rebellions of 1870, 1882, and 1911 in Juchitán, which appeared to have had many causes, resulted primarily from one, "which is the real one, and which is regional autonomy . . ." (Rivera Cabrera and Gómez n.d.-a, 17). They argued for independence for the Isthmus, whose residents "had created their own soul, now perfectly defined," and who therefore "heartily detested their current political subordination" (Rivera Cabrera and Gómez n.d.-b, 3).

The 1911 "Che Gómez" rebellion involved carnage and killing "without pity or mercy" (Nuñez Ríos 1969, cited in *ES* 12 Nov. 1972). Oral histories of the event recount bitter confrontations, the burning of houses, large numbers of deaths, and the gathering of the bodies of the dead from the river: "I went to collect those bones with my grandmother . . . Everything was bones, only bones in the mouth of the river. Yes, pure bones, and there were skulls, many of them had been broken open by machetes . . ." (López Rui Marín and Salinas 1980, 5). During the early period of the Mexican Revolution, according to historian Alan Knight, the uprising in Juchitán "constituted the biggest armed movement in the country, bar Zapatismo," its scope and violence indicative of Juchitecos' "fierce commitment to self government and local autonomy" (1986, 376, 378).

To President Porfirio Díaz, the threat of rebellion in Juchitán in 1889 "gives hope to the disrupters of order" nationwide. Referring to national rumors of land conflict in Juchitán, Díaz observed that "they have served as a stimulus to discontented people, and in other places they could lead to assaults upon the public peace, as occurred in a conspiracy that has just been discovered in Chihuahua . . . Among the documents and plans that were discovered there were references to an imminent rebellion in Juchitán . . . and they [the Chihuahuans] capitalized upon it to inspire resolve in those who were wavering."[3] According to the granddaughter of a Juchiteca combatant in 1866 battles against the French, who invaded Mexico under Louis Napoleon, "these [Juchiteca] women were the ones who rang the church bells and cried out that the Juchitecos should attack . . ." (Martínez 1985, 21, cited in Campbell, 1990b, 136). In his 1937 article, Adolfo Gurrión noted that "it has been repeated from mouth to mouth that a Juchiteco mother [Na Gada] collected rocks in the folds of her dress to hurl at the invaders" (30).

Observing local social customs in the decade before the invasion, French traveler Charles Brasseur expressed horror at the seminude "obscene promiscuity" of Juchiteco men and fascination with Zapotec women: "She was a Zapotec Indian with bronze-colored skin, young, slender, elegant, and so beautiful that she enchanted the hearts of the whites . . . I also remember that the first time I saw her, I was struck by her proud and arrogant demeanor" (Brasseur 1981 [1861], 159, cited in Campbell 1990b, 128). German traveler G. F. Von Tempsky, planning a visit to Juchitán in 1858, explained that the city was "reputed for its hostility against white strangers, or strangers of any kind" (1993 [1858], 119). A government official reported that "the violence of the rebels had become so notorious that by merely declaring 'I am a Juchiteco' they could get whatever they wanted in any nearby town" (Campbell 1990b, 50), and the owners of the Marquesana hacienda lamented the "insatiable greed of a barbarous town which possessed no other title but brute force" (Campbell 1990b, 60). Claiming a long historical sweep for this barbarism, Governor Benito Juárez, opening a session of the Oaxaca State Congress in 1850, reminded the legislators of "the state of immorality and disorder in which the residents of Juchitán have lived since very ancient times": "You know well their great excesses . . . their depredations . . . their attacks against the agents of the Spanish Government . . . their crimes . . . You have been witnesses to these scenes of blood and horror. You know all this . . . this is not the first time that the State has been faced with such scandals by them" (1993 [1850]). Fearing further subversive activity, Juárez later prohibited "all unauthorized public meetings promoted by the 'sound of drums, conches, or bells'" (de la Cruz 1983a, 21).

Two centuries earlier, Magdalena María, one of the local women who was arrested in the wake of the Tehuantepec rebellion, "was convicted of having sat on the dead Spanish *alcalde mayor* and pounded his corpse with a stone while scornfully reproaching him" (Campbell 1990b, 74–75). Rebels remained in arms for a year, inspired by the battle cry *"haremos Tehuantepec"* (we will take Tehuantepec) (Manso de Contreras 1987 [1661],

14, cited in Campbell 1990b, 74), and the claim that "Up to now Indians have been subject to the Spanish, now the Spanish will be subject to the Indians" (González Obregón 1907, 29, cited in Campbell 1990b, 74). As a result of her deeds in the uprising, Magdalena María was sentenced "to have her hair and one hand cut off, to be flogged 100 times in public, and for the amputated arm to be hung to the gallows near the site of her alleged crime" (Campbell 1990b, 74–75). According to Spanish observers, Zapotec women were the boldest stone throwers in the rebellion, and when Catholic leaders sought to control the rebels, "women threatened the churchmen with death if they did not return to their refuge in the local convent" (Campbell 1990b, 72).

Economic Self-Sufficiency and Political Resistance

These enduring representations of Isthmus Zapotec ethnicity emerged in a context of Isthmus Zapotecs resistance to outside incursions and a peripheral yet relatively prosperous economy. During the precolonial period, the Isthmus functioned as a location of retreat and defense for Zapotecs from the Valley of Oaxaca in the face of outside invasion and cultural domination. This defensive position originated when colonists arrived from a weakened Zapotec empire in the Valley of Oaxaca (Tutino 1993, 43–44) in the fourteenth century. By the late fifteenth century, while facing challenges from the Mixtecs, who occupied their former territory, the Zapotecs also confronted the Mexicas (Aztecs) from the north, who sought political sovereignty and the power to demand tributes.

In the face of these threats, Isthmus Zapotecs forged strategies of resistance. Their stance, reproduced through combinations of armed resistance and diplomatic negotiation, sustained the Zapotec presence in the Isthmus in the face of hostile incursions during the colonial period and provided some of the economic and cultural tools with which Isthmus Zapotecs resisted state and national authority in the nineteenth century. In the precolonial period, these actions included armed opposition, which was strong enough to prevent defeat by the Mexicas, and the negotiation of a dynastic union that created "an alliance of unequals" (Tutino 1993, 44), allowing Mexicas free passage through the region and acknowledging their rule, while at the same time preserving Zapotec control over the peoples of the region (Tutino 1993, 44). In the face of subsequent colonial incursions, one form of resistance occurred through the creation of a "Zapotec Christianity" of belief and ritual, a religion that was "Christian in its vision of cosmic questions" and its justifications of Spanish sovereignty, "while insistently Zapotec in the continuing emphasis on the powers that ruled and regulated daily life in an agrarian society" (Tutino 1993, 46).

The possibility of sustained resistance resulted in part from the Isthmus Zapotecs' maintenance of a monopoly over basic foodstuffs, along with their control of the production of goods essential to the regional commercial economy, such as cloth and salt. This relative self-sufficiency, based in agriculture and commerce, was made possible by the repeated waning of the colonial presence in the Isthmus, and it facilitated what Tutino described as the "consolidat[ion] of a colonial culture of resistance, adamantly Zapotec" (1993, 48–49). This resistance was further visible in the violent response to increased tribute demands in the rebellion of 1660, as well as in Zapotec control of water resources and cloth production a century later (Tutino 1993, 50–52). According to Tutino, the 1660 revolt was triggered by a doubling of tribute demands (1993, 49). Tutino found, however, that the preexisting tribute demands had been low, by colonial standards, and that "the revolt convinced the colonial State that the Isthmus Zapotecs had their own definition of bearable colonial demands, along with a clear willingness to defend their views" (1993, 50). Ironically, the brutal defeat of rebels in the Isthmus city of Tehuantepec, along with the presence there of the region's Spanish community, stimulated a gradual process of accommodation with colonial authorities in that city. As a result, by the late colonial era Juchitán became the primary locus of Zapotec power and resistance (Tutino 1993, 50–51).

The colonial and nineteenth-century Isthmus economies experienced "periodic incursions and subsequent recessions of state power and commercial economy," and the resulting middle ground between isolation and subjugation "allowed Isthmus Zapotecs to learn to adapt, accommodate, and even profit from those developments without being crushed by them" (Tutino 1993, 60). The possibility of economic room for maneuver for indigenous people within a peripheral but relatively strong regional economy persisted in the nineteenth and twentieth centuries in the

Isthmus. Leticia Reina offers several reasons for this persistence in the nineteenth century, including the variety of ecological niches in the Isthmus, the relatively limited levels of both production and control on the part of Isthmus haciendas, the limited reach of liberal property legislation from Oaxaca and Mexico City, and the regional system of roads and of market interchange and distribution (Reina Aoyama 1993, 140, 144–46). Together, these characteristics provided an economic context in which ethnic identities and practices could be maintained and elaborated.

This nineteenth-century room for maneuver, however, was repeatedly challenged. Successive waves of expansion on the part of the Marquesana hacienda, along with the attempted privatization of communal salt flats, threatened Isthmus Zapotec agriculture and trade. In addition, outside investors, merchants, and government authorities sought to control property and commerce by attacking the prerogatives of the church in the Isthmus, prohibiting textile trade with Guatemala, enforcing tax collection, appropriating land for colonization schemes and the trans-Isthmic railway, and imposing political authorities (Hart 1987, introd., chap. 1; Henderson 1981; Reina Aoyama 1992, 1993; Tutino 1980, 1993).

The Zapotec pueblo's willingness and ability to resist these outside intrusions took the form of petitions, land invasions, illegal use of private salt flats and pasture, smuggling, and attacks on persons and businesses, in addition to armed rebellion. In 1827, armed peasants in a village near Juchitán burned two cattle ranches and repudiated civil authorities who had not resolved their land claims. This prompted local landowners to request a permanent military guard-post. In response to the growth of British textile production, Juchitecos smuggled machine-made fabrics through Guatemala, illegally exchanging salt and other local products for the imported goods (Campbell 1990b, 108–13). In 1829, faced with state government recruitment of local men for the army, Juchitecos refused to serve, and women persuaded the townspeople to occupy municipal buildings and free the conscripts. In 1834, Juchitecos took up arms behind José Gregorio Meléndez to reject the property rights of Cortés's heirs and other Europeans. In the 1840s, Juchitecos worked their ancestral salt flats despite the Oaxaca government's having officially granted the flats to an outsider. In 1848, they "defiantly pastured their cattle on Maqueo and Guergue's haciendas," and Meléndez led renewed raids on the salt beds, challenging not only outside property rights, but government tax revenue as well (Campbell 1990b, 113).

Nineteenth- and Twentieth-Century Rebellions

In 1848, in an effort to co-opt opposition, Governor Benito Juárez appointed Meléndez to head the state's military forces in the Isthmus. However, Meléndez broke with Juárez and declared the Isthmus independent from Oaxaca. Under his leadership, Juchitecos then attacked and robbed the salt mines, killed or removed from office several managers and administrators from Oaxaca, and attacked the local jail, freeing those who had been taken prisoner.[4] They directed their anger against the properties and representatives of Oaxaca and of the local elite, especially Maqueo, the owner of the Marquesana hacienda (Campbell 1990b, 119). They also sent letters to the governor explaining the injustices that needed correction and their desire for peace.

After two years of rebellious activity, military forces sent by the governor killed many rebels and burned one-third of the town. In the face of this brutal attack, Meléndez and the rebels fled to the nearby state of Chiapas, then returned to challenge the state forces, living in the countryside with the support of local inhabitants. When Meléndez's forces reached the town of La Venta, the center of the Marquesana hacienda, they killed the manager, a Spaniard, and burned the estate (López Gurrión 1982, 65). In the face of Meléndez's endurance, Juárez was said to have ordered the unconditional surrender of the rebels or their total annihilation (López Gurrión 1982, 69). In 1851, Juárez sent an army large enough to force a surrender, pardoned those who swore allegiance to the Oaxaca government, and installed a municipal council loyal to that government and to the Oaxaca-based commercial elite (Tutino 1980, 97–99). Even after the surrender of most of his supporters, Meléndez attacked Tehuantepec in 1852 and formulated a separatist plan for the Isthmus that was enacted by Santa Ana when he briefly returned to national power in 1853 (Tutino 1980, 99).

Juchitecos resisted European intervention in a series of bloody battles against the French, who had invaded Mexico under Louis Napoleon. In an important regional battle in 1866, Juchitecos defeated the French against great odds, after burning and abandoning Juchitán, laying siege to it when the French occupied it, and then defeating the enemy in a swamp area as they fled. While this was only a minor battle in a national war and received little subsequent attention in Mexico City, it has occupied a prominent place in Isthmus Zapotec historical accounts.

Juchitán also played a prominent role in the political imagination of Porfirio Díaz. As indicated in the passage quoted above, Díaz saw Juchitán as the quintessential location of subversive activity. Díaz's impression of the Juchitecos derived from his own experience in the Isthmus before he became president, as well as that of his brother, Félix Díaz, who was governor of Oaxaca in the early 1870s. As president, Díaz saw Juchitecos take up arms in opposition to his trans-Isthmic railway plans and in response to hacienda attacks on the town's communal lands (Knight 1986, 374; López Gurrión 1982, 70). Earlier, Juchitecos had rebelled in the face of his brother's efforts to shut down their contraband trade and force them to pay state sales taxes. In the course of this conflict, Félix Díaz had attacked the town, executed prisoners, and carried off the image of Juchitán's patron saint (Berry 1981, 123). Two years later, a group of Juchitecos tracked Díaz down on the Oaxaca coast (Henderson 1981), where they lynched him after beating him and stabbing him with bayonets. "Then, cutting off his genitalia and sticking them into his mouth, they sent the corpse into the district seat of Pochutla . . ." (Berry 1981, 127).

In 1911, at the beginning of the Mexican Revolution, Juchitecos rejected the imposition of a political boss sent by Governor Benito Juárez Maza (son of the former governor and president) and defended by the governor's local conservative supporters. This imposition occurred in the context of continued efforts on the part of Oaxaca governors to protect landed interests in the Isthmus and to assert state political control by appointing *jefes políticos* (head political authorities) in Juchitán and Tehuantepec (Henderson 1983, 6; Hernández López 1972; Nuñez Ríos 1969; Rojas 1962). Rallying behind José F. Gómez, a popular lawyer and elected municipal president known for defending the claims of the town's poor, Juchitecos prevented the new administrator from entering the town, attacked the local barracks, and defeated reinforcements sent from outside (de la Cruz 1983b, 68–71; Henderson 1983, 6; Henestrosa de Webster 1985, 374–78; Hernández López 1972; Nuñez Ríos 1969; Rojas 1962). In Knight's telling, "it was noted that 'the Gómez forces . . . seem to comprehend the populace generally,' and they drew on reinforcements from nearly a score of Juchiteco villages to the east of the town. For three days they controlled Juchitán . . . and, as was customary in such moments of popular insurgence, a tax-collector and magistrate were killed" (1986, 375–76).

In the midst of the rebellion, Gómez began negotiations with the new national government of Francisco Madero, who shared the Juchitecos' animosity toward the conservative Oaxacan elites and felt pressed to intervene by the threat of widening rebellion. On his way to visit President Madero, with a pass of safe conduct signed by the president himself, Gómez was apprehended and murdered by Juárez Maza's troops. In Mexico City, according to Knight, this violence was attributed to the habitual passions and savagery of the provinces in general and Juchitecos in particular: "family enmities were blamed; it was another *tierra caliente* vendetta." However, the targeted political nature of the killing was clear, as "none of the police escort had been injured, while Gómez' corpse was found to have fifty-two gunshot wounds" (1986, 377). Within several months, "some 2,000 were under arms, controlling the country between Juchitán and Reforma, raiding the Pan-American Railway, effectively cutting Chiapas off from the rest of Mexico" (Knight 1986, 377). In the years during and immediately following the rebellion, according to John Hart, Isthmus rebels responded to decades of foreign encroachment "by expelling hundreds of American landholders and companies . . . [and] reestablishing much of their pre-Porfirian land tenure system" (1987, 8).

The rebellions in Juchitán in the nineteenth and twentieth centuries contested the content and limits of outside authority in public and violent forms.[5] In a context in which neither state nor national governments in Mexico could enforce property decrees or create effective rural police forces (Tutino 1986, 257), these rebellions constituted significant threats to the establishment of centralized political authority. The political and economic relationships fought over were by no means resolved, and they remained ambiguous until the 1930s. However, in contrast to the unevenness and fluidity of political authority, several aspects of Juchitecos' conception of themselves, as well as of others' conceptions of them, either took shape or were significantly reinforced in the crucible of the violent rebellions. These included perceptions on the part of Juchitecos of the Zapotec pueblo as multiclass and of the Isthmus Zapotecs as a rebellious people threatened physically by Oaxacan military authorities.

In addition, Juchitecos saw outsiders—Oaxacan, Mexican, European, and U.S.—as perpetually seeking to impose economic and geopolitical claims on the Isthmus. In turn, these outsiders viewed Juchitecos as foreign, lawless, and violent, attributing to women in Juchitán both arrogance and seductiveness as well.

During these and subsequent years in Juchitán, images of rebellious-ness, tenacity, and strength, along with intrusion, conflagration, and bru-tality, were repeated and elaborated in ballads composed in local can-tinas, in jokes and *mentiras*,[6] and in idioms, ritual practices, and family banter. They also appeared prominently in the poems and legends central to regional, and at times national, literary life, as well as in the historical narratives, literary magazines, and paintings produced by Juchitecos in Juchitán and Mexico City throughout the twentieth century. In virtually all of these accounts, Juchitecos emphasized the ferocity and heroism of their parents and grandparents and the activism of Zapotec women in the midst of combat, along with the unique and sensual character of Ju-chiteco social experience. In so doing, they responded to outside charac-terizations of savagery and barbarism with their own emphasis on the centrality of passion, violence, and eroticism in political and cultural affairs. The ritual contexts of these observations and the Zapotec lan-guage in which they were articulated underscored continuities in ethnic practices and their rootedness in daily life.

Class and Gender Alliances

An unusual alliance facilitated the endurance of nineteenth-century cul-tural forms in twentieth-century daily life and politics in Juchitán, an alliance that COCEI both benefited from and challenged. In the nine-teenth century, when outside power-holders became too intrusive and threatened the Juchiteco elite, that elite turned to mass support. In turn, the notables' ability to gain such support "depended on their defense of the Zapotec peasant vision of shared access to resources" (Tutino 1993, 59). Thus, the multiclass nature of the nineteenth-century Juchiteco rebellions—their distinctly Juchitán-versus-outside character and the corresponding elaboration of a multiclass ethnic identity—derived from the elite's awareness that there was a price for peasant support and their willingness to pay it. In and of themselves, the components of this bargain—peasant defense of subsistence autonomy, and power seeking on the part of local elites—were common in nineteenth-century Mexico. However, it was rare for the two classes to ally and to share common *ethnic* identities. In most places in Mexico, ethnic identities over time became primarily peasant identities, while local elites cast aside Indian language, spoke Spanish, and adopted Mexican "national" culture (Tutino 1993, 59).

Thus, an important aspect of what has distinguished ethnic identity in Juchitán from that of most other Indian regions of Mexico in the course of the late nineteenth and the twentieth century has been its multiclass character, and this has played a central role in its vitality in the face of nationalist and urban pressures. Alongside great differences, including elite familiarity with and participation in outside economic and cultural practices, rich and poor Juchitecos wore Zapotec dress to Zapotec markets and festivals, spoke to their children, conducted commerce, and buried their dead in Zapotec, and took pleasure in common forms of ethnic display. This multiclass identity, furthermore, played important political roles in Juchitán, as subsequent chapters will show: in the consolidation of regional autonomy under a postrevolutionary political boss; in the economic and electoral mobilization of peasants and workers by elites in the 1960s; and in the ongoing presence of forms of support for COCEI among some of the movement's middle-class and elite opponents.

Gender is also a key factor in explaining the tenacity of ethnic identity in Juchitán. Women in Juchitán possess greater autonomy in particular arenas of their lives than do women in most other indigenous cultures in Mexico (Burguete 1985; Campbell 1990b, 488–89; Chiñas 1983). Juchitecas of all classes have acted to preserve ethnic identity in order to safeguard and elaborate this autonomy and the margins of economic and social maneuvering room it has fostered. These margins of autonomy can be seen in women's ownership of market and business enterprises, both small- and large-scale, as well as their control of family economic resources. In addition, it is widely perceived as legitimate in Juchitán for women to participate in and pay for social obligations and celebrations independently of men. Campbell notes that "Zapotec women have considerable control over their own standards of physical beauty" and that Juchitecas gain forms of pleasure and power from "their great pride in Zapotec ethnic attire, the considerable degree of solidarity among women, the sexual freedom of widows and some other single women,

Zapotec women's strong character, personal dignity, and social self-confidence . . ." (1990b, 287–88). Lynn Stephen argues that the autonomy of women in Juchitán derives from the cultural understanding of sexuality and of women's control over their bodies, finding evidence for this in the extraordinary openness of and tolerance for an alternative male gender role in the city, as well as in the large physical size of women in Juchitán, their physical and social forthrightness, and their free physical contact with other women in public dances and fiestas (1990a).

As a result of this unusual physical presence and the economic and social power of Juchitecas, Zapotec society in Juchitán has been represented historically—by foreigners, Mexicans, and Juchitecos themselves—as an exotic matriarchy, a social order dominated by strong and proud women and suffused with an otherworldly eroticism. This recurrent romanticization, partially contradicted by familiar daily oppressions of women, has consistently reinforced images of Zapotec ethnicity as different, barbaric, and enduring. At the same time, it has performed a variety of often contradictory, social and political functions, alternately lending value and pleasure to the political status quo and fueling radical mobilization, providing women with a means to exercise power and disguising gendered violence and exclusion.

Zapotec Ethnicity in the Twentieth Century

The strength of ethnic identity and practice in Juchitán in the twentieth century has been extraordinary for a Mexican city. For example, while in 1980 it was not unusual for the majority of the inhabitants of a small Mexican village or town—of, for example, two thousand to ten thousand residents—to speak a common indigenous language in addition to Spanish, in most cities of more than forty thousand the proportion of bilingual speakers would likely not exceed 20 to 30 percent, and this might include several languages (INEGI 1984). In Juchitán, in contrast, the 1980 census reported that 79 percent of Juchitecos spoke an indigenous language, and the vast majority of these could be assumed to speak Isthmus Zapotec (INEGI 1984, chart 1, 15). Similarly, Juchitán is remarkable for the high percentage of women who wear traditional Zapotec dress and for the size and importance of its central market, where hundreds of Zapotec women sell virtually everything that is eaten or used to adorn or maintain households in the region, from mangos to iguanas to enormous piles of dried shrimp, from palm mats to plastic containers. Women from all social classes can be seen attending to their market purchases in traditional dress. The son of one prominent Juchiteco family tells of returning from college in Mexico City with his friends. Upon seeing his mother leave the house to do her shopping, the friends exclaimed, with confusion and disapproval, "But she looks like an Indian!"

Ritual customs and celebrations around life-cycle events, such as births, baptisms, comings of age, weddings, and funerals, occupy a large portion of Juchiteco families' nonwork time and energy, as well as contribute substantially to the food, craft, music, clothing, and jewelry enterprises that form a significant component of the regional economy. Ritual networks connect the city and provide frequent and direct means of communication among families in disparate neighborhoods, who can be seen setting out, extravagantly adorned, to cross the city on foot to attend fiestas. Together with the central market (for women) and local bars (for men), these fiestas provide one of the principal means for exchange of information and the fostering of various kinds of family, neighborhood, community, and political solidarities (Chiñas 1983; Covarrubias 1986 [1946]; Royce 1975). In addition to this system of fiestas, ritual life in Juchitán is focused around a cycle of *velas*, or large, elaborate, several-day celebrations involving a variety of processions, masses, food preparation, drinking, and dancing, and organized on the basis of neighborhoods and families. The velas provide "a forum for musical and verbal performances, ritualized dancing, stylized religious processions, and displays of women's aesthetic clothing," and they stand out as perhaps the most opulent and intensely cultivated of such festivals in contemporary Mexico (Campbell 1990b, 205–6).

Zapotec culture in Juchitán boasts a large repertoire of songs and romantic poetry. According to Miguel Covarrubias, who traveled in the region during the Charis period, literature and music played extremely important roles in Juchitecos' lives, and the Isthmus Zapotecs "cultivate language with an unusual intensity" (1986 [1946], 310, cited in Campbell 1990b, 203). These activities occur in ritual celebrations, during civic functions, and in the many cantinas scattered throughout the city. Campbell characterizes Juchiteco political speeches as "showcases for eloquent verbal performances, often including lively jokes in the Zapotec language" (1990b, 203), and sees the cantinas as "a main stage for the Zapotec troubadours who sing their own compositions (often in Zapotec) or popular tunes . . . interspersed with spicy jokes and *mentiras* (didxax-hiihui'), a genre of Zapotec story-telling which emphasizes fantasy and imagination" (204–5).

Zapotec identity in Juchitán withstood the destructive pressures of Mexican national culture in the nineteenth and twentieth centuries partly because economic advancement in the city—to the visiting college students' surprise—was never equated with the casting off of indigenous language and other traditions, as it has been in other parts of Mexico, as well as in other Isthmus cities. Indeed, the Juchiteco student's mother was the daughter of a Lebanese immigrant man and a Juchiteca woman. Lebanese immigrants, who came to Juchitán at the end of the nineteenth century (Royce 1975, 191), as well as later migrants from other parts of Mexico, frequently adopted local customs and learned to speak Zapotec. Tarú, the opposition leader who became municipal president in 1971, and who was seen at that time as the "genuine" leader of the pueblo, was also a member of a Lebanese-Juchiteca family.

In Juchitán, middle- and lower-middle-class families have generally lived in communal courtyards in poor neighborhoods, participated in family and neighborhood traditions, and considered themselves to be part of "the poor people." The bourgeoisie in Juchitán, in contrast to economically similar groups in other parts of Mexico, has generally not rejected its indigenous identity and has ensured that its children speak Zapotec and participate in customary rituals, even as they learn to function in the educational and business environments of wealthy Mexicans.[7] While the resulting cultural mixing can take varied forms, it serves to consolidate both wealth and Zapotec ethnicity. The matriarch of a prosperous local family, for example, took her place daily at the fabric counter of the family's clothing store, wearing traditional *huipil* (blouse) and *enagua* (skirt) as she recommended patterns, measured cloth, and gossiped in Zapotec. In the evening, in contrast, among family and friends, she might reminisce in Spanish about drinking champagne on French ocean liners and wear an embroidered dress typical of Indians in the Oaxaca Valley and popular among international tourists. Her son, a COCEI sympathizer, founded the Simone de Beauvoir private school in Juchitán, where Zapotec language formed a prominent and innovative part of the curriculum. Juchitecos of all classes participate in the vela celebrations, and while there is some stratification of velas by economic level, there is considerable mixing. The velas are organized by vela societies, local associations of neighbors and family groups that plan, pay for, and run the festivals, and the planning and attending of velas occupies a prominent place in daily social life in the city.

In addition to shaping the characteristics of daily life, Isthmus Zapotec culture has played a role in Mexican "high" culture since the 1920s, which in turn made the elites' continuing ethnic identification possible and appealing. A number of Juchitecos gained access to educational and political opportunities in Mexico City through the patronage of Porfirio Díaz, in return for their victories against the French and their early support for Díaz, and they in turn provided opportunities for others in subsequent years (Campbell 1990b, 193). A generation later, in 1923, Isthmus youth formed the Association of Juchiteco Students in Mexico City. The organization published a periodical, sponsored cultural events, and organized the first vela in Mexico City. In 1929, Andrés Henestrosa published a book of Zapotec legends, *Los Hombres Que Dispersó la Danza*, which was a great literary success. In subsequent years, he and other Juchiteco intellectuals and writers gained national attention in Mexico City for their writing, and they published a literary magazine, *Neza*, from 1935 to 1939.

On the one hand, these activities went on in Mexico City and concerned the ways in which Juchiteco professionals there dealt with their ethnicity. In Covarrubias's words, "There they join the rabidly sectarian, melancholy colony of émigré Juchitecos who speak Zapotec among themselves, meet in cafes, and give full vent to their homesickness" (1986 [1946], 161, cited in Campbell 1990b, 196–97). On the other hand, these intellectuals connected the national and the local, providing a written history and literature "in which Juchitán invariably figured as a kind of indigenous promised land . . ." (Campbell 1990b, 199). At a time when the new postrevolutionary state was proclaiming support for indigenous culture and well-being as a pillar of national identity, it was possible for Henestrosa and his contemporaries to believe that they could simultaneously participate in the national culture and strengthen a local, indigenous one (López Monjardin 1983b, 77). The presence of this active Zapotec participation in the national culture reinforced the value of Zapotec identity for local elites in this period and contributed to the compatibility between—and the advantages of combining—their goals of economic advance and the retention of ethnic characteristics.

Shifting Hegemonies

Despite broad continuities over time, Zapotec cultural discourses and economic practices were woven together in different ways, and with different relationships to local and outside power, over the course of the past hundred years. The configuration of multiclass pueblo versus outside, central to nineteenth- and early-twentieth-century rebellions, shifted during the establishment of General Charis's rule in the 1930s to one of innovative coexistence of local and outside. In this period, which continued through the 1950s, elite Zapotecs succeeded in guaranteeing considerable autonomy, and a measure of well-being, for ordinary Juchitecos. Their brokering between nation and region secured for local use the very domains of agriculture and commerce that had been sought by outsiders during the decades of regional rebellion. Elites themselves profited from the consolidation of agriculture, craft production, and commerce in a better-than-average peripheral economy, efforts that were aided by modest federal investment in economic and social infrastructure.

This arrangement of identities and alliances changed yet again in the 1960s as basic political and economic patterns—of party, elections, land, and development—were hotly contested, with elites seeking higher levels of industrial growth and mobilizing Juchiteco peasants and workers in public campaigns in defense of private property and opposition to the PRI. Through these efforts, Zapotec elites wanted to foster closer connections to the national economy and polity, but on their own terms. While they pursued economic advance, they sought simultaneously to maintain forms of autonomy vis-à-vis national political institutions and to preserve their status as the legitimate leaders of the pueblo and arbiters of Zapotec style.

In the 1970s and 1980s, COCEI transformed the process and meaning of these elite efforts and successfully appropriated Zapotec culture—including its elaboration and leadership—for a poor people's movement. This ethnic appropriation was a crucial ingredient in COCEI's success. In defending themselves against COCEI's class-based mobilization, elites identified increasingly with "national" Mexican culture, economic practices, and political authority. COCEI's claim to Zapotec ethnicity, in contrast, made available for radical politics a common language, a remembered history, dense market and ritual networks, and abundant artistic and cultural representations that reconfigured customary boundaries between "popular" and "high" culture. In this way, the forms of regional autonomy that were secured during the mid-century years of boss rule facilitated COCEI's subsequent reconstruction, in the 1970s, of discourses of nineteenth-century rebelliousness. Furthermore, as COCEI's political and intellectual leaders drew on and reinvented Zapotec identity, cultural meanings and practices themselves became objects of public contestation, interwoven with the issues of political sovereignty, land ownership, wages, and municipal services that were central to the movement's organizing campaigns.

In the course of the cultural and political shifts of the late nineteenth and the twentieth century, interaction with various outside cultures was central to the construction and reconstruction of Zapotec discourses. For example, the formal literary and artistic component of Zapotec culture, as important to COCEI's cultural project as the (related) cultural practices of peasants and workers, grew out of interaction between Juchiteco artists and writers and Mexico City cultural elites in the 1930s and the 1960s. The entry of Mexican and European texts, which served as important inspirations, contributed to the pleasures of local artistic activity and the outside appeal of local work, but did not displace local aesthetics and imaginations. These cultural relationships, in turn, offered crucial protection to COCEI in moments of repression, as national artists, intellectuals, and journalists publicized the movement's situation in the capital. Similarly, Juchitecos' ability to incorporate outside immigrants and practices as different from their own as Lebanese settlers, Western childbirth practices, and multinational retail chains, and make *them* part of Zapotec culture, provided complex pathways for both accommodation and resistance in contemporary idioms.

Thus, in citing continuities between nineteenth- and twentieth-century discourses, I make no assumption of either continuous presence or automatic reproduction. Rather, Zapotec culture could define and unify a pueblo in the 1970s because arrangements between the regional boss and the central state—arrangements themselves fashioned by the conjuncture of past regional rebellions and contemporary state-building—allowed certain forms of social life to occur in Juchitán. Zapotec culture could foster radical politics in the 1970s because reformers in the 1950s and 1960s, in the Isthmus and elsewhere in Mexico, favored new forms of economic development and political administration, because student radicals pursued socialist political visions, and because outside authorities responded initially with violent repression. In the context of this history, innovation occurred in the intersections of formal political mediation, informal political practices, and multiple locations of cultural construction. As a result, Zapotec identities of rebelliousness and barbarism and Zapotec defenses of autonomy in the face of encroachment—which themselves crystallized in the course of nineteenth- and early-twentieth-century rebellions—took on new political meanings and transformed key power relations in Mexico in the 1970s and 1980s.

3

Cacique Rule and the Zapotec
Domain of Sovereignty, 1930–1960

"The PRI Doesn't Exist in the Isthmus" [1]

During the years from 1934 to the early 1960s, Juchitecos succeeded in establishing and maintaining a "domain of sovereignty" (Chatterjee 1993, 6) distinct from the hegemony of the new national state. The political arrangements between Juchitán and the outside that characterized the rule of General Heliodoro Charis, the regional political boss, insured that officials were not imposed by outside authorities, landholdings and natural resources remained in local hands, and the language and rituals of Zapotec daily life flourished among ordinary and elite Juchitecos. In all of these ways, Charis's cacicazgo secured resources and practices for which Juchitecos had repeatedly taken up arms since the mid-nineteenth century. Resistance on the part of state-level elites to national reform initiatives also limited the reach of outside authorities and contributed to Charis's enduring strength in Juchitán.

Oral histories reveal the price of this strength, which included violence against Charis's political opponents and their families, the enrichment of the boss and his associates, and partial denial of land and labor rights to peasants and workers. They also reveal the absence of the PRI from boss politics and the presence of fierce political opposition to boss rule on the part of reform movements. [2] While people's memories of Charis indicate ambivalence toward the figure of the boss in these respects, they demonstrate widespread praise for the way in which he wielded images of Indian savagery and ignorance to local advantage against politicians in Mexico City.

Popular and official mythology coincide in establishing a clear boundary between the years of Charis's boss rule and subsequent decades, when politics was dominated first by mobilizations within the PRI and then by COCEI radicalism. During my field research, an older, COCEI-supporting market woman observed that "he got all the things we have" and "when he died, all things died here." Her son-in-law, a young, COCEI-supporting oil worker, revised this to say, "when he died, politics began here." In the course of this new politics, according to a teacher who became active in the PRI in the 1960s, "people became aware of the necessity of seeing" practices and possibilities that had been obscured during Charis's rule.

In his discussion of the formation of anticolonial nationalism, Partha Chatterjee argues that a realm of autonomy, self-definition, and control with regard to cultural matters was established in India before the nationalist political battle began. Chatterjee points to issues of language, historical narrative, family and community structure, and education to show the ways in which a particular cultural rendering of the Indian past and of Indian identity and daily life paved the way for explicitly political campaigns decades later (1993, 6–9). In applying this concept to Juchitán, I expand the notion of domain of sovereignty to include forms of political and economic, in addition to cultural, activity. "Domain of sovereignty" aptly describes the developments of Zapotec culture and Juchiteco politics that were in no way radical or oppositional, but that established the possibility of autonomous, locally initiated activity— fostering, from the beginning of the postrevolutionary system, a counterweight to national power.

This insight is useful for examining the historical antecedents of a regionally and ethnically based poor people's movement, as well as for thinking about democracy in terms of voice and autonomy, rather than formal procedures alone. While COCEI's politics differed significantly from nationalist mobilizations elsewhere in the world, with respect to the identity of Juchitecos as both Zapotecs *and* Mexicans and the movement's willingness to act within the Mexican nation, COCEI gained much of its force from its identity as a movement of Zapotecs combating outside domination. And while the Zapotec domain of sovereignty did not precisely follow Chatterjee's designation of a spiritual as opposed to material domain, it established the bases for identity and resistance that Chatterjee demonstrates in the early, cultural stages of Indian nationalism. What Juchitecos saw and the political pathways available to them in the decades after Charis's death in 1964, when much about the economy of the region and its relationship to Mexico City began to change, grew out of who they understood themselves to be and how they practiced politics. These understandings and practices were shaped by the domain of sovereignty that had been constructed and defended during the Charis cacicazgo.

Charis the Boss

Charis's local prominence began in the late teens, when he established a base in the area of Monte Grande, in the hills outside of Juchitán. At this time, the minority Reds, in alliance with Oaxaca elites, maintained political control of Juchitán. Remembering his first meeting with Charis, Justo Pineda, a political opponent, told a friend that he "met a big Indian named Charis, alone in the mountains hunting." As an Indian and one of the leaders of the more popularly based Greens, Charis was a local political outsider. However, Charis backed the successful national leader Alvaro Obregón in the later years of the Mexican Revolution and led a battalion of Juchitecos in his support. As Obregón himself ascended, Charis rose in military rank and assumed a prominent post in the central Mexican city of Querétaro.

In the 1920s and early 1930s, support for Charis grew in Juchitán. The claims of the Greens to represent local autonomy and well-being in resistance to outside intervention were clearly articulated in Charis's Plan de San Vicente (1982 [1920]). According to Pineda, what distinguished Charis was that "he got together with people and mixed with people. They really loved him." After an incident in the 1920s in which Charis gathered supporters, attacked the town hall, and freed prisoners, Pineda continued, "The whole pueblo started to say 'Charis,' which was a very unusual last name. It began to sound familiar." In the 1930s, Charis returned from a series of national military campaigns and used his twin successes as a popular local figure and a leader of the national revolutionary army to establish himself as the regional political boss for the following twenty-five years. "Taking advantage of his political influence," in the words of Victoriano López Toledo, another of Charis's long-standing opponents, "the first thing that he [Charis] did was work for the unification of the pueblo, and he succeeded in ending the division that had existed for so long in Juchitán" between the Reds and the Greens.

The general's accession to power was brought about by a combination of armed rebellion and political compromise, arranged during a campaign visit by presidential candidate Lázaro Cárdenas. In 1932, two local doctors backed the candidacy of a popular Charis supporter for municipal president. When Governor López Cortés imposed his own candidate, the doctors fled to the mountains and waged a short-lived armed campaign against state troops (López Nelio n.d.-b), resulting in the rebels' deaths. This willingness to resort to arms in support of popular claims to self-government facilitated the subsequent political compromise and Charis's ascent to power.[3] During Cárdenas's 1934 campaign visit to Juchitán, Charis's friend and second-in-command, Luis Pineda, wrote and delivered a speech emphasizing local support for Charis and Charis's loyalty to the governor. Charis's willingness to acknowledge the governor's power paved the way for the local victory of his candidate, Pineda, and, shortly thereafter, Charis's position as national senator.[4] In Pineda's account, "Charis told me to say in the speech that the pueblo of Juchitán wasn't fighting with the state government and that the crowd there was proof of it. Cárdenas liked this and promised that unity would lead to improvements for the region, with schools and roads. The governor then allowed Charis to run Juchitán." After that, municipal presidents in Juchitán changed yearly, according to the law. Like other regional caciques of this period, Charis did not generally hold public office, but rather placed loyalists in key positions of power.

Charis's ascendancy in 1934 signified a temporary alliance between regional, state, and federal governments. Initially, this included a popular (Green) local government (finally defeating the more Oaxaca-oriented Reds), the conservative state elite (previously allied with the Reds), and a newly radical federal government led by Cárdenas. Charis could successfully strike this bargain because he had both local support and extensive ties in Mexico City, and because neither state nor federal authorities wanted to face continuing popular revolt in the Isthmus. Furthermore, the exchange of regional autonomy in return for support for the postrevolutionary state served the ongoing federal need to establish centralized control over regional political domains.

With the eclipse of the Reds, Charis came to ally with the Oaxaca elite in support of what became the status quo. In Juchitán, this meant a skillful combination of the maintenance of grassroots support for the popular general and the safeguarding of elite landed and political interests. In this context, Juchiteco Greens and Reds alike came to identify themselves as Charistas, although they were nominally members of the PRI as well.

Through his ties to the federal government, Charis became known for bringing the first municipal services to Juchitán. He repeatedly petitioned for electricity, water, schools, hospitals, and roads, and received a number of these, including the school in the center of the city and the first public hospital in the region. In many accounts, it was the petitioning that was most significant. According to his contemporary and supporter Honorato Morales, Charis "didn't get potable water, but he asked for it for six years. He asked for drainage for thirty years, but didn't get it. He always asked. Some things they gave him and some they didn't." Even according to one of the families he attacked, "some things Charis did were good and some were bad . . . Before, nobody thought there would be irrigation. He asked for irrigation—it's his accomplishment."

Oral histories offered by Juchitecos, both ordinary people and political elites, suggest a more ambiguous postrevolutionary past than the myths about Charis's control and benevolence acknowledge, in terms of the formal politics of the period and people's understanding of the dynamics of Charis's power. According to one market woman, for example, "Charis brought everything we have: light, water, schools." According to another, in partial contrast, "if someone lived well, Charis sent someone to kill him, so that there wouldn't be a man who stands tall, macho, except him." To a campesino and his market-vendor wife, Charis "was a good guy, he asked for schools, irrigation, and water" and "he didn't rob," while their neighbor in the market, a younger woman, retorted, "yes, he robbed, but nobody knew." Others in the PRI and COCEI described Charis's strong-arm tactics, which banished whole families from town, as well as the formation of civic opposition movements early on in Charis's political tenure. To his critics, "he was a bandit" in the years before he assumed political power, one who "with his friends . . . took money from the Huaves [a neighboring ethnic group]." In office and out, he was "despicable and vulgar, he used and raped young girls, he killed others for political reasons so that he could be the only one, but he didn't kill face to face, rather hidden."

Charis kept for himself the land that Obregón had awarded to his troops, and he arranged for the assassination of Rosalino Matus, a peasant who pressed for distribution of the land to its rightful owners (Campbell 1990b, 211; López Nelio n.d.-a). Charis also controlled some of Juchitán's valuable salt mines, where he dominated the unions, provided substandard equipment, and ordered the shooting of a rival union leader.[5]

Similarly, Charis opposed Cárdenas's efforts at land reform in nearby Santiago Laollaga, forcing the president to arm local citizens as part of his *defensa rural* and providing arms himself for supporters of the hacienda (Binford 1983, 298).

Charis spoke Spanish badly, having learned it in adulthood, and brought Luis Pineda with him for reading, writing, and public speaking. The figure of the poorly educated, Zapotec general arguing for the needs of his people in Mexico City earned him enormous local loyalty, and a whole body of anecdotes arose concerning the contact between the Indian and the national politicians.[6] "General Charis had no schooling," said the COCEI-supporting oil worker quoted above, "just sheer courage." He succeeded, according to the market-vendor mother-in-law, much as she had herself, "even though he didn't know how to explain things well, a bit in Zapotec and a bit in Spanish."

Charis's limited linguistic abilities lay at the center of many stories of his interaction with outside authorities. According to one of his soldiers, for example, he defended a number of his men when the military chief of operations in Monterey wanted to throw them out, because they spoke only Zapotec: "Charis told him that he couldn't: 'the language suckled them, general, you can't take it away from them; it suckled them, with it they grew up, it is everything for them, that's why you can't prohibit them from speaking it . . .'" (de la Cruz 1992, 65). In a story recounted by writer Andrés Henestrosa,[7] when Charis decided to address the crowd assembled to greet presidential candidate Avila Camacho in 1940, his enemies laughed at him, "and his friends were pained, because our representative was speaking a Spanish so elementary, primitive" (de la Cruz 1992). Henestrosa may be alluding more to his own discomfort, as a member of the Juchiteco elite and a national intellectual, than to the discomfort of Juchitecos generally. In his telling, however, Charis rescued the situation—and turned the implicit racism of the laughter to his advantage—by turning to Avila Camacho and saying to the crowd, "Friends, so that you are not pained by me, who doesn't know how to speak Spanish, and so that enemies are not happy and laugh at me because I don't know Spanish, I am going to ask you to give us a school where the Juchitecos can learn Spanish" (de la Cruz 1992, 67). "This oratorical recourse," according to Henestrosa, "earned him great applause from friends and enemies."[8] In these applause, furthermore, as well as in the admiration of the soldiers, lies recognition of Charis's skill in maintaining the Zapotec domain of sovereignty and fostering among Juchitecos the ability to interact with the outside on their own terms.

Though he has generally been portrayed as the undisputed regional cacique for twenty years, Charis faced significant challenges throughout his tenure. Some of these challenges, such as the imposition of a candidate for municipal president by outside authorities in the early 1940s, underscored the conflictual relationship between Juchitán and outside political authorities and the tenacity of local resistance. Contemporary observers tell of watching Charis march by with hundreds of supporters, then the outside candidate with eight, and of Charis subsequently bowing to the presidential order, only to return to power a year later. Other oppositions to Charis grew out of conflicts within the Zapotec domain of sovereignty itself. According to López Toledo, who led the Front for Democratic Renovation, the predominant anti-Charis political movement in the Isthmus, Charis's initially honorable political activity "degenerated to the point that he acted as the boss of the Isthmus region" by the mid-1940s. Upon his return to the Isthmus from military service, López Toledo "sensed the unrest of his neighbors, of citizens in general, who no longer supported the bossism of General Charis and wanted a change in the politics of the pueblo." In keeping with what would become the guiding principle of political reformers and moderates in Juchitán, they "wanted others with advanced ideas to take the reins of politics."

During the same years, some national leaders sought to establish a more reformist government in Oaxaca. Both the regional and the national oppositions to the predominant Oaxaca and Isthmus political arrangements spoke in the name of anti-machine politics: the establishment of "modernizing" administrations of businesspeople[9] and professionals who would support freer commerce, economic growth, urbanization, and education.[10] Under the leadership of López Toledo, the Front for Democratic Renovation gained considerable Isthmus-wide support in an explicitly anti-Charis and anti-machine campaign. The Front emphasized the corrupt, uneducated characteristics of Charis's appointees, whom it characterized as politicians, and fought for the entry into politics and administration of educated businesspeople and professionals.

In 1944, López Toledo was designated the official candidate for the municipal presidency in Juchitán by "modernizing" governor Edmundo

Sánchez Cano, who opposed the Oaxaca political and commercial elite with much the same vision López Toledo brought to Juchiteco politics. According to the accounts of contemporaries, López Toledo won office with majority support, but was ousted less than a year later when Sánchez Cano fell, to be replaced by a governor more to the liking of the Oaxacan upper class, Eduardo Vasconcelos. For several months, López Toledo refused to leave office in Juchitán and ran his own municipal government "parallel" to the official one, so that there were in effect two local governments. When it became clear to López Toledo that the situation would not be resolved through negotiation, he stepped down and left Juchitán.[11] In 1950, the federal government attempted for a second time to weaken the Oaxaca elite by appointing Manuel Mayoral Heredia as governor, and the Front for Democratic Renovation again had access to outside political authority and local office. This time, López Toledo and the Front opposed Charis's candidate for federal deputy and eventually succeeded in preventing him from receiving the nomination. Mayoral Heredia, however, was ousted in 1952 and replaced by General Carrasquedo, again an ally of the Oaxaca elite, and Carrasquedo in turn supported Charis.

These accounts of attempted reform in Juchitán and Oaxaca make clear the centrality of state and national relations for politics in Juchitán. Federal reform attempts at the state level in the 1940s and 1950s provided support and access to office for the modernizing coalition in Juchitán, but the rapid failure of these state-level efforts fatally undermined the Front's ability to challenge General Charis. Sánchez Cano fell, as did Mayoral Heredia, in the face of broad alliances of Oaxacan students, professionals, politicians, and businessmen, including many who might have benefited from the new development plans, but who chose instead to support Oaxacan autonomy by opposing federal interventions. As a result, the conservative Oaxacan commercial elite maintained its power, and supported cacique politics in Juchitán, until the end of the 1970s. The authority of the outside, however, was mediated by the practice of "shared" municipal administrations. When Luis Pineda became the first Charista municipal president, the resulting municipal government consisted of five Charistas and four representatives of the state PRI.[12] This sort of arrangement, which continued throughout the years of Charis's rule, was one of the ways in which Juchitecos negotiated the presence of the PRI in the city, and it shows the centrality of elections and municipal administration in brokering the ongoing tension between Juchitán and the outside.

During this period of cacique politics, the ruling political group, which included landowners and teachers, by and large left businesspeople alone. Juchiteco businesspeople, in turn, generally made individual arrangements with politicians and were not active in public politics, with the exception of the minority who supported reformist movements. In the words of one local politician, "The businesspeople made accommodations . . . No one from among them came to be a political leader . . . The businesspeople didn't participate in politics, they had no political strength." One of the reasons Juchiteco businesspeople could seek individual accommodations with local political authorities was that the role of the national state in economic development in Juchitán, while significantly greater than in the Central Valley of Oaxaca and most of the rest of the Oaxaca, was minimal in comparison to its promotion of dynamic national bourgeoisies in some regions of Mexico. For the most part, economic activities during this time changed slowly, with gradual commercial growth centered around the railroad line in Ixtepec, steady activity at the salt mines, and, in Juchitán, the consolidation of craft activities in the hands of local entrepreneurs. Because there was little change in agricultural activity before 1960, furthermore, and land was available to peasant families, the ruling political group by and large left peasants to their own devices. At the same time, politicians began providing the private sector with infrastructure projects that would both promote its growth and facilitate more direct state involvement in later development projects.

In this configuration, the PRI as an official party, though nominally in existence since 1929, was at best only beginning to function in Juchitán by the time of Charis's death, and it was by no means a mass-based party. Although all politicians, including Charis, were nominally priístas, Juchitecos discuss the absence of the official party during the Charis years explicitly. According to Ta Jorge,[13] an older campesino, "there wasn't a party. The designation of candidates, nothing more." In response to the question, "Did you vote for the PRI?" another older campesino answered, "No. In those days Charis was in charge. We voted for Charis, nothing else. There wasn't PRI or COCEI." Mario Bustillo, who led the PRI in the 1970s and 1980s, said that during the Charis period it was difficult to go to Oaxaca, and communication with the capital city was minimal. "I think that they left Charis alone," Bustillo continued. "He put in people. There weren't sectors or, properly speaking, the party itself. Yes they were there in the statutes, but they didn't function."

According to Esteban Peralta, a PRI politician active during and after the Charis years, the sectors, as the PRI's mass organizations were called, were all part of "the PRI as a whole," but they existed "in name only, nothing more. They met to get instructions before elections . . ." Peralta's recounting of the relations between labor unions and the PRI, and his rationale for their existence, indicates the lack of clarity concerning the location of political authority. Unions existed, he said, "only to manipulate people, to have them unionized so as to use them politically, to attract people so as to make a majority, even though the majority didn't matter, since things were run from above, the name of the new governor came from the national PRI in a wax-sealed envelope. Here they let Charis control things." According to López Toledo, Charis would designate leaders for all the organizations, "so it would look like the machinery was functioning." Jaime Ferra, a municipal president at the end of the Charis period, said about politics during the years of boss rule, "There was order, not organization."

Neither peasants nor workers in Juchitán were organized into Mexico's centralized peasant (CNC) and worker (CTM) confederations for two reasons. First, there were no large *ejidos* (collective peasant landholdings) or industries—the economic enterprises around which the CNC and the CTM initially formed—in the southern part of the Isthmus in the 1930s, when the mass organizations were consolidated by Cárdenas. Second, Charis saw no need for such organizations and ignored the directives to form them that arrived periodically from Mexico City.[14] When ordered to establish a branch of a national organization, Charis would appoint a supporter as leader of the organization, instructing that person to fill out and sign documents as necessary. In this way, leaders of local PRI-affiliated organizations, including the local branch of a national women's confederation, were seen as keepers of the seals and documents, not as active participants, and there was no incorporation of peasants, workers, or women into organizational or party politics.

The absence of strong affiliates of the large national confederations does not indicate an absence of organizations based on occupational groups, but rather a local domain of sovereignty in politics that was constructed and maintained apart from national confederations. Regional agricultural and livestock organizations indeed played active roles in political and economic battles during the Charis period and in the 1960s, and they subsequently became focal points for conflict between the PRI and COCEI. These regional organizations, however, enjoyed considerable independence from the national and state PRI. Party leaders in Juchitán recount that efforts to form more substantive sectors of the party began in the post-Charis years of the late 1950s and early 1960s, although even then the results were largely insubstantial.[15] PRI-affiliated organizing efforts among peasants and workers gained greater force only in the 1970s, when active sectors were seen as necessary for combating COCEI's radical mobilization.

Leaders of both COCEI and the PRI have made exaggerated claims for peasant well-being within the Zapotec domain of sovereignty under Charis. Similarly, most scholars of Isthmus society argue that the economic prosperity of local elites during these years—before the economic growth that resulted from highways, the dam, and oil facilities—coexisted with a relatively secure life for the region's peasants, artisans, and few workers (López Monjardin 1983b, 74). Campbell finds that Isthmus Zapotecs "lived in endogamous villages with diversified and vigorous local economies which provided for most basic needs," and that "most peasant producers maintained control of land and their tools of production" (1990b, 174, 175). One consequence of this view of economic life is that COCEI's radical mobilization in the 1970s can then be explained as the straightforward result of attacks on peasant well-being (COCEI 1983). However, a closer look suggests that these conclusions about self-sufficiency and well-being are based on little evidence and conflict with the way people remember the past.

Economic security for Juchiteco peasants was partial and problematic during the Charis period. Even in the nineteenth century, Juchitán had not exhibited the pattern of relatively egalitarian political and economic life that was still characteristic of many similarly small towns with homogeneous ethnic traits. Wealthy Juchitecos were involved in salt production, agriculture, and commerce, including trade in dyes, textiles, and salt with Europe and Guatemala. As a result, economic differentiation among Juchitecos was marked, though both landed and commercial holdings in Juchitán were relatively small, in comparison to other regions of the country. When discussing their own economic history in interviews, Juchitecos first emphasized the difficulties associated with the present, including dramatic price increases, but then went on to say quite directly that the past had in fact been a time of greater poverty: "[they were] hard times. Things cost less, but we had no money." People indicated that they were poorer in the earlier period, in terms of access to food, clothing, shelter, education, and health care, even as they might remember the past as "a nicer time, a cheaper time." Furthermore, many men had to migrate for work in the dry season during the Charis years. In an older peasant's words, "There wasn't irrigation. It was sadder then. As soon as the rainy season was over, we had to leave to go somewhere else." While he was gone, he remembered, his wife lived with his mother: "If there was not enough to eat there, she'd go to her own mother's house. Sometimes there wasn't even breakfast." Thus, the cultural and economic domain of sovereignty in Juchitán during the Charis period included the absence of peasant men, who were forced by the lack of local work to migrate, and the poverty of those left behind.

In reflecting on the Charis period, a younger market woman emphasized the poverty of the past, as well as the intertwined cultural and economic differences between past and present: "The old people used to bathe naked in the street. There were no bathrooms. People bathed anywhere. There was no plumbing. Also no shame. Before, nobody would laugh. Now people laugh. It was better before. No, those were hard times. Now anybody has a bathroom." Similarly, Doña Mariana, a prominent and prosperous local midwife, spoke frequently of her discomfort with the male nudity she encountered during the Charis years in the poor neighborhoods of the city. She also criticized people's habit of eating with their hands, though she later confided that she had eventually come to understand the pleasurable aspects of such a practice. The observations of the young market woman and the older midwife, like those of the migrating peasant, underscore the dual character of the autonomies of the Charis period, during which many Juchitecos were both poor and "backward" by elite local standards, while at the same time they experienced a valued form of community life. The comments of the two women, neither of whom wore traditional dress on a daily basis, also demonstrate the openness of even those Juchitecos critical of local cultural practices to the potential value of those practices.

The ambivalence of people's memories of the past, and their clear indication of greater poverty in the earlier time, suggest that scholars are right in terms of cultural autonomy and economic *survival*, but wrong in terms of absolute levels of economic well-being. Autonomy during the Charis period included the need for large numbers of peasant men to migrate for six months at a time, and survival included hunger. On the other hand, as data presented in the next chapter will indicate, health indices since the 1960s reveal lower levels of infant mortality and of adult morbidity and mortality in Juchitán than in most poor regions of Mexico. Campbell presents the most persuasive evidence for well-being in a discussion of Isthmus ecology—the combination of "ocean and riverine fisheries, salt sources, extensive, flat farming and pasture lands, and tropical forests (which provide wood, animals, and vegetable products)," along with proximity to major north-south and east-west trade routes (Campbell 1990b, 186). These resources indeed distinguish the Isthmus from the more limited ecological and commercial opportunities of many other indigenous regions of Mexico.

Furthermore, there was little explicit consciousness of exploitation during Charis's rule, or, at least, little that is remembered in the 1980s by poor families who lived through the earlier period. Then, there appears to have been some correspondence between what people expected from local economic and political arrangements and what they got. People were in fact getting new kinds of goods from the national government, such as hospitals, schools, and roads. In addition, they were governed for the first uninterrupted period of several decades by a local hero who was seen to represent the poor, within the complex dynamics of cacique politics.

Thus, between 1930 and 1960, in the absence of the sorts of social and economic transformations that occurred in regions of large-scale land reform and industrialization, daily life in Juchitán continued to reflect the ethnic practices and forms of agriculture and craft production of preceding decades. Changes occurred—changes that would be significant in later forms of political resistance and rebellion—but they occurred slowly, and in the short run they reinforced past practices. During these years, Isthmus Zapotec literature and art developed a presence on the national cultural scene, a presence that would play a role in stimulating renewed waves of artistic activity in Juchitán in subsequent decades, and then offer direct financing and protection for COCEI in the 1970s and 1980s. Economically, modest local fortunes were accumulated through the financing of sesame crops and the control of craft production and marketing, and urban infrastructure projects were initiated. Local leaders during the Charis period successfully maintained control of most local resources and, as described above, secured considerable local political autonomy as well. The absence of attack from the outside, finally, allowed these phenomena to come together in a sense of autonomy and self-determination that had not existed during the more tempestuous and violent years of rebellion.

In this context, cacique politics in Juchitán allowed elite interests to be defined as the general interest. Elites acted as arbiters of Zapotec style, often as a means of competition among themselves, as well as to safeguard their status and bring themselves pleasure (Royce 1975). The general outlines of language, dress, ritual, and historical opposition to the outside were shared among elites and ordinary people, all of whom understood themselves to be members of one pueblo. This particular configuration of ethnicity and class was facilitated not only by the shared Zapotec culture and the participation of the bourgeoisie in the elaboration of that culture, but in addition by the local availability of land, the presence of new public-works projects, and the continuing identification of conflict with issues that pitted Juchitán against outside authorities and interests.

Rethinking Boss Politics and Corporatism

Victoriano López Toledo and the Front for Democratic Renovation never fully succeeded in ousting Charis,[16] whose power gradually diminished at the end of the 1950s and ended with his death in 1964. However, the conflict between supporters of an established political boss, including the city's peasants and workers, and an opposing group of professionals, reformers, and aspiring bosses became the mainstay of municipal politics in Juchitán. The Mexican system of one-party rule provided no mechanism for resolving this conflict. The political battles of the late 1940s and early 1950s concerned competing visions of politics and economic development, and this kind of conflict would occur again in the 1960s and continue unresolved for the next twenty years. Should the pueblo look "modern," as that was defined nationally and internationally, with thriving businesses and efficient public administration? Or should Juchitán's economy and culture continue to revolve around small-scale agriculture, handicrafts, and a sprawling central market, with an accompanying politics of Zapotec alliance and coercion? This choice, furthermore, did not involve distinct pathways of "Western" or "Zapotec," but rather concerned how the two would interact, what weight and meaning being Zapotec would assume in a changing Mexico. Juchitán itself constitutes one of a small number of locations where indigenous people have participated in urban, national life *and*, by resisting the customary imperatives of that life, fostered spaces for alternative arrangements.

Conflict over competing visions of development also involved attempts to establish a procedurally workable system of government, which by the late 1950s had come to mean a PRI that could mediate diverse interests. From 1956 to 1965, these procedural issues took center stage in local politics, temporarily eclipsing the divide between politicians and reformers. The planning of a dam and irrigation district for the Isthmus, together with subsequent efforts to oppose the formation of an ejido, provided some basis for unity between the previously opposed camps. However, in Charis's absence, there was no agreed-upon system of candidate selection or municipal administration. As a result, the 1960s was a period of intense conflict over political procedures and their relationship to administration and development.

Why didn't reform efforts succeed in Juchitán in the 1940s and 1950s? In the 1930s, when Cárdenas was promoting large-scale reform and the incorporation of peasants and workers into mass organizations elsewhere, Charis was taking power for the first time in the Isthmus and Juchitecos were working out the parameters of boss rule. In the 1940s and 1950s, when reform efforts were indeed attempted in Oaxaca and Juchitán, there was no longer a national policy of mobilizing the lower classes and challenging established elites. Furthermore, the success of Cárdenas's mobilizations and reforms depended in part on the development of grassroots radicalism, in labor and *agrarista* movements alike. In Juchitán, in contrast, Charis maintained mass support and the reform movement was an elite, minority phenomenon. The federal government, moreover, generally left local politicians alone when they were strong enough to maintain order. During this period, being strong enough meant, among other things, being able to *traer gente*, to demonstrate popular support, and that was one of the things Charis could do best. In this situation, the Oaxaca Valley commercial elite's opposition to reform anywhere in the state successfully forestalled occasional federal reform initiatives.

Thus, in Juchitán a shrewd and strong boss could consolidate power because of the federal government's need for control over diverse regions during a tumultuous postrevolutionary period. After the national regime allowed him to take power over state opposition, the boss and state politicians found that they could coexist quite comfortably, in the absence of reform efforts that threatened them both. The boss's continuing ability to publicly demonstrate mass support earned him power within Juchitán and credibility outside. Some businesspeople and professionals, organized in the Front for Democratic Renovation, had a different vision of politics, or could gain in specific ways by new development policies, and wanted to oust him, while most did quite well by coexisting. The power of the regional cacique and that of the state elite reinforced one another, allowing the consolidation of a cultural and political domain of sovereignty, but preventing the establishment of a coalition focused on economic growth and the development of more democratic processes of political mediation within the PRI.

The postrevolutionary history of Juchitán thus provides convincing evidence that Mexican politics cannot be accurately understood as the establishment and breakdown of an institutionalized one-party regime exercising control through corporatist mass organizations. While the implicit bargain struck by Cárdenas, the governor of Oaxaca, and General Charis was typical of the arrangements that underlay the early years of the "institutionalized state," the dynamics of this arrangement—with its reliance on bargaining, autonomy, and ethnicity—are not acknowledged in the usual corporatist picture. The nature of the relationship between the central government and the region after 1930 was neither institutionalized, nor corporatist, nor controlled from the center, in the way these terms are commonly used to describe Mexican politics. The regional cacique did not form an effective political party within the PRI, official mass organizations did not supplant local ones, and the PRI did not function to mediate conflict among elites or between elites and masses.

Contrary to the corporatist picture, which assumes a complete reorientation of political affiliations under Cárdenas (Hamilton 1982), the political commitments and relationships found in Juchitán drew heavily on those that had been established in the course of nineteenth- and early-twentieth-century rebellions. In the process of resisting economic incursions by Oaxacans, Europeans, and others, Juchitecos had come to see themselves as a unified pueblo and to be defined by Oaxacans as criminal and barbaric. The multiclass alliance that resulted from this local history, and produced a regional domain of sovereignty, was not reinforced by the political practices of the PRI, and it broke down in the 1970s partly as a result of the economic projects and political policies of the party and the regime.

The corporatist analysis does not examine elections before the late 1970s, viewing them as affirmations of political decisions reached in the center and seeing the apparent significance of elections since the late 1970s as a new phenomenon. Such an analysis characterizes the Díaz regime, like the postrevolutionary one, as a successful form of centralized political and economic control. The history of Juchitán, in contrast, demonstrates that elections that matter, and competition over local office generally, have long been important focal points for negotiations over power, both internally and between Juchitán and the outside. The designation of local political officials by state and national authorities was hotly contested before and during the Díaz regime, often in the form of violent rebellion. After the revolution, electoral competition was central to the installation of Charis as regional boss, to reform attempts in the 1940s and 1950s, and to efforts to establish a political party and allocate regional power in the 1960s. This does not mean that elections were fair or that the winners necessarily took office. Rather, elections affected the allocation and exercise of power in complex direct and indirect ways— through the massing of supporters, the holding of public office, negotiation over economic and administrative policies, and the formation of ethnic and regional identities. The question of votes and how they would count related directly to the different ways in which the PRI was formed and developed as a political party in successive decades and to the way in which opposition was enacted. The use of parallel local governments as a means for expressing the endurance of opposition and of shared city councils, which allowed representation of opposing camps within the official party, demonstrates that forms of opposition autonomy and non-corporatist representation were central to the politics of the midcentury period.

In contrast to the active, hegemonic PRI and weakened ethnicity of the state-centered model, Juchitán had no institutionalized political party between the 1930s and the 1970s, but exhibited a vibrant indigenous ethnic life, including language, ritual, poetry, music, and painting. In contrast to the national peasant and worker confederations of the corporatist model, Juchitán housed only weak branches of the confederations, but active local land and livestock associations unaffiliated with the center. Rather than the supposed corporatist peace of the 1930–60 period, Juchitán during these years experienced ongoing conflict between a regional boss and reformist civic oppositions. On the state level, in contrast to the economic development and political institutionalization of the corporatist model, diverse Oaxacan elites mobilized repeatedly and successfully against technological and industrial change and against the reform governors designated by the central government. These mobilizations in turn consolidated elite control of markets, cacique control of regions, and diverse regional ethnic identities and practices—precisely those patterns that were supposed to wither away under the hegemonic corporatist state, and which continue to challenge and shape national politics today from such locations as Oaxaca, Guerrero, and Chiapas.

The conflict between cacique-based politics and reform coalitions, unacknowledged in the corporatist analysis of this period, characterized regional politics in the Isthmus and in the state of Oaxaca from the 1940s to the 1980s. Its lack of resolution during the life of General Charis left local elites with no base upon which to establish a political party that could incorporate diverse groups and mediate conflict among them in the 1960s. The absence of such a political party at the local level in many regions of Mexico made it near impossible for the national electoral reforms sponsored by Carlos Madrazo in the mid-1960s to succeed. These reforms, in turn, particularly the institution of a primary system within the official party, might have established mechanisms of political competition for solving local disputes and linking center to region during the subsequent years of conflictual economic transformation.

The rigid and closed political party that evolved, with considerable turbulence, by the end of the 1960s in Juchitán was distinctly not the PRI of the corporatist or state-centered analyses—it did not incorporate ordinary Juchitecos, it did not mediate local interests, and it did not provide mechanisms of communication and control between Juchitecos and the state and national government. The PRI of the late 1960s, in turn, elicited an opposition much like the earlier Front for Democratic Renovation, with a base of support among middle-class and elite businesspeople and professionals. In their efforts to rework the domain of sovereignty to their own advantage, elites in the 1960s began a process of explicit politicization of daily life that took on a life of its own and ultimately forged new discourses of democracy and development. This elite-led politicization occurred through mass mobilizations and electoral participation and through critiques of corruption, poverty, and failed economic development. The persistence and complexity of the debates in *El Satélite* during the 1960s and 1970s demonstrate that Juchitecos were well aware of the broad significance of politics. The state-centered model does not acknowledge the existence of these debates or their effects in shaping people's beliefs about politics. Furthermore, again in contrast to the state-centered model, this debate was carried on outside of and in explicit critique of official, national politics.

Contrary to the corporatist state analysis, with its emphasis on mass incorporation, elite quiescence, and insignificant elections, it was a group of middle-class and elite citizens within a noncorporatist PRI that first articulated the very critique that COCEI would put forth several years later and that first mobilized peasants and workers to vote against the official party. This political effort, as Chatterjee argued for Indian nationalism, occurred after a domain of sovereignty had been achieved in linguistic, artistic, ritual, and family arenas. In this context, a radical grassroots movement of Zapotec students, peasants, and workers in the 1970s could successfully appropriate the cultural and economic components of the domain of sovereignty to forge a mass-based, counterhegemonic project. A mid-twentieth-century politics of boss rule, and of elite cultural and economic predominance, thus shaped a Zapotec pueblo that could later reshape the discourses of nineteenth-century Indian violence and barbarism to challenge both outside authority and the indigenous elite.

4

The Politics of Reform, 1960–1973
"Transcendental Steps toward Progress" [1]

By the 1960s and 1970s, Juchitán's increasing integration with the national economy and polity threatened the forms of autonomy around
which the relationship between ethnicity and class had been constructed
since the 1930s. During the Charis period, the dynamics of regional
life complemented and enabled the hegemony of the postrevolutionary
state. In this context, the multiclass Zapotec alliance had secured autonomy from the outside, elite cultural authority and prosperity, and a degree of well-being for peasants and workers. In the 1960s, in contrast,
these pillars of the domain of sovereignty began to be challenged by
state-led development projects, competition within the newly important
PRI, and shifts in Zapotec artistic and cultural discourses. As a result, local
elites sought to rework the components of boss rule to fit the new circumstances. Their goal was to adjust to new forms of economic development
and new beliefs about civic politics and administration, while maintaining ethnic autonomy and elite leadership of it. To carry out these economic and political transformations, they welcomed increasing involvement on the part of government authorities and outside businesspeople in
regional affairs.

In prominent public campaigns, Juchiteco elites promoted privatization of land, mechanization of agriculture, and industrialization. In addition, political reformers pressed for "clean" government, in the form of
transparent competition and accountable administration. These efforts
culminated in the 1971 election of a moderate, reformist municipal government in opposition to the PRI. The leader of this opposition campaign, Manuel Musalem Santiago, or Tarú, simultaneously represented
the aspirations of an ambitious private sector and reproduced many of the
attributes of the midcentury domain of sovereignty. Tarú signified a

larger-than-life figure, elite ethnic leadership, Zapotec language, and a public politics suffused with ritual celebration. However, Tarú and his supporters misread the state of both the Zapotec domain of sovereignty and the national hegemony, each of which had changed in complex and contradictory ways since the 1930s. Tarú's coalition, with its promises of elite-led economic and political development in accord with Western norms, foundered on its assessment of each component of such a plan. Moderate reformists in Juchitán wrongly assumed that ethnic identities had remained constant and elite political authority intact. They mistakenly believed that change within the PRI could be achieved through internal pressure and underestimated the economic and cultural effects of large-scale industrial and agricultural development on Juchitecos. All together, they understood as an elite project a set of issues involving Juchitecos across classes, at a time when boundaries between Juchitán and the outside were rapidly shifting: what would be the place of Zapotec life, of the Zapotec domain of sovereignty, in the changing Mexican nation?

The Political Economy of Reform in Juchitán

The political movements of PRI moderates in the 1960s, like those of COCEI radicals after 1973, responded to widespread economic transformations in the Isthmus. However, different forms of economic change underlay reformist, as opposed to radical, initiatives. The 1960s was a period of land concentration, infrastructural development, and new agricultural products, though also of slowed and even negative economic growth. After 1973, economic-development efforts disrupted patterns of work and the panorama of municipal life more rapidly, with industrial projects, oil processing, and commercial expansion fostering a two-track economy of oil-led urban expansion and low-productivity, small-scale agriculture.

Juchitán's location at the intersection of two recently completed highways, the Trans-Isthmic and Pan-American, led to its steady growth as a regional commercial center after 1960 (Campbell 1990b, 241–42). The construction of the Benito Juárez Dam and an electric plant in the early 1960s, as well as a rice-processing plant and sugar mill in the 1960s and 1970s, respectively, accelerated this process. Between 1960 and 1980, local merchants expanded the textile and all-purpose stores that had characterized the city's retail trade, and both local entrepreneurs and investors from Oaxaca established hardware, furniture, automobile, appliance, building-material, and stationery businesses. In the 1970s, several national and international retail chains, such as Sears, opened branches in Juchitán, and beer distributorships and soft-drink bottling plants expanded. The construction of a refinery, the modernization of the port of Salina Cruz to serve as a Pacific base for oil exports, and the redevelopment of a trans-Isthmic rail and trucking system connecting Gulf and Pacific ports in the 1980s provided both temporary and permanent jobs and again stimulated commercial development in the Isthmus. The population of Juchitán grew throughout this period, from 13,814 in 1950 to approximately 80,000 in 1988,[2] with the largest growth rates for the years from 1950 to 1980 occurring between 1960 and 1970 (Jhabvala 1982, 51).

Throughout these decades, the region occupied a middle position in Mexico economically. Its indices of economic production and standard of living were considerably lower than those of larger urban and industrialized areas, but higher than those of other peripheral indigenous and agricultural regions. In 1960, 33 percent of the gross domestic product of the Isthmus consisted of secondary-sector activities, while for Mexico as a whole, including its many regions of small-scale agriculture, the figure was 27.7 percent (Jhabvala 1982, 20). The value added per capita in the Isthmus was twice that of the state of Oaxaca as a whole in 1960, and 75 percent greater than the state as a whole in 1968 (Jhabvala 1982, 20, 39).[3] Similarly, Juchitecos experienced a higher standard of living (that is, a somewhat less extreme level of poverty) than did the inhabitants of the other regions of the state of Oaxaca, except the capital city itself, and a higher standard of living than residents of other relatively poor southern states as well. The city occupied a middle position in Mexico with regard to such matters as protein consumption and availability of electricity and running water (Jhabvala 1982, 109, chart 20; Ortiz Wadgymer 1971, 94, chart 7), as well as general health indices.[4] This middle position reflected the achievements of nineteenth-century rebellions and the twentieth-century domain of sovereignty in maintaining regional control of resources and establishing effective local networks of distribution. It also meant that the Isthmus had the infrastructure perceived to be necessary for industrial growth and that Juchitecos were well enough off to defend their economy over decades.

Despite expectations of industrial expansion, the Isthmus economy experienced forms of negative growth in the 1960s (Jhabvala 1982, 83). The absence of industrial expansion was particularly vexing to local businessmen, professionals, and politicians, who viewed such growth as a prerequisite for economic well-being and social advance. While the proportion of manufacturing in the *national* economy increased in the course of the decade, it decreased in the Isthmus, with the gross product per capita decreasing steadily as well.[5] During these years, furthermore, the municipality of Juchitán experienced an unusually high rate of population increase (Jhabvala 1982, 51, chart 4). Renewed attempts at reform within the system in the 1960s thus took place at a time when the city was expanding in size, but expectations for economic growth were not being met. Furthermore, while local reformers expected that the flaws in the economy could be corrected with the right combination of political pressure and technical expertise, a report produced in the early 1970s by an Isthmus-wide development commission documented continuing economic failure, citing low agricultural yields, inferior livestock, poor technology, and insufficient credit as causes (Rueda Jiménez 1976, 124–26).

In its most inclusive sense, the reform agenda in Juchitán sought recognizable improvements in political accountability, economic well-being, and cultural voice, and it addressed the lives of ordinary people as well as elites. Reformers sought forms of economic development and political competition that would benefit entrepreneurial and professional middle-class and elite Zapotecs, allowing them to expand their economic activities in a well-administered, modernizing city. However, because of their strong Zapotec identity, reformers also acknowledged the suffering of the pueblo and at times spoke for economic improvement and political empowerment for the region's peasants and workers. Both aspects of the reform movement were spurred by the spectacular failure of new agricultural and industrial programs and the corruption of the PRI and the agrarian bureaucracy.

The politics of reform in the 1960s and early 1970s in Juchitán was integrally related to the task of creating a politics to replace boss rule. This problem occurred throughout Mexico, as the central figures of regional political authority died and the relationships between region and center that had coincided with the hegemony of the regime in the 1930s faced new pressures and challenges. In the 1960s, battles over political procedures and reformist initiatives precipitated explosive civic mobilizations in numerous states.[6] In Juchitán, the functioning of the PRI as a political party was repeatedly contested as various political factions maneuvered to assume the power of the boss, national and local officials attempted and then abandoned internal primaries, and opposition groups tested strategies within and outside the official party. Two dramatic campaigns, in which Zapotec elites mobilized the region's peasants and workers, stood out in this process. First, in an Isthmus-wide campaign in the early 1960s, elites used identity-based discourses to oppose a presidential decree that would have turned most of the Isthmus irrigation district into an ejido. Such an ejido arrangement, which was canceled, would have protected peasants from land grabs on the part of wealthy landowners. Second, in 1971, after years of political challenge within the PRI, elites sought to recreate the Charis cacicazgo on new terms. To do so, they mobilized the pueblo behind a charismatic opposition leader, suffusing municipal life with ritual celebration and promising honest public administration. As hopes for reform met with obstruction, however, reformers denounced existing political and economic institutions and called for change in increasingly radical terms.

The Anti-Ejido Movement

The political movement in defense of private property, led by Zapotec elites and supported by mass mobilizations, simultaneously drew on Juchitán's legacy of resistance to outside incursions and abetted the efforts of large landowners to expand their holdings. In 1962, with the completion of the dam and accompanying irrigation district, President López Mateos announced that the land surrounding Juchitán would become an ejido. While the land in Juchitán had been legally classified as communal—owned and regulated by the community, but used like private property—it had functioned in practice like private property and, before the 1960s, was relatively inexpensive and available to those willing to work it (Binford 1985, 179–85). When the introduction of irrigation led to increases in land prices (Binford 1985, 186), peasant families began to sell some of their holdings to meet expenses in crisis situations,

making up for lost income by increasing their participation in the growing commercial economy. An ejido arrangement would have guaranteed
that land remain in peasant families, at least legally. It might also have
provided credit and other agricultural supports and offered possibilities
for collective production.

In response to the ejido decree, prominent members of the city's economic and political elite, many of whom were landowners, formed an
association to fight the decree (Binford 1985, 185–88).[7] Their campaign, which involved the establishment of anti-ejido committees in each
Isthmus town, linked businessmen and politicians who had been on opposing sides in past municipal political conflicts, but who generally stood
to gain if land became legally marketable as private property. Committees in Defense of Small Property mobilized three thousand to five thousand supporters in protest meetings, rallying peasants with historical
references to the defense of land rights and rhetorical threats of armed
rebellion, as well as filing petitions and legal claims against the ejido
resolution (López Gurrión 1982, 151, cited in Campbell 1990b, 223).

The anti-ejido committees gained peasant support through arguments
that land in Juchitán had always functioned as private property, as well as
rumors that land would be distributed to families from other parts of the
state. Fears of losing land were strengthened by the negative experiences
of residents of the nearby town of Jalapa del Marqués, which had been
displaced by the dam's reservoir (Campbell 1990b, 223), as well as by the
fact that peasants had lost land in the course of railroad and highway
projects in previous decades (Campbell 1990b, 265n 35). In addition,
landowning peasants may correctly have reasoned that as members of
an ejido they would be subject to considerable bureaucratic decision-
making at a time when ejidos in other regions were not receiving strong
government support. Some may have felt as well that they would prefer
to have full control over their land, including the right to sell it, as the
irrigation district developed. In this way, Juchiteco attitudes toward the
ejido project mirrored those of peasants in Namiquipa, Chihuahua, who
rejected the legitimacy and value of the ejido that was pressed on them in
the 1920s, arguing instead for local autonomy based on prerevolutionary
property arrangements (Nugent 1994, chap. 4). Indeed, the effort on the
part of state and national authorities to promote ejido reform in Juchitán
conflicted with local experiences and beliefs in ways that officials did
little to address (Binford 1985, 188).[8] As a result, Juchiteco peasants

opted to oppose outside incursions, rather than seek the long-term protections potentially offered by the ejido arrangement. In so doing, they minimized the tensions between agrarian capitalists and small producers, adopting a political discourse that joined all local landholders in an alliance against the state (Binford 1985, 196).

After meetings, petitions, and analyses by professionals sent from Mexico City, the anti-ejido association succeeded in pressuring President Díaz Ordaz to reverse the decree. In a widely publicized ceremony in 1966, the president issued almost four thousand private-property titles to those who demonstrated "ownership" of communal land. These titles covered twenty-five thousand of the thirty thousand hectares of irrigated land within the municipality of Juchitán. As a result of this reversal of the ejido decree, most of the irrigated land in the Juchitán district remained in private hands, to be freely bought and consolidated in subsequent years. However, in reversing the decree and converting communal land to private property, President Díaz Ordaz acted illegally, and the steep political costs of any legal resolution of the conflict maintained the status of the land in official limbo, a situation that complicated agricultural transactions and kept the issue volatile. Meanwhile, the private-property solution, followed in practice despite official findings of illegality by President Echeverría's Ministry of Agrarian Reform in the 1970s, made possible the gradual sale of peasant property and the consolidation of large landholdings that exceeded legal limits, with the result that ten years after the anti-ejido effort, the land issue became the center of COCEI's political program.

The Agrarian Agencies

The construction of the Isthmus irrigation district not only changed patterns of land ownership, but brought peasants into direct contact with state agencies, as agricultural planners sought to recoup the costs of constructing the dam and irrigation system and foster the regional economic benefits that the project had promised. While this economic effort was largely unsuccessful during the thirty-year history of the district (Binford 1983, chaps. 3, 5; Campbell 1990b, 227–39), it transformed agricultural relations in the region, through the construction of first a rice-processing plant, which rapidly failed, and then a sugar mill, which functioned with some success after initial difficulties, but eventually closed in the early 1990s. Both efforts were accompanied by pressures on small and medium landowners to abandon corn cultivation for rice and cane, resulting in considerable state control over peasant production, as well as in peasant indebtedness, with debts in turn providing outside agencies with increased leverage in production decisions (Binford 1983, chap. 3; Warman 1972).

Agricultural development projects failed in a number of different ways, generally related to the inappropriateness of new crops and the contradictory effects of irrigation.[9] In addition, the projects brought corruption on the part of government officials and the leaders of producer organizations, as new authorities used their positions to obtain land illegally or to engage in corrupt deals. Ordinary growers, in contrast, depended on proper methods, good weather, and a reasonably functioning bureaucracy for success, which varied from year to year (Campbell 1990b, 234–35). As a result, the cane project neither pacified peasants nor won their support for the PRI. Instead, it produced competing cane "mafias" within the official party and politicized and alienated many peasants as they experienced the negative consequences of government agricultural credit and supervision (Campbell 1990b, 237).

Government involvement thus produced contradictory results—new forms of production from which some small- and medium-scale producers indeed benefited, as well as dissatisfaction and political opposition. In addition, the very inefficiency and unevenness of the system provided peasants with room for maneuver in maintaining indigenous social arrangements and nonindustrial farming methods (Campbell 1990b, 238). Peasants manipulated available agrarian services to resist development, selectively accepting and adapting such inputs as credit, insurance, and new crops to maintain their smallholdings and way of life. As peasants did this, officials of the agrarian bureaucracy exhibited open disdain for the Zapotec culture peasants defended, and the publications of agrarian agencies and researchers were rife with references to the need to abolish traditional practices and mentalities (Ortiz Wadgymer 1971, 87; SARH n.d., cited in Campbell 1990a, 267n 42). The assistant director of the Tehuantepec Office of the Ministry of Agriculture (SARH) blamed agricultural problems on "local customs" and described Zapotec peasants as "savage" (Campbell 1990b, 229), thus drawing on the tropes of otherness and barbarism long employed by outsiders. Such assertions underscored the foreign origin of development projects and the extent to which, in addition to threatening peasant livelihoods, they attacked popular Zapotec culture explicitly. Engineers assessing the problems of the irrigation district labeled that culture "degenerate" and insisted that it was inadequate for the tasks of development:

The type of dwelling . . . and the clothing have not been modified and have only been impoverished through time, the same as religious traditions, fiestas, and forms of government, that after apparently constituting an adequate social structure, have degenerated in customs that contain very little of what originally was essential and, instead, generate wastage of money, laziness, and conflicts with grave consequences for the impoverished economies of the region's inhabitants . . . *It is evident that there is a wide gap between the culture they possess and that necessary for their development* . . . (del Conde and Piedra n.d., cited in Campbell 1990a, 229, italics mine)

Although they disagreed in part about the suitability of Zapotec culture for development, reformist Juchitecos and outsiders alike saw industrialization as the key to well-being. Writers in *El Satélite* related economic change directly to local politics, observing that "before it was the high rates of return on capital [that attracted investors]; today, more than that, [it is] security, the stability of the region . . . in which they are going to invest millions of pesos." *El Satélite* also emphasized the potential effects of economic stagnation on the region's poor, who, in the absence of industrialization, would "run the risk of finding themselves with nothing." In that situation, "cattle rustling, assault, and robbery will be the only way out for many people who find no other resources" (21 Sept. 1969). As a result, "All of us, absolutely all, with one single voice, clamor for industrialization" (29 June 1969). This clamoring was articulated in a distinctly modern, Western idiom. "Like a plane," a columnist wrote, "we are ready with all the necessary equipment. We are lacking only fuel and the personnel for takeoff." Like modernized politics, furthermore, this takeoff could be honest and accountable: "What we ask is that all be done through a study. That it be planned . . . so that in the near future we won't be sorry" (26 Oct. 1969).

Several articles in *El Satélite* in 1968 outlined the technical and bureaucratic failures that would plague the irrigation district in the future, despite these early hopes, and serve as rallying points for mass mobilizations. One article documented the rice fiasco, arguing that the debts it produced left peasants worse off than they had been with past systems of usurious loans. Furthermore, in many cases where peasants could not repay their debts, the bank took possession of land titles (17 Mar. 1968). Two other articles presaged the explosive agricultural issues of the next decade, the amassing of large landholdings and authoritarian control of the local Communal Land Commission (Comisariado de Bienes Comunales), with the newspaper calling on authorities "to unmask the new monopolists" (22 Sept. 1968). Observers became increasingly hostile to state agricultural agencies in the early 1970s (17 Jan., 17 Oct. 1971), and *El Satélite* regularly reported cases of unethical and incompetent treatment of peasants. As a result of unfair agrarian policies, according to writers in the newspaper, "the mantle of poverty embraces ever more families who are dispossessed of their land" (25 Apr. 1971). Many Juchitecos concluded that what was needed to fight this "agrocracia" was radical change in the banks and the return of land to those who were forced to sell it (2 May, 25 Apr. 1971). The agricultural situation also focused attention on the inability of local organizations to deal with the new, state-led system of agricultural development. *El Satélite* reported extensively on the control of the Regional Livestock Union by a handful of corrupt leaders and the union's failure to aid peasants with pressing problems (14 Feb., 22 Aug. 1971). Similarly, when elections were finally held for the Communal Land Commission, powerful local leaders packed the meeting with nonpeasant supporters, thereby manipulating the elections in their own favor. In this situation, according to the newspaper, the real peasants "found themselves like strangers, silent and crestfallen, thinking about their land. Looked all around, they said, 'Well, and those who are supposed to fight for us? Don't bother, *compadres'*" (28 Feb. 1971).

As this response indicates, the process of agricultural transformation in Juchitán had led to a situation in which peasants were harmed by economic projects administered by outside officials, while the local organizations that had served to regulate agrarian affairs in the past no longer addressed peasant needs. The arrangements between elites and peasants that had characterized the years of cacique rule, with elites maintaining economic and cultural authority while peasants enjoyed relative well-being and autonomy, could no longer be met by either party to the bargain. Elites needed new relationships to outside political and bureaucratic officials, as well as access to outside financial resources, in order to maintain their predominant economic position locally, while peasants needed new leverage and skills in order to protect their land and family economies. Debates about economic development and poverty spurred widespread contestation over political procedures, the meaning of a political party, the identity of the pueblo, and the designation of successors to the postrevolutionary cacique.

Efforts to Form a Political Party

Beginning in the late 1950s, and intensifying after Charis's death in 1964, politics in Juchitán centered around the issue of how to create a political party. In the boss's absence, there was no agreed-upon system of candidate selection or municipal administration and little formal organization, apart from local land, livestock, and business associations with few links to the outside. Those who had been closely associated with Charis sought to maintain control of his political machine, now fully identified with the PRI. In elections in 1965 and 1968, political conflict centered around processes of candidate selection and "independent" candidacies within the official party. In each case, efforts to forge political options distinct from those of the past foundered on the strength of machine politics, the weakness of national reformers, and increasing municipal corruption.

As a result of the policies of PRI president Carlos Madrazo, who led the movement to establish more democratic procedures within the national party, several candidates competed openly in a primary election to choose the PRI mayoral candidate in Juchitán in 1965.[10] This effort generated extensive local participation, and it has long been remembered in Juchitán as a key moment of attempted political reform. Its results were contested and ambiguous. According to some accounts, precandidate Ricardo López Gurrión won the primary, but was arbitrarily denied the candidacy by higher PRI authorities. According to others, López Gurrión had not lived in Juchitán long enough to qualify to run, having only recently returned from years of residence in Mexico City. All agreed that López Gurrión's supporters burned ballot boxes during the general elections, resulting in their annulment and the appointment of an administrative council. New elections were held six months later, with PRI authorities this time supporting a more popular candidate. Juchitán's first experiment with democratic primaries within the PRI was thus neither a success nor a failure. The primaries took place, their fairness was contested, elections were held and disrupted, and the appointment of an administrative council and temporary leader was followed by the appointment of a new candidate and new elections. However, reformer Madrazo was killed in a suspicious plane crash, and the national experiment with internal primaries was subsequently terminated, largely because of widespread regional opposition.

Besides being a period of turmoil within the PRI in Juchitán, the 1960s was a time when Isthmus traditions of critical journalism and artistic commentary experienced new vitality. Leopoldo de Gyves Pineda, a retired military officer, wrote in regional newspapers of the need for new party leaders and more effective approaches to development. De Gyves followed in the tradition of Facundo Génico and his outspoken newspaper, *La Voz del Istmo*, which was known in the 1950s and 1960s for supporting Isthmus separatism and Zapotec culture, as well as for criticizing local authorities and opposing the PRI (Campbell 1990b, 278). De Gyves's critique also reflected the efforts of a group of Juchiteco students and young intellectuals who began to publish the journal *Neza Cubi* (the New Road) in the mid-1960s. *Neza Cubi* was a descendant of the earlier literary journal *Neza*, published by Juchiteco writers in Mexico City in the 1930s. The younger generation of Juchitecos renewed the intellectual attention to Zapotec culture and art that had occurred in the earlier period. In keeping with the increasingly critical national political culture of the 1960s, they took the new step of combining their emphasis on Zapotec art with commentary on contemporary social and political affairs. In discussing such local problems as the regional agricultural situation and the ineffective government handling of a massive flood, the *Neza Cubi* writers made new connections between the development of a self-conscious ethnic identity (the task of the earlier, nationally prominent intellectuals) and the economic and administrative problems of daily life in Juchitán (the concerns of the 1960s reformers).

Pressured by the termination of internal primaries and escalating conflict within the PRI, and inspired by the new critical discourse, reformers established the Juchitán Civic Committee (Comité Cívico Heroes 5 de Septiembre) as a base for challenging old-style, machine politics. The Civic Committee entered electoral politics in 1968, when Mario Marín, who had been defeated in the 1965 primaries, was named candidate for municipal president by federal officials. Marín's designation occurred without even the limited, sector-based selection procedures that were supposed to have replaced local primaries. A coalition of local groups, including the Civic Committee and López Gurrión and his supporters, formed a leadership committee and carried out a series of meetings and then a plebiscite to choose an alternative candidate. They intended for this candidate to be "independent" within the PRI, so as to pressure state and national authorities to restructure the slate headed by Marín. When outside authorities refused, however, the Civic Committee launched its candidate, de Gyves, in municipal elections as an independent opposition to Marín. In the face of an official victory for Marín, the committee characterized the elections as fraudulent and claimed victory for de Gyves. Popular opposition to Marín's taking office brought the military to Juchitán for the first time for an inauguration, foreshadowing the repeated military interventions and occupations of the following two decades. In this instance, soldiers surrounded Marín's house, the PRI office, and City Hall in order to install the new municipal president.

While municipal corruption was not a new phenomenon, Marín's administration was the one most often cited for beginning the widespread and public corruption of the PRI that is said to have occurred in the years after Charis's death. The three-story building that Marín constructed on the town square during his term in office, which later housed both Sears and Banamex, became a prominent public symbol of PRI corruption. A treasury scandal ultimately brought state auditors, which was seen by Marín's opponents as a commitment to administrative reform on the part of outside authorities. Despite findings of fraud, however, the treasurer remained in office with Marín's support. Denunciations of corruption in *El Satélite* highlighted the factionalism and corruption of the PRI and invoked the involvement and unity of the pueblo. In addition, in a rhetorical form that became increasingly common during these years, the newspaper manipulated for antiregime purposes the very designation of the pueblo as ignorant that had historically been wielded against Juchitecos by outsiders. Emphasizing the need for accountability and questioning the motives of a government that withholds information, the newspaper asserted that "the pueblo has a right to be informed of the amount of the fraud." "In this," it continued, "the members of the Chamber of Deputies, as representatives of that pueblo which they so often invoke, have an obligation to announce the extent of the fraud, and whether it is going to be returned. Or is it a State secret? *Or is it that it's not worth the effort to inform the pueblo because it is ignorant?* If that's the way it is, then say so" (27 July 1969; italics mine). By making strategic use of the historical trope of ignorance, *El Satélite* drew on the cultural politics that underlay the Charis cacicazgo, when the "ignorant" Indian mediated skillfully between Juchitán and Mexico City. However, in its effort to renew the multiclass alliance of the Charis years behind new goals, *El Satélite* employed the trope of ignorance in order to reject, rather than embrace, its characterization and to press for forms of honest public administration foreign to the machine politics of the Charis era.

Mobilization and the Ousting of the PRI

During Marín's term in office, the reformist Civic Committee continued to grow. The committee emphasized its local origin and its independence from outside officials, and it pressured government authorities to further an agenda of clean politics and regional development. For the 1971 elections, the committee joined with other local groups—the association of small-property owners, the local livestock association, small-business people, market people, and several groups of workers—to form the United Democratic Front, designating Alejandro López López as candidate and Manuel Musalem Santiago (Tarú), who was a more popular leader, as the head of the campaign. In light of its 1968 experience, in which acting as an independent group within the PRI did not bring tangible results, the Democratic Front formed an alliance with the Popular Socialist Party (PPS), a national, quasi-opposition party that had begun to grow in the Isthmus. This resulted in the second elite-led mobilization of the post-Charis period, a moment of passionate and festive community activism that transformed public politics in Juchitán.

In the course of this campaign, Juchitecos gathered in celebrations and demonstrations wearing pink, the color of the PPS, and the pueblo was repeatedly identified with Tarú in political slogans and in accounts of daily life and ritual. It was said that supporters of the opposition said "Tarú" as they greeted each other and shook hands (Campbell 1990b, 190–91), and *El Satélite* reported that a baby, thought dead at birth, cried "Tarú, Tarú, Tarú" after being slapped on the buttocks and coming to life. The newspaper also reported that a sick man, kneeling at the altar, bargained with the candidate: "Tarú, you have my vote, but help me, I need to get up to go to your rallies." The Democratic Front attracted ten thousand supporters, an extremely large gathering at the time, to its campaign rallies. As a result of this electoral participation, according to *El Satélite*, the pueblo was being mobilized: "The civic-mindedness of the pueblo, which in previous years had remained asleep, is awakening" (24 Oct. 1971). Despite the clear outpouring of support for the Front, however, election officials declared victory for the PRI candidate, Esteban Peralta, in a move that evoked memories of outside political impositions before the revolution and during the Charis years. The Democratic Front countered with mass mobilizations and protests, and this, in turn, led to the annulment of the elections and the appointment by the governor of a civil administration headed by Tarú.

Tarú's appointment to office was experienced as a popular victory of enormous symbolic and practical importance, signifying resistance to PRI rule, a triumph of democracy, and the beginning of competent and efficient municipal government. It involved masses of Juchitecos in elections and located the pueblo simultaneously within formal politics and outside the official party. Tarú's victory established the notion of popular sovereignty as an event, a defining moment when a grassroots movement gained control of public administration and public space. Furthermore, it made of elections a form of cultural elaboration in which the daily acts of ordinary people—the colors they wore, the fiesta rituals they celebrated, the arguments they sustained, and the makeup and finery they applied—played a conspicuous and consequential role, much as they would in the campaigns and victories of COCEI. These elections, in turn, reinforced the belief among Juchitecos that democracy meant that the end result corresponded to the popular will, rather than that fair electoral procedures were strictly upheld.

The Tarú administration was the last in a succession of opportunities for reform within the system—reform that would accommodate rather than oppose regime authority, look within rather than outside the PRI for long-term legitimacy, and speak in the language of community and nation rather than ethnicity and class. In addition to problems of land ownership and agricultural production, pressing issues included Juchitán's woefully neglected physical and social services (*ES* 15 Aug. 1971, 1 Sept. 1968) and the glaring abuses of fiscal, judicial, and police authority that occurred regularly on the part of government officials (*ES* 25 Apr. 1971). With the inauguration of the Tarú government, fiery condemna-

tions of the corrupt PRI and exploitative agrarian bureaucracy temporarily subsided, giving way to analysis of particular problems and how
they might be resolved. At this point, reformist elites looked to progressive policymaking rather than mass mobilizations for solutions, although
their observations were suffused with the imagery of an angry pueblo.

Opposition victory renewed discussion about a path to fiscal and political integrity within the system, a possibility virtually discarded during
the preceding year. The question of whether Juchitecos would return to
the ranks of the PRI was a plausible and compelling one. Along with
continued calls for planned industrialization—"We welcome the grand
captains of national industry!" (*ES* 23 Jan. 1972)—opposition victory
brought action with regard to municipal services and to conflicts over
land tenure and state involvement in agricultural production. *El Satélite*
reported attention on the part of agrarian authorities to problems concerning land ownership, rice production, and sugar processing in Juchitán and surrounding areas. The newspaper attributed this action to
promises on the part of President Echeverría to address injustices in the
countryside. Throughout the region, peasants mobilized to defend land
rights, and the minister of agriculture, Augusto Gómez Villanueva, visited the Isthmus and sent teams of inspectors to investigate peasant
claims (*ES* 30 Jan. 1972).

Political discussion in the wake of the Tarú victory exhibited a new
recognition of the potential unevenness and inequality of economic development. An editorial arguing for integrated planning criticized the
unequal distribution of wealth in Mexico and provided examples of this
process in Juchitán (*ES* 21 May 1972). In reporting the inauguration of
new airplane service in nearby Ixtepec, the newspaper simultaneously
praised the governor for this "transcendental step toward progress" and
noted that the vast majority of the local population did not have the
economic means necessary to make use of the new service. In discussing a
land conflict between two nearby towns, one an agricultural town and
one a fishing town, *El Satélite* observed that there were always victims in a
modernization process, as the least-skilled workers were replaced by
machines and other workers. The newspaper argued that the land claim
of the agricultural town should be favored, because its agriculture and
livestock had begun to develop successfully. The fisherman, in contrast,
would not have the skills necessary to participate in a new fishing industry. *El Satélite* also suggested that "local dialects and customs" often slowed

economic change and thereby "imped[ed] people's integration in the process of socioeconomic development" (28 May, 20 Aug. 1972). The proponents of moderate reform and of electoral mobilization in the 1960s and 1970s thus identified some of the difficulties and contradictions of the development process they advocated, and they simultaneously valued and worried about Zapotec cultural practices. When, in the end, the Tarú administration neither fostered development nor attended to these difficulties, the students and peasants who formed COCEI built on just these identifications, placing them within a more radical analysis of structural economic inequality and cultural marginalization.

In the eyes of many Juchitecos, opposition victory could make the system stronger by stimulating the PRI to reform itself. In their analysis, the pueblo arose not so much against the party as against the "mafia" of leaders who ran it, and the defeat was a lesson for the PRI. The PRI was "our party," the party even of those who opposed it (*ES* 24, 2 Jan., 30 July, 5 Mar. 1972). The compelling question of the day—"Will the pueblo want to return to the ranks of the PRI?"—was answered with the assertion that the pueblo would indeed return if the party changed (*ES* 13 Feb. 1972) and included those Juchitecos who were "marginalized in today's economy" (*ES* 2 Jan. 1972).

However, even as some looked to a strengthened PRI, others began to forge new cultural and political pathways. Macario Matus, an intellectual who would later head the Casa de la Cultura in Juchitán and support COCEI, urged Juchitecos to record their history "from all angles." He encouraged the young to go to the archives and the old to retell and write down the events and customs of their past. Matus called for an organization unaffiliated with the PRI or the government to carry out this task, insisting that the representation of culture had to be carried out independently of official power (*ES* 1 Oct. 1972). In their work on India, Partha Chatterjee (1993) and Ranajit Guha (1988) show such efforts to be precursors of explicitly political struggles. In their analyses, the call to history "implied in effect an exhortation to launch the struggle for power, because in this mode of recalling the past, the power to represent oneself is nothing other than political power itself" (Chatterjee 1993, 76). In her analysis of historical memory and mobilization around land issues among the Cumbales in Colombia, Joanne Rappaport similarly observes that figures of the past were made meaningful to the Cumbales "only within the context of the identity of their movement, whose program developed *after native historians began to interpret local history"* (1994, 156, italics mine). In Juchitán, while moderates wrestled with a Zapotec path to reform, students, intellectuals, artists, and neighborhood storytellers set out to represent a Zapotec past, and their historical efforts indeed promoted radical political mobilization.

The PRI against Tarú

Meanwhile, the PRI fought back against Tarú's reformism, successfully resisting pressures for change with a dual strategy: the official party obstructed or violently attacked the Tarú administration in virtually every area of its activity, and it worked to establish a new local political boss in Juchitán. Those politicians who remained members of the PRI, thus identifying themselves with old-style boss politics, pressured representatives from the party's national committee to call new elections to replace Tarú, who had been appointed by the governor (*ES* 11 Feb. 1973). While national and state officials refused to oust Tarú, they withheld the municipal budget, so that the Tarú administration did not have funds to pay its staff or continue public-works projects.[11] In the summer of 1973, the PRI gathered two thousand supporters to a demonstration demanding the immediate removal of Tarú. In response, hundreds of women rallied to support the popular leader, threatening that blood would flow if the PRI organized another demonstration. After this, Tarú supporters began to guard City Hall nightly. The PRI responded with violence on what Juchitecos called "the Night of the Stones." While thousands listened to Tarú discuss municipal activities and the treasury problem, several hundred priístas gathered at the party office, then marched to City Hall with torches and rocks, attacking Tarú supporters there. During the attack, windows were broken, and goods were stolen from Sears, located on the town plaza, as well as from a bank and stationery store (*ES* 5, 19, 26 Aug. 1973).

Local students who supported Tarú organized a meeting to discuss the attacks on his administration and the events of the Night of the Stones. At the meeting, the students also reported on their case against Dr. Braulio Barragán, the head of the local public hospital, who illegally charged students for medical certificates. The link between the defense of Tarú and the campaign against Dr. Barragán, which was COCEI's first organizing effort, underscores the connection between the failure of reform and the rise of radicalism (*ES* 26 Aug., 2 Sept. 1973). By resisting change at this time, the PRI categorically opposed the efforts that had characterized the reformist development agenda since the mid-1960s. In so doing, it set the stage for the successful growth of COCEI, whose class analysis of economic exploitation and political authoritarianism came to accurately characterize the policies of the official party and of state agencies in the eyes of a majority of citizens.

Even during Tarú's administration, local institutions central to interest mediation continued to fail to represent their constituents, experiencing conflicts over leadership, procedure, and goals. In 1972, only the members of the Communal Land Commission succeeded in electing a new leader who might represent peasant concerns. Similar attempts to elect more representative leaders engendered conflict in livestock, student, and professional organizations, where charges of corruption and personalism abounded (*ES* 14 May, 16 July, 27 Aug., 12 Nov. 1972). Eventually, Tarú resigned after shooting a man in a dispute, and the first councilman of his administration took over as municipal president, signaling that he would rejoin the PRI if the "bad elements" in the party were replaced by honest ones. During the following year, *El Satélite* exposed corruption in the Tarú administration, including personal use of municipal resources and efforts to amass large landholdings with the collusion of the new head of the Communal Land Commission. As a result of these activities, Tarú came to be identified, in the emerging class analysis, with the rich and corrupt, and a decade later he became a leader of the reformist, business-oriented group within the PRI.

Beyond Tarú's personal dealings, however, the inability of his administration to implement change derived from the form of popular mobilization behind Tarú and the ambivalence of local elites toward the reform agenda. Many members of the Zapotec elite supported Tarú because they believed he could reassert their predominant social and political position, not because they supported the political and economic transformations championed by reformers. At the same time, the masses of peasants and workers backing Tarú had responded to a call to ethnic identity and to a condemnation of the dislocations and poverty they were experiencing, but they had not been partners in the reformist discourse, and their electoral mobilization had included no programmatic or organizational components. Tarú could reproduce neither the commitments linking boss and ordinary people characteristic of the midcentury domain of sovereignty, nor the local economy that had ensured elite prosperity during the same period. As a consequence, when Tarú moved to implement economic and political reforms, his elite support dropped (Royce 1975, 199). At the same time, Tarú was not accountable to peasants and workers, and they did not form an ongoing, mobilized base of support for his administration.

The PRI in the 1970s: A New Form of Caciquismo

As the Tarú administration faced attack and fell, local priístas began to form an alliance around Mario Bustillo Villalobos, resulting in his subsequent role as political boss. This role combined skill in local-level politicking, a steadfast identification with the PRI, and links to party and government officials in Oaxaca and Mexico City. In addition, the new cacique role involved an ability to funnel outside initiatives through local networks, to back party hard-liners, and to oversee the repeated use of violence on the part of the regime and paramilitary groups. In the course of two decades, Bustillo served as president of the local PRI, mayor, and state and federal deputy. While there is some evidence that Bustillo was less corrupt and more closely connected to ordinary Juchitecos than previous PRI politicians, he was not a reformer. Rather, Bustillo gained control of the existing party apparatus and then handed over the city government to the most corrupt municipal administration in memory in the next municipal elections. During his own administration, he supported hard-line governor Manuel Zárate Aquino and oversaw the greatest use of government violence in Juchitán's recent history. After this demonstration of support for higher authority, outside officials consistently supported Bustillo's role as regional boss. They valued him for his political stance and skills and preferred him to a more extreme local politician who advocated greater violence and a vehemently antistate position.

Bustillo's talents included a well-developed ability to "do politics," to get out into the streets and neighborhoods of the city, meeting, talking to, and helping out people when they needed it. In Juchitán, as in other parts of Mexico, ritual kinship roles of various sorts were central to this political networking (Stephen 1990b, 43–60; 1991, chap. 7). In addition to being a full-fledged godparent, one could be godparent (sponsor) of the band or the flowers or the dinner at various life-cycle and religious celebrations. Bustillo and his wife were said to routinely undertake an astonishing number of these obligations, establishing and reinforcing personal ties that could be marshaled for political advantage. In this, Bustillo resembled Charis. In addition, both Bustillo and Charis had reputations for forthrightness and honesty, after a fashion; they were seen as trustworthy in protecting individuals and families who supported them. Both were viewed as closely connected to common people in Juchitán's poor neighborhoods. Both were seen as simple men, not highly educated, yet able to hold their own in state and national political arenas. This ability to wield power despite humble origins won them popular support. Charis had not learned to read, and had made his name as a general during and after the revolution. Bustillo was a practical dentist, one who had learned his trade on the job. Both could speak the language of the pueblo, in the twin senses of speaking Zapotec—which most elite Juchitecos could do—and speaking to the concerns of poor people.

This closeness to the pueblo was facilitated by a characteristic of the Zapotec elite generally, which was particularly pronounced in Charis, Bustillo, and Tarú alike. In Juchitán, most of the elite lived among people of all classes and participated in the quotidian cultural life of the pueblo. In this, they differed from the nationalist middle classes described by Chatterjee, among whom "the popular is . . . appropriated in a sanitized form, carefully erased of all marks of vulgarity, coarseness, localism, and sectarian identity" (1993, 73). In Juchitán, in contrast, middle classes and elites lived more or less immersed in the "vulgar" and "coarse." While these aspects of Zapotec culture were at times criticized as dissolute or as obstructing of progress, they were also, like the tropes of barbarism and ignorance of earlier decades, enjoyed and celebrated across classes as constitutive of Zapotec identity.

While Charis and Bustillo shared immersion in popular culture, there were also key differences between them. These differences reveal the ways in which the components of culture and politics that reinforced national hegemony in the 1930s had shifted and unraveled in subsequent decades. Charis was a charismatic general, a fighter, a friend of the generals who ruled Mexico in the 1930s and 1940s. He carried out his politics in broad strokes, cutting deals in Mexico City for schools or roads and securing autonomy in exchange for a general level of support for the central government. Locally, he did not depend on outside support to buttress his claim to rule, and, aside from one term as senator, he generally did not hold formal political office. Bustillo, on the other hand, was a dentist, a small-time wheeler-dealer, and he knew how to "do politics" in a second sense as well. In addition to knowing how to communicate with ordinary Juchitecos, he knew how to talk to government officials and functionaries. His friends in Oaxaca and Mexico City were the officials and administrators of a host of agencies and party organizations that had opened up offices or sent representatives to the Isthmus since the 1960s. Bustillo occupied official posts for much of his political career, and he had far less room for local maneuver than Charis. He was there not to assure allegiance to a distant government, but rather to see to it that the multiple economic and political programs of that government—from irrigation, sugar production, and the provision of credit and insurance to the establishment of new party organizations, women's committees, and cultural activities—were carried out with a minimum of economic loss and political violence. In order to serve these outside purposes, Bustillo had to funnel the outside—literally and figuratively— through his network of political associates and grassroots supporters and to make the pathways by which the outside encroached seem at least partly invisible.

Bustillo's differences from Charis—his less charismatic stance and his ability to oversee the multiple interventions of the central state—similarly differentiated him from Tarú. In an account of local customs and Zapotec style during the heyday of Tarú's campaign and administration, anthropologist Anya Peterson Royce presented biographies of Tarú and Bustillo (1975, 186–202). In her analysis, Royce underscored Tarú's stunning success as a leader of the pueblo and expressed skepticism about Bustillo's political future, arguing that Bustillo lacked important attributes of Zapotec identity and style. While Royce was wrong about the political future of the two figures, the differences she discerned between Tarú and Bustillo, like those distinguishing Bustillo and Charis, describe the differences between caciques of the postrevolutionary decades and those of the 1970s and 1980s. Tarú, while he cast himself as a reformer, would probably have made a successful cacique in the Charis mode, manipulating outside authorities and presiding over a domain of sovereignty in Juchitán. Bustillo, in contrast, could manage the multitude of interconnections that linked Juchitán and the outside ever more tightly.

Royce emphasized how hard Bustillo had to work in politics and social relations, because of his lack of wealth, social position, and education. His lack of elite status denied him the automatic support of upper-class Zapotecs, who in Royce's view held the key to political power in Juchitán. Royce identified the source of Bustillo's political strength in his thorough loyalty to the PRI and his corresponding willingness to put in hours doing party and community work that others didn't care to do. In contrast, Royce attributed Tarú's political success to his charisma, his outside education and connections, and his family status. Tarú gained popular support because of his relations with the many employees in his large businesses and because of his ability to inspire ordinary Juchitecos with visions of a proud Zapotec future. He gained support from upper-class Zapotecs because he supported their challenge to the outside PRI and from non-Zapotec businesspeople because they thought that as a businessman, he would act in their interest. In addition, because of his privileged upbringing, he could comport himself effortlessly in both the Zapotec and non-Zapotec worlds. Like Charis, Tarú had achieved status outside Juchitán, in his case by becoming a pilot. In Royce's words, "Tarú had at his disposition . . . a hundred years of influence, of the acquisition of money and power, all that was necessary was to activate them" (1975, 197).

Looking back from the early 1970s, before the formation of COCEI, and ignoring the vast transformations of agriculture and commerce that were already under way, Royce evaluated Tarú and Bustillo according to the politics of the past. Tarú, like Charis, might have been suited to brokering a domain of sovereignty between Juchitecos and the outside, and supporting upper-class Juchitecos in their dominant position within that domain. He might also have gained the loyalty of ordinary Juchitecos, so long as they were permitted to maintain the degree of economic and cultural autonomy to which they had been accustomed, as they had been permitted to do during Charis's cacicazgo. What Royce didn't see, however, was that a different kind of brokering was necessary to maintain power in the Juchitán of agricultural agencies, state intervention, and COCEI.

In the course of the 1960s, regional processes of economic change, cultural elaboration, and political construction had intersected forcefully with new, national political and economic trends. Juchiteco politics was no longer a matter of securing autonomy against the outside, of gaining the allegiance of a population left more or less alone under the banner of elite Zapotec leadership. The pueblo was under attack. It was being pressured, controlled, and manipulated by numerous government programs and officials, and work was fast becoming urban and salaried. Zapotec elites themselves pursued the economic opportunities opened up by development projects and commerce, the very forces that were disrupting the lives of Juchiteco peasants and workers. These peasants and workers would soon identify themselves with COCEI, in opposition not only to the PRI and the central state, but to the local Zapotec elite as well. In this situation, Charis's descendant was not Tarú, but Bustillo. Bustillo's nonheroic ability to talk to ordinary people and work tirelessly within the discredited PRI, manipulating officials, agencies, procedures, and rhetoric, gained him the leadership of that beleaguered party. His willingness to ally with unpopular outsiders, to tolerate more violent repression than the city had seen since the revolution, and to coexist with the most corrupt and the most nondescript of PRI politicians enabled him to secure this position through the years of unresolved class conflict in the 1970s, and to maintain a position of influence and prominence as PRI politics changed in the 1980s.

Bustillo carved out a shifting terrain of PRI support alongside the groundswell of peasant and worker mobilization behind COCEI. Bustillo was thus different from Charis not only because of his personal background and the transformed economic context in which he operated, but because the pueblo no longer supported a regional cacique, but rather rallied behind a popular movement with class-based demands for radical change. At the same time, Bustillo's ability to "do politics" in both senses— his ability to talk to Juchitecos and to outside officials—explains a good deal about politics in Juchitán, as well as about the tenacity of this new form of caciquismo nationwide. Bustillo's skills enabled the PRI to maintain some peasant and worker support in Juchitán, so that it could win perhaps 30 to 40 percent of the vote in fiercely contested municipal elections in the 1980s.[12] Bustillo's commitment to doing politics, furthermore, contrasts with the more distant relationship between PRI reformers and the pueblo and thereby highlights the source of their weakness. Reformers failed repeatedly in Juchitán to achieve their goals because, in their emphasis on investment, production, and an electoral politics of rationally acting citizens, they neglected to invest their own time and effort in developing close ties to ordinary Juchitecos. As a result, when reformers sought to win local political contests, they needed direct and strong outside support—not support that could be funneled through the pueblo, in Bustillo's fashion, but support that took the form of outside authorities overturning local PRI victories, appointing leaders and administrators, and beginning to carry out public-works projects—as indeed occurred at key moments in the 1980s.

This sort of intervention, however, revived long-standing hostilities on the part of Juchitecos toward outside authority, thus further limiting the ability of the reformers to gain popular support. In addition, alliances between reformers and outside officials required moments of extraordinary openness at the national level, when state and national politicians were willing to negotiate new deals and stand behind their promises. While reformers had skills in bringing to fruition such alliances at particular moments, Bustillo and the local PRI politicians knew how to work things out with the national politicians and functionaries who were more likely to be around for the long haul.

Cultures of Politics

The ongoing failure of the PRI to foster representative and accountable leadership was seen as a source of public disorder, instability, and political violence in Juchitán. The abuses of authority on the part of PRI officials pressed Juchitecos to redefine the pueblo, construct notions of accountability and class, and suggest new forms for legitimate political activity. In her work on nineteenth-century Mexico, Florencia Mallon demonstrates that liberalism formed a central component of popular political cultures, even as these cultures were internally complex and rooted in local experiences (1995, 19). In Mallon's view, Western ideas about democratic citizenship and political participation motivated and defined popular political action and thereby significantly shaped mid-nineteenth-century politics. In colonial and postcolonial India, in partial contrast, Chatterjee observed that "the state itself is being made sense of" in terms far removed from liberal political theory, so that "notions of representation and the legitimation of authority" take on quite distinct meanings in popular domains (1993, 225). The observations of both Mallon and Chatterjee are apt in Juchitán, where both Western and non-Western discourses shaped cultures of politics. Understandings of the Zapotec pueblo were brought to bear on particular aspects of democratic theory at different times, so that democracy was treated more as a collection from which meanings and practices could be borrowed and adapted than as a formula for government.

The debates about politics in Juchitán in the 1960s and 1970s argued variously for competitive democracy, for accountable government, for parties with deep social roots, for freedom from coercion and violence, and for radical economic change. The complexity of this discourse demonstrates the indirect pathway by which a radical political movement was constructed, not simply out of the failure of reform, but from the ways in which political institutions, procedures, and meanings were experienced and evaluated. The culture of politics in Juchitán, furthermore, consistently resisted the colonizing aspects of Mexican political ideology and the political practices of the PRI. The resources of the domain of sovereignty enabled Juchitecos to develop an indigenous discourse of political development and forge spaces for democratization in daily life and popular culture.

In a 1968 radio speech reprinted in *El Satélite*, an unnamed reformer argued that current conditions surrounding elections "make the exercise of democracy into a threat of disorder." Representatives of the state PRI arrived in Juchitán without any real knowledge of the local scene, the reformer said, and allied with local factions who sought power as a means to personal enrichment. In this situation, political parties "do not fulfill their mission" (1 Sept. 1968). The PRI chose the worst candidates for office, and those who worked for the benefit of the pueblo counted least for the official party (*ES* 15 Mar. 1970). When leaders of the opposition PPS protested against electoral fraud in 1968, observers predicted that they would provoke bloodshed, thus creating "a rallying point for rebellion among Juchiteco citizens" (*ES* 24 Nov. 1968). According to commentators, it was up to the political parties to win over the abstainers—those at the margin of politics—by offering better incentives to vote in the form of real programs (*ES* 10 Nov. 1968). However, even when the PRI claimed to reorganize itself statewide, "we are seeing the same faces." Others took this critique further, arguing that parties were the very source of political corruption, and "it is for that reason that responsible men repudiate all registered political parties." The pueblo itself had to put forth the ideal candidate (*ES* 22 Aug. 1971).

The perceived poverty and corruption of political parties was linked in public commentary to the lack of accountability on the part of public officials. In this context, according to a writer in the newspaper, there was no point in opposing even disruptive change: "Now is not the time to think about political stability" (16 Nov. 1969). When both the mayor and the chief of police refused to take responsibility for violent attacks against their political opponents, *El Satélite* posed the issue of accountability in terms of government-sponsored violence: "When can we hold them responsible, only when they personally commit a crime?" So far as political violence is concerned, "no one is responsible" (17 Aug. 1969). Government corruption, furthermore, did not go unnoticed by ordinary Juchitecos: "The population, even though it is said that most of them are illiterate or don't understand anything, cannot easily be taken in" (14 Sept. 1969). By invoking ordinary people in this way, moderates simultaneously denied the ignorance of the pueblo, attributing such claims to unnamed others (probably allied with outsiders), and placed the pueblo at the center of claims about legitimacy.

At times, moderates argued that well-developed parties and regular elections were central to democratic politics. Parties were the proper agents to exercise power, and opposition parties, not the PRI, could promote good government by "changing the PRI for other parties or placing other parties in posts of public administration, and in that way demanding honesty in administration" (*ES* 18 June 1978). At other times, however, moderates described party politics as obstructing a more direct relationship between citizens and state. In this case, establishing popular sovereignty did not mean guaranteeing electoral competition, but rather ensuring that the leaders with popular roots indeed governed. While this could be achieved through elections, it could also be reached by other forms of political negotiation. For example, in 1971 the governor's annulment of fraudulent elections and subsequent appointment of an administrative council headed by Tarú fulfilled the mandate for popular sovereignty. By this logic, a powerful state could achieve democracy by enlightened decision-making or by permitting competition that the ruling party always won.

Juchitecos were well aware of the broader economic and political context in which local politics was enmeshed. According to an editorial, Mexico's political and economic structure couldn't be changed in one pueblo, without a national uprising like the 1910 revolution, a fact that was demonstrated by the recent failure of guerrilla movements. Thus, change had to come through a politics of persuasion (*ES* 1 Dec. 1974): ". . . we live in a bourgeois democratic country and as such have to accept its institutions" (*ES* 19 Jan. 1975). In this situation the resolution of conflict was most likely to come through an extraordinary candidate who emphasized unity and conciliation (*ES* 10 July 1977). COCEI leaders agreed with moderates that change depended not primarily on procedures but on extraordinary leadership, and they also shared the belief that the absence of nationwide mobilization limited the possibilities for grassroots successes. However, where moderates emphasized dialogue as the path for change in this context, COCEI leaders emphasized confrontation. Neither group viewed party competition and procedural democracy as the primary pathway to political and socioeconomic change.

The range of views about competitive democracy in Juchitán reflected the city's history of interwoven elections and rebellion, militant leaders and deal making, and regional autonomy and interdependence. For Juchitecos in the nineteenth and early twentieth centuries, rebellions followed political impositions disguised as electoral victories, and these rebellions were seen to have secured degrees of local economic and cultural autonomy. Between 1930 and 1960, caciquismo and political deal-making at the state and national levels guaranteed some continuing economic and cultural autonomy, even as they preserved local elite power. In the 1960s, efforts at democratic competition failed to control corrupt municipal officials or to stimulate economic growth, and the largest popular successes, the anti-ejido campaign and the Tarú victory in municipal elections, occurred through combinations of mass mobilization, electoral competition, and the intervention of higher officials at moments of crisis. In the course of this history, procedural democracy was one strand among many political forms, a strand that safeguarded particular people's interests and promoted their goals. Juchitecos in the 1960s and 1970s knew this, and they spoke about democracy, and made strategic use of this discourse, in light of this knowledge.

As a result of this variety of experiences with electoral competition, writers in *El Satélite* in the late 1960s argued less for formal democracy than for the formation of new political approaches and organizations. "If peasants had an organization," they reasoned, "it would be their representatives who would defend them in this situation" (27 July 1969). A 1971 report on the formation of a new bus drivers' union discussed the right of workers to organize and the need for such organizations in preventing

overt class conflict. Low-wage policies, in contrast, "only lead to deepening further and further the abyss that separates capital from the work-
force," with the result that "at any moment the fuse burns and open war
between these forces appears." *El Satélite* also counseled businesspeople to
look to organizations to protect their rights, pointing out that they would
be more effective in fighting corrupt municipal practices if they acted
collectively (18 Apr. 1971). Even in the face of these challenges, however, PRI leaders did not act to "interpret the longings of a pueblo that
seeks a complete change of politicians" (*ES* 22 Aug. 1971).

All together, *El Satélite's* writers issued a call to arms: "Peasants, wake up,
don't accept a trifle for your lands!" (27 July 1969). In a situation of
corrupt parties and failed administration, independent organizations
served the interests of their members and of the society as a whole. Such
organizations, furthermore, had legal rights: "No one can shut the door
on an organized group, so long as that group acts within the Constitution
and legal norms" (*ES* 25 Apr. 1971). This critical analysis suggested a new
solution, one that produced the Tarú victory and thus transformed Juchitán's political future: a new politics outside of the PRI.

The Meaning of an Official Party

Even as parties were questioned, events and commentary during the
1970s illuminated the resonance and complexity of the notion of an
official political party in local experience. In the course of the 1971
electoral campaign and its aftermath, news articles and editorials in *El
Satélite* exposed the internal workings of the PRI and rejected that party
outright, supporting the alliance of opposition groups. At the same time,
however, the leaders of the opposition groups saw themselves as working
largely within or alongside the PRI, even as they organized outside it—
they were working for what the PRI claimed publicly were its goals, and
what the opposition leaders thought should have been its goals. Bere
Lele, an unsigned column in *El Satélite*, outlined the ambivalent relationship between Juchitecos and the PRI that would continue to characterize
moderates in the city for the next twenty years. The column said that the
PRI had been so discredited that for many people it was most honest to
say, "I'm independent, I don't have a party." In order to change this, the

state and national executive committees of the PRI needed to work intensely to get rid of corrupt local members, something they had already tried to do many times, without success. Since Mexicans were priístas at heart, though, there was a continuing need to "make this party into a party of the pueblo and for the pueblo" (21 Oct. 1973).

In effect, Juchitecos had no party in the 1970s, and the ambiguity of their political affiliation was central to the political conflicts of the decade. Juchitecos had left the PRI, which they had entered, to the extent that they had entered it at all, as a formation of the Charis cacicazgo, and thus of a particular relationship between themselves and outside power. That relationship had protected local political and cultural autonomy, but had been disrupted by the economic changes of the 1960s. However, even as they recognized their break with the party, Juchitecos called for reform of the official party. They did this despite their awareness that reform had failed repeatedly and despite the fact that there had never really been a PRI in Juchitán. The PRI existed as an idea to which some Juchitecos repeatedly returned. Like many Mexicans, Juchitecos spoke of a public politics that could unite nation and pueblo, and this discourse continued until at least the 1980s. It derived from the experiences and memories of Charis politics, from beliefs about the multiclass Zapotec pueblo, from nationalist claims about an official party, and from ideas about democracy and good government. Part of the commitment to an official party was a nostalgia for a cacique past during which, in popular myth, "nothing happened," an assertion of the absence of political conflict in the recent past that could be sustained because Charis's rule had so successfully mediated complex antagonisms. For some Juchitecos, this form of unified public politics would come to be symbolized by COCEI, while others would continue to look for it in the PRI. Both groups sought identity and unity, indeed a politics of successful mediation, more than procedural democracy in the 1960s and 1970s.

The ambiguity of political affiliation and of beliefs about democracy in Juchitán underscores the extent to which meanings of politics and democracy are locally constructed and vary considerably from theoretical norms and procedures. In Juchitán in the 1960s and early 1970s, the boundaries between citizen and pueblo, pueblo and PRI, and PRI and democracy were fluid and changing. Examination of the PRI from this perspective, as a contested set of ideas and practices central to the political life of Mexicans, illustrates why individuals need not have been either fully inside or fully outside of official institutions. In a situation of economic disruption, cultural reconfiguration, and ambiguous political meanings, Juchitecos assumed numerous relationships to formal politics and the politics of the official party. The notion of a better PRI, to which many Juchitecos kept returning, also signified the possibility of a better, more reasonable outside. By the 1960s, Juchitecos could entertain the idea of being part of the nation. This meant modifying the hostility to the outside of the period of rebellions and "barbarism," as well as the autonomy and distance from the center of the midcentury domain of sovereignty. Such a reconfiguration of the relationships between the Zapotec domain of sovereignty and Mexican nationalism—indeed a restructuring of past forms of resistance—was an implicit component of the reformist project of the 1960s.

Juchitecos' changing understanding of the relationship of the pueblo to national political institutions and practices can be seen in a series of observations that appeared in *El Satélite* between 1976 and 1978. In a 1976 analysis of voter abstention, the Bere Lele column observed that the corrupt and repressive practices of political parties "lead the pueblo to distance itself further from the ballot box each day" (25 Apr. 1976). In 1977, discussing the local PRI's attacks on any form of opposition, Bere Lele reported that "the pueblo takes refuge in COCEI" (13 Mar. 1977). Finally, in a commentary on the upcoming municipal elections, the columnist concluded that "to vote for the PRI as it is today is to cease to be a good Juchiteco" (*ES* 16 Dec. 1979). Thus, the possibilities for formally democratic politics changed repeatedly in Juchitán—from rejection of voting to experimentation with radical politics to voting as an oppositional act—in the course of a decade of radical mobilization and national electoral reform.

Violence and Rebellion

Leaders of the anti-ejido campaign in the early 1960s had rallied peasants with calls to rebellion. Similarly, the absence of honest elections in Juchitán in 1968, just after the student uprising in Mexico City, was characterized as a potential prelude to political instability and rebellion.

The threats, coercion, and intimidation at the heart of PRI politics in 1971, according to an *El Satélite* author, would "lead the pueblo to rise up against the institutions, possibly to the point of the threat of guerrilla war" (24 Jan. 1971). In 1972, under the headline "When a People Awakens," *El Satélite* described the anger behind peasant support for Tarú and how it was fostered by a situation in which the extreme poverty of newly landless peasants coexisted with the enrichment of a privileged few (6 Feb. 1972). In subsequent years, moderates in Juchitán recognized the contradictory and inherently violent nature of Echeverría's national "democratic opening." In their view, Echeverría opposed reactionary caciques and landowners with peasant-student alliances, but at the same time allowed the use of police and thugs to repress the resulting protest activities. As local examples, they pointed to threats and reprisals in Juchitán, such as a blacklist of student activists and police harassment of the director of *El Satélite* (*ES* 12 May 1974).

In the course of the 1970s, according to writers in the newspaper, violence became pervasive in Juchitán, its purpose to "imprison and assassinate all members of the opposition, without regard to the means" (17 Oct. 1976). These writers identified the violent and authoritarian characteristics of the Mexican regime and the growing similarity between uses of violence in civilian-controlled Mexico and the military regimes of South America: "They are violating human rights" (21 Mar. 1976). In the view of local observers, violence in Juchitán reflected similar practices elsewhere in Mexico. Several weeks before one of the largest killings in Juchitán, when eight COCEI supporters were gunned down, the Bere Lele column observed that peasants had recently been murdered in Sonora and Veracruz and that this could happen in Juchitán. After the local slaughter, Leopoldo de Gyves Pineda again emphasized the ties between violence in Juchitán and in other states and the unwillingness of police to properly investigate the local incidents (*ES* 9, 23 Nov. 1975, 8 Feb. 1976).

The newspaper also reported on specific instances of improper police activity in Juchitán, including an attack on a public meeting by the state police, the shooting of a student who refused detention without justification, and the disappearance of COCEI leader and Ministry of Agrarian Reform official Víctor Pineda Henestrosa at the hand of the Eleventh Infantry Battalion. The newspaper charged that police and soldiers interfered in political activities, disrupting meetings of opposition parties and detaining opposition leaders (23 July 1978, 7 Aug. 1977). Local political authorities, furthermore, were seen as directly responsible: "In this city, with the direct or indirect intervention of the authorities imposed by the PRI, many fellow Juchitecos have been assassinated" (13 May 1979).

In response to this pervasive violence, *El Satélite* called for respect for civil liberties. The pueblo had to be guaranteed "its rights of assembly and to support the candidates they choose" (29 May 1977). "They can't be prohibited from meeting" (16 Jan. 1977). Peaceful demonstrations were constitutional, and it was the job of the army to watch and to protect demonstrators from attack. The language of civil liberties signified the culmination of increasingly vehement reformist opposition to the regime. Paradoxically, it also signified what would come to link reformists to the regime in the subsequent decade, a rhetorical rejection of violence and militancy. Despite occasional reference to the ineffectiveness of nonviolent politics, moderates responded to violence by insisting on the necessity for a pacific public politics: "Everything must be based on persuasion, on dialogue" (*ES* 27 Mar. 1977). This rejection of violence, couched in calls to dialogue, served two clear purposes: it discredited the regime and its instruments of coercion, and it strictly delimited the realm of legitimate behavior for opponents of the regime. At the same time, the moderates' uncovering of violence at the heart of official political authority reinforced and legitimated the discourse of rebellion among Juchitecos.

From the Domain of Sovereignty to Failed Reform

General Charis succeeded in establishing an enduring form of rule because he based his power on the maintenance of indigenous forms of economy and community life—on combining allegiance to the new central state with a domain of sovereignty that approximated, at least in part, that for which earlier rebels had fought. At the same time, cacique rule repressed political opposition, prevented fair elections, wielded considerable economic and political power over peasants, and resisted the "modernizing" agenda of urbanization and free enterprise promoted by some educated elites. The reform movements of the 1960s drew on these different historical legacies. They sought to unite the multiclass pueblo and to secure new arrangements with the outside (the goals of the rebellions and the Charis cacicazgo) for the purposes of expanded political competition, clean government, efficient administration of state economic projects, and economic growth (the goals of the anti-Charis reformers). In the 1960s, reformers claimed that such an agenda, including the possibility of new peasant and worker organizations, would lead to the alleviation of poverty and the construction of a new, shared civic life.

Tarú and his supporters, in looking to the period of Charis's rule, sought to maintain elite Zapotec political and cultural leadership. Even as this elite effort failed, the revitalization of opposition politics that accompanied it strengthened the reformist political voice in Juchitán and linked it to the identity of a Zapotec pueblo. This linkage was facilitated by the explicit turn to Zapotec cultural awareness and artistic innovation on the part of the city's young intellectuals. In this cultural context, where attention to indigenous language, ritual, and art was seen as a source of local pride and a link to fashionable national discourses, to speak of reformist change—a discussion usually linked to "modern," nonethnic economic and political projects—could mean embracing, rather than rejecting, the Zapotec past. Thus, ethnicity in Juchitán was not simply a static phenomenon that would fuel the political solidarity of the Charis cacicazgo, the reformist opposition behind Tarú, and then COCEI. Rather, it was a changing construction of elite cultural roles and conceptions, artistic themes and networks, and daily language and ritual practices that contributed in specific ways to successive political movements.

Just as the reform movements of the 1960s and early 1970s grew out of past Zapotec rebellions and reform movements, the failures of these efforts can be traced in part to the structure of political power developed after the revolution. The postrevolutionary combination of indigenous political boss and distant central state—which itself responded to earlier demands for autonomy, and facilitated successful state formation in the 1930s—enabled regional political elites consistently to oppose reform and to defeat both local challenges and national initiatives. The increasingly powerful central state, in turn, while adept at sponsoring large-scale economic projects, failed repeatedly to offer the level of backing to reform movements that might have enabled them to succeed despite this regional opposition. As a result, reform in Juchitán—in terms of political accountability, economic well-being, and cultural voice—occurred only in the presence of a mobilized, radical political movement.

The Language of the Pueblo

The difficulties and ultimate failure of the movement for change that had culminated in Tarú's gaining office—an effort to transform local politics through electoral participation—altered the ongoing discussion in Juchitán about the nature of power and the role of elections. At this moment, after a decade of fragmented and competing discourses, marked by mixtures of continuity and innovation, a counterhegemony began to coalesce, providing a new, alternative political and cultural understanding. If Tarú spoke in the voice of caciques past, and Bustillo in the voice of caciques to be, neither spoke the "language of the pueblo." What this language was, how it might be discerned, and how politics would be affected by it were central concerns of the moderates writing in *El Satélite,* as well as of Juchiteco students in Mexico City and at state and regional universities and secondary schools. These observers of the local scene knew that Juchitecos were changing before their eyes. They wondered by what means people could express their will and ensure good government. They asked whether elections were a goal in themselves or whether they were one potential method among several for establishing self-government. They deliberated about the proper relationship between citizens, political parties, and the state.

Some observers continued to exhort the PRI to change. They condemned the party's use of threats, thugs, and guns, pointing out that this made citizens more hostile and resolute in their opposition, a reaction that occurred across social classes. People had to be free to vote as they chose: "It is necessary and urgent that [PRI authorities] change their tactics and let citizens decide for themselves what they want" (*ES* 5 Aug. 1973). Voting became more important than ever in 1971, when abstention gave way to participation, with a 20 percent increase in turnout. This change demonstrated the possibility of "awakening civic consciousness" with honest candidates who "understand the language of the pueblo" (*ES* 11 Feb. 1973).

What was the proper politics for officials who indeed heard and understood the language of the pueblo? Was it a new language? Would politicians represent the people, or was the pueblo itself seeking power? How could the pueblo exercise power? What was the difference between old and new politics? A pueblo that spoke its own language would be able to act not only "in defense of its interests," but also to bring about "a more effective means for power to reach the real pueblo" (*ES* 12 Aug. 1973). In this effort, traditional political parties were of little use; it would be difficult for a party to choose a candidate whom the pueblo would accept (*ES* 23 Dec. 1973). As a result, potential candidates felt greater pressures to campaign as independents. In the view of reformists, existing political institutions might be able to accommodate these changes if the state legislature amended the constitution to allow independent groups to participate in elections without allying with a recognized political party, and if the Federal Electoral Commission recognized the victories of independent groups (*ES* 2, 9 Dec. 1973).

Students suggested an alternative approach: a class-based party, with a political platform and a defined ideology (*ES* 8 Apr. 1973).[13] While they accepted the critique of the PRI and the agrarian bureaucracy voiced in *El Satélite* since the late 1960s, the students reached conclusions substantially different from those that emphasized reform of the PRI, honest municipal administration, and economic development projects. Redefining the pueblo in class terms as the peasant and worker majority, they challenged the view that independents behind Tarú supported genuinely progressive politics. The reformist agenda, in their analysis, was the product of conflict among elites who used the issue of municipal government to fight among themselves for a bigger share of the pie.

From this perspective, the reformist agenda could not properly address the needs of the poor. The students related the structure of the national system to local events in explaining the persistent failure of reform in Juchitán. They observed that the rule of the PRI and the president's control over politics and the economy not only supported capitalism at the national level, but led to specific local economic exploitations: large landowners and state agencies acted to perpetuate peasant poverty, and merchants paid workers less than the minimum wage. Furthermore, economic power that originated at the national level entered the local political domain directly as local economic elites "form[ed] political groups to fight for power," deceiving Juchitecos in the process. In this situation, peasants and workers needed an independent organization with a program that reflected their own interests (*ES* 8 Apr., 30 Sept. 1973).

As they watched COCEI form and grow in the course of the decade, moderates and reformers grappled with this conclusion and its consequences. Supporting such an independent, class-based organization meant rejecting the existing political system. The reformers who articulated the development agenda and supported Tarú had denounced the PRI and the agrarian bureaucracy in the strongest terms, and they had gone on to locate the source of corruption and failure at least partly in the nature of the political process and the unevenness of economic development. However, what they wanted most of all to solve these problems was a reformed electoral and legislative process, with a new PRI at the center. They wanted to be part of the nation on acceptable terms, which for them could mean electoral democracy and a PRI strong enough to dominate the system, governing legally and wisely. As a result of the failure of the Tarú government to bring about systemic change, these same reformers realized quite clearly that the PRI was not likely to change.

The students' class-based program thus made sense, and most of the writers in *El Satélite* never rejected it outright. They argued with and about COCEI for the rest of the decade, praising its goals and successes, warning against its radicalism and inexperience. They condemned the violence with which right-wing priístas opposed COCEI, but praised PRI candidates who seemed honest and willing to act moderately and decently. They urged COCEI to pursue an electoral path. As they recognized the source of COCEI's strength in its roots among Juchitecos, they argued for a PRI that could be equally rooted. In so doing, they accepted COCEI as a genuine expression of the will of the pueblo, with rights to participate in politics; if the PRI wanted to succeed, it would have to become as good as COCEI.

A manifesto published to protest violence against two local journalists, signed both by future COCEI leaders and by future PRI moderates, exemplified this stance. Addressed to the governor and the president, the letter opposed what it characterized as related political and economic exploitations. It denounced "the violence of the exploiters of the pueblo, of those tempted by economic power." This violence, practiced by "the powerful against the economically and politically weak," had been tolerated by the State Office of the Public Prosecutor (Ministerio Público del Estado), which should have acted to represent the interests of the society as a whole. In the face of this attack, the pueblo "is committed to fighting for respect for its rights, for the just application of the law" (*ES* 16 Dec. 1973). Here, at a time when "the just application of the law" constituted a radical challenge to elite power, the language of class conflict took center stage in Juchiteco politics. In the past, political discourses and reformist initiatives had consistently articulated an inclusive, multiclass vision of politics and culture. Now, in contrast, explicit recognition of politically sanctioned violence and of exploitation of the poor stimulated a poor people's struggle against both the state and the Zapotec elite.

5

Mobilization and Repression in the 1970s

"Embodying the Defiance of the Pueblo" [1]

Ay!, didxazá, didxazá,
diidxa' rusibana naa,
naa nanna zanititlu',
dxi initi gubidxa ca

Ah, Zapotec, Zapotec!
language that gives me life,
I know you'll die away
on the day of the death of the sun
—Juchiteco poet Gabriel López Chiñas[2]

Con valor y con balazos, así se pudo ganar.

(With bravery and bullets, that's how we were able to win)
—peasant from the Alvaro Obregón settlement[3]

In the 1970s, ordinary people in Juchitán's neighborhoods stated clearly that they were poor people (*los pobres*) and that they were exploited in specific ways by local commercial enterprises and government agricultural programs. They said that they were ruled by a municipal government imposed through fraudulent elections and military force and that they supported COCEI because it fought unequivocally for their well-being. Juchitecos participated in local politics—attended meetings and marched in the streets with raised fists, voted, joined communal work projects, and contributed financially—in order to carry on this struggle. In so doing, they forged new and enduring forms of leftist politics that brought elections, representations of violence, negotiation with state officials, and indigenous cultural elaboration to the forefront of grassroots organizing. Such strategies, worked out in practice in Juchitán, anticipated changes that would characterize leftist politics in Mexico and elsewhere in Latin America in subsequent decades. Through these means, Juchitecos reshaped regional power relations, achieving an unprecedented degree of autonomy for their political and cultural efforts and successfully pressing outside political officials to become more responsive and accountable in matters of economic policy.

This process of political mobilization was neither orderly nor homogeneous. Despite the discernible set of common claims and actions that made a social movement visible and strong, political mobilization in Juchitán consisted of multiple, fragmented phenomena on the parts of both COCEI and the Mexican state and regime. As Gavin Smith observes in his study of land invasions in the Peruvian highlands, grassroots mobilization is powered not by "the solidarity of a group having identically shared perceptions" but rather by "a discourse between participants holding partial perceptions" that interact to create the momentum for political action (1989, 215–16). In characterizing the historical memory that shaped land invasions among the Cumbales in southern Colombia, Joanne Rappaport similarly finds that the "sources and the final products of Cumbal's historians are thus palimpsests in which the distant past, the recent past, and the present are layered, in which the political maneuvers of ancient chiefs and the labors of artisans of just thirty years ago complement each other, and in which written and oral modes of communication are interwoven with practical action" (1994, 7).

In his analysis, Smith emphasizes not only the diversity of perceptions within social movements, but the disorderly nature of political phenomena themselves. As he confronts the task of describing a land-based movement that linked geographically dispersed participants along shifting paths of conflict and negotiation, Smith concludes that "the requirements of post hoc account-giving . . . [tend] to conform to the structural requirements of narrative over and above the structural requirements of the movement being described" (1989, 27). Such an understanding of politics—based on the relationship between fragmented narratives and incomplete events—corresponds to the lessons of my fieldwork in Juchitán's courtyards and market stalls. What ordinary people "remember at first," in response to questions about the history of grassroots mobilizations in which they have participated, "is a generalized struggle and possibly the name of one surrogate hero or another" (Smith 1989, 216).

What they next remember is not the narrative of strategy and events that the interviewer often seeks, but rather aspects of the way their own experiences and memories intertwined with those of their neighbors and with public events. This form of memory, partial and relational, characterizes "events that were essentially incomplete, uncertain as to their outcome and unclear in the role played by participants" (Smith 1989, 228).

Thus, explaining political mobilization and regional democratization necessitates investigating the interaction between nonunitary parties to political contestation. During COCEI's first decade of mobilization, both movement and state were fragmented, and domination, resistance, and change occurred in the midst of this fragmentation. Accordingly, in order to understand the 1970s in Juchitán, I analyze the overlapping modalities of violence, negotiation, culture, and formal politics out of which COCEI constituted itself and engaged in political struggle. I tell partially chronological but partially parallel stories of origins (the many different ways people became involved in COCEI), direct-action mobilization, the land battle that was regarded as COCEI's founding event, and COCEI's electoral participation. I also discuss the ongoing violent repression that characterized COCEI's first decade of mobilization and the negotiations with regime officials that accompanied the movement's vehement anti-regime stance.

To analyze these overlapping yet separate modalities of activism, this chapter and the following two chapters employ different approaches. The origins and force of COCEI in the 1970s, discussed in this chapter, can best be understood by examining separately the fragmented domains of its activity during a time when the movement gained undeniable presence, but achieved little change in formal political relations. COCEI's activities in the 1980s, in contrast, corresponded to clear cycles of electoral politics, mass mobilization, repression, and reform and can thus be recounted through a more conventional chronological and analytic narrative. Finally, COCEI's internal strengths and limitations in both decades emerge best through thematic analysis of the ambiguities and contradictions that animated and shaped radical politics from within.

While the approach undertaken in each chapter privileges one aspect of the events it describes over others, each is particularly suited to the matters under discussion and to illuminating the changing *balance* between incompleteness and coherence that characterized COCEI over two decades. By varying my approach in this fashion, I seek to avoid the dangers of conventional narrative that Smith vividly portrays and to take his advice to downplay "the role of leadership and the role of unity" (1989, 27) in peasant resistance. The forms of presentation and analysis I have chosen enable me to explain COCEI as simultaneously strategic and coherent, on the one hand, and fragmented and contradictory, on the other. By emphasizing both aspects of politics, and seeking flexible ways of presenting and privileging one or the other, I avoid, in part, flattening politics into a "narratable history" in which, at the expense of lived complexity, "the role of participants becomes clearer, the outcome more certain, and the event itself more complete" (Smith 1989, 228).

The Formation of COCEI

COCEI formed in the context of continuing national conflict about the structure of politics and paths for reform in postrevolutionary Mexico. The tragic conclusion of the student protests of 1968 in Mexico City revealed the regime's willingness to practice massive repression and led to reevaluations of the nature of the regime and strategies for change on the part of both the left and the subsequent Echeverría administration. In the early 1970s, President Echeverría responded to this deepening crisis of representation and regional succession throughout Mexico by providing new opportunities for peasants and workers to organize politically in their neighborhoods and workplaces, outside of the existing framework of government-sponsored mass organizations. This led to increases in radical grassroots mobilizations throughout the country (Hellman 1983 [1978]; Foweraker and Craig 1990).

In Juchitán at this time, the local PRI supported nascent political boss Mario Bustillo in an effort to reestablish political authority within the party and the city. As the new cacicazgo was elaborated, the activities of the official party continued to involve only a limited group, for the most part ignoring both the provision of municipal services and the development of mass-based organizations. Opposition to caciquismo developed in tandem with its growth, much as it had during General Charis's rule in the 1940s and 1950s. The new activities began in Mexico City, among Juchitecos gathered in the Association of Juchiteco Students, a social organization that had functioned in the past primarily as a springboard for political and business careers. As a result of the interaction of Zapotec identity with a cosmopolitan, national setting, "the Association of Juchiteco Students had a certain prestige in Juchitán . . . People had confidence in it."[4] In the early 1970s, a group of students within the association challenged the current leadership, arguing that the organization should address social and economic problems in Juchitán and play a more active role in the daily life of the city. This challenge involved class as well as political differences, with students from poor and lower-middle-class backgrounds opposing the predominantly wealthy leadership (Campbell 1990b, 293–94). For poorer students, the experience of urban university life exposed them to new currents of political radicalism and, simultaneously, to a process of discovery and examination of their own ethnic identity (Campbell 1990b, 294–95).[5]

Two sets of events in the 1960s influenced the change among Juchiteco students in Mexico City. The first was the appearance of *Neza Cubi* (the New Road), the Zapotec journal of literature, art, and current affairs. A group of students and young intellectuals began to publish the literary and political journal at just the time that local leaders in Juchitán were challenging the candidate-selection procedures of the PRI and new political groups were forming. In *Neza Cubi*, the intellectuals infused the recuperation and elaboration of Juchitán's cultural heritage and the promotion of a new generation of local artists with an explicit commitment to exposing the marginalization of Juchitán's poor peasants and criticizing the failures and inequalities of economic development.

The members of the association were also influenced by the student movement of 1968. Before the repression at Tlatelolco, tens of thousands of students, primarily in Mexico City (though in other cities, including Oaxaca, as well) mobilized around issues of educational policy and democratic control of the universities, forming citywide coordinating committees and shutting down universities. In the course of this mobilization, the students broadened their analysis to question and oppose the authoritarian politics and antipopular economics of the postrevolutionary system, taking their activism beyond the universities and into the streets. In the weeks preceding the opening of the 1968 Olympic Games in Mexico City, the students succeeded in attracting widespread attention, disrupting the life of the city, and bringing about a virtually uncontrollable political crisis that the regime acted to resolve through violent repression (Hellman 1983 [1978]; Zermeño 1978).

This event took on profound significance in Mexican politics, marking for many the demise of the stable and orderly postrevolutionary system, or, more accurately, the end of the myth of stability that had followed the tempestuous reforms of the Cárdenas years. One of the many effects of the student movement and its repression was a rethinking on the part of leftist student leaders of the path for revolutionary change in Mexico. Where the Mexico City-based mass movement had kindled the possibility of rapid transformation at the national level, the intransigence of the regime and the relative ease with which its violent repression destroyed the student movement led many participants to conclude that change would come about only as the result of long-term, grassroots political organizing. In this view, shared by COCEI leaders, revolutionary activity had to begin by addressing the daily needs of peasants and workers in local communities, developing consciousness and organization through direct-action tactics, and avoiding manipulation by the regime through political parties, national organizations, and elections.[6]

With this political understanding, the new group of student activists in the Association of Juchiteco Students began organizing to gain control of the association, winning elections in 1973 (Gutiérrez 1981, 253). In the final months of that year, the students from Mexico City, together with others from two regional postsecondary agricultural and technical schools, organized a successful campaign in Juchitán to oust the head of the public hospital, Dr. Barragán, who had been charging younger students illegally for health certificates needed to enroll in local schools. These demonstrations against Barragán, which also functioned as rallies in support of the Tarú government, brought together a wide range of local political groups. When the demonstrations did not succeed, the students took over the public hospital. In response, the governor removed the hospital administrator from his post, and the Ministry of Health funded the Association of Juchiteco Students to run a health campaign in the outskirts of the city (*ES* 23 Sept., 7 Oct., 4, 11 Nov., 9, 16, 23 Dec. 1973).

COCEI formed out of the association after this success.[7] The progression of the hospital campaign, from public demonstration to building takeover—from legal action outside the realm of official politics to action that was technically illegal and on the border between permissible and not permissible—remained COCEI's strategy throughout the 1970s and 1980s. The talent of the movement's leaders lay in judging when and where to employ these tactics and how far to push them. In its first two years of activity, COCEI gained widespread popular support for strikes, marches, occupations of government offices, and skilled negotiations that improved living and working conditions.[8] In response to these activities, an article in *El Satélite* observed that if COCEI's student leaders didn't sell out to the "buyers of conscience" then "this pueblo will always be behind its children" (23 Sept. 1973). This identification of students as children of the pueblo served to characterize COCEI as a genuinely local opposition for two decades. The students "took the suffering of the peasants as their banner, then also the workers . . . their goals were to satisfy concrete claims and needs. This took fire, especially among the poor."[9]

The Coalition, as COCEI was also called, moved quickly to challenge the economic and political status quo in numerous arenas and to gather a wide range of groups behind its campaigns for better living and working conditions. At the end of 1973, the students addressed peasant concerns directly for the first time, by opposing a new tax on cultivated crops, and they won the annulment of the taxes in January of 1974 (Ornelas Esquinca 1983, 122; *ES* 6 Jan. 1974). COCEI leaders and supporters remember this successful campaign as the beginning of COCEI's identity as a peasant organization. COCEI went on to fight successfully for control of the Communal Land Commission, the elected body responsible for overseeing land use and the distribution of credit in the region (Ornelas Esquinca 1983, 123). Throughout these and subsequent activities, COCEI leaders' willingness to negotiate, along with the willingness of some state and national authorities to negotiate with them, contributed to the radical movement's ability to survive.[10]

In March, the students organized workers at the government-owned rice-processing plant, which had recently closed without paying its workers the indemnifications to which they were legally entitled. The workers succeeded in obtaining the indemnifications and the right to return to work when the plant reopened. In May, the Coalition met with representatives of the Treasury Ministry to secure the cancellation of fines issued to 234 peasants who had not registered their property in the ministry's office, and it began to pressure the Banco Agropecuario to cancel the debts owed by peasants to government banks (Ornelas Esquinca 1983, 123).

In July of 1974, the Coalition held a demonstration protesting the

Ejidal Bank's protection of a small group of agriculturalists who rented poor people's land and then obtained credit from the bank that had been denied to the small landowners. In August, COCEI began to organize workers of the Companía Maderera de Comitán in Niltepec, a town not far from Juchitán. The workers there sought recognition of an independent union and the right to strike, as well as removal from the region of military forces backing the wood companies. COCEI's meeting in Niltepec attracted supporters from Juchitán and other surrounding towns, and the participants agreed to form an Isthmus-wide peasant-student movement. In September the Coalition won the conflict at the rice plant, where the workers obtained their demands for reinstatement, indemnification, and an independent union, and in November the Coalition won a labor dispute in the local corn mills, securing a wage increase and benefits for workers. At this time, *El Satélite* reported the existence of orders to imprison the Coalition's leaders.[11]

As the local PRI responded with hostility and violence to COCEI's challenges, Juchitecos confronted a situation of rapidly escalating class conflict. In this situation, moderate priístas played a role that at times complemented that of COCEI's increasingly militant supporters. The moderates' position in Juchitán had earlier been articulated in opposition to boss rule, in the 1940s and 1950s. In the following decade, it had assumed the form of vehement criticism of the official party and the regime, culminating in the Tarú campaign against the PRI. As a result of these actions, moderates shared many of COCEI's goals, and, indeed, had been among the first to articulate them. Furthermore, COCEI itself had emerged from locations and experiences at the intersection of the moderates' critique and the intransigence of the regime: the politicization of culture in *Neza Cubi*, popular responses to the 1968 massacre at Tlatelolco, and the conflicts within the Association of Juchiteco Students. However, COCEI's own beliefs and practices went beyond the procedural democratic norms of elections, dialogue, and maintenance of civil liberties that moderates claimed to support. As a result, moderates were faced with the choice between a state whose practices and methods they found abhorrent, but whose basic form and substance they wanted to reform, and a radical movement employing approaches they rejected, such as confrontation, threats of violence, and antistate ideology, in pursuit of goals with which they sympathized.

COCEI's militant and at times illegal approaches were potentially acceptable to moderates in Juchitán in light of the failure of earlier reform efforts, and, equally importantly, because of their local origin and their embeddedness in Zapotec language and cultural forms. COCEI was seen as a genuine response on the part of the pueblo to the economic and political exploitation that the moderates themselves had exposed. As a result, faced with a local world at odds with their convictions, moderates discussed and rethought their positions on basic political issues, such as democracy, opposition, and violence. Their willingness to support a radical grassroots movement, even as most middle-class and elite Juchitecos fiercely opposed radical politics and tacitly supported ongoing repression, strengthened COCEI at key moments in its development, bringing votes, degrees of local tolerance, and support from some officials in Mexico City.

The Political Economy of Radicalism

The economic context in which the radical COCEI formed and grew was distinctly different from that in which reformist economic critiques and political campaigns had taken shape a decade earlier. COCEI arose during a period of increased aggregate economic growth, increased disruption in patterns of landholding, commerce, and industrial work, and some improvements in basic living conditions. The gross product per capita for the Isthmus increased at the substantial rate of 3.9 percent per year between 1968 and 1981, in contrast to a slightly falling rate for the previous decade (Jhabvala 1982, 43). Indeed, in contrast to the 1960s, which was a period of increased expectations, failed development projects, population increase, and slowed economic growth, the 1970s was one of rapid industrial and commercial expansion. In 1974, construction was begun on an oil refinery in Salina Cruz, initiating a period of oil-led economic growth, inflation, and an increasingly dual economic structure, whereby dynamic oil and commercial sectors coexisted with a peasant economy of ox-drawn plows, smallholdings, and family craft production. During this period, the most dynamic sectors of the economy, such as oil, transport, and fishing, were linked increasingly, through federal investment, to the national and international economies, to the detriment of local savings, investment, and economic linkages. These sectors demanded workers with specialized skills, often drawing on other regions to provide them, and they were centered around Salina Cruz, which expanded rapidly during the years of Mexico's oil boom (Fauvergue 1982; Jhabvala 1982, 41–46; Prevôt-Schapira and Rivière D'Arc 1983).

One of the main effects of this oil-led expansion on Juchitán was a marked increase in the size of the commercial and service sectors of the city's economy, which had already been expanding since the construction of the highways. When combined with the steady concentration of land and the gradual, if often unsuccessful, conversion to new, more mechanized forms of agriculture, the demand for services generated a process of increasing urbanization.[12] As a result, more and more peasants and their generally literate children worked for wages in stores, restaurants, factories, offices, banks, and repair shops in Juchitán, as well as in the oil and related facilities of Salina Cruz. The proportion of Juchitecos working in agriculture decreased by approximately half from 1960 to 1980, from about two-thirds to about one-third of the economically active population, while the proportion working in industry, construction, commerce, and services almost doubled, from about one-fourth to about one-half of the working population.[13] In the words of a successful local entrepreneurial couple in the mid-1980s, "Juchitán was virgin territory, despite being ugly. People came here to make money . . . [they] started coming here in 1975. They came despite COCEI and made money, and they'll keep coming. Even with the crisis, more money passes through Juchitán than any other place. . . ."[14]

During this period, a number of indices of living standards improved dramatically. The proportion of Isthmus families lacking basic protein sources dropped substantially between 1970 and 1981, in keeping with improvements in Mexico as a whole,[15] and the availability of water and electricity approximately doubled during the same years, to include more than 80 percent of Isthmus households.[16] This relative well-being, particularly unusual for an indigenous group, was one of the ingredients in the success of COCEI. Most Juchitecos, even though impoverished by their own and outside standards, were healthy enough, and sufficiently able to survive economically, to sustain themselves and their families in the course of a long-term process of political mobilization.

Accurate data on land ownership in the Juchitán irrigation district was difficult to obtain.[17] It was generally agreed that many families owned more than the legal limit, with large holdings ranging from fifty to two hundred hectares, a size that was relatively small compared with holdings in other parts of Mexico, but large for the Isthmus.[18] However, COCEI claims of monopolization and threats to peasant survival notwithstanding (COCEI 1983, 3–4), the process of land concentration did not completely exclude peasant families from ownership and cultivation, but rather diminished the size of their holdings.[19] This process upset family economies, threatened long-established habits of survival and well-being, and probably caused considerable anguish. At the same time, land concentration did not happen so rapidly that it absorbed most peasant land in the 1960s and 1970s, and the process was not a threat to peasants' physical survival. As families increased in size and sold land, Juchitecos worked increasingly in the city's rapidly growing commercial and service economy.

In the 1970s and 1980s, researchers who studied the Isthmus economy characterized the economic changes that occurred after 1974 as the detrimental effects of an oil-led, dual economy, and they identified an untrammeled, state-led process of capitalist expansion as the impetus for COCEI's formation and growth (Binford 1983; Campbell 1990b, 217–273; Fauvergue 1982; Prevôt-Schapira and Rivière D'Arc 1983, 1984; Warman 1972). In their analyses, the oil-driven economy, which built upon the infrastructural and agrarian changes of the preceding decade, signified a qualitative shift in the basis of economic activity and a wholesale change in the economic parameters of people's daily lives. In contrast, I will show in chapter 7 that the effects of commercialization and oil-led economic growth were more uneven than researchers claimed. What Juchitecos described in interviews about their economic experiences, in contrast to the homogeneous pictures presented by macroanalyses of the Isthmus, was unevenness, contradiction, and room for maneuver. Their battle to create new democratic forms occurred, as García Canclini suggests is increasingly common in Latin America (1989), in a hybrid economy and culture in which elements of "tradition" and "modernity" were starkly juxtaposed. Thus, it was not primarily direct challenges to survival caused by relentless capitalist transformation that inspired and sustained COCEI's radicalism, but rather Juchitecos' recognition of economic exploitation and poverty and their perception of threat to their cultural identity and way of life.

Poor Juchitecos and the Formation of COCEI

Juchitecos' accounts of their involvement with COCEI emphasized the prominent role of leaders and of concrete achievements, particularly in the early years of the movement's organizing. Their fragmented narratives reflect just the sort of experience and commentary that Smith (1989) found in the Peruvian highlands. Juchitecos indicated that they supported COCEI because they trusted the organization and because it worked for them. This form of identification with a radical political movement proved to be extraordinarily strong and enduring, in part because it was intimately connected with ethnic identity and practice. Identification with radical politics was also facilitated by the loose form of organization within COCEI, as well as by the fact that COCEI leaders neither criticized local culture nor advocated development projects, which would have required new forms of work and discipline.

COCEI offered concrete help to people who suffered numerous exploitations and had few avenues of recourse. COCEI leaders came to speak to people in Zapotec in their homes, communities, and workplaces, offered assistance, and achieved a series of material and symbolic victories through protest mobilizations. Like leftist activists and radical priests elsewhere, the founders of COCEI accompanied their discussions and actions with a radical critique of the existing structure of power relations. In discussions twelve years later, Juchiteco peasants, workers, and market women repeatedly cited these early contacts with COCEI leaders as the defining characteristic of their relationship to COCEI and radical politics. When I asked them about their support for the organization, Juchitecos praised the young male leaders of COCEI and explained what these leaders had done for them and for others in the first years of the movement's history. In these discussions, people generally presented the movement as one unchanging force for good. They would list some of the gains that COCEI had achieved, particularly those earlier ones that had affected them personally. They generally did not mention ways in which the movement had changed, moments of important strategic choices, or disagreements among leaders or between themselves and leaders.

As a researcher from the United States interested in the dynamics of political consciousness and mobilization, I had expected my interviews to elicit comments about experiences and strategies within COCEI and how these had changed in the course of two decades. However, I was unable to gain such information in a wide variety of interviews. It is of course likely that some people chose not to inform me about these sorts of conflictual matters because I was a foreigner. However, many of the people I talked to in the course of eighteen months were open to my presence and very interested in helping me learn about COCEI. After many months of sitting, talking, and especially listening in the courtyards of poor Juchitecos, I concluded that the absence of such narrative and analysis was not, for the most part, a consequence of my position as foreigner. Rather, it revealed the extent to which Juchitecos' ties to COCEI were based not on a narrative of objectives and strategy, but on interrelated, partial experiences of material interest, cultural discourse, and family relationships.

The comments of peasants in two small agricultural towns near Juchitán, Alvaro Obregón and La Venta, illustrate the type of founding experience that people describe as constitutive of their relationship to COCEI and COCEI leaders. In June of 1974, the Coalition leaders began working with peasants in Alvaro Obregón, acting on a land claim that had been pursued by the peasants for a decade, since the death of General Charis. In the years following the Mexican Revolution, the peasants had been awarded more than seven thousand hectares of land through a grant to Charis, as a reward for their support of Obregón during the revolution. However, after Charis's death, his widow and daughter claimed the land and sold valuable salt flats and some of the land to a local landowner and former Charis ally, Federico Rasgado (Campbell 1990b, 310). Rasgado employed armed guards to prevent peasants from fishing and gathering firewood and paid salt workers less than the minimum wage, denying them social security and threatening them with violence.

In allying with the Alvaro Obregón peasants, the Coalition thus joined a struggle that concerned both land and the political legacy of Charis, who had told the peasants that all they needed was "six hectares and a bullet" to protect the land (Campbell 1990b, 310). Between 1974 and 1977, Rasgado's gunmen were implicated in the killing of COCEI supporters outside the COCEI office, and peasants in Alvaro Obregón were repeatedly beaten. In 1977, Alvaro Obregón peasants, together with other COCEI supporters, as well as peasants from other regions, occupied the headquarters of the Ministry of Agrarian Reform in Mexico City for fifteen days. These efforts finally bore fruit later that year, when a presidential decree awarded one thousand hectares to the peasants, a major victory for COCEI and one of the movement's few successful efforts to secure ejido land rights for peasants (*Por Esto!* 23 July 1981; *ES* 16 June, 28 July 1974).

In recounting the origin and significance of the entry of COCEI onto the scene, Alvaro Obregón residents told a story about the relationship between poor families and COCEI that was told to me repeatedly, in bits and pieces, throughout the city of Juchitán and environs. In this account, the student leaders of COCEI came and talked to peasants throughout the region. The young men interpreted peasant concerns as the results of unjust government and economic exploitation and convinced peasants to join with them in fighting against these injustices. In the words of Antonio López Luis, set to music in ballad form,

In nineteen hundred seventy-four two leaders arrived, Hector Sánchez and Daniel López Nelio. They were valiant men, defending the rights of the poor campesinos and attacking the exploiters and the landlords.

Hector Sánchez said to the campesinos: The legal cases that were cast aside by that traitorous leader, we are going to take them up. Join together *compañeros* and we can move forward.

Daniel López Nelio answered him: We are the leaders, we come to form the Coalition to defend the rights of the poor campesinos and attack the landlords, monopolists, and exploiters. (*Por Esto!* 23 July 1981)

This dramatic musical account, which emphasizes the bravery and mobilizing potential of leaders, coexists, in the multifaceted fashion described by Rappaport, with somewhat different comments on the organizing process in an interview with the songwriter. In the interview format, López Luis placed more emphasis on the process by which peasants formed an organization and fought for their land. In this telling, it was the campesinos who emerged at center stage: "Now the rich are frightened of the campesinos, because little by little our organization is growing, with pride because now it is becoming famous throughout Mexico" (*Por Esto!* 23 July 1981).[20]

The residents of the *agencia* of La Venta, a political dependency of the municipality of Juchitán, recount another, similar founding story. In 1978, COCEI helped the parents' association in La Venta oust the head of the local school, Professor Hermán Matus Vera, for misuse of funds. As a result of this action, much like the initial COCEI involvement in Alvaro

Obregón, many La Venta residents saw the potential efficacy of challenging unjust practices (*ES* 8 May, 26 June, 28 Aug., 4 Dec. 1977, 7 May, 9 July 1978). Subsequently, COCEI helped them elect members of their group to run the local government for six consecutive years. Antonio Rodríguez, a peasant from La Venta, dated the beginning of awareness about COCEI in the town to a series of visits from Héctor Sánchez and other COCEI leaders during the COCEI campaign for mayor of Juchitán in 1974. Rodríguez said that Sánchez was the first person to arrive in La Venta with an "open" ideology, one that sought to defend the causes of people who had a low standard of living. Rodríguez said that he and Sánchez talked a lot about wages, working hours, and the lack of benefits for peasants who worked for others, as well as about credit and other protections for peasants. According to Rodríguez, Sánchez and other COCEI leaders carried out meetings, marches, and demonstrations in La Venta, bringing people from Juchitán to support the COCEI members there, "so that the pueblo could elect its own leaders." In the 1980s, COCEI helped La Venta residents construct and manage a new potable water system and a community health center, each of which was administered by committees of local residents who took active, ongoing interest in the new activities. Several years later, in discussing the decision of workers at a local department store to seek COCEI support for their grievances, Rodríguez and Ana María Díaz, another La Venta resident, concluded that people followed COCEI "because COCEI knows how to watch out for their interests disinterestedly."[21]

COCEI supporters in Juchitán gave similar reasons for backing the movement. According to Ta Juan, an older peasant who had performed different kinds of manual work in the course of his life, the Coalition watches out for poor people: "so that the rich leave a little for the poor." Ta Juan cited the very limited buying power of peasant wages, the high price of corn and meat, "and then one needs clothes, and to pay the electricity and water, how can it cover this?" Furthermore, with the high cost of school registration and required contributions for school improvements, he sends only one of his two school-age children to secondary school. Poor people used to accept things, he said, but now COCEI is opening their eyes, so things can't continue the way they were before. In Ta Juan's account, poor people go to COCEI with their problems—mistreatment in the workplace, rises in irrigation rates—and COCEI helps them. Na Marisela, who has a market stall in the street outside the central market, said her husband began to support COCEI when the organization backed a strike at the limestone factory where he worked, helping the employees get better wages. According to Armando, an oil worker, COCEI helped workers by getting benefits they didn't have before, and gradually people realized that COCEI helped poor people.

Origins stories focused not only on material gains, but also on "being heard." Ta Mauricio, also a campesino, observed that Polín,[22] COCEI leader and mayor of Juchitán in the early 1980s, "would have a movement anywhere. Whenever you have a problem, you go to Polín, he takes care of it." Another COCEI supporter said that "when people go to Polín to tell him about something, that's what he addresses." Both of these comments indicate people's conviction that Polín literally followed their words. COCEI, in turn, according to Ta Mauricio, got the government and employers to heed its words: "When COCEI goes to the governor, the governor listens."[23] In these ways, the "language of the pueblo" was quite literally heard and spoken by COCEI leaders.

Material gains and new forms of voice were often combined, such as in union organizing. A middle-class family, most of whose members have some sympathy for COCEI, but support the PRI, told of their Tía Paulina's conversion to COCEI. In the course of teachers' mobilizations and strikes in the mid-1980s, COCEI members convinced her—a member of the democratic movement within the teachers' union and a priísta—to accompany them to demonstrations in support of the teachers in Mexico City. She went, against family advice, and returned a COCEI supporter, with concessions from the government in hand. According to her family, she was a valuable asset for COCEI, because she was a "democratic" teacher with the capacity to draw other democratic teachers.

COCEI also gained supporters through family networks. Providencia, whose husband works in the bank and who herself runs a small neighborhood grocery store, expressed strong support for COCEI during the year and a half that I knew her and frequented her family's courtyard. Like many Juchitecos, she supported COCEI without closely following its activities. For example, she would know that there was a strike at a local department store, but ask me for details when I visited. Having heard a long, anti-COCEI presentation of the conflict on the radio, Providencia concluded that the radio account must have been false, or why would COCEI have been out there protesting? According to Providencia, her family first began supporting COCEI after the "disappearance," by the army, of Víctor Pineda Henestrosa, a COCEI activist who became a local official of the Ministry of Agrarian Reform. Pineda had married Providencia's cousin, and when he was abducted by the army this cousin came to the family and convinced them to support her and COCEI in demanding information about his whereabouts. After that, Providencia's family began to hold dances for COCEI at her house, and she saw all of the COCEI leaders frequently there. Once her family began to support COCEI, in solidarity with their cousin, they saw that COCEI did good things.

Elena, who sells electronic equipment, provides another example of the centrality of family connections to COCEI's bases of support. Elena's mother, a very successful market vendor, supported COCEI because her son (Elena's brother), one of the few local professionals who openly backed COCEI, was a student in the House of Juchiteco Students in Mexico City when the movement formed. Rafaela, the most politically articulate member of a large family that strongly supported COCEI, explained that after her father, she was the first in her family to support COCEI. This had resulted from her father's teaching her about "how the struggle is." At the same time, Rafaela and her sisters told me, only partly in jest, that it is good to support COCEI because "COCEI gives husbands," an observation borne out by the marriage of their brother to a woman from a family that hosted the COCEI section meetings in another part of the city. (Rafaela's own subsequent marriage ended tragically, in a dramatic illustration of the hidden side of Juchitán's culture of female autonomy. Rafaela was shot by her husband, who then left Juchitán and was never apprehended.) Rafaela and her sisters also introduced me to the technologies of grassroots voter fraud, as they used duplicate voting credentials to vote twice, and to the elaborate fashion rituals of voting, for which they spent several hours adorning themselves, in their case in Western rather than traditional dress.

Providencia's relationship to COCEI indicates one prominent initial pathway to COCEI support, that of family connections. Such forms of communication and solidarity often occurred through networks of ritual celebration, as well as political and social activities, such as dances, that drew on ritual practices. Antonio Rodríguez's account demonstrates another path, that of ideology combined with practical gains, including both material protections and the achievement of self-government. Tía Paulina similarly supported COCEI for civic reasons, in her case COCEI's defense of democratic procedures within labor unions. Rafaela's relationship to COCEI, through her father's notion of political struggle and her own and her siblings' experiences of marriage and adornment, combined several of these characteristics, ideological, material, and cultural. Ta Mauricio's comments on COCEI, like those of several others above, emphasize the successes of COCEI leaders in solving people's problems and offering a very personal form of help and leadership. This help developed out of intense, ongoing discussion and activism in people's courtyards and neighborhoods. COCEI leaders undertook these activities as men who had grown up in these neighborhoods, who had left as students and then returned, and who spoke, joked, and explained their ideology in Zapotec.

Local Associations

Part of COCEI's initial success derived from the weakness of official peasant and worker organizations in Juchitán.[24] In mobilizing support, COCEI did not have to break strong bonds tying workers and peasants to the PRI through the national peasant and labor confederations, the CNC and CTM. However, COCEI did encounter such bonds in specialized local associations. Conflicts over control of the Communal Land Commission (Comisariado de Bienes Comunales) and the Livestock Association (Asociación Ganadera) were central to COCEI's organizing efforts and defined an important aspect of its strategy and goals. Both struggles were electoral, with the radical movement seeking to win democratic elections for leadership positions in the local groups. In both cases, COCEI sought to control organizations with symbolic, if not always actual, roles in allocating resources and defining the path of regional agricultural development, and, in both, COCEI acted in the name of popular sovereignty to reclaim local institutions that had been controlled by the particular elite individuals and groups for decades.

In 1973, members of the Livestock Association, which monitored the buying and selling of livestock, acted to oust the association's president, Ricardo López Gurrión. Members accused López Gurrión of making improper use of the association's truck, pocketing funds, and abetting local rustlers. In keeping with its analysis of agrarian corruption, *El Satélite* applauded what it characterized as "raising the flag of democracy" in the face of "those who even now keep trying to swindle the pueblo" (28 Oct.

1973). After failing to oust López Gurrión through a series of pressures in 1973 and 1974, a COCEI-supported opposition slate won in association elections in January 1975. In response, the defeated leaders attacked the offices of the association, stole its documents and seals, and appointed its own leaders, and they secured a legal stay that enabled them to continue functioning. The COCEI winners of the elections retook the offices and, despite lack of support from the Ministry of Agriculture, proceeded to function as well. From that time on, the two offices and two associations coexisted in Juchitán, with incidents of PRI-sponsored violence continuing to subvert democratic procedure and the transaction of business through the end of the decade.[25]

The Communal Land Commission administered land designated as communal, which included most land in Juchitán until the 1960s. Before land became scarce with the building of the dam, the commission was officially in charge of assigning land to new families as well.[26] With the inauguration of the irrigation district, the commission became responsible for soliciting credit on behalf of landholders, a function crucial to peasant survival and well-being. A COCEI slate won elections in the Communal Land Commission three times, in 1974, 1975, and 1978. In 1974, students and peasants in COCEI opposed Land Commission president Juventino Ramírez, challenging the propriety of many of his actions, including the distribution of recently acquired land and a land grant to Tarú. In its campaign to win control of the Land Commission, COCEI faced threats from gunmen as well as an injunction obtained by Ramírez to stop the investigation. The COCEI slate won elections held in March, and the legality of the victory was upheld by a representative of the Agrarian Commission. When elections were held again in July of 1975, a group of prominent landowners actively campaigned for the PRI slate. Despite this, COCEI's candidate won 71 percent of the 716 votes cast. In the next Land Commission elections, held in 1978 and supervised by the Ministry of Agrarian Reform, peasants elected a COCEI supporter to succeed the outgoing COCEI-affiliated president.

Landowners, however, challenged the victory with the support of local deputy Mario Bustillo and the local Agrarian Reform delegate. After numerous legal maneuvers on the part of the landowners, as well as COCEI protest mobilizations in Oaxaca and Mexico City, authorities in Mexico City refused to recognize the COCEI slate, claiming election irregularities. They called for new elections, which were never held. As a result, since 1978 there has been no officially recognized Communal Land Commission in Juchitán.[27] In the 1980s, however, the credits that had in the past been distributed through the commission began to be distributed through independent groups of peasants, which were generally sponsored by either COCEI or the PRI. In this way, COCEI came to administer credit resources that were central to peasant agricultural production and peasant family economies. The closing down of one local institution, the Communal Land Commission, as a result of COCEI's successful campaign to control it through democratic elections, thus led to the creation of another space for COCEI autonomy and influence.

COCEI's successful challenges to the leaders of the Livestock Association and the Communal Land Commission represented a clear break with the past. Until COCEI's actions, the leaders of the two organizations had maintained the corrupt and authoritarian practices that had been attacked by progressive groups in Juchitán since the 1940s, and they had succeeded in preventing the emergence of clearly articulated lower-class interests in local institutions. COCEI's ability to challenge this elite, PRI-affiliated control indicates the extent to which the opposition movement could disrupt existing forms of interest mediation and begin to achieve a radical reorientation of regional life. By engaging directly with the most local institutions of Juchitán's economy, COCEI gained symbolic and practical experience in electoral competition and in administering the everyday activities upon which Juchitecos' livelihoods depended. Furthermore, the lack of definitive recognition of COCEI's electoral victories and the continuing violence surrounding them demonstrated clearly to Juchitecos the institutional limits COCEI faced, the contradictory impulses within the regime, and the risks of violence inherent in political activism.

The Land Issue

COCEI sought control of local land and livestock associations as part of its larger goal of reversing the promotion of commercial agriculture and the resulting dispossession of peasant landholders. An atmosphere of violence and crisis prevailed in Juchitán throughout the mid-1970s as COCEI pursued land claims through mass mobilizations. In response, paramilitary groups shot COCEI supporters dead in the streets, and police and army troops occupied the region to protect the agricultural activities of large landowners. Concurrently, officials of the Echeverría administration decided repeatedly in COCEI's favor with regard to the status of the region's land, and Juchiteco peasants came very close to achieving a massive reform that would have reactivated the 1964 ejido decree, which had designated the Juchitán portion of the Isthmus irrigation district an ejido.

The land mobilizations occurred at the end of Echeverría's presidency and the beginning of the administration of López Portillo, during a period of the rise and subsequent decline of widespread peasant mobilization in Mexico. At the same time that COCEI was mobilizing to reclaim and protect local landholdings in the southern Isthmus region, peasant land invasions in the Yaqui and Mayo Valleys in the northern state of Sonora succeeded in gaining large-scale land redistribution and establishing ejidos that developed into economically and politically powerful cooperative ventures (Baird and McCaughan 1979, 52–59; Fox and Gordillo 1989; Sanderson 1981, chap. 7). In Juchitán, implementation of the decree would have redistributed large landholdings, established new institutions of collective decision-making, and provided a basis for collective activities in production, marketing, and representation. Leigh Binford has shown that federal agencies consistently responded to COCEI's pressures with decisions that supported the movement's claims about land. However, the same agencies did not follow through by enforcing their findings. This apparent contradiction in state policy resulted in ongoing police and paramilitary violence, on the one hand, and, on the other, "the maintenance of . . . [an] ambiguous situation in which, contrary to the opinion of the Agrarian Reform Ministry, landowners continue to appeal to the titles as legal sanction for the purchase and sale of land" (Binford 1985, 198). As a result, Juchitán was under a virtual state of siege by 1977.

In 1974, a land invasion in the *agencia* of La Ventosa initiated COCEI's campaign to challenge the private-property titles distributed by Díaz Ordaz in 1966. Peasant grievances centered around ownership of ejidal or communal land by people who were ineligible for such land because of their private wealth or who owned more than the legal limit of thirty hectares. In response to peasant challenges, landowners urgently demanded support for their titles from agrarian authorities. The conflict led to a meeting of regional government agencies and political groups, as a result of which a resolution was sent to the Department of Agrarian Affairs and Colonization (DAAC, renamed the Ministry of Agrarian Reform, or SRA, in 1975) requesting "an investigation of the origin and validity of the [1966] titles expedited by the DAAC." The resolution also asked that the DAAC determine whether or not there was land monopolization (meaning ownership of land beyond legal limits) in the region (Binford 1985, 198–99n 47). As a result of its investigation, the DAAC upheld COCEI's interpretation of the private-property titles in its final report, rejecting the private-property designation as illegal within the territory of communal land. Furthermore, the engineers documented monopolization as well as noncultivation, both of which were grounds for land expropriation and redistribution (Binford 1985, 198–99n 47).

Throughout the struggle over land in Juchitán, grassroots mobilization and negotiation were intertwined with state and private violence against COCEI supporters. In the spring of 1975, one hundred Juchiteco peasants met with the secretary of agrarian reform, Augusto Gómez Villanueva, pressuring him to execute the 1964 decree, and he agreed to send a commission to investigate and apply the laws governing land ownership (*ES* 1 June, 7 Sept. 1975). In October, a prominent COCEI activist, Víctor Pineda Henestrosa, was appointed head of the Agrarian Affairs Office (Promotoría Agraria), a local branch of the federal agrarian bureaucracy. This appointment indicated federal support for COCEI and suggested that COCEI's agrarian demands might be met before the end of President Echeverría's term in 1976. The following month, however, in a clear indication of the deep fear and hostility this elicited among landowners, eight COCEI supporters were killed at a demonstration commemorating the first killing of a COCEI supporter one year before (Ornelas Esquinca 1983, 130–31; *ES* 2, 16 Feb., 23 Mar. 1975).[28]

During the 1975–77 period, COCEI filed a suit against the private-property titles with the district court, but this was never acted upon. COCEI proposed the creation of a commission that would oversee agricultural production in Juchitán and assume responsibility for the resulting profits until the status of the land was settled legally. This proposal was rejected by the government and landowners. As a result of government unresponsiveness, COCEI acted to block the granting of credits to large landowners through demonstrations and land invasions. These efforts achieved some success in disrupting production, which proceeded under the protection of the police and the army (COCEI 1983, 4), as ongoing military oversight became a quasi-permanent feature of daily life in the fields.

1976 marked a crucial year in the land battle. For a time, it looked like the ejido decree and a program of collective agriculture might both become reality. At a January assembly called by the Communal Land Commission, peasants voted to establish a collective ejido, a form of collective agricultural production that had been promoted by President Echeverría as a way to modernize ejido agriculture and improve production. Representatives of the Ministry of Agrarian Reform, along with representatives of most of the region's agrarian agencies, attended the meeting and pledged their and President Echeverría's support (*ES* 4 Jan. 1976). The prospect of a collective ejido elicited considerable discussion and opposition, as well as continuing violence against COCEI. Before a key meeting between COCEI and the State Agrarian Commission, a group of the landowners attacked the house of COCEI leader Cesar Pineda, where COCEI leaders were meeting with the Communal Land Commission and representatives of the (federal) Ministry of Agrarian Reform. The attackers shot at the house for six hours without any intervention on the part of the municipal police (Ornelas Esquinca 1983, 131). In the face of this violence, editorials in *El Satélite* contrasted the efforts of the rich to maintain their exploitative position with the rights of peasants to work the land as they chose and to seek a more equal distribution of income (11, 18, 25 Jan. 1976).

El Satélite's editors also supported the collective ejido because they believed it would promote the kind of modernization the newspaper supported: "There would be profound changes, as much in the consciousness as in the customs and way of life of the campesino family; whoever wants to progress has to accept the new situation" (1 Feb. 1976). While COCEI shared *El Satélite*'s opposition to inequality, the newspaper's critical attitude toward local agricultural practices and culture differed sharply from COCEI's defense of this way of life, establishing the lines of future cultural division between COCEI and moderates within the PRI. *El Satélite* and COCEI agreed, however, that the landowners who opposed the effort were provoking violence and bloodshed: "Señores, you yourselves arm to the Coalition . . . you, the exploiters, are the ones who make the peasants seek their rights with the young men of the Coalition . . ." (16 Feb. 1975). In its evocation of impending bloodshed, *El Satélite* linked the ferocity of state violence to the likelihood of a violent response on the part of campesinos, thereby strengthening COCEI's own discourse of explosive class and indigenous violence.

In the end, the forceful combination of peasant mobilization and government findings in favor of peasant claims did not lead to land reform. *El Satélite* reported efforts to oppose the ejido plan, in the form of a local committee to defend private property, along with the use of state police against peasants and COCEI. Agrarian Reform minister Félix Barra García first seemed responsive to COCEI claims, but subsequently refused to meet with peasants (*ES* 29 Feb., 28 Mar., 18 Apr., 20 June 1976). While large-scale agrarian reform was always an unlikely result, it did occur in Sonora at precisely this time,[29] as well as in other regions, and it seems clear that such a move was being considered for Juchitán as well. Binford cites intense resistance on the part of regional elites (1985, 198), which was indeed the case, but this was true in Sonora as well (Sanderson 1981, chap. 7). In the case of Juchitán, the best explanation for the lack of land reform can be found at the state level, where government and private-sector actions had been crucial to the promotion and foreclosing of reform in Juchitán during the nineteenth- and early-twentieth-century rebellions and throughout the Charis cacicazgo of the 1940s and 1950s. In Oaxaca, the mid-1970s was a period of widespread popular mobilization and government intransigence, and municipal president Mario Bustillo was a staunch supporter of hard-line governor Zárate Aquino. Together, they were able to veto land reform for as long as Zárate Aquino managed to stay in power. By the time Zárate Aquino was forced from office in 1977, President Echeverría, who had promised changes in land tenancy in Juchitán and initiated the process of investigation there, had completed his term. López Portillo, in contrast to his predecessor, responded to the leftist mobilization and political turmoil of 1976 by opposing further land reform and favoring business interests.

Despite the lack of progress on the overall land issue, one large concession occurred in 1977, soon after the killing of Juchitecos and the fall of Zárate Aquino. As described above, 1000 hectares of the land claimed by Federico Rasgado in Alvaro Obregón was given by presidential resolution to the peasants there, who had been fighting to regain the land since 1964 (*ES* 3 July 1977). Since this land battle had been a COCEI priority, López Portillo's resolution of the dispute in COCEI's favor represented a significant concession following a period of repression. In addition, during this period, COCEI successfully pressured the Rural Credit Bank to turn over a 250-hectare cattle ranch to local peasants and cancel the debt left by the ranch's previous owners. These were just the sort of minimal concessions typically offered by the Mexican regime to calm unrest, often with the result, when combined with repression, of stifling dissent. In Juchitán, however, this response to seemingly uncontrollable mobilization served to strengthen peasant opposition.

Land-related activities continued in 1977 and 1978, even though it gradually became clear after 1976 that large-scale changes were unlikely in the short run. In 1978, fifteen hundred COCEI peasants invaded one thousand hectares of land in Juchitán, and four hundred peasants in Tuxtepec, a city in the northern part of Oaxaca, led in part by COCEI, took over five thousand hectares there. The latter were subsequently removed by Tuxtepec police and army troops (Ornelas Esquinca 1983, 113). In that same year, COCEI itself suffered military violence, when Víctor Pineda Henestrosa, the COCEI militant who headed the local agrarian agency, was "disappeared" by the army. Images of Pineda Henestrosa, including a photo of his elderly grandmother holding a photograph of him, played a central role in COCEI's political and cultural iconography thereafter. An editorial in *El Satélite* evoked images of impending violence, characterizing what had in the past been seen as the violence of the Zapotec pueblo now as the violence of peasants, understood as an economic class. The newspaper observed that everyone knew there had been a presidential decree making the land in Juchitán an ejido and that sooner or later the land would go to the *ejidatarios*. Six thousand peasants were waiting for land, the editorial continued, and in the future their number would double, "and then nobody will be able to keep poor peasants from carrying out justice with their own hands . . ." (16 Apr. 1978).

COCEI leaders, even as they pursued a nonviolent path to class consciousness and political power, explicitly recognized the limits of dialogue and the potential necessity for violence in achieving change. In a 1975 discussion of possibilities for progressive reform, for example, Guillermo Petrikowsky, a COCEI sympathizer, had concluded that the absence of substantive change, coupled with the presence of state-sponsored violence, would be met by violence on the part of the oppressed: "the pueblo, in the end, after exhausting all parliamentary means, devoted to the law, will finally respond to aggression in the same language [of violence] . . ." (*ES* 30 Nov. 1975). Leopoldo de Gyves Pineda recognized not only the inevitability but the value of such violence: "We salute the violence of the poor peasant." De Gyves praised the political mobilizations that peasants were initiating across Mexico, in the form of land invasions and the occupation of offices of the Ministry of Agrarian Reform, and he hoped for signals from president-elect López Portillo that the president would support peasant claims. These activities constituted rebellion, in de Gyves's view, and they necessitated violence: "Our warmest welcome to the violence of the humble campesino, who, filled with wrath and hunger, rebels against his enemies, the exploitative landowners and the corrupt authorities who practice deception from the highest public offices" (*ES* 26 Dec. 1976).

While such rhetoric continued to fuel COCEI's mobilizations, the land battle became less central to COCEI's organizing activities in the 1980s. In the face of regime intransigence concerning land reform, COCEI, like other grassroots peasant movements, began to focus on issues of agricultural production and marketing, such as credit, inputs, and prices, rather than land ownership itself. In addition, in the 1980s, COCEI focused increasingly on types of activity it had carried out alongside the land battles of the previous decade—the defense of workers' rights and the improvement of municipal services. These efforts had generally been more successful than the land campaigns because, in contrast to demands for restoration of the ejido decree, individual battles could be won in an incremental fashion. Furthermore, the shift away from land issues in the 1980s responded not only to regime policy, but to generational changes that accompanied the ongoing process of economic transformation in the region; in the 1980s, fewer Juchitecos looked to land to secure their futures than had done so a decade earlier, while more worked for wages in the urban economy.

Despite these many changes, the land issue remained a cornerstone of COCEI's identity and discourse. The campaign that had galvanized Juchiteco peasants in the 1970s became a central image in the movement's subsequent efforts to occupy public office, defend economic well-being, and develop and promote Zapotec cultural practices. The land-reform mobilizations were not understood primarily as failures, but rather as efforts that established COCEI as a powerful people's movement and defined its confrontational relationship with the regime at all levels, from local associations to national offices. The land campaigns, along with the violence and military occupation that accompanied them, were experi-

127

enced, codified, and remembered as the founding experiences of radical identity and practice—even when participants themselves did not remember the ejido decision or when they did not see land as having been taken from themselves illegitimately. A discourse of attacks on peasant land and heroic mobilizations coexisted with a broader range of family experiences with land tenancy, just as a discourse of violent repression coexisted with imageries of fierce and self-sufficient Zapotecs. Juchitecos constructed COCEI to encompass these partially contradictory discourses and experiences and bring them to bear on new situations. In contrast to Sonora, where land invasions resulted in a new form of ownership and production, and where radical politics then grew from (and was also limited by) these collective economic efforts, COCEI built on its experiences in the land struggle in the 1970s to achieve unprecedented successes in the municipal arena in the following decade.

Oaxaca in the 1970s and 1980s

Oaxaca state politics directly influenced COCEI's growth through the availability of allies for both Juchiteco elites and COCEI. During the land battle in Juchitán, dramatic mobilizations on the part of grassroots movements in the state's Central Valley increased the force of COCEI's own claims, while the violent responses of state officials and elites effectively prevented redistribution. At the same time, state-level events responded to different dynamics from those at play in Juchitán, and COCEI's alliances with a coalition of grassroots groups in Oaxaca disintegrated rapidly in 1977. Furthermore, the state-level conflicts receded in local memory, popular and official, much more quickly than the land battle in Juchitán in which they had been enmeshed. Radical politics in Juchitán, in contrast to Oaxaca, grew out of shared indigenous identity in an urban location, innovative cultural elaboration, and a linear historical narrative of barbarism, autonomy, and resistance. As a result, while the grassroots coalition in the state capital rapidly lost force at the end of the 1970s, COCEI could sustain itself within a complex network of local institutions and courtyards during a period of restrictive government policies.

Between 1968 and 1970, when student mobilizations occurred in many Mexican cities, leftist students in Oaxaca fought for changes within the university and formed alliances with grassroots groups in the city.

While these activities led to swift repressive action on the part of Governor Víctor Bravo Ahuja, the situation changed dramatically with the designation of Bravo Ahuja as minister of education in Mexico City and the naming of Fernando Gómez Sandoval to the governorship. A former rector of the University of Oaxaca and a relatively progressive politician, Gómez Sandoval presided over a period of marked opening toward popular movements of peasants, workers, and students between 1970 and 1974.[30]

Leftist students formed the Coalition of Workers, Peasants, and Students of Oaxaca (COCEO) in 1972, a year before COCEI was formed in Juchitán. Like COCEI in the Isthmus, COCEO pursued a multifaceted organizing strategy, seeking to unite a range of poor people's groups into an explicitly class-based, militant popular movement in the state's Central Valley. Between 1972 and 1974, peasant land invasions achieved repeated successes in gaining control of communal and ejidal land that had been taken over by large landowners (Zafra 1980). In 1974, small, independent unions in a range of commercial and service industries in the Central Valley gained legal recognition and won strikes, securing higher wages and the payment of benefits (Yescas Martínez 1980). Also in that year, a number of the peasant communities that had been involved in land invasions sought to win power in municipal elections (Zafra 1980).

While mounting protests and organization on the part of the private sector did not succeed in pressuring Gómez Sandoval to change his policies, they did secure the nomination of a known hard-liner, Manuel Zárate Aquino, for the governorship in 1974. The Echeverría administration, which had encouraged Gómez Sandoval's openness to popular organization in clear opposition to the state's private sector, thus retreated in the fashion of alternating conflict and concession that had been practiced by the federal government toward the state elite since the 1930s. When Zárate Aquino took office, he acted immediately to oppose the widespread mobilizations, making use of military intervention to defeat labor strikes, opposition to bus rate hikes, mobilizations against fraudulent municipal elections, and urban land invasions (Santibañez Orozco 1980, 317–18).

After these successes, Zárate Aquino set out to defeat the leftist student movement within the university, which had supported the grassroots movements and provided them with aid and counsel. Because of the university's legal autonomy from the state government, the governor could not act directly, but had to depend on the university groups who supported him winning an internal struggle. This difficult task proved to be the governor's undoing. As conflict in the university escalated, the national Ministry of Education (SEP) supported the Democratic University Movement, which represented the leftist groups, installing and providing funds to an alternate rector sympathetic to the popular movement. Continuing opposition on the part of opponents of the Democratic University Movement led to increasing mobilization and confrontation, culminating in an attack by police and others on the central university building in January 1977, and police shooting at a crowd of student demonstrators in March (Santibañez Orozco 1980, 318–20, 326).

In Oaxaca, as in Juchitán and in other parts of Mexico, the economic and political practices of regional elites and Mexico City authorities were under attack in increasingly militant, public, and threatening ways. As the Ministry of Education's support for a progressive rector at the University of Oaxaca indicated, regional and national elites often disagreed with each other, as well as among themselves, about how and when to encourage, tolerate, or violently repress popular-movement initiatives. This can also be seen in the support provided by federal labor boards for COCEI's claims on behalf of workers, in direct opposition to the interests and convictions of Isthmus economic elites. Furthermore, the fact that it was indeed the same man, Bravo Ahuja, who opposed the Oaxaca popular movements as governor but supported the Democratic University Movement at the University of Oaxaca as national minister of education, indicates that it is not only individual histories and ideologies that create conflicts and contradictions among policymakers, but institutional position within a divided and changing regime as well.

Throughout his term, Zárate Aquino chose repression in responding to popular mobilization. In August 1977, he opposed a strike by bus employees that had been declared legal by federal authorities, sending in police to disrupt the strike on its first day. In October, as a result of this conflict, bus lines to the coast were shut down, and service to the Isthmus was soon curtailed as well (Ornelas Esquinca 1983, 104; Santibañez Orozco 1980, 326). Zárate Aquino now simultaneously faced several explosive conflicts: over municipal elections, internal university affairs, the bus drivers' strike, and Isthmus student mobilizations. Nationally, the peso had been devalued twice in the fall of 1976, and presidential power had recently been transferred from Echeverría to López Portillo. The Oaxaca crisis figured prominently in the national press, and the Permanent Commission of the Congress in Mexico City sent a committee to investigate. In all these conflicts, the federal government pursued a strategy at odds with that of Zárate Aquino: through the Ministry of Education, it sought a referendum in the university and negotiations in the Isthmus, and through the Federal Board of Arbitration and Conciliation, it favored a negotiated solution to the bus strike.

The governor, in contrast, supported the hard-liners fully in each case, refusing all negotiation, and he responded to the mounting crisis by authorizing police violence in Juchitán, rural villages, and the state capital (Ornelas Esquinca 1983, 104; Santibañez Orozco 1980, 328). In response, students in Oaxaca sequestered and burned buses, trucks, and cars. Groups supporting Zárate Aquino fought back by forming civic committees and organizing a citywide business strike (Santibañez Orozco 1980, 325–28). As a result of this escalating conflict, Zárate Aquino was removed from office, to be succeeded by a general, Eliseo Jiménez Ruíz. Heladio Ramírez, who would promote reform at the state level and in Juchitán as governor in 1987, was then designated president of the state PRI. Jiménez Ruíz, a military man, had led the counterinsurgency campaign against guerrilla leader Lucio Cabañas in Guerrero earlier in the decade (López Monjardin 1986b, 19), while Ramírez, a leader of the National Peasant Confederation, brought reformist commitments to representing the needs of campesinos.

Unified opposition to Zárate Aquino gave way after his resignation to infighting on the left that effectively ended the popular movement in the university and the capital city (Ornelas Esquinca 1983, 61–80, 105–9). As a result of the failure of COCEI's alliance with COCEO, as well as the difficulties encountered by COCEI in joint activities with other peasant organizations, COCEI leaders concluded that the movement's strength lay in the Isthmus and in Juchitán. This lesson did not preclude future alliances with other peasant movements or with political parties—much like negotiations with state authorities, such alliances were in fact crucial to the organization's successes in the 1980s—but it led to a retreat to Juchitán and a focus on municipal concerns for the remainder of the decade. The retreat to Juchitán, in turn, emphasized the strength, resilience, and fertile nature of the local environment for radical politics.

Despite the strategic usefulness of this move inward, COCEI's difficulties in alliance building constituted one of the most dramatic and enduring failures of innovation for the movement. Such failure was intimately tied to the movement's internal characteristics and successes: the ability of COCEI leaders to speak the language of the pueblo with artistry and humor; their skillful combining of respect for local needs and practices with a relative absence of internal democracy; and the personal, familial, and cultural pathways by which Juchitecos joined COCEI. These characteristics, which grew from the autonomy that Charis had secured for local cultural and political life during the midcentury years, would continue to hinder alliance building in the 1980s.

Similarly, the elite political events of the mid-1970s in Oaxaca repeated some of the dynamics between region, state, and federal government that had characterized politics in the 1940s and 1950s, with national reformist initiatives facing fierce resistance in the state capital. In the earlier period, oppositions to boss rule on the part of the Juchitán Democratic Front gained office only when federal officials designated reformist governors in the state capital. In these instances, however, the "modernizing" governors were rapidly unseated by multiclass civic oppositions, with corresponding retreat on the part of the Democratic Front. In the 1970s, in contrast, reformist Gómez Sandoval stayed in office, while hard-liner Zárate Aquino was ousted. Although Jiménez Ruíz reinforced the hard-line position, the balance between reformists and hardliners, and between the state and federal governments, had shifted discernibly, as evidenced by the Jiménez Ruíz/Ramírez pairing. This shift, in turn, provided increased maneuvering room for COCEI in its engagement with elections and municipal government in the years to come.

Elections

COCEI's most innovative strategic choice in the 1970s, in terms of its interaction with both Juchitecos and the regime, was its decision to participate in municipal elections and to place considerable rhetorical emphasis on its democratic claim to municipal sovereignty. Beginning in 1974, soon after its formation, COCEI fielded independent candidates with little chance of officially recognized victory at a time when virtually all Mexican radical movements rejected such participation (Haber 1993, 218).[31] Much like COCEI when it addressed state and national politics, these groups perceived elections as tools of the state and the ruling class, so that genuine opposition could come only from mass mobilization and the development of radical consciousness.[32] COCEI's unique decision to combine such nonelectoral mobilization with participation in *municipal* elections accounts in significant part for the movement's endurance, which surpassed that of most other popular movements in the 1970s.

Despite the left's principled critique of electoral politics, participation in elections was in many ways an obvious path for grassroots organizing in Juchitán. Since early in the century, municipal elections there had involved contestation over local sovereignty, with popularly based oppositions either winning elections and governing the city, or rebelling in the face of electoral fraud and influencing local politics as a result.[33] Even when the coincidence of a strengthened central state and Charis's enduring rule precluded the taking up of arms, electoral contestation crystallized important political and cultural projects in the city and influenced negotiation over political authority. COCEI's own entry into electoral politics followed the experiments with primaries in the 1960s, as well as the 1971 mobilization behind Tarú and the unprecedented defeat of the PRI.

COCEI thus entered the competition by building on a recent history of renewed electoral mobilization, in a context where the significance and practice of elections were up for grabs. According to COCEI leaders, this electoral strategy responded to pressure from peasant and worker supporters, based on their experiences of elections in Juchitán, rather than to the views of the leaders alone.[34] Moderates writing in *El Satélite* also urged COCEI to participate, as a result of their own historical critique of boss politics and failed development and their ongoing advocacy of elections as a means to reform. Thus at this point, as in subsequent years, COCEI's electoral activity responded to multiple constituencies, as it emphasized the idea of popular sovereignty and provided a goal around which to organize. Official declarations of PRI victory, along with violent attacks on protest demonstrations, served to highlight political imposition and repression and thereby further the cause of radical organizing.

Because leftist parties were illegal for most of the 1970s, COCEI acted independently of political parties by necessity as well as conviction. In this way, the exclusion of the left from electoral competition reinforced the independent character of grassroots opposition. Successful grassroots organizing in the 1970s, in turn, prompted the regime to attempt to control leftist political activity by channeling it into political parties and electoral campaigning in the 1980s. As a result, COCEI's participation in elections came to afford the movement a degree of protection from repression, through effective use of the democratic rhetoric of the regime and the media attention that accompanied it.

COCEI entered the 1974 elections in competition with both the PRI and the Popular Socialist Party (PPS), an officially recognized opposition party with some claims to an oppositional stance. After some speculation that the Juchitán Democratic Front and COCEI would combine forces for the elections, COCEI announced the candidacy of one of its founding members, Hector Sánchez. The reformist Democratic Front had publicly opposed COCEI during the preceding months, and in any case unity between the two groups would have been difficult. In the words of the columnist Bere Lele, politics in Juchitán had changed since the formation of the Democratic Front in the previous decade: "today we are no longer dealing with an electoral politics, but with a class struggle . . ." (18 Aug. 1974, 16, 23 Feb. 1975).

Official election results gave 3,086 votes to the PRI, 2,405 to the PPS, and 1,021 to COCEI. This represented one-third of an electorate of approximately 20,000 eligible voters.[35] Three days after the elections, COCEI held a meeting to protest electoral fraud. The demonstrators were violently attacked outside the house of municipal president Mario Bustillo, and a pregnant COCEI supporter, Lorenza Santiago, was killed. This was the first killing of a COCEI supporter since the organization had formed at the end of 1973, and it marked the beginning of a rapid escalation of violence against the movement. In response, COCEI held a demonstration in front of the Cámara de Diputados in Mexico City, calling for the annulment of the elections and the arrest of Bustillo for Santiago's murder. In Juchitán, COCEI made an agreement with the PPS to oppose the fraud, and, after more violence against COCEI supporters, the two groups together took over City Hall. Two days later, however, in what COCEI leaders considered a decisive betrayal, the leader of the PPS convinced his supporters to leave the building, and COCEI was subsequently removed from City Hall by the army.[36]

COCEI participated in municipal elections again in 1977, and in all subsequent municipal elections as well. In 1977, at the end of Bustillo's term in office, COCEI candidate Leopoldo de Gyves Pineda (a member of the Juchitán Democratic Front who had initially opposed COCEI, but came to be one of the movement's most prominent supporters) opposed priísta Javier López Chente. López Chente had won out over a new, young group within the PRI, led by Jesus Pineda López, the president of the local PRI. Pineda's group, consisting primarily of younger men who had returned recently to Juchitán from study and work in Mexico City, advocated a renovation of the official party through honest and responsive politics, and it represented a potential alternative to corrupt business-as-usual within the PRI. Indeed, Bustillo, despite his willingness to countenance unprecedented levels of violent repression, was also recognized by many Juchitecos as having been less corrupt and more closely in touch with local families than his predecessors, and initially he had some connections to the Pineda camp. Despite the efforts of the reformers, however, López Chente won the candidacy through his willingness to ally with another precandidate, Vicente López Orozco, who was disqualified because of past criminal behavior, and the two proceeded to preside over the most corrupt municipal government in recent memory.

El Satélite drew a direct connection between the elections of 1974 and those of 1977, marshaling the voice of the martyred Lorenza Santiago to "rise up even more powerfully to tell her countrywomen to continue fighting" for local democracy (20 Nov. 1977). Pointing to the government's promises of fair elections in 1977, with open procedures at the polling places, the newspaper joined COCEI in denouncing the official PRI victory, and a succession of fruitless meetings were held with authorities of the Electoral Commission in Oaxaca. COCEI's efforts brought police surveillance of protest meetings, and attacks on COCEI's inauguration-day march resulted in the death of a COCEI supporter and the sacking of stores around the central plaza. Later in January, candidate de Gyves Pineda, characterized by a friend as "a classic recalcitrant Juchiteco, a warrior, to the point of suicide," led a protest march in several towns just north of Juchitán. As a result of this effort to challenge the official electoral results, de Gyves Pineda, a retired officer, was arrested, tried, and imprisoned by the military.

In response to the regime's use of police power to keep COCEI from office and delegitimate its protest activities, COCEI began to organize the section committees that would become central to its political activities in subsequent years.[37] The section committees served as centers for discussion and mobilization, and they also took on the function of adjudicating disputes among neighbors. These section committees represented the continuation of a form of local organization that had existed previously in Juchitán, but had been subservient to municipal authorities and had come to be characterized by corrupt section leaders who charged high fees for their services (Campbell 1990b, 321). In 1978 and 1979, the reestablished committees repaired a bridge, fixed roads, and pressured authorities on public-health issues (*ES* 1 July 1979), and they also judged and resolved such issues as marital disputes, personal quarrels, labor conflicts, and legal matters, many of which were supposed to be handled by municipal authorities.

The section committees, formed in response to electoral repression and serving as the focal point for neighborhood electoral mobilization, demonstrate COCEI's success in combining electoral and nonelectoral forms of activity in the same organizational networks, as well as the movement's ability to transform preexisting institutions into focal points for radical politics. As a result of COCEI's remaking of the committees as staging areas for citizen complaints, public-works projects, and political mobilizations, "poor villagers began to view COCEI as the de facto political leaders of Juchitán" (Campbell 1990b, 322). In addition, these centers of political leadership in turn contributed structure and practical experience, including alternative locations for social and cultural activity, for COCEI's subsequent period of opposition municipal government.

In 1979, COCEI leaders debated whether to participate in legislative elections, the first national elections in the period of the *reforma política* (political reform), when leftist parties were legalized and some forms of proportional representation expanded. COCEI leaders also debated whether to gain legal status in municipal elections by allying with a national party in 1980. Formally, legal status would bring with it the protection guaranteed by the political reform: participation in the registration process, representation at the polls, and access to grievance procedures. At the same time, alliance with a national party represented a potential loss of independence for COCEI and form of support for the regime. In contrast to most strategic decisions faced by COCEI, which were cloaked in secrecy, the debate about whether or not to ally with a national party, as well as to participate in state and national elections, was made public in a series of newspaper articles. The articles were written by two COCEI supporters, one of whom spoke for the dominant COCEI view of nonparticipation, and one of whom, who was also a member of the

Mexican Communist Party (PCM), argued for the Communist Party's position of working within the system.

In the debate, supporters of the dominant position within COCEI argued that COCEI should reject elections, which they saw as manipulated by the regime, in favor of mass mobilizations that challenged the regime head-on. This dominant position, in effect presented as COCEI's position, denied in theory what COCEI had been doing in practice since its formation—combining electoral participation with direct action. In addition, the majority argument rejected just the sort of simultaneous engagement with local *and* national electoral processes, including political parties, that would begin to characterize COCEI's successful political strategy a year later and, by the end of the decade, represent the philosophy of much of the Mexican left.

Those who argued against elections distinguished between participation in official politics and practical efforts to address problems that people faced daily at the local level. In calling themselves a mass movement, they meant not only that they wanted to better the lives of peasants and workers, but that they would act outside of and against the regime and the state with the revolutionary goal of gaining access to power. As a member of the Communist Party, in contrast, Alberto López Morales argued that the reforma política itself provided an opportunity to establish a new form of opposition politics, and he urged COCEI to ally with a party and participate in legislative elections.[38] López Morales argued that taking elections seriously and trying to pressure the state from within was a valid and necessary part of a revolutionary struggle, alongside mass organizing, the development of consciousness, and attention to people's most pressing problems (*ES* 29 Apr. 1979). What López Morales imagined is what indeed occurred in Juchitán in subsequent years: sustained participation in official politics on the part of an independent opposition that continued to act in the interest of its constituents.

The Bere Lele columnist in *El Satélite*, speaking for the moderates, put the matter more bluntly: the government had been pushing COCEI into clandestine activity, and the organization needed to take advantage of the new law to secure legal status. That way, it could mobilize more citizens throughout the Isthmus (26 Mar. 1978). Bere Lele envisioned a competitive party system that would encourage debate and participation. As a moderate with great faith in electoral democracy, he also anticipated immediate change through elections, given that "hundreds and thousands of citizens want a radical change in the administration of justice in this city and in many other Isthmus towns" (5 Aug. 1979).

For COCEI, in its antielectoral discourse, mass mobilization meant staying out of electoral politics, which did not provide for genuine competition, took energy away from productive activity, and served the interests of elites. The reforma política was designed to "strengthen the Mexican political system," as its creators stated explicitly (*ES* 15 Apr. 1979). It represented a controlling tactic of the state, providing a means to legitimize some leftist groups and delegitimize others, labeling as guerrillas those who refused to participate (*ES* Apr. 1979). Legitimation, furthermore, revolved around political parties, the object of particular hostility and wariness on the part of COCEI. Focusing on the dangers of party politics and ignoring its own immersion in municipal elections, COCEI insisted that "education and organization [for radical politics] can and must take place at the margins of elections" (*ES* 22 July 1979).

The debate itself, however, illustrates the ambiguity of these margins and represents a dividing line between two different leftist positions. More than a disagreement about electoral participation per se, the debate concerned whether and how a regional grassroots movement would engage with national politics. Before 1979, COCEI indeed participated in elections in practice, but rejected them in theory, and its participation occurred overwhelmingly in the regional context. Beginning in 1980, in contrast, COCEI not only participated in municipal elections, but engaged directly with national political actors in the process—allying with a national party and competing in national and state legislative elections. Through changing electoral discourses and practices on the ground, COCEI thus forged a path that would be recapitulated by much of the Mexican and Latin American left in the 1980s and 1990s—from grassroots politics "at the margins of elections" to grassroots politics publicly engaged with national politics. This path developed in interaction with, but ultimately separate from, the direct-action tactics of the land battle in Juchitán and the multifaceted mass mobilizations in Oaxaca. Both of these campaigns achieved great successes in organizing and in fostering new forms of political awareness among ordinary people, but they failed to gain significant material or political concessions. In contrast, in the electoral domain—by way of internal disagreements, as well as partial contradictions between its discourse and practice—COCEI forged the capacity to engage with the national regime through municipal elections in the 1980s.

Repression

Shuncupe laacabe, ruutica cobardeca laacabe sica rati bicu

(Poor ones, those cowards kill them as if they were dogs)
—anonymous Juchiteco[39]

Throughout its existence, COCEI has faced violent repression. This repression was particularly fierce between 1974 and 1977, when COCEI supporters suffered repeated violent attacks by the right wing of the local PRI along with hired thugs, resulting in the deaths of more than twenty supporters. Repression took the form of harassment and arrests of leaders, harassment and attacks on the families of leaders, attacks on offices, military and police responses to COCEI mobilizations, and repeated killings at public demonstrations. These attacks were made at various times by prominent priístas themselves, gunmen hired by local priístas, members of right-wing paramilitary groups, local and state police, and the military. Until the late 1980s, attacks on COCEI appeared to be made with the sanction of government officials at all levels, who never pursued the attackers. The savagery of the violence unleashed against COCEI, tolerated and at times perpetrated by the regime, made the repression of the 1970s, intertwined with the early activities of COCEI leaders and the land campaign, into foundational experiences that provided lasting images of the relationship between poor Juchitecos and the Mexican regime. These images were embedded in a discourse that was distinct from that of the barbarous, rebellious, and Indian pueblo, but that coexisted with it. In this case, COCEI-supporting Juchitecos became "the poor ones," treated like animals, gunned down in the streets. In their own representations and those of outside allies, they were the victims of elite and state violence and exploitation, in need of precisely the explosiveness that they and others had long attributed to their nature. Indeed, the inhumane ways in which they were treated legitimated the fierceness of their response.

This coexistence of pain and rebellion evokes the mixture of hardship and heroism attributed by nationally prominent Juchiteco writer Andrés

Henestrosa to the founding of Juchitán (1993 [1929]). In searching for a home for dispersed men who had been saved from catastrophe, Saint Vincent rejected the first place he landed, where the air was clear, the land fertile, and the jungles beckoning with fruit, and looked instead "for an area where the air was thick and dirty, the land arid, the water deep, [and] the rain unruly" (Henestrosa 1993 [1929], 39). There, overcome with relief, Saint Vincent established a city "for hardworking men who live next to a dead river." The settlers had to dig wells seven fathoms deep to quench their thirst and to "rip the chest of the earth after scarce rains to obtain its fruits" (Henestrosa 1993 [1929], 39). In 1929, Henestrosa wrote that "the bravery, uproar, and misfortune of its first settlers are repeated in all the movements of its current inhabitants" (1993 [1929], 40). In the 1960s and 1970s Juchiteco artists and intellectuals drew on these representations of Juchitecos' nature to describe and animate radical politics in the face of violence.

In May 1974, COCEI leaders Daniel López Nelio and Oscar Matus were beaten, the former by the municipal treasurer and others, the latter by the municipal police. In November, Hector Sánchez was attacked by PPS members during his electoral campaign. Also in November, at a COCEI demonstration protesting electoral fraud, opponents opened fire in front of the house of the official victor, Mario Bustillo, killing Lorenza Santiago. Two armed attacks occurred in December, one when priístas attacked COCEI activists and the other when the mayor's bodyguard attacked a group of peasants.[40]

A year later, at a demonstration outside the COCEI office marking the anniversary of the first killing of Lorenza Santiago, paid gunmen opened fire and killed seven peasants and one student. Slightly more than a year after that, in February 1977, state police attacked a COCEI demonstration in front of the Juchitán jail, where COCEI supporters were protesting the jailing of thirty-seven student activists. The police opened fire and continued shooting, following people as they fled. Two children and three COCEI activists were killed, and approximately one hundred people were injured in the shooting. The description of the scene in the Mexico City publication *Punto Crítico* evoked the ferocity and all-pervasiveness of violence:

. . . suddenly the line of state police, under the command of an agent of the federal Ministry of the Interior, fired in the air with its M-1 automatics. After the confusion of the first shots, the people regrouped in an orderly manner. That was when the federal agent gave the order to fire and 50 policemen took three steps forward and fired into the crowd in repeating bursts. Then children, women, and men started to fall, to be picked up by their *compañeros* and pulled out of the line of fire. A group of women who hid in the Sta. Cruz 3 de Mayo Church was dragged out and beaten by the police. In the midst of this torment, Héctor Velázquez, treasurer of the rice plant union, was wounded and disappeared. He did not reappear until the 24th, together with two other workers, 100 km from Juchitán, tortured, mutilated, and dead. (*Punto Crítico* 71, 15 Mar. 1977, cited in Ornelas Esquinca 1983, 104)

After the attack, a letter in *El Satélite* reported a meeting in nearby Ixtaltepec attended by teachers from the schools affected by the student strikes, along with the municipal presidents of Ixtaltepec and Espinal. According to a teacher present, "they signed the death sentences of the leaders of the student groups and of COCEI, there was a lot of money to pay the police who might carry out a massive assassination" (*ES* 27 Feb. 1977).

In 1978 and 1979, at the same time that leaders of COCEI were writing frequently in the local newspaper and the organization was gaining increased legitimacy in the city, protests against repression were increasingly couched in the language of human rights and were carried out in more public, national, and religious forums. In February 1978, more than one hundred peasants gathered in front of the headquarters of the United Nations in Mexico City to protest police repression in Oaxaca. A COCEI hunger strike then returned to the same place in September. Family members of COCEI supporters who were prisoners or had disappeared gathered in the Church of San Vicente, the central church in Juchitán, in May 1979, asking for the help of the bishop of Tehuantepec, Arturo Lona Reyes, in securing the release of the prisoners. In September 1979, COCEI supporters joined with two thousand others in occupying the Mexico City Cathedral as part of the National Committee in Defense of Prisoners, the Disappeared, and Political Exiles. Through these efforts, COCEI gained the attention of the human-rights groups that were just beginning to form in Mexico and elsewhere. As with its willingness to enter into national electoral politics in the early 1980s, COCEI's use of human-rights discourses in the late 1970s demonstrated its emerging skill in combining intensely local experiences—rooted in characterizations like those of Henestrosa that set Juchitecos apart from Mexicans—with national and international political discourses.

Several different groups were responsible for the violence in Juchitán. Activists in the local PRI were intent upon reasserting control of the city after two years of opposition government under Tarú, and some local elites, particularly large landowners, initiated violence against COCEI as well. Individual priístas and landowners at times carried out this violence themselves, and they made use of regional paramilitary groups as well. Municipal president Mario Bustillo and Governor Zárate Aquino readily employed violence against the new opposition movement, in the form of attacks by the local and state police. The federal army was involved in repression in Juchitán throughout these years, but in a role different from that of the local and state police. The army attacked citizens when they were involved in overtly political actions, such as building takeovers, land invasions, strikes, and demonstrations, while police repeatedly beat, shot, and jailed COCEI supporters who were not at the time of attack involved in public political actions. Some of the activities in which the army intervened were technically illegal, though most were not, and all were nonviolent. Army interventions did not generally result in reported injuries or deaths, while police activities frequently did. According to COCEI, the identity of local military troops changed in 1976. Before then, the Eighth Battalion, consisting of men from the region, had been stationed in Ixtepec. Some of these men sympathized with the activities of the reformist opposition groups in Juchitán, against whom they had to act at various times. The Eleventh Battalion came to Juchitán from northern Mexico in 1976 with training in anti-drug-trafficking tactics, and their arrival corresponded to the ongoing military presence and limitations on civil liberties that characterized municipal life during 1976 and 1977 (Alfaro Sánchez 1984, 130).

The army intervened in Juchitán with the official purpose of "maintaining order" at times of crisis and opposition mobilization, such as in 1977, following the massacre outside the jail. In doing this, the army restricted rights of assembly and harassed COCEI supporters and others—but, again, these actions did not result in reported violence. Finally, the army was involved in two sets of incidents directed at individual COCEI leaders, while police attacks more frequently involved nonleaders. In 1978, the army twice arrested Leopoldo de Gyves Pineda, the second time sentencing him to three years imprisonment, and soldiers abducted

Víctor Pineda Henestrosa, resulting in Pineda Henestrosa's permanent disappearance, and presumably his murder. This last was the only reported case of injury or death carried out by the military.

Repression in Juchitán contributed directly to the development of collective understandings about power and to the rootedness of COCEI in people's daily lives. The absence of efforts on the part of government officials to oppose attacks and killings made visible the hostility of the state not only to the visions and claims of peasants and workers, but to their lives and physical safety as well. In retelling the history of COCEI and their own involvement with the movement, Juchitecos invoked the names of those who were killed at demonstrations and described the instances of harassment that they themselves experienced. Women vendors in the central market recounted examples of denial of places in the market and destruction of market stalls by PRI officials; urban squatters told of attacks on the COCEI housing development; peasants described attacks in the fields; and students described arbitrary arrests and physical mistreatment by police. Often, a family's involvement in politics began as a response to the injury or arrest of members of kinship networks or neighborhoods, as in the case of Providencia's involvement with COCEI following the disappearance of her brother-in-law.

The mass killings at demonstrations, in particular, were perceived as a direct regime attack on the pueblo and evoked a response of solidarity and political support. Priísta Felipe Martínez, a Juchiteco sociologist who became municipal president of Juchitán in 1987, described how these attacks affected the community identity of Juchitecos:

If for Juchitecos one is Juchiteco above all, and if one has roots in a strong sense of belonging to the community, then to feel massacred, persecuted, and beaten by soldiers and police creates a collective consciousness of solidarity. In addition, knowing that other Juchitecos have been persecuted inspires fierce indignation, as well as moral solidarity with them. Since the massacre of 1977, the *coceístas* [COCEI supporters] have been surrounded by martyrs. (Martínez López 1985, 62)

Such repression in Juchitán resulted in ongoing, ritualized attention to the dead, with the image of *muertos* becoming a central element of COCEI's narrative about itself: "Thus, coceístas painted demonstration placards and banners with the images of their dead compañeros, female relatives of 'disappeared' coceístas wore pictures of them around their necks, Juchiteco intellectuals wrote hagiographic essays, and the leader-

143

ship began to talk of fighting on behalf of the deceased" (Campbell 1990b, 317). A local poet prefaced his work with a quote from Salvadoran poet Roque Dalton, "each day the dead become more unruly" (Campbell 1990b, 317), and writers in *El Satélite* also observed that violence in Juchitán "has awakened thousands of our compatriots, who are fighting for new paths to the future" (*ES* 23 Oct. 1977, 13 May 1979).

The overarching pattern of violence in Juchitán coexisted with varying degrees of openness to COCEI on the part of regime officials, including instances of negotiation between COCEI and national authorities. Violent repression occurred not only during the years when López Portillo's Alliance for Production signaled support for businessmen and landowners, but also during the preceding years, when the Echeverría administration exhibited relative openness to independent organizations. COCEI supporters were beaten and killed even as Echeverría promised attention to COCEI demands and agrarian officials found in COCEI's favor on land issues. Intense violence was one among several strategies of a regime characterized by disagreement at the national level and antagonism between state and national officials. While the federal government was willing to employ soldiers in response to political challenges and mass mobilization, its direct practice of violence was restrained in comparison to the private and police violence enacted by local and state authorities and elites. Military occupation, limitation of civil liberties, and threats of physical harm, all wielded at times from Mexico City, coexisted with national moves to promote land reform, respond to COCEI's direct-action campaigns, and initiate more open forms of electoral competition. Juchitecos' ability to interpret and withstand violence derived from their ability to negotiate the shifting fault lines of this national politics.

Negotiations with Government Officials

Despite its stance as an independent organization, as well as ongoing hostility and repression from all levels of government, COCEI has maintained contact and participated in negotiations with government officials at the state and national levels during the 1970s and subsequent decades. In his study of the Popular Defense Committee of Durango, Paul Haber observes that such negotiation was a crucial element in the formation and survival of the Durango movement, although it was rarely acknowledged publicly (1993, 222, 224). Jonathan Fox, Gustavo Gordillo, and Luis Hernández have noted the interactions between regime officials, promoters of government programs at the regional levels, and grassroots activists in a number of states: in Oaxaca, with regard to the establishment of local food councils (Fox 1993); in Nayarit, in the early stages of the formation of the Lázaro Cárdenas Union of Ejidos (Fox 1992; Hernández 1990); and in Sonora, during the growth of the Union of Collective Ejidos of the Yaqui and Mayo Valleys, as well as the subsequent formation of the Unión Nacional de Organizaciones Regionales Autónomas (UNORCA) (Fox and Gordillo 1989). Support for radical movements on the part of regime actors can often be traced to their experiences in the student movement of 1968. Even those on opposite sides of the fence, when it came to radical change, shared a common language of educational background and student politics (Fox 1990a). Among regime actors who supported significant reform in the interests of poor people, furthermore, some did so for reasons of social justice, while others believed that the ability of the Mexican regime to survive depended on such reform.

Little information is available about negotiations between COCEI leaders and state officials. COCEI leaders have consistently refused to discuss these matters, even with researchers to whom they have granted extensive interviews (Campbell 1990b, 296). This is indicative of the extent to which existing lines of communication between radical leaders and state officials are obscured, and deliberately hidden, by images of confrontation between poor people's movements and a monolithic state, just as electoral participation is in some sense "hidden" by the debate about whether or not COCEI should participate. However, images of confrontation and nonparticipation coexist with other kinds of private and public knowledge. During conflicts and mobilizations in Juchitán, the occurrence of meetings between COCEI, its local opponents, and government officials or representatives of government agencies was common knowledge, though the content of the meetings was generally secret. For example, observers in Juchitán reported frequent meetings between COCEI leaders and officials of the Echeverría administration, such as Secretaries of Agrarian Reform Augusto Gómez Villanueva and Félix Barra García.[41] COCEI leader Hector Sánchez stated in a series of interviews that Echeverría had promised resolution of the land tenancy question in favor of COCEI (*ES* 10 Apr. 1977), and reevaluations of the land situation were indeed carried out during these years, with officials supporting COCEI's claims about the legal status of the land.

However, the occurrence of meetings of another kind is more obscure. These meetings did not focus on negotiation over specific political or material issues, but rather concerned the existence of COCEI, the terms on which it might be permitted to act, and the kinds of responses that might be expected from the regime. According to a regional PRI politician, there were two such meetings between COCEI and government officials, one with President Echeverría in Cancún in 1976, and another with Governor Jiménez Ruíz in Oaxaca in 1977.[42] In addition, COCEI reports a meeting with officials of the Ministry of the Interior in 1977, concerning recent events in Oaxaca. What differentiates these meetings from negotiations over particular issues is their attention to the question of the terms on which COCEI's continued existence would be acceptable to the regime (though the regime could not necessarily enforce its terms). While this question was part of more focused negotiations concerning land, labor, and elections, the occurrence of these meetings suggests a willingness on the part of officials to explicitly acknowledge COCEI's continuing existence at particular moments, and on the part of COCEI leaders to negotiate with government officials concerning mobilization strategies.[43]

The 1976 Cancún meeting with Echeverría allegedly took place during López Portillo's presidential campaign, in order to avoid conflict during López Portillo's visits to Oaxaca and Juchitán. According to the PRI politician, Echeverría sent first Bravo Ahuja and then Gómez Villanueva, both of whom had been involved in previous dealings with COCEI, to Juchitán to offer concessions to COCEI leaders in exchange for a promise of cooperation during the campaign visit. After COCEI leaders refused, the PRI politician from the region succeeded in convincing them to meet with Echeverría in Cancún and present their demands, all of which were agreed to by Echeverría, but only one of which was carried out.[44] The demands included the ousting of municipal president Mario Bustillo for his alleged role in the killing of COCEI supporters the previous November, indemnification of the families of the dead, and land redistribution. Eventually, the indemnifications were paid, and an investigation of the land situation was ordered, but in the end no changes in land tenure were implemented, and Bustillo completed his term in office.

In 1977, Antonio Salazar Salazar, the representative of the national PRI

146

in Oaxaca, allegedly sought a meeting with COCEI, and at the meeting offered COCEI support for its efforts if it would officially join the PRI. This meeting appears to have had the same purpose as one reported in another source as a 1977 meeting between the Ministry of the Interior and COCEI, in which the ministry tried to persuade COCEI to act strictly by legal means, without direct-action pressure tactics (Ornelas Esquinca 1983, 107). At the latter meeting, COCEI in turn asked for the legal settling of agrarian problems, which the ministry refused (Gutiérrez 1981, 259–60). At the former meeting, COCEI insisted on meeting with the governor, who, in the words of the politician, treated them "like guerrillas," acting like a military man and not a politician and telling them that if they did not change their tactics, he would destroy them. According to the regional politician, a more serious discussion might have resulted in an agreement.

During my field research in Juchitán, I did not gain access to the kind of information that would enable me to assemble a more detailed account of the ongoing interactions between COCEI leaders and regime officials, or between local business elites, PRI politicians, and regime officials. Such interactions constitute the most hidden aspect of the story of radical politics and democratization recounted in this chapter and the next. An account of them would reveal the ways in which violence and bloodletting in Juchitán occurred in much closer proximity to dialogue—however partial, angry, disingenuous, and failed—than is suggested by any of the public accounts of COCEI's history.

Fragmentation and Innovation

COCEI emerged from the 1970s having forged new grassroots practices out of a diverse set of "incomplete, uncertain" (Smith 1989, 228) projects that overlapped and diverged according to differing dynamics. In the results it achieved, COCEI was representative, and indeed a forerunner, of much of the reshaping that occurred on the left in Latin America in subsequent years. Moves toward electoral participation, engagement with national political processes, and attention to cultural representation and elaboration occurred "on the ground" in Juchitán, through debate and contradiction, enmeshed in local conjunctures. Juchitecos themselves described these phenomena in terms of particular experiences of protest, electoral participation, material gain, family connection, or violence, rather than through a narrative of political strategies and outcomes.

In the course of the 1970s, COCEI simultaneously lost municipal elections and took on symbolic and practical duties of governing through neighborhood section committees, the local Livestock Association, and the Communal Land Commission. In the latter associations, COCEI's electoral challenges produced ambiguous outcomes, as the regime recognized newly created organizations or disbanded existing ones in order to outmaneuver COCEI's successes. COCEI rallied peasants in defense of land even as the role of land was changing in an increasingly hybrid local economy and culture. This battle, too, produced contradictory responses on the part of the regime, while it came to signify COCEI's origin and integrity in popular discourse. As COCEI's mobilizations challenged the PRI and regional elites with increasing force, police and paramilitary groups attacked COCEI supporters without opposition from public officials. This repression, in turn, brought support for COCEI from Juchiteco moderates. In the face of regime-sanctioned violence, furthermore, COCEI maintained contacts with regime officials that remain unacknowledged to this day.

Outside Juchitán, COCEI played a central role in statewide mobilizations that empowered reformists at the expense of hard-liners in Oaxaca and Mexico City, a shift that aided COCEI at key moments in the subsequent decade. In the course of its state-level activities, however, the movement failed to develop an enduring capacity to ally with other radical groups and alienated leftist activists and politicians from other regions and from Mexico City. During the same period, COCEI rejected elections ideologically and assumed a militant antiregime and antielectoral stance, while at the same time it made municipal electoral campaigns a cornerstone of its organizing.

Out of these incomplete, and contradictory, phenomena, COCEI forged a movement that could foster and maintain support internally and that could go on in the course of the 1980s to engage increasingly with national political processes. COCEI established its own autonomy and gained authority through its day-to-day rootedness in local family networks and concerns. This rootedness, in turn, enabled the movement to incorporate complex and contradictory understandings and thereby to move flexibly from one issue to another and include Juchitecos with differing identities. These contradictory understandings were articulated and mediated through an explicit cultural project, including a separate (Zapotec) language with which to talk about exploitation and repression and connect them to ethnic identity. In so doing, COCEI rearticulated tropes of barbarism long present in Juchiteco culture, but wedded in preceding decades first to Zapotec boss politics and then, in the 1960s, to civic activism. Through its political and cultural elaborations, COCEI experimented with how to act in formal politics, how and in what ways to be democratic, how to wield internal and external authority, and how to secure forms of voice and autonomy for Juchitecos. Elections were an insightful and shrewd component of this experimentation, a visionary use of local history and practice to leap over then-current leftist beliefs.

Campesino (photo by Jeffrey Rubin)

Woman at party (photo by Jeffrey Rubin)

Market vendors (photos by Jeffrey Rubin)

Woman and child in family courtyard (photo by Jeffrey Rubin)

Wedding celebration in family courtyard (photo by Jeffrey Rubin)

(photo by Shoshana Sokoloff)

Midwives

(photo by Jeffrey Rubin)

(photo by Jeffrey Rubin)

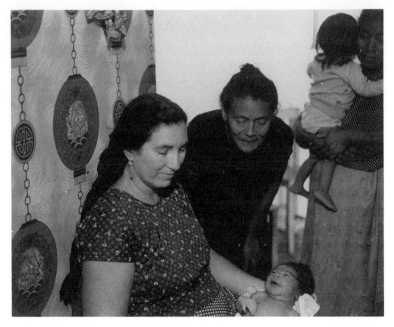

(photo by Shoshana Sokoloff)

Inauguration of COCEI health center (photo by Jeffrey Rubin)

COCEI demonstration (photo by Cindy Karp/Black Star)

6

Leftist Government in the 1980s and 1990s
"The Pressure of Zapotec Is Much Stronger" [1]

In 1981 COCEI won municipal elections in Juchitán and became the only leftist government in Mexico. As a result of this COCEI administration and subsequent events in the course of the decade, peasants and workers and their organizations in Juchitán gained greater influence in regional politics, economy, and cultural life, and, correspondingly, regional and national power holders became more accountable to the majority of the population. The process of transformation and democratization in Juchitán occurred through locally constructed political meanings and the elaboration of alternative cultural projects, and it developed in interaction with violent imagery and practice that appropriated tropes of Juchiteco barbarism. When the Ayuntamiento Popular took office in 1981, it "symbolized indigenous self-government, an ethnic millennium" (Campbell 1994, 169). On inauguration day, in the words of COCEI leader Mariano Santana, "the streets of Juchitán were adorned with red flowers, and in the Municipal Palace the red flag of the COCEI flew at full mast. After a long road with many sacrifices and obstacles we had realized a Zapotec dream: to be the government [*ser gobierno*]" (Campbell 1994, 169).

COCEI's ability to "be the government" derived from the combination of its partially urban character, its rootedness in ethnic identity and language, and its participation in elections during a period of uneven democratic opening. Juchitecos experienced the complexities of urban life, including multiple forms of direct government involvement in daily affairs, at the same time that they preserved and elaborated one predominant ethnic identity. As COCEI made use of these characteristics to press the boundaries of acceptable electoral and nonelectoral political activity in the 1980s and appeared on the verge of getting "out of control," regional elites and national authorities responded with mixtures of violence and negotiation. Part of this combination of responses resulted from the political role of Juchiteco moderates, whose shifting stances, based alternately on class, ethnicity, and civic politics, provided maneuvering room for the radical movement. COCEI itself constructed activism out of varying positions in each of these areas, shifting its emphasis from multiclass unity to class conflict, from literary representations of ethnicity to celebration of daily cultural practices, and from impartial administrative procedures to machinelike patronage.

In their work on democratization, O'Donnell and Schmitter offer a broad definition of democracy: "Democracy's guiding principle is that of citizenship. This involves both the right to be treated by fellow human beings as equal with respect to the making of collective choices and the obligation of those implementing such choices to be equally accountable and accessible to all members of the polity" (1986, 7). Accordingly, "if political democracy is to be consolidated, democratic practice needs to be spread throughout society, creating a rich fabric of democratic institutions and authorities" (O'Donnell 1988, 283). During the past decade, the combined effects of electoral competition and neoliberal economic restructuring in Latin America have shown that formally democratic procedures are not sufficient for establishing the forms of citizenship O'Donnell and Schmitter describe. Situations of popular empowerment and regional reform, conversely, have at times fostered autonomy and accountability in the absence of formally democratic procedures (Fox 1990b, 1992, 1994b). In assessing the democratic character of power relations, it is thus necessary to examine not only electoral competition, but the relationships between elections and the ways in which people experience power in other spheres of their lives. In Juchitán, processes fostering democratic voice and accountability occurred both inside and outside of formal politics, including not only local government, labor unions, and economic policymaking, but language use, information exchange, religious practice, and Zapotec ritual celebration as well. Through the interaction of the fragmented domains of mobilization in the 1970s and cycles of electoral participation and municipal administration in the 1980s and 1990s, COCEI has forged a tempestuous and multifaceted regional democracy. In so doing, Juchitecos have once again shaped a domain of sovereignty within the nation. In contrast to the domain of sovereignty of the Charis period, the arrangements of the 1980s and

1990s have assumed a different form, with new class, ethnic, and national alliances. But they have also preserved and expanded many of the autonomies that had been sought through rebellion in the nineteenth century and achieved through coexistence with the nation in the twentieth.

The Left Governs and the Right Reorganizes: 1980–1983

After the 1977 political reform put democratization on the national agenda and legalized leftist parties, COCEI formed an alliance with the Mexican Communist Party, gaining an official place on the municipal ballot in 1980.[2] This alliance provided a national forum from which to denounce electoral fraud following the 1980 elections. In the face of national publicity as well as direct-action mobilizations that included the occupation of two foreign embassies in Mexico City, the Mexican government acknowledged that there had been fraud in Juchitán and annulled the elections. In special elections held three months later, COCEI was declared the winner with 51 percent of the vote, and Juchitán became the first and only city in Mexico governed by the left.

A coincidence of regional and national events made possible the annulment of the 1980 elections and the subsequent COCEI victory. On the national level, the López Portillo administration placed considerable emphasis on newly invigorated electoral competition. Mexico's 1977 political reform had been designed in large part as a strategy for controlling the independent popular movements that had formed in the 1970s, as well as to fortify the quasi-democratic image of the regime. Between 1980 and 1983, policy decisions under both President López Portillo and President de la Madrid permitted opposition victories of the left and right in a number of relatively large cities in Oaxaca, as well as in other states, particularly in the north. This strategy meant encouraging the electoral participation of COCEI and possibly tolerating a leftist victory.

National economic and geopolitical factors also influenced this period of political opening in the Isthmus, which began during the expansive years of Mexico's oil boom. At this time, it was expected that increased political competition, to the extent that it occurred, would take place in the context of unprecedented industrial and commercial growth. Thus, the national government would possess sufficient fiscal resources to reward multiple constituencies. The political opening also coincided with intense conflict and increasing leftist success in Central America, with Guatemalan refugees fleeing into Mexico in record numbers and regional conflict appearing likely to widen. These economic and geopolitical pressures had conflicting effects on the regime's willingness to accept leftist political participation in the Isthmus. While militant conflict would endanger the regime's economic plans and political control, violent repression in the Isthmus would scare investors and weaken Mexico's foreign policy, which was based on support for leftist movements in Central America.

Locally, COCEI was strong and able to mobilize considerable mass support in protest activities in 1980, while the PRI was divided, its historical conflict between machine politicians and reformist challengers continuing to fragment the party, despite the consolidation of Mario Bustillo's political leadership in the 1970s. In addition, the PRI and its outgoing municipal president were discredited, with accusations of corruption and inefficiency coming from across the political spectrum. The PRI candidate in the 1980 elections was a longtime politician and leader of the weak local branch of the National Peasant Confederation (CNC), and he did not gain strong support from priístas allied with the business and professional wing of the party. In the 1981 contest, however, the appointment of a progressive priísta by the governor was seen as an imposition from the outside and alienated the party's base in the city.[3] The splits between reformists and hard-liners within the official party facilitated COCEI's electoral victory. At the same time, the multiclass nature of Zapotec ethnicity, COCEI's success in claiming the identity of the pueblo, and the partial support on the part of moderates for radical politics established a degree of openness to COCEI victory among priístas. Lack of support for PRI candidates resulted in abstentions, as well as some votes for COCEI. As in 1971, when the majority of voters had supported Tarú, there was sentiment across classes that it was time to throw the PRI out of office and that COCEI deserved a chance to govern.[4]

Events at the state level also played a central role in the 1981 opening. Both political and business leaders were in a situation of disorganization. Oaxaca's two major business groups were engaged in a struggle for control of the State Federation of Chambers of Commerce and could not act as a unified force against COCEI. At the same time, a new governor, Pedro Vásquez Colmenares, had just taken office, arriving from Mexico City without a developed base in Oaxaca politics. He was not the preferred candidate of the business elite and needed to establish his own political support, and he sought to represent the national political opening at the state level. A repressive approach to Juchitán, likely to provoke violence, was both risky and undesirable at the beginning of his term (Bailón Corres 1985, 6; 1987).

The 1981 democratic opening was perhaps the most significant event in COCEI's fourteen-year history. Despite harassment and subsequent violent repression, COCEI's two and a half years in office provided the opportunity for an Ayuntamiento Popular, a people's government, and secured for the movement a claim to municipal sovereignty and the enduring support of large numbers of Juchitecos.[5] The inauguration of the Ayuntamiento Popular offered a glimpse of transformation after almost a decade of conflict and violence. The COCEI of fragmented narratives and enduring mobilizational power had triumphed in an altogether unprecedented way. Its victory transformed municipal life, infusing both public politics and daily activities with festivity, innovation, and conflict.

At the same time, the formal political opening that brought COCEI to power was limited and uneven. Despite his ostensible support for COCEI's right to govern in Juchitán, Vásquez Colmenares cut off much of the municipal budget as soon as COCEI took office, and both state and federal agencies opposed loans and credits to the Ayuntamiento Popular. Such a combination of formal support and withdrawal of resources mirrored the state and federal governments' policies toward the Tarú administration a decade earlier. In response, COCEI organized a march from Juchitán to Oaxaca, pressuring the governor to agree to negotiations before the marchers reached the capital city. The municipal budget increased only gradually, and well-publicized pressure tactics of this sort were needed repeatedly to secure the basic necessities of municipal administration. Locally, Juchitán's businesspeople attempted a commercial strike against COCEI, but only a handful of enterprises participated, and the strike was a failure.[6] Local PRI leaders initially found no effective way to respond to state and national support for COCEI's victory, which was based on strategies that responded as much to national as to local concerns. By permitting a COCEI victory in Juchitán, the regime hoped to give credence to its claims of democracy, to promote the sort of regional and state-level reform that national authorities had attempted for decades in Oaxaca and the Isthmus, and to weaken the radical movement, by "giving COCEI enough rope to hang itself."[7]

In office, the COCEI government acted with unprecedented speed and success to lessen the neglect that Juchitán had suffered under a succession of corrupt PRI administrations. Working together with city residents, municipal officials repaired unpaved streets, constructed and staffed local health clinics, established a public library on the central plaza, and rebuilt the crumbling City Hall. They took on two of the largest local employers, a beer distributor and a Coca-Cola bottling plant, and, after bitter strikes, secured higher wages and better benefits for workers. In addition, they pressured employers throughout the city to begin to pay the minimum wage and provide workers with the benefits to which they were legally entitled.[8] The COCEI government negotiated with state and national authorities to secure agricultural credit and crop-insurance settlements for peasant farmers, and it used a percentage of the funds thus obtained, in the form of "contributions" from peasants, to fund the movement itself, a practice that elicited criticism from COCEI opponents.[9]

During the Ayuntamiento Popular, COCEI sponsored the invasion of a large tract of government-owned land, where several hundred families built houses. This squatter settlement, the Colonia Rodrigo Carrasco, became one of the focal points for COCEI activity in subsequent years. In 1985, a market was built and inaugurated there, and in 1986 a health center and training program for nurse's assistants established. COCEI negotiated with Oaxaca housing authorities for ownership rights and water services, in exchange for payments to the state on the part of individual families. In addition to the Colonia's function as a COCEI neighborhood, its open spaces served repeatedly as gathering points for COCEI celebrations and demonstrations, particularly after the movement was forced from City Hall.

In 1982, COCEI participated in elections for federal deputy. This was the first time its leaders agreed not only to ally with a national political party, but to compete for office beyond the municipal level. While COCEI did not have sufficient support in the electoral district, which included twenty-two municipalities, to win a majority seat, its candidate gained a place in the national legislature as a member of the United Socialist Party of Mexico's (PSUM) proportional representation list.[10] This achievement served important symbolic and practical purposes. For COCEI supporters in Juchitán, having a representative in the legislature indicated that their movement was strong and effective and contributed to their sense of multifaceted COCEI success during this period. In terms of political power and negotiation, a COCEI deputy provided an additional, direct means for COCEI to publicize its situation in Mexico City, a tactic of continuing importance in limiting the state's use of repression. Participation in legislative elections in alliance with the PSUM also marked a new stage in COCEI's alliance with the national party. In 1979, COCEI had rejected participation in national politics, and its relationship with the Communist Party in the early years of the Ayuntamiento Popular was characterized by antagonism, with COCEI repeatedly asserting the primacy of its own activity in advancing leftist politics. COCEI's participation in the national legislature indicated an increased willingness to acknowledge the usefulness of a national party in furthering grassroots politics.

In addition to opposing the economic and political privileges of the PRI and its supporters, the Ayuntamiento Popular laid claim to the public spaces of the city, encouraging supporters to make use of areas where they had not previously gathered, such as the plaza in front of City Hall (López Monjardin 1986a). COCEI literally changed the language used in public institutions in a way that simultaneously facilitated people's use of those institutions and reaffirmed their cultural identity: "Today in the municipal court, matters are resolved in Zapotec, which PRI would not accept for many years. That is, PRI forced our people to speak Spanish, whether they could or not, in judicial affairs. Today, this policy has been discarded, and Zapotec is spoken in the courthouse, police station, and mayor's office" (López Nelio 1993, 234).

The Ayuntamiento Popular also fostered a new atmosphere of participation and activity, with political meetings, public gatherings, street theater, and an Ayuntamiento radio station changing the panorama of municipal life—in Juchitán's central plazas, in businesses, and in people's neighborhoods and courtyards. COCEI intellectuals affiliated with the Cultural Center published a sophisticated literary magazine that reached national and international audiences. COCEI journalists, along with national and international visitors and reporters, produced commentary not only for foreign audiences, but for avid Juchiteco readers as well. Bright red graffiti, posters, and multicolored murals covered city walls, beat-up pickup trucks circled the city publicizing COCEI events, and City Hall itself was covered with bright political banners, including COCEI's own flag waving from the rooftop (Campbell 1994, 175). COCEI's neighborhood committees, spread throughout the city, held weekly meetings to address both neighborhood administrative and judicial issues and COCEI's ongoing campaigns. Festive and militant demonstrations featured the "expression of a ritual elegance that had previously been available only to the rich through their *velas* [yearly ritual celebrations]" (Campbell 1994, 177). During the Ayuntamiento Popular, the Cultural Center conducted classes and workshops on poetry, painting, and photography, combining Zapotec and outside styles, and it offered political lectures, poetry conferences, films, and art exhibitions (Campbell 1994, 180). The scope of these activities indicated COCEI's presence and its ambition—to reshape power relations by fostering resistance and innovation throughout the city's physical and social geography.

Through the Ayuntamiento radio station (Radio Ayuntamiento Popular, or RAP), COCEI sought to disseminate a multitude of COCEI views and popular voices (Alfaro Sánchez 1984; López Mateos 1993). Initiated in 1983 despite the denial of an official operating permit, the station's broadcasts included an early-morning program on agricultural issues, a children's show that emerged out of a children's radio workshop, and newscasts that presented labor news from around the country and analyzed regional politics in the context of national and international events. The station's most popular show featured Zapotec culture, combining poetry, folktales, legends, and music. According to Manuel López Mateos, a founder of the station, the Ayuntamiento Popular's radio station fostered an ongoing dialogue between COCEI leaders and intellectuals, on the one hand, and ordinary Juchitecos, on the other: "It was not enough to give radio time 'to the people.' It was the people of town—peasant *compañeros*, workers, students, neighborhood residents, merchant *compañeros*, teachers, and fishermen's wives who made up the staff of RAP. Elements of the people and not an elite made RAP work" (1993, 261). Furthermore, at a time when conflict in Central America was increasing dramatically, with the Sandinistas governing in Nicaragua, guerrilla movements making significant headway in both El Salvador and Guatemala, and Guatemalans crossing Mexico's southern border in increasing numbers, COCEI expressed its solidarity with the region's leftist movements in speeches and public events and timed its literacy work to coincide with the Sandinista's well-publicized literacy campaign. These actions transformed politics and public space, evoking images of revolutionary change in the minds of COCEI supporters and opponents alike.

During the Ayuntamiento Popular, the COCEI government also emphasized the regional nature of its activities. COCEI articulated the demands of peasants throughout the Isthmus, organizing workers and supporting strikes in an independent Isthmus union, and announced its intention to participate in the 1983 municipal elections in municipalities throughout the region (Bailón Corres 1985, 11). During its two and a half years in office, the Coalition invaded agricultural land in at least six different Isthmus towns, and its Regional Peasant Union of the Isthmus (UCRI), formed in 1983, drew together peasants from twenty towns and began to constitute a powerful force in regional agrarian politics (Campbell 1990b, 391–92). While COCEI was able to keep only a small amount of the land it invaded, these efforts were powerful symbols of the movement's intentions and mobilizational capacities. In all these efforts, furthermore, COCEI bypassed the traditional power structure of the local PRI and negotiated directly with state and national authorities.

COCEI's advances, especially efforts opposing ownership of land beyond legal limits and demanding payment of the minimum wage, challenged the existing development model by claiming a greater share of wages, land, and services for peasants and workers. It did so, furthermore, by marginalizing local PRI authorities and party bosses. These efforts provoked considerable turmoil in Juchitán and met with some success, and COCEI's plans to field candidates and make economic demands on an Isthmus-wide basis became increasingly credible. In the face of elite opposition, furthermore, COCEI favored militant rhetoric and action, including veiled threats of violence to property that were occasionally carried out, further alienating opponents. COCEI's exercise of municipal patronage angered the middle class in particular and led to accusations of arbitrary and illegal practices. When the state government cut off the municipal budget, COCEI responded by pressuring local businesses to make contributions to the municipal treasury. These payments, like the portions of agricultural settlements COCEI kept for its own use, became a major point of controversy among the movement's opponents.[11]

In response to COCEI's strength and successes, local PRI politicians and businesspeople formed new groups that could fight the radical movement on the local level and pressure state and national authorities to intervene. The right wing of the PRI organized the Committee for the Defense of the Rights of the People of Juchitán. Unfettered by official constraints, this group waged a virulent anticommunist campaign, invoking the image of Central American-style conflict in the Isthmus and making free use of violence and intimidation. The committee challenged precisely the animation and politicization of municipal life that COCEI promoted. In an unsigned pamphlet enumerating COCEI's crimes (*Juchitán: ¡Un Pueblo Que Clama Justicia!*), the committee described an atmosphere in which Salvadorans sent messages encouraging Juchitecos to undertake subversive activities and COCEI mayor Leopoldo de Gyves incited violence on the COCEI radio station. The Ayuntamiento Popular converted City Hall "into a refuge for Central Americans and delinquents, ordering them to commit all sorts of crimes." Making free use of the tropes of savagery and barbarism employed in the past by outsiders to attack Juchitecos, the local authors of the pamphlet asserted that Juchitán was submerged in "terror and anarchy," that it was a "no-man's land," a "communist paradise," and a breeding ground for vice and prostitution, where the CIA-agent director of the Cultural Center and the leaders of COCEI engaged in "bizarre" (homoerotic) sexual acts (Anonymous 1983, 6, 13, 15, 16, 22, 26, 35).

Between the spring of 1982 and the summer of 1983, in a climate of rapidly escalating violence, members of the committee disrupted COCEI meetings and shot at the organization's supporters and leaders, resulting in approximately five deaths and many injuries. While this did not diminish the militancy of COCEI supporters, it fostered an atmosphere of extreme tension and provided an effective means for convincing outside authorities of the need for intervention. In a legislative session in Oaxaca discussing the crisis in Juchitán, Governor Vásquez Colmenares charged that the situation "threatens to degenerate into a state of chaos and anarchy, provoked by COCEI" (Anonymous 1983, 31).

Business leaders in Juchitán also acted to oppose COCEI in 1983, electing a new, young executive committee to head the previously weak Chamber of Commerce. Turning this organization into a focal point for unified opposition to COCEI demands, they gained support from state and national business confederations.[12] According to the president of Juchitán's Chamber of Commerce at the time, business groups in the capital and across the state of Oaxaca joined in efforts to oppose COCEI because they were afraid COCEI would spread and become unstoppable. A national business newsletter characterized COCEI as "Sandinismo on a smaller scale" and charged the Ayuntamiento Popular with assassination, guerrilla activity, support for Christian Marxists, and extortion, as well as being "the center of [subversive] operations for the entire southeast"

(COPARMEX 1983). Finally, both middle-class opponents and political moderates,[13] including some who had initially sympathized with COCEI, responded negatively to the configuration of class, cultural identity, and civic politics that COCEI emphasized in the Ayuntamiento Popular. Faced with a politics emphasizing militant class conflict, Zapotec popular culture, and backroom influence and patronage, the middle class and moderates concluded that COCEI consisted of illiterate rabble-rousers, the city was no longer safe, and government should be placed in the hands of the "educated."[14]

By 1983, then, PRI politicians and businesspeople in Juchitán had formed new organizations that could act more effectively in opposing COCEI than could those that existed in 1980. In addition, hostility to COCEI's economic, cultural, and political projects and practices had crystallized among potential supporters as well as opponents. The pressures exerted by these groups coincided with state and national changes. The more conservative Oaxacan business leaders had won control of the state federation, and they joined with the Juchitán Chamber of Commerce to organize a business strike in May 1983, enlisting the support of local chambers of commerce statewide to pressure the state and federal governments to remove COCEI from office. Drawing on a historic Oaxacan alliance between big business and the Oaxaca branch of the PRI's national confederation of middle-class groups (CNOP), they obtained the participation of market retailers, bakeries, transport services, and small industry in the capital city (Bailón Corres 1985, 12). During the same period, Miguel de la Madrid assumed the presidency and replaced López Portillo's minister of the interior with his own more hard-line choice. De la Madrid also spoke for a market-oriented politics and economy allied with those of the United States, rather than the more economically and culturally nationalist project supported by Echeverría and López Portillo. The de la Madrid administration, its term coinciding with the national economic crisis, responded first to political competition by permitting PAN (the conservative National Action Party) victories in major northern cities, but then acted to oust COCEI. After the closing down of political reform in Juchitán, no further opposition victories were permitted in Mexican cities for several years.

In its foreign policy, Mexico supported leftist movements in Central America and opposed U.S. intervention in the region (Karl 1986). It did this by emphasizing Mexico's difference from Central America, so as to discredit the Reagan administration's imagery of revolution sweeping through Mexico and laying siege to the U.S. border. Juchitán's location just over the Guatemalan border posed a potential contradiction to Mexico's claim. A militant and regionally expanding COCEI, by appearing to demonstrate the spread of revolution, could have served U.S. interests and brought increased intervention in Central America and in Mexico. At the same time, however, bloody repression in Juchitán, as Mexican leftists pointed out, would have been used by the United States to discredit Mexico's claims of difference vis-à-vis its authoritarian neighbors. Such discrediting of the regime's domestic politics would have substantially weakened its foreign-policy position and in that way abetted U.S. intervention.

Also at this time, Isthmus oil-production activities and revenues reached an all-time high, with a trans-Isthmic pipeline bringing crude oil from the northern Isthmus to the newly constructed refinery in Salina Cruz. The nearby port city had just been designated one of a handful of priority development poles in Mexico.[15] In addition, the Mexican regime had invested heavily in a trans-Isthmic rail and highway system, which passed alongside Juchitán. The regime's economic plans in the Isthmus affected its responses to COCEI in contradictory ways. On the one hand, the availability of increasing economic resources made it possible to respond to the demands of newly recognized political forces without withdrawing resources from old ones. Threats of disruption, on the other hand, cut two ways, largely because of COCEI's skill in challenging economic elites and state agencies through direct-action tactics. To prevent COCEI from governing, given the movement's militancy and its extensive support, was risky. COCEI's responses to repression might complicate oil processing and export, as well as scare away foreign customers for new economic enterprises, such as the trans-Isthmic transport system. At the same time, however, COCEI's vehement hostility to existing economic development plans, as it translated into militant actions on the part of the COCEI municipal government, made allowing COCEI to remain in office risky as well. The expanding economy, like the Central American situation, thus put conflicting pressures on the Mexican regime. In its decisions about recognizing COCEI's electoral victories and its responses to the COCEI government in office, the regime steered a course between these competing dangers. It did this by ousting the militant COCEI from office, but refraining from the most brutal forms of repression, which might have engendered increased disruption and violence.

In the summer of 1983, a violent incident provided the state government with a pretext for throwing COCEI out of office and appointing a PRI administrative council to run the city.[16] COCEI refused to leave City Hall and called out a massive demonstration, while federal troops arrived to patrol the streets and set up several permanent barracks in the city. In defending and publicizing its claims to public office, COCEI deployed much the same resources it had used throughout the Ayuntamiento Popular. The movement drew on local patterns of communication, protest, and ethnic display, as well as national and international networks of support and media attention, to stage an enormous protest demonstration, which it followed with ongoing, nonviolent resistance to the military occupation.

COCEI supporters from Juchitán and surrounding towns arrived daily in truckloads to prepare food and guard City Hall. Correspondents from national publications, as well as from international newspapers and magazines, such as *Time*, the *Wall Street Journal*, and San Diego and Toronto dailies, reported on the demonstrations and the subsequent standoff between COCEI and the military. After three months of such activity, during which polarized political discussion filled the city's streets and courtyards, new elections were decided in favor of a young, professional PRI candidate. The army then attacked City Hall, removed COCEI supporters, and instituted a period of repression, during which arrests and beatings of COCEI supporters became commonplace. Four COCEI leaders, jailed without charges or trial, were named prisoners of conscience by Amnesty International (1986, 47–63). The army set up a barracks inside City Hall and stood guard on the building's balconies for five years, a military role unprecedented in contemporary Mexican politics.

Militancy and the Ayuntamiento Popular

Much of the political commentary on the part of local COCEI opponents during and after the Ayuntamiento Popular focused on charges of arbitrariness on the part of the COCEI government. These allegations included acts of expropriation, unequal enforcement of the law, and favoritism in the distribution of patronage. Although no one claimed that the PRI had behaved less arbitrarily in the past—most agreed that its abuses had been significantly worse—the charges of arbitrariness and procedural illegality were leveled with great vehemence against the left. In addition, COCEI's approach to workplace and agricultural issues was based on mass-mobilization tactics and involved both threats and occasional use of violence. Many middle-class or moderate sympathizers faulted the Ayuntamiento Popular for this violence and for its unwillingness to negotiate with local businesspeople and offer them basic guarantees of a secure environment in exchange for reforms. According to them, if COCEI had demonstrated an ability to run the city, it would have been able to stay in power longer, consolidate middle-class support, and carry out more reforms.[17]

These criticisms on the part of moderates demonstrate the limits of their support for COCEI. Moderates were willing to consider the need for violence and illegality as they confronted PRI intransigence and repression in the 1970s. However, faced with COCEI's militancy and its radical policies in office, moderates paid less attention to issues of substantive reform and called increasingly for dialogue, nonviolence, and, especially, guarantees for what they would consider equal treatment for COCEI and PRI supporters of all classes by the municipal government. In numerous interviews, moderates and some middle-class Juchitecos acknowledged many of the achievements, as well as the moral authority, of COCEI, but criticized its methods. Teresa, for example, whose father had been a prominent PRI politician under Charis and afterward, charged COCEI with attacking particular politicians its leaders disliked, rather than rich people generally. Furthermore, she claimed, the movement's leaders were willing to appease rich people who paid them off. Elena, a member of an educated, middle-class family who had gone to school with the COCEI leaders, said she broke with her classmates because they used COCEI money for personal ends and because, when they got loans for peasants, they charged the peasants a percentage.

Elena said she was not surprised when COCEI won the 1981 elections. The movement had "always had support, since the beginning. We accepted this. The surprise was that the PRI would accept the defeat." COCEI, she went on, "had a good part of the middle class in 1980 and '81. They had the opportunity to consolidate as a party and group, but they abused their power. They turned their back on the people of the middle class." What bothered her family was that "you had to be a COCEI supporter, and contribute a percentage, be financially committed, to get anything from the COCEI government." At the same time, Elena acknowledged that COCEI helped people in direct ways, while the PRI didn't, and that "what is important to the person is the help, not the charge." In addition, she said that in some situations COCEI did treat all Juchitecos equally, while the PRI never did. She noted that her daughter participated in cultural activities at the Casa de la Cultura, a COCEI stronghold, and that COCEI obtained credit benefits for priístas and asked for, but didn't insist upon, the corresponding contributions.

In contrast to Elena's moderate view, which characterized COCEI's actions with relative accuracy, a young student guest in Elena's mother's house presented views similar to those of most COCEI opponents. He said that COCEI succeeded by fooling ignorant people and that it worked together with Russians to set up a clandestine radio station. This right-wing view complemented the common refrain, heard in the streets of Juchitán during periods of extreme public conflict, that characterized COCEI supporters as murderers, thieves, and drug users (*marijuanistas*). An elderly, PRI-supporting couple with a modest house in a poor neighborhood complained of the laziness of COCEI supporters and their desire to get something for nothing:

COCEI takes things from the rich and gives them to the poor . . . This is wrong because rich people don't sleep . . . so that they will be able to earn money . . . The people in the *septima* [one of Juchitán's poorest neighborhoods] just sleep with their wives and have babies, then they want to take things from the rich.

The couple went on to argue that people are deceived or forced into joining COCEI. The couple's niece, a prominent schoolteacher in Juchitán and a supporter of the PRI administration's cultural programs, added that "COCEI supporters incite violence. Violence is bad and doesn't resolve anything."

Elena's mother took a position closer to that of these PRI supporters and her young visitor than of her daughter. "COCEI leaders," she said, "had their opportunity and threw it out. They presented a bad image, filled City Hall with food and slept there." She emphasized repeatedly how filthy City Hall was, an image which contrasted dramatically with that of a family of COCEI-supporting middle-class women, who reminisced at length about how nicely COCEI fixed up City Hall, how during the tense days after COCEI had been officially thrown out of office, but remained in City Hall, COCEI leaders worked all night, and the women prepared food and coffee. In Elena's mother's view, right-wing extremism had played a necessary role in ridding the city of the Ayuntamiento Popular. "It would have been hard to get rid of COCEI without El Rojo," she said, referring to the founder of the Committee for the Defense of the Rights of the People of Juchitán and one of the PRI's most violent local bosses.

In contrast to middle-class criticism, COCEI's supporters were generally pleased by the movement's successes in office and by its approach. Most of them felt strongly that COCEI acted consistently in the collective interest of poor workers and peasants and cited examples of the particular ways in which the organization helped individuals. They spoke of COCEI's integrity and effectiveness without criticizing the organization's militancy with respect to local elites. They expressed ongoing satisfaction with existing forms of popular participation during the Ayuntamiento Popular and with the involvement and attentiveness of the movement's leaders, who in their eyes made well-informed decisions based on interaction with supporters.

Middle-class and moderate opposition to COCEI involved intertwined issues of material interest, identity, and civic politics. While it could be argued that moderates opposed COCEI when their class interests were tangibly threatened by the Ayuntamiento Popular, such an approach overlooks both the complexity of material interest and the centrality of cultural representation and political vision in the lives of Juchitecos. In each of these areas, the views of COCEI and of Juchiteco moderates and middle classes both coincided and diverged. With regard to class, for example, moderates and some middle-class Juchitecos exhibited a willingness to recognize the needs of the poor and their claim to material well-being. They also recognized as inevitable and just the potential "explosiveness" of those in need. In this way, moderates shared some of COCEI's goals. However, middle classes and moderates, unlike COCEI, also supported a discourse of modernizing development, which favored market relations and private property, criticized local cultural practices as backward, and advocated cleanliness and education as paths to economic well-being for poor people. This form of economic development was endangered by COCEI's radicalism. Discerning the material interests of moderates is further complicated by the fact that small- and medium-business people, in contrast to the very rich in Juchitán, might well have benefited from the forms of redistribution and small-scale economic activity that COCEI advocated.

In the realm of civic politics, moderates and some members of the middle class shared with COCEI its condemnation of PRI corruption and boss politics. Moderates supported COCEI when it pressed for fair elections in local associations and municipal government and when it instituted "transparent" and efficient procedures for public administration. However, moderates and some middle-class Juchitecos vehemently opposed COCEI's own versions of boss politics in its exercise of municipal authority.

In terms of Zapotec identity, moderates and middle classes shared with COCEI an identification with the Zapotec pueblo. It was this identity that enabled moderates to tolerate class-based demands in the name of popular well-being. Moderates, middle classes, and COCEI also shared identification with the literary and historical aspects of Zapotec culture, including pride in local generals, politicians, and rebellious leaders, as well as in the artistic achievements of Juchiteco essayists, poets, and painters. Moderates and middle classes, however, distinguished between what they saw as the beneficial and harmful characteristics of Zapotec cultural practices, embracing those aspects of ritual, crafts, and ornamentation over which Zapotec elites had long exercised leadership, but condemning a range of practices with regard to education, work, food, drink, and sex that they saw as suffused with vice and indecency and as incompatible with economic development. COCEI, in contrast, largely accepted and celebrated those same daily practices and acted to defend family economies as they existed rather than to propose new forms of work or "development."

In all of these areas—economic policy, civic politics, and cultural representation—the Ayuntamiento Popular moved in precisely the directions that most troubled moderates. Moderates and middle classes then criticized COCEI and its supporters for opposing the rich, for extracting coercive contributions and practicing favoritism, and for fomenting laziness, alcoholism, ignorance, crime, and filth. Some of these accusations were indeed on target. COCEI's rhetoric and policies favored attacks on private wealth and state power, employed both democratic and undemocratic administrative procedures, and celebrated daily Zapotec cultural practices.

Would COCEI have been permitted to stay in office if it had taken a less militant stance and negotiated with middle-class citizens and with local businesspeople? And could it have continued to represent poor Juchitecos in a radical and autonomous way if it had moderated its stance on some or all of these issues of class, civic politics, and ethnicity? These questions were asked frequently in Juchitán and on the Mexican left in the years after the army removed the Ayuntamiento Popular from office, and responses continue to be relevant to the choices of COCEI in Juchitán and leftist grassroots movements elsewhere. The relative moderation that occurred on COCEI's part during and after the 1986 elections suggests that the movement might have been able to stay in office if it had changed its militant stance. COCEI's success in governing Juchitán since 1989 further supports this view, particularly in light of agreements it made with the Salinas administration, which brought considerable social-welfare funds to the city. In these years, COCEI negotiated more openly and successfully with elites and the regime, moderated its dogmatic and militant postures, and at the same time maintained its grassroots support.

Nevertheless, while it is plausible that a more moderate stance in 1981 would have avoided the escalating violence and regime intervention of 1983, moderation at that point would also have weakened the prospects for lasting reform. The three-year tenure of the militant Ayuntamiento Popular, with its clear goals and successes in transforming public spaces and daily life, was a key symbolic and practical ingredient in enduring radical politics. In the form it took, as well as the way it was removed from office—the massing of thousands of supporters around the besieged City Hall and the occupation of the city by the army—the Ayuntamiento Popular established the possibility of leftist sovereignty and radical change, as well as images of military repression, in the minds of COCEI supporters. A more moderate stance at this point would have greatly diminished COCEI's cultural and symbolic power.

In addition, the militancy of the Ayuntamiento Popular scared local elites and the regime into enacting reform. There is no reason to take the commentary of local elites about their willingness to reach accords with COCEI at face value. Juchiteco businesspeople sought to oppose the COCEI government with a strike the moment it took office, and they rejected attempts at mediation. Businesspeople and others who claimed to have been rebuffed by COCEI's style and tactics would likely have acted to oppose any substantive reform, however clothed in legal and conciliatory procedure. The regime, in its turn, would have jumped in quickly to weaken the unprecedented attempt at leftist government. Such efforts to squelch the radical COCEI by way of its participation in the electoral process would have been consistent with the regime's policy of achieving domestic political control through electoral reform. In addition, it would have been consistent with the regime's and the local PRI's attacks on the opposition Tarú administration in the early 1970s. In this context, the ability to threaten was essential to the promotion of reform.

Finally, the militancy and radicalism that had rallied Juchitecos behind COCEI in the 1970s, sustained them through violent repression, and pressured the regime to recognize COCEI's electoral victory made it difficult for either COCEI leaders or supporters to envision a policy of moderation and conciliation during the Ayuntamiento Popular. While they participated in elections and negotiated with the regime, COCEI leaders at this time espoused a militant Marxist ideology and looked toward Central American revolutionary efforts as promising pathways to change. They captured public attention through imagery of radical cultural and economic changes in locations throughout the city, from outlying neighborhoods to the central plaza, from the sprawling market to adjoining City Hall. Furthermore, even if a policy of moderation had been an option for leaders, COCEI would have jeopardized popular support if it had rejected the militant identity and practice that it had previously championed. In this context, COCEI's militancy saved it from potential dangers of electoral politics—co-optation and demobilization—by demonstrating sufficient power, autonomy, and cultural excitement to generate mass commitment and compel regime negotiation. At the same time, the militancy of the Ayuntamiento Popular had clear costs, including repression and military occupation, and COCEI leaders learned these lessons as well. The experiences of the Ayuntamiento Popular—the successes and limits of its militancy—constituted a key moment of experimentation, innovation, and learning in a path from the massive and violent mobilizations of the 1970s to negotiation, democratization, and reform after 1986.

State Repression and a New Reform Project: 1984–1989[18]

After months of severe repression following the military's removal of COCEI from City Hall, a variety of activities that would characterize the regime's subsequent strategy in Juchitán emerged. These included a public military presence, state investment in municipal services and infrastructure, respect for most civil liberties most of the time, elections that sometimes permitted opposition victories, and reform of the local PRI. The regime implemented these strategies in a context of continuing class conflict, including the presence of a strong, unco-opted opposition movement. In Juchitán, unlike most other instances of leftist organizing and state repression in Mexico, the repressive actions of the regime neither destroyed nor substantially weakened the opposition, which continued to negotiate with political officials and state agencies from a position of strength.

After the army occupied Juchitán in the summer of 1983, it established three permanent barracks in the city, two of them located at the dividing lines between the center of the city and the poor neighborhoods where COCEI enjoyed its greatest support, and one inside City Hall. In the course of 1984, constant patrolling of the city by armed vans gradually diminished, but the military continued to maintain a clear public presence, with soldiers standing guard around the clock on the balconies of City Hall, jogging daily through the city's streets and plazas, and resuming formal patrols during political demonstrations and on election days. Along with an ongoing state police presence, administered from its own new headquarters, this represented an extraordinary level of armed surveillance for a Mexican city.

During this time, which coincided with the national economic crisis of the mid-1980s, the Mexican government invested unprecedented millions of pesos in Juchitán, building a bridge, beginning the construction of a sixty-bed hospital and a new market, remodeling City Hall and other public buildings around the town plaza, cleaning irrigation canals, and extending the small network of paved streets (Fuentes Valdivieso 1985). These investments provided some new services and many jobs. In public events, the new municipal government emphasized its professional character and its ties to Mexican national culture. At the same time, in response to COCEI's success in using ethnicity to mobilize political support, PRI speeches were conducted in Zapotec with new frequency. A commentary on the local radio program *Encuentro* in 1985 indicated the difficulty of maintaining such a dual cultural discourse. At the ceremonies marking the first anniversary of the PRI municipal government, the students of a local bilingual school sang the national anthem in Zapotec. Describing this performance, the radio commentator began by condemning prostitution and then went on to identify the Zapotec performance of the anthem as illegal and to label the musical event as political prostitution.

The regime-sponsored remodeling of Juchitán's central plaza, which continued for several years, was a particularly noteworthy undertaking, representative of the regime's vision of how the city should change in order to avoid the recurrence of radical mobilization and takeover. Lively restaurants and other businesses were removed from the arcades of the central plaza adjacent to City Hall and replaced with the post office—which had previously been housed in an obscure building on a side street—and other public offices. Juchiteca flower sellers, whose bundles of multicolored displays had overflowed from a corner of the plaza during the Ayuntamiento Popular, were moved two blocks away from the central plaza, and the taco stands that had been the center of evening gatherings of music, gossip, and general hanging around were moved to the street behind the public buildings, out of sight of City Hall. A municipal bookstand, and a municipal library that had been established by COCEI, were purged of the publications of the Ayuntamiento Popular and of left-wing books generally. During the period of repression, three of the streets surrounding the central plaza, which in the past had been hubs of commerce and transportation, were closed to traffic, thus emphasizing the character of the plaza as a place for officials, rather than ordinary Juchitecos, and the fourth side was kept wide and open, possibly as a quick access route for the two nearby military outposts or for an eventual rerouting of the Pan-American Highway through the center of the city. In these ways, the overlapping of commerce, festivity, milling about, literary production, and government that had characterized the city center during the Ayuntamiento Popular, when City Hall was literally surrounded by petty commerce and socializing, was replaced by a formal central plaza housing only government offices, with the market that adjoined City Hall kept largely out of view.

After several months of repression, members of COCEI were gradually and unevenly permitted to exercise their rights to free speech and assembly. These rights were limited by a tacit understanding that the plaza in front of City Hall was off-limits, by police harassment and assault of COCEI activists, and by the continuing imprisonment of four COCEI leaders. However, compared to the repeated killings of the 1970s, the repression of the mid-1980s was restrained. The military crackdown of

1983 and 1984 sought to intimidate rather than destroy COCEI, and paramilitary right-wing violence occurred less frequently and with less intensity than it had in the 1970s. While half of COCEI's most important leaders were imprisoned, the other half resumed their organizing activities within months, and those in prison were released after a year and a half.

In 1985, COCEI mounted an active campaign for federal deputy, mobilizing supporters in meetings and marches throughout Juchitán and surrounding towns over a period of three months. COCEI also defended workers in a labor dispute, fought an increase in irrigation rates, and negotiated with housing authorities in Oaxaca to regularize land ownership and services in COCEI's squatter settlement. While it was again clear the COCEI would not win a majority in the legislative district, the campaign for federal deputy demonstrated COCEI's survival and continuing strength. Furthermore, because COCEI was assured a place on the PSUM's proportional representation list, the campaign resulted in a popular victory and the maintenance of an important channel for national publicity. Like the national elections of 1982, the 1985 contest concerned neither winning a majority nor gaining a position of political power, goals which in Juchitán revolved around municipal government. Rather, the national elections served purposes common to minority oppositions in majority-controlled systems—mobilizing support, presenting platforms, developing political consciousness, and participating in national political debate. In addition, this electoral activity was worthwhile for COCEI because it brought additional protection from repression, including a public platform from which to denounce abuses.

Participation in national legislative elections for the second time also marked the strengthening of COCEI's relationship with the Unified Socialist Party of Mexico (PSUM). After initial years of antagonism between the allies, COCEI's respect for the PSUM and the working relationship between the groups continued to improve, although tensions persisted and occasionally worsened. In 1983, COCEI made use of PSUM support in fighting the regime's moves to oust the Ayuntamiento Popular, and its leaders acknowledged the national party's reliability. During the 1984 repression, however, COCEI leaders questioned the PSUM's willingness to act at the national level to denounce the military occupation of Juchitán and press the regime to release the movement's imprisoned leaders. In 1985 and 1986, the groups routinely cooperated in electoral campaigning, and in 1986 COCEI joined with two other national leftist parties, in addition to the PSUM, in a statewide Democratic Coalition.[19]

In 1986, COCEI once again participated in municipal elections and subsequently joined a coalition municipal government, headed by a priísta, in an arrangement overseen by the governor of Oaxaca. This and subsequent coalition governments were startling outcomes in a situation that had been characterized by militant class conflict for a period of thirteen years, and they marked the establishment of democratic electoral competition in Juchitán. The way the coalition governments came about illustrates the relationship between elections and other forms of political negotiation and conflict in Juchitán, including the regime's commitment to internal PRI reform in Juchitán and the strength of local PRI resistance.

In May 1986, Mexico City authorities surprised Oaxacans by designating Heladio Ramírez, the most progressive of the precandidates and a longtime supporter of peasant claims within the CNC, as the official candidate for governor of Oaxaca. This choice represented a challenge to the conservative economic elite in the state, an elite that had seen the governor it supported removed from office in 1977, after extensive leftist mobilizations, but had subsequently maintained much of its political power. The designation of Ramírez, like the appointments of reformist governors in the 1940s and 1950s, represented a clear effort on the part of national authorities to recognize some of the claims of opposition groups in Oaxaca and, in the 1980s context, move the state's politics to the left. Ramírez, in turn, chose a young member of the reformist wing of the PRI in Juchitán as candidate for municipal president there, demonstrating the regime's commitment to reform of the local party.

PRI political leaders in Juchitán responded by physically threatening the newly appointed candidate and his family. After a delegation of priístas arrived at his house brandishing weapons, the candidate resigned, and local PRI officials replaced him with a nondescript schoolteacher whom they could easily manipulate. The business and professional group in Juchitán, which had allied with Ramírez, then formed its own organization, much as reformists within the PRI had done during the Charis cacicazgo, as well as in the late 1960s and in 1971. Supporters of the dissident group, which they called MIPRI (the Integrated PRI Movement, but also "my PRI"), refused to back the official candidate and campaigned actively for abstention and for annulment of the elections. Looking ahead, they sought to demonstrate strength before the 1986 elections in order to gain support from the governor for political changes in Juchitán in the future.

Despite recent repression, COCEI entered the 1986 municipal elections with the same strong support it had maintained since the 1970s and ran a short, orderly campaign. The number of people voting in Juchitán had increased 84 percent since 1981, a result of efforts on the part of both the PRI and COCEI to mobilize voters and a clear indication of the increasing centrality of elections to political contestation. COCEI's candidate, an accountant who taught at the regional technological institute, was older and more established professionally than COCEI's previous two candidates, and his campaign emphasized a moderate rather than militant approach, made overtures to the middle class, and promised accords rather than confrontation with business. With Ramírez as the incoming governor, COCEI leaders thought they had a good chance of being allowed to win these elections. They negotiated with Ramírez and his allies repeatedly over electoral rules and procedures and received support for several key demands. As in the first 1980 elections and in 1983, however, the PRI was declared the winner with 56 percent of the vote,[20] despite evidence of fraud in the preparation of the list of registered voters and the issuing of ID cards necessary for voting. This official defeat signaled the possibility of a regime policy of denying recognition to opposition victory in Juchitán under any circumstances.

In response, COCEI blocked the international Pan-American Highway repeatedly, stopping traffic between the states of Oaxaca, Chiapas, and Veracruz, as well as between much of southern Mexico and Guatemala. Members of COCEI also carried out hunger strikes in the halls of the National Legislature and in the state capital and staged demonstrations in front of Juchitán's City Hall. These actions, which led to long negotiations with state and national authorities, resulted in the annulment of PRI victories in several towns surrounding Juchitán, providing the first official acknowledgment of regional strength for COCEI. In Juchitán, COCEI's pressures for annulment coincided with similar views on the part of businesspeople and the new governor, though each group had different goals for subsequent political arrangements. After refusals on the part of both the PRI and COCEI to participate in a coalition government headed by the newly elected PRI municipal president, as well as a PRI occupation of City Hall protesting the coalition proposal, Ramírez named as municipal administrator an Oaxaca-based Juchiteco sociologist, Felipe Martínez, who had written a book about the conflict in Juchitán (Martínez López 1985). In the book, Martínez had argued that the strength of COCEI arose more from PRI weakness and errors than from an enduring mass base, thus suggesting that reform of the PRI would enable the party to regain support in the city. After lengthy negotiations, both the PRI and COCEI agreed to participate in a coalition government, with half the offices in the city government going to each group.[21]

The Reformist Agenda

Events in Juchitán suggested that when state legislators removed COCEI from office in 1983, policymakers in Mexico City hoped to resolve the political conflict in Juchitán through what they called economic and political modernization. This approach mirrored the philosophy of the reformist Front for Democratic Renovation in the 1940s and 1950s, as well as the views put forth by Juchiteco moderates in the late 1960s and early 1970s. Through massive investment, policymakers in the mid-1980s intended to put an end to the pervasive lack of basic services in Juchitán, such as paved streets, drainage, and public lighting, improve public facilities, such as hospitals and markets, and provide the infrastructure for commercial and urban development, such as a branch off the Pan-American Highway that would pass through the center of the city. Politically, national and state leaders would press for the definitive ascendance of well-educated businesspeople and professionals to positions of political authority in Juchitán. These new leaders, aware of the economic costs of corruption, extreme poverty, and explosive class conflict, would work to clean up both municipal finances and the streets of Juchitán. MIPRI, for example, supported proposals to plant trees in Juchitán, and joined in the PRI government's "campaign of the thousand brooms," a largely rhetorical effort to address the presence of garbage in the city's streets.

In addition to establishing new standards of cleanliness, the new leaders spoke of extending public services, educating the "ignorant poor," combating alcoholism and prostitution, and calming political tensions. Such efforts would foster a good investment climate and regain support for the official party. In the view of these 1980s reformists, many of whom were the same people who had been arguing for such change in the 1960s and 1970s, poverty and class conflict in Juchitán arose more from the correctable problems of corruption, lack of professional training on the part of political leaders, and ignorance and vice on the part of the governed than from characteristics inherent in the economic system. In contrast, COCEI leaders did not advocate development or criticize local cultural practices, a stance that distinguished them not only from reformists, but from other Mexican leftists as well.

In placing various tropes of cleanliness at the center of their discourse, reformists identified themselves with the long line of outsiders who had criticized the barbarism of the pueblo. Indeed, the reformists themselves were made up of an uneasy alliance between businesspeople and professionals who had come to Juchitán from the outside and those who were native-born Juchitecos. While the two groups shared commitments to a "good investment climate," the outsiders were much more willing to take on COCEI—and local customs—directly, while Juchiteco businesspeople for the most part kept away from the Chamber of Commerce and sought individual accommodations. The outsiders did not understand this reluctance on the part of Zapotec businesspeople to take strong public action against COCEI. In the words of a Chamber president, "Why don't locals come to the Chamber? I don't know. We're defending their interests. They should come. But they don't. It's not logical."

Despite their not attending the Chamber of Commerce meetings, Zapotec reformists did share many of the views on cleanliness, culture, and development of their non-Zapotec counterparts. However, they were more aware of the extent to which this cultural stance weakened their local authority, as well as their ability to cultivate amicable business relationships. Their authority was also weakened by their criticism of "uneducated" Zapotec bosses, such as Charis and Mario Bustillo. Juchitecos from wealthier backgrounds, including many who supported MIPRI, pointed repeatedly to Bustillo's poor speaking ability and his family background, much as members of the Front for Democratic Renovation had criticized Charis—for precisely those characteristics that won both of them grassroots support. In the puzzled words of the non-Zapotec president of the Chamber of Commerce, Bustillo "is a simple dentist who never succeeded much in his profession. I can't answer where his power comes from. He's very skillful—but at what? Culturally—

nothing. He doesn't even know how to speak well . . . [he is] incapable of a rich vocabulary with distinct tones and words . . ."

One of the central criticisms of PRI politicians made by 1980s reformers, most of whom were businesspeople and professionals, was that PRI politicians sat around in the party office and didn't do anything, while the reformers themselves were busy in their workplaces being productive. In the eyes of the above-cited businessman, "There are few intellectuals in the PRI . . . Few are disposed to waste time in the PRI." What the reformers didn't see or couldn't acknowledge was that PRI politicians weren't doing nothing, they were doing *politics*: gossiping, debating, visiting, and helping out ordinary Juchitecos. As a result, they gained supporters in the pueblo to an extent that consistently eluded the reformers. Correspondingly, the reformers' tropes of cleanliness and education, together with their refusal to "do politics," limited their own ability to generate grassroots support.

While their reform plan was being carried out in the years after 1983, regime authorities assumed that the presence of the army would prevent the opposition from physically seizing power, an act that it could carry out with majority support. At the same time, the army would avoid confrontation and both civil and military authorities would act to permit the exercise of most civil rights, so as to avoid provoking and thereby strengthening the opposition. In this scenario, domestic conflict would be calmed, economic growth sustained, and Central American-type conflict averted. And this would be achieved by way of a set of reforms that had repeatedly been advocated by local moderates and by the central government, in roughly similar form, since the 1940s.

The future desired by the reformers and by the regime occurred only in part. Juchitán indeed became a more "orderly" place, from the perspective of both grassroots mobilization and formal politics, after 1986, though there continued to be massive demonstrations, political killings, and opposition government. The price the regime paid for COCEI's apparent adherence to the formal rules of the game was recognition of the grassroots movement as a legitimate regional political force, an extraordinary phenomenon in the context of postrevolutionary Mexican politics. This legitimacy was evidenced first by the inclusion of COCEI in the governing coalition in 1986 and then by recognition of COCEI victory in municipal elections in 1989, 1992, and 1995. In addition, during these years, violence against COCEI was met with prompt negotiation and arrests, in striking contrast to official tolerance of such violence in the past (Campbell 1990b, 415, 424–25).

The Limits of the Regime

The Mexican regime could not control politics in Juchitán on its own terms after 1983 because of the economic crisis it faced, the policies it favored, and the resistance of the local PRI to reform. Its control was also limited by the dual class and ethnic loyalties with which Juchitecos supported COCEI, as well as by COCEI's continuing commitment to direct-action mobilizations. Despite the regime's efforts to gain support for economic investment, continuing economic crisis repeatedly brought the ambitious projects begun in 1984 to a halt. In 1986, for example, neither the hospital nor the market had been completed, rerouting of the highway had not begun, and drainage had been extended only several blocks. While these efforts advanced in subsequent years, they continually faced severe economic constraints. In addition, the regime's policy choices favored improvements in public image, such as reconstruction of the public buildings around the central plaza, which addressed middle-class concerns, rather than efforts to extend education, health care, potable water, or drainage to Juchitán's poor neighborhoods. As a result, people attributed what changes they saw to the success of COCEI in scaring the government into action, noting at the same time that they themselves, and poor people generally, benefited little.

Public investment and even the possibility of temporary jobs did not easily buy off COCEI supporters. The movement's organizing success of the 1970s and early 1980s, based on ethnicity, class consciousness, and municipal self-government, fostered the development of steadfast loyalty. The national focus of attention on the conduct of elections and limits on the exercise of violent repression in Mexico also protected COCEI. This continued the protection and encouragement the movement had gained from earlier national-policy openings, Echeverría's *apertura democrática* (democratic opening, when opposition movements independent of the PRI were officially permitted to exist) and López Portillo's reforma política. Furthermore, COCEI continued to take advantage of the regime's economic and political projects in the Isthmus, making use of the tensions and transformations of economic development, as well as political conflict within the PRI, to continue its disruptive direct-action efforts. The very existence of state projects and goals provided the sort of environment in which the leaders of COCEI had proven themselves most adept at fostering popular mobilizations and successful negotiations in the past.

Finally, the regime could not achieve control in Juchitán because the local PRI had successfully resisted political reform for forty years, despite state and national pressures. This had endangered what reformers saw as the long-term interest of the party. However, the local political system, with its ongoing links to state and national networks, served effectively to enrich a political class, provide a handful of leaders with authority and prestige, and, for the most part, maintain public order. In the 1940s and 1950s, the governors who allied with reformers against regional bosses and the conservative Oaxaca business elite were ousted from office, and the proposed reforms of PRI president Carlos Madrazo in the 1960s were abandoned on the national level and in Juchitán after brief experimentation. When COCEI formed in the 1970s and reform was perhaps most necessary, it was least likely, because the old-style political leaders were those most capable in the short run of taking charge and opposing the new movement. National leaders supported the establishment of Mario Bustillo as a new political cacique, and he and his supporters, willing to countenance and promote right-wing violence, played a central role in removing COCEI from office in 1983.

Despite the subsequent initiation of a new round of reform efforts on the part of national authorities, the old-style politicians continued to participate actively in managing both repression and municipal administration in Juchitán. The regime's strongest public stand for reform of the local PRI occurred in 1986, when it acted decisively to support the reformist MIPRI group, going so far as to impose the coalition PRI-COCEI government despite local PRI bosses' occupation of City Hall in protest. Between 1986 and 1989, conflicts among supporters of the PRI's right wing indicated the possible weakening of this political force. The 1989 elections, however, were indicative of the local PRI's apparent inability to develop a cohesive reformist stance. After considerable factional battling in the selection of a PRI candidate, a wealthy, non-Zapotec businessman, originally from northern Mexico, was chosen, indicating the ascendance of the reformers. However, supporters of a rival PRI candidate held a demonstration in front of City Hall and burned their voting credentials.

Another PRI group vandalized the candidate's office, and observers reported a resurgence of middle-class and elite decisions to support COCEI, much as had occurred in 1980 and 1981 (Campbell 1990b, 416, 421–22).

The 1989 candidate-selection process, like those in 1986 and 1980–81, underscored the dilemmas of insider-outsider political identities for the PRI in Juchitán. Non-Juchitecos by birth, along with Juchiteco businesspeople and professionals, were generally seen as political outsiders and failed to gain the support of local politicians and their allies. At the same time, candidates who played active roles in the local PRI and supported local bosses, generally seen as insiders, were opposed by reformists in the party and by Juchitecos seeking honest and efficient local government. In a context where cultural issues were prominently articulated by COCEI, the former PRI politicians risked being seen by potential PRI supporters as insufficiently Zapotec, the latter as insufficiently educated. In elections in the 1980s, the PRI tried each option with little success.

Democracy and Municipal Administration in Juchitán

In exchange for recognition by the regime and considerable economic resources for municipal projects, the 1989 COCEI administration agreed to participate in President Salinas's program of concertación social. This program offered substantial economic and political support to established oppositions in return for a reduction of militant tactics, along with public acknowledgment of negotiation and coexistence with the regime. In this way, Salinas's need to respond to a major regime crisis—the massive grassroots electoral support for Cárdenas in 1988—resulted in a new opportunity for COCEI, along with the risks attendant to accepting government funds. Critics of participation in concertación social, especially Cárdenas and the opposition Party of the Democratic Revolution, saw the program as a means to weaken the new party. It was also an effort to limit the number of surviving grassroots oppositions in Mexico by strategically allying with the stronger ones and then seeking to demobilize them by expanding their cooperation with the regime. At the same time, the regime remained free to repress and marginalize less powerful oppositions and continued to do so. Arguments for COCEI's participation in concertación were similar to those for allying with the Mexican

Communist Party in elections a decade earlier—that such participation responded to the immediate needs and interests of supporters of the grassroots movement and that COCEI had always achieved gains and strengthened itself by taking advantage of the opportunities and concessions that the regime offered, while at the same time maintaining its militancy and independence.[22]

COCEI leaders' relative moderation after 1989 represented a significant change in the movement's public rhetoric and practice. Hector Sánchez, COCEI municipal president from 1989 to 1992, was one of the most militant COCEI leaders during the Ayuntamiento Popular, and he remained one of the least willing to form cooperative relationships with either the regime or outside leftist activists through most of the 1980s. However, during his administration, Sánchez reached out to the middle class and made overtures to the private sector concerning guarantees for investment. Sánchez led COCEI to its participation in concertación social (against the wishes of a number of other COCEI leaders, and in a fairly nondemocratic fashion) (Campbell et al. 1993, 280), and he welcomed President Salinas to Juchitán by proclaiming COCEI's willingness to act within the legal structure established by the regime and the constitution (Campbell et al. 1993, 282).

In his speech, Sánchez followed this theoretical acceptance of federalism with criticism of the regime. "On the national scene," he said to Salinas, "Mexicans in the rural areas as well as in the city continue to endure misery," and he went on to cite modernization without protection and electoral violence as ongoing problems (Campbell et al. 1993, 282). After signing the concertación accords, which brought funds from the National Solidarity Program (PRONOSOL) to Juchitán, Sánchez's municipal administration functioned in some of the ways critics of the Ayuntamiento Popular from across the political spectrum had advised a decade earlier, taking care to treat COCEI and PRI supporters equally and initiating competent programs of municipal administration and economic development. For example, much to the approval of outside leftist critics, who favored innovative development efforts, Sánchez used some of the funds from concertación agreements to purchase agricultural equipment, which the *municipio* then loaned out to surrounding towns.

While those who opposed concertación wondered if COCEI's cooperation with the Salinas administration would lead to the demise of radical politics, supporters of Sánchez's activities said he was laying the ground-work for a strengthened COCEI, one that would simultaneously remain radical and gain increasing multiclass support. Forms of moderation in municipal administration, furthermore, did not signify the end of mass mobilization or of gains for ordinary Juchitecos. During the 1986–89 coalition government, for example, COCEI invaded private land and built another squatter settlement, and it won strikes at two large Isthmus beer distributorships and a major interstate bus company. In addition, it secured credit and crop-insurance settlements for peasants, higher wages for salt collectors, and indemnification for peasants and fishermen whose lands and lagoons had been damaged by a PEMEX pipeline and oil spill (Campbell 1990b, 416–17). COCEI also began to successfully organize workers at the new Pacific-coast resort of Huatulco, located about 150 kilometers from Juchitán. During the 1989–92 Sánchez administration, COCEI leaders used funds from the National Solidarity Program to pave streets and install drainage throughout much of the city, improving the local infrastructure most relevant to people's daily lives to an extent unprecedented in the city's history. Furthermore, through efficient management and the use of volunteer labor, the Sánchez administration stretched the development money to pave even more streets than had been funded. As a result, Juchitecos from across the political spectrum praised the honesty and efficiency of the development efforts, which earned great credibility for COCEI.

COCEI's moderation, its presence in office for a third term, its extensive use of government funds, and its close relationship with regime officials all raise questions about the movement's present and future. COCEI's willingness to negotiate publicly with the Salinas administration solid-ified the movement's officially acknowledged role as a regional political force. It brought continued funding to the COCEI administration and contributed to the process of formal democratization. At the same time, the centralization of power among a small group of leaders and the mate-rial comfort enjoyed by those leaders led to growing criticism of internal power relations in the 1990s. During Sánchez's administration, charges of COCEI corruption were aired for the first time on the left, in the weekly magazine *Proceso*. Because this article consisted almost verbatim of the claims of COCEI's right-wing opponents in Juchitán, its conclusions lacked credibility. However, together with the observations of Campbell and others in Juchitán (Campbell 1990b, 427), this article constituted the first public speculation among COCEI supporters of corruption within the movement. The appearance of the armed, antistate Zapatista uprising in Chiapas in 1994 further underscored COCEI's cordial relations with, and dependence on, regime officials. At the same time, the presence of ex-COCEI mayor Leopoldo de Gyves at the Zapatistas' National Democratic Convention highlighted COCEI's prominence as an example of grassroots autonomy in Mexico and its role in promoting just the sort of engaged civil society that the Zapatistas advocated.

In the midst of these crosscurrents, and in striking contrast to its own past and to most places in Mexico, Juchitán exhibits a vibrant democratic politics, including honest and competitive elections, an administration responsive to a wide range of citizens, efficient administration of extensive social-welfare funds, and active and innovative Zapotec cultural institutions.[23] In the face of obstruction on the part of successive Mexican administrations, COCEI has stimulated political debate, dramatically increased voter turnout, and improved living and working conditions. At the same time, the workings of democracy in Juchitán exacerbated old tensions and generated new ones. COCEI today faces difficult choices concerning cooperation with the central government, conciliation with local middle-class and business groups, and representation of poor Juchitecos during a period of regional economic decline.

Perceived moves to the center on the part of the Sánchez administration and the subsequent COCEI government of Oscar Cruz have disturbed longtime COCEI supporters, despite the COCEI administration's achievements in securing agricultural and workplace benefits. While COCEI successfully negotiated new private-sector investment in Juchitán—a Coca-Cola plant and a commercial shopping center—businesspeople have continued to criticize the movement's mass-mobilization activities. Furthermore, despite COCEI's new openness to investors, some development-minded Juchitecos worry that larger state-sponsored plans for new roads and an industrial corridor in the Isthmus will circumvent Juchitán entirely, in retaliation for its democratic successes. In this case, the very democratic politics that empowers peasants and workers may scare away investors, who find more quiescent workers elsewhere.

COCEI's terms in office have also witnessed the growth of organized dissent within the movement. Groups of activists have challenged the perpetuation of a small group of leaders, along with the absence of open processes of discussion and decision making. Many of these criticisms were acknowledged publicly for the first time by ex-COCEI mayor Leopoldo de Gyves de la Cruz in a speech at the twentieth-anniversary celebration for the Casa de la Cultura in Juchitán. Furthermore, during COCEI's terms in office, there have also been conflicts between COCEI and the PRD over the autonomy of the grassroots movement within the party. COCEI's 1990 decision to participate in President Salinas's program of concertación social and to welcome the president to Juchitán caused deep strains in the COCEI-PRD alliance. These strains continued through and beyond the 1994 presidential campaign, with the state PRD attacking COCEI and explicitly seeking to restrict its influence.[24] (While COCEI insisted on joining the PRD as an organization, maintaining its autonomy within the party, PRD officials sought to limit COCEI activists to individual roles.)

As these examples indicate, democratic politics in Juchitán is simultaneously competitive and explosive, exclusionary and responsive. Despite complaint and conflict, Juchitecos have secured significant political and cultural rights and established a framework for formal democratic practices and negotiation over economic issues. They have done this, furthermore, during a period of increasing economic inequality and considerable manipulation of elections nationwide. This achievement of democracy in Juchitán demonstrates a number of points that have not been at all clear or well understood about Mexico in the 1980s and 1990s: that the PRI and the regime are capable of reform in specific cases; that reform, when it occurs, may depend on the existence of radical, grassroots oppositions, and on virtually uncontrolled class conflict; that elections matter, even when they are fraudulent; that participation in elections increases the chances for survival of popular movements; that democratization is related to but quite distinct from elections, and involves political, economic, and cultural arenas; that ethnicity can form the basis of the fiercest and most successful popular resistance to the Mexican regime; that grassroots opposition can be strengthened by images of indigenous explosiveness, the absence of institutionalized forms of organization and decision making, and actual and potential acts of violence; and, finally, that grassroots movements can survive and grow, can avoid co-optation even as they achieve concessions, and can become recognized regional powerholders.

Decentered Democracy

Resistance to the power of the regime occurred in many locations in Juchitán. Some of them involved formal politics and resulted in large part from the regime's policies of uneven political opening. Others, which will be discussed in the next chapter, arose amidst the complex internal dynamics of COCEI itself. In addition, through daily practices of accommodation and resistance, Juchitecos fostered numerous additional locations of voice and autonomy that contributed to making the growth of COCEI possible and making the movement strong. The existence of these diverse spaces of resistance is another indication of the unevenness of the Mexican state's presence in formal politics and people's lives in the Isthmus and thus of the uneven and changing nature of its hegemony. Such spaces existed because whole domains of civil society remained largely outside of the state's control, because state-sponsored organizations demonstrated degrees of autonomy from political authorities, and because some aspects of state organization or policy contradicted others. In addition to fostering points of opposition within civil society and the regime, furthermore, these spaces served to promote and embody a multifaceted process of democratization: not uniquely or even primarily the establishment of competitive elections, but places in people's personal and community lives where they could speak, act to make change, and hold those with more political, economic, or cultural power than themselves accountable for at least some of their actions. This multifaceted nature of democracy in Juchitán distinguishes the process of democratization there from a purely linear history, thus mirroring the fragmented fashion in which Juchitecos themselves recounted the origin and pathway of COCEI's activism.

The Catholic Church in the Isthmus was one example of a space for resistance. Before and during the early years of COCEI's organizing, local priests influenced by liberation theology began forming lay groups to analyze the social and economic problems of indigenous people in light of biblical teachings (Bichido 1983; López Nelio 1983). When COCEI succeeded in voicing the concerns of Juchitecos, the church shifted its consciousness-raising activities to surrounding areas and non-Zapotec indigenous groups. The church did not forge an explicit alliance with COCEI, but rather contributed to the environment in which COCEI arose and indirectly supported COCEI's radicalism by beginning to organize

195

other groups in the region. In addition, and more directly relevant to COCEI's survival, Arturo Lona Reyes, the bishop of Tehuantepec and one of the few radical bishops in Mexico, consistently supported COCEI's legitimacy and defended the organization from repression. At moments of extreme conflict, local priests in Juchitán and surrounding towns read the bishop's letters during mass. In discussions, they stated clearly that the church had no political affiliation and would explicitly support no political organization, while making it equally clear that the church supported COCEI because it fought for the well-being of poor people.[25]

Several democratic spaces created by contradiction and resistance within the regime contributed to COCEI's own ability to organize. The democratic movement within the national teachers' union fought to establish democratic procedures for leadership selection and for the union's exercise of power within the educational system, procedures that challenged the union's corrupt leadership. By encouraging teachers to join together and fight abuses of power locally, as well as press for representative union congresses at state and national levels, the democratic teachers' movement served as a nurturing ground for political discussion, mobilization, and internal democracy. It included PRI supporters as well as supporters of opposition parties. Mexico's minister of education gave the democratic movement important organizing opportunities early in its history when he acted to weaken the corrupt union leadership. By decentralizing the educational bureaucracy, he sought to limit the leadership's considerable power in national educational and political affairs (Cook 1990, 205–7), a move that simultaneously limited its ability to repress grassroots challenges within the union. In this way, tensions within the state, with their own historical origins, combined with the politicization of people's work experiences to produce an explicitly oppositional organization, as well as alternative beliefs and practices regarding democracy. These beliefs and practices then influenced, and were influenced by, other political discourses both within COCEI and among PRI moderates.

Tía Paulina's shift from supporting the PRI to COCEI by way of her participation in the democratic teachers' movement, mentioned above, exemplifies the importance of this space for opposition politics in Juchitán. The mobilizations of the teachers' movement provided a forum in which COCEI could interact with middle-class Juchitecos who had initially rejected radical politics and win some of them over. Another teacher, in discussing the democratic teachers' movement with a government-employee friend, emphasized the key role of the movement in establishing job rights based on seniority and went on to observe that some prominent members of the democratic teachers' movement would not support the PRI candidate for municipal president in 1986, because he was a member of the nondemocratic wing of the union.

Paradoxically, the oil workers' union, a corrupt union entrenched within a state industry, also supported opportunities for radical politics in Juchitán, in that it provided a limited but significant number of COCEI-supporting families with secure incomes and benefits. While the extremely hierarchical union excluded many Juchitecos by demanding high payments to leaders for jobs, the union then guaranteed those jobs, irrespective of the political affiliations of workers. Numerous oil workers in Juchitán, each part of an extended family that benefited from his income and benefits, supported COCEI without endangering their oil-related jobs, either in the northern Isthmus cities of Minatitlán and Coatzacoalcos or in nearby Salina Cruz. Thus, by virtue of its autonomous power base, the regime-affiliated union could offer protections to oil workers—by ignoring their lives outside work—that were not shared by workers in other government agencies and private enterprises and that directly affected the economic base of radical organizing. The nondemocratic union, product of a nondemocratic regime, thus provided a key ingredient of democracy—the ability to exercise political dissent and opposition without suffering economic retribution.

Juchitán's central market, as well as the state agrarian bureaucracy, provided economic space for COCEI by supporting Juchiteco families, even as these families engaged in radical politics. At the same time, the market and agrarian agencies became focal points for COCEI activities. Many energetic market women, COCEI and PRI supporters alike, secured considerable incomes through market activity—enough to provide houses, education, and bits of investment capital for numerous family members. While market women who supported COCEI were harassed during periods of PRI municipal government—their locations changed or stalls vandalized—they were neither excluded from the market nor deprived of substantial income. Several sections of the market, devoted to particular kinds of merchandise, were COCEI strongholds throughout the 1980s. In addition, the market played a preeminent role in shaping economic and cultural relations in Juchitán. Situated adjacent to City Hall, so that it appeared to be part of the government building itself, and radiating outward through all surrounding streets, the market ensured that the main location for fulfilling daily household needs was a Zapotec one, where indigenous language and dress were assets. The market offered a plethora of locations for public and private conversation, and many of the products sold there came from local, small-scale networks of production and distribution. This enabled a wide range of women to generate information and income, even from scarce resources, and thus facilitated the relative economic well-being and political awareness of poor Juchitecos.

Similarly, despite COCEI's ongoing attacks on agrarian agencies, agricultural banks offered credit and insurance to both COCEI and PRI supporters throughout the 1980s. Paradoxically, again, the regime's unwillingness to recognize COCEI's victory in local Land Commission elections in 1978, which resulted in the effective dissolution of that institution, forced banks to deal directly with small groups of peasants in allocating credit. In so doing, the banks generally recognized such groups irrespective of political affiliation. In part, it was COCEI's strength in defending its supporters that accounted for the relative equality experienced by COCEI and PRI supporters in their market and agricultural activities. As part of its local direct-action campaigns, for example, COCEI pressured the banks to extend credit to groups of COCEI peasants. However, the ability of COCEI supporters to survive and prosper in the local economy is also indicative of the partial autonomy of the market and the agrarian banks from state authorities, autonomy that enabled them to continue to support Juchiteco families even at the height of those families' militant opposition to local elites and to the regime.

The availability of information in Juchitán, the result of a rich history of literary and journalistic production, constituted another space for resistance and for COCEI activism. The production and circulation of information was facilitated by the physical geography of the market and the thriving urban economy. The combination of Zapotec language use, local artistic production, COCEI events and publications, local newspapers and radio programs, and state and national newspapers enabled Juchitecos to receive a considerable array of information. They received not only information that contradicted the official pronouncements of the regime, but information that acknowledged and debated the disagreements in direct and lively fashion. This availability of information, while strengthened considerably by COCEI's own literary and journalistic production, preceded COCEI in Juchitán, having achieved a notable level with the publication of *El Satélite* between 1968 and 1979, as well as with the publication in nearby San Blas of the muckraking local newspaper *La Voz Del Istmo,* which appeared during the 1950s and 1960s (Campbell 1990b, 278). Furthermore, commentary on local social and political events had long been presented in the poetry, music, and painting that had been central to Juchitán's cultural life. After *El Satélite* ceased publication, the events of the Ayuntamiento Popular and subsequent COCEI activities were covered in *Hora Cero,* a leftist newspaper published in Oaxaca. Mexico City newspapers and periodicals from across the political spectrum, which covered local events during periods of crisis, were also available and read in Juchitán.

The presentation of information at the local level was not unproblematic. Alberto López Morales failed twice in the mid-1980s in his efforts to publish an independent weekly paper in Juchitán. López Morales managed to publish a half dozen or so issues each time, but found that neither the PRI nor COCEI was willing to tolerate his critical stance. López Morales's presence in the city, however, resulted in the almost continuous appearance of dissenting viewpoints since the late 1970s, when he had argued for COCEI's participation in national elections. In the mid-1980s, López Morales and other moderates found a place on a local radio station, where they hosted an afternoon broadcast of interviews with prominent regional figures on important issues of the day, accompanied by commentaries by the hosts. This show, *Encuentro,* was broadcast at midday and reached Juchitecos of all classes and educational levels.

Encuentro was broadcast on a radio station whose owner, Humberto López Lena, identified himself as a moderate and supported MIPRI, although he had also headed the local Chamber of Commerce in 1983, when it played a significant role in bringing about the ousting of the Ayuntamiento Popular. At some points in the 1980s, López Lena refused to carry COCEI material, while at other times, as a result of his efforts to combat local PRI bosses, he accepted it. This dual role of moderates, who sometimes opposed PRI bosses and tolerated COCEI, but at other times led attacks on COCEI, grew out of their contradictory responses to radical politics in the 1970s and their efforts to advance a modernizing agenda in the 1980s. Their changing strategy resulted, on the one hand, in a radio program that brought some information and debate on controversial issues to all Juchiteco households. On the other hand, it placed limits on the sustained presentation of critical information, through such actions as opposition to López Morales's newspapers and efforts to shut down the radio station of the Ayuntamiento Popular.

The very existence of a continuing moderate discourse in Juchitán's media and politics itself fostered a space for radical politics. This discourse, a product of the challenges and accommodations of the Charis years, contributed to the rise of COCEI through mobilizations and critiques in the 1960s, and it defended the movement in the face of violent repression in the 1970s. In addition, despite the withdrawal of moderate support for COCEI during the Ayuntamiento Popular, moderates repeatedly declined to support PRI candidates and even voted for COCEI before and after the first period of COCEI government. Moderates' ongoing pressure for reform within the PRI, despite the continuing difficulty of this process, in fact contributed to COCEI's strength, and moderates were well aware of this. Unlike situations of extreme class conflict in Central and South America, moderates in Juchitán were willing to play this role, and class conflict in the city did not result in their polarization and disappearance, ideologically or physically. In response to the presence of moderates, furthermore, COCEI was able to manipulate its own identities as a class- and a pueblo-based movement, emphasizing the former in its direct-action mobilizations, but making use of the latter to gain support among moderates when PRI bosses or government officials acted in ways that moderates found particularly objectionable.

Moderates thus played several roles in local politics from the 1960s to the 1980s in Juchitán. At different moments, they formed new political organizations, influenced public opinion, and provided agendas for governing. In the 1960s and early 1970s, moderates actively promoted opposition political organizations, articulating a critique of the regime and a reform agenda. Between 1974 and 1984, they influenced the course of local politics in a second fashion, by commenting on the actions of others and shaping public opinion, particularly among the literate middle class, and by promoting their view through their connections with state and national policymakers. This influence assumed two forms. When COCEI suffered violent repression and denial of civil liberties in the 1970s, moderates defended the organization, whereas when COCEI governed Juchitán between 1981 and 1983, moderates opposed the movement, strengthening the position of those who had always opposed it and contributing to the removal of COCEI from office and the occupation of the city by the Mexican military.

Moderates also played a central role in local politics in a third fashion, by providing readily available discourses that other political actors could use to advance their goals. Their most critical view of development, set out between 1971 and 1973, provided one such discourse. The moderates' thoroughgoing condemnation of party and bureaucracy provided an analysis and language with which COCEI could mobilize support for a new form of opposition with new political tactics. The debate carried out in *El Satélite* between 1974 and 1978, which stressed democratic procedure and legal order (even as they recognized the potential need for radicalism and violence), provided a second instance of a discourse that originated among moderates and later served other political actors. The moderates' combined emphasis on reform and on procedural democracy provided a readily available vehicle for the regime's mid-1980s reform project. At this time, moderates again formed new political organizations, such as MIPRI, and participated directly in local politics and administration, this time in alliance with the regime.

The enduring discourse of moderates in Juchitán was reinforced by an equally enduring, though less clearly articulated, discourse on the part of PRI supporters across classes. Many priístas acknowledged, in partial ways, the legitimacy of COCEI and the validity of its claims. This reservoir of openness to COCEI's politics, situated within discourses and practices of fierce opposition to the movement, accounts in part for the limits to polarization and violence in the 1980s. This openness, always contested and always reemerging, constituted a form of resistance to the claims of the PRI that occurred within the PRI itself. Tía Ramona, boasting about the PRI at her COCEI niece's goading, talked about how nicely kept City Hall was under PRI administration, then said that the PRI was continuing what COCEI in fact had started. A group of unemployed men who backed a local PRI strongman, passing the time in the courtyard of a Zapotec midwife who spoke little Spanish, observed that COCEI did good things for people and thus *earned* its support. A prominent entrepreneur and official of the Chamber of Commerce argued that the original source of problems in Juchitán was exploitation on the part of local businesses, which had not paid the minimum wage. He also noted that the government had done nothing for the city until the formation of COCEI. In a family discussion in her middle-class household, Elena held to the theoretical possibility of supporting a COCEI candidate. "You won't vote for COCEI even if its candidate is a good person," a visitor insisted, "because of the trajectory the movement has followed." In response, Elena insisted repeatedly that she might: "I could say at a particular moment, I vote for the person not the party." Thus, around the same courtyards, tables, and business meetings where priístas gathered to line up behind a PRI boss, accuse COCEI of thievery and communism, or plan a business strike to oust the movement from office, voices of resistance to the PRI's besieged and partial claim to rule emerged.

The local projects stimulated and protected by COCEI itself were another example of spaces for resistance and democratization. The politics of health care and water in the small town of La Venta were particularly clear examples of this. COCEI supporters in La Venta constructed a health center, supplied it through government grants and international donations, and secured the labor of young doctors doing field placements as part of their medical training. La Venta residents achieved this through local organizing, as well as through pressuring and negotiating with health authorities in Oaxaca, and a local health committee managed the center in a participatory fashion.

Similarly, a new water system was constructed and managed by the residents of La Venta, with the help of COCEI leaders from Juchitán. I was present in La Venta during a crisis in this process of local control, when the PRI government in Juchitán acted to take over the water service. What I saw was an intense process of discussion and conflict in La Venta between PRI supporters who felt obliged to honor the municipal government's edicts and COCEI supporters who wanted to maintain their control over the water system, which had been running well. As part of this process, the water committee and some of its supporters—older women, an older man, a younger woman, and younger men—gathered in a local yard to figure out how to keep, quite literally, the keys to the system. The older women, in traditional dress, took the lead in this discussion and designated one of themselves to confront the local PRI official who was supporting the municipal government. Despite the partial defeat for local control that resulted, the ongoing cooperative planning and administration carried out by the local women and men, including their efforts to defend the autonomy of the water system, constituted a clearly discernible space for new forms of participation and resistance. Without political rhetoric and without the ongoing presence of COCEI leaders, these La

Venta residents oversaw the design, implementation, administration, and defense of sophisticated municipal projects that provided important services for all local residents. Such activities occurred in Juchitán itself as well, with the establishment of neighborhood markets, health centers, and libraries, and they encouraged innovation among Juchitecos and accountability on the part of regime officials.

Finally, COCEI's control of the cultural arena stimulated numerous, interrelated spaces for autonomous and radical activity in Juchitán. COCEI's cultural project included publication of artistic and historical materials, the promotion of written and oral forms of Zapotec language, the fostering of artistic activity at the Cultural Center (Casa de la Cultura), and the elaboration and celebration of ritual practices in both social and political contexts. Juchitán's Cultural Center, funded by the Mexican Ministry of Fine Arts, provided a rambling, culturally rich, and Zapotec physical space not only for predominantly leftist artists, but for the children of all social classes. In 1993, the COCEI municipal government secured funds from the National Solidarity Program to completely renovate the Cultural Center. In its steadfast and sophisticated promotion of Zapotec art since its founding in 1972, the Cultural Center offered a striking alternative to the more secular, homogeneous cultural programs directly sponsored by the regime and the PRI municipal government. For example, in 1985, on a night when the Cultural Center sponsored a program of Zapotec music and theater in its airy and elegant courtyard, the PRI municipal government hosted a traveling band that played pop music on the street in front of City Hall and ended its concert with a lively rendition of "New York, New York." The Cultural Center, furthermore, played an active role in the artistic and historical publications of the Ayuntamiento Popular and COCEI, while PRI officials in Juchitán did little to promote new forms and uses of Zapotec art.

By combining artistic activity and radical politics in the same institution and building, but maintaining a degree of separation sufficient to make possible continued funding and multiclass participation, the Cultural Center served as a fertile ground for autonomous voice and dialogue among Juchitán's artists and young people.[26] Furthermore, COCEI's sponsorship of artistic activity facilitated resistance in another key way, through its relations with artists, intellectuals, and journalists in Mexico City. The influence of these figures, itself a product of the state's complex relationships with artists, political radicalism, and indigenous cultural representation, protected COCEI from violent repression by publicizing the movement's activities among influential elites in the capital.

The spaces described above, each of them embedded in the complexities and contradictions of both the regime and daily life, functioned as sites of resistance and as "islands of democratization,"[27] not only achieving forms of autonomy and accountability in distinct spheres, but contributing to the expansion of these phenomena as well. The existence of these spaces resulted from the often circuitous and contradictory workings of power in Mexico. For example, the centralization of state power that contributed to the strength of labor unions in Mexico in the 1930s also resulted, in subsequent decades, in the autonomy of the oil workers' union. This autonomy, which permitted the union to protect the jobs of its workers irrespective of political affiliation, contributed to the economic well-being of some COCEI supporters in Juchitán, thereby providing a form of support for antistate radicalism. At the same time, in another location, conflicts over union autonomy, in the form of the central state's opposition to the power of the teachers' union hierarchy, also resulted in an opportunity for workers to develop oppositional, democratic practices, this time within the union itself.

Within the economic bureaucracy, the imperatives facing state agrarian agencies to deliver economic results with minimum political disruption permitted those bureaucracies to largely ignore political affiliation in the distribution of credit. In the cultural arena, state policies that promoted indigenous cultural representation in the 1930s, in the service of postrevolutionary nationalism, thereby fostered linguistic and literary projects that nurtured subversive cultural and political activities in Juchitán in the 1960s and 1970s. With regard to the media and to left-leaning nongovernmental agencies, the very ambiguity of the regime's relation to these groups—the multifacetedness of their presence and the regime's toleration of some forms of dissent—provided opportunities for the funding, elaboration, and defense of radical artistic and community-development projects.

Democratization in Juchitán was facilitated by COCEI's repeated exercise of limited political sovereignty. However, democratization can be said to have occurred in Juchitán not primarily because of elections and the transfer of municipal office, but because poor Juchitecos in the 1980s had more voice, and could hold those with power more accountable, in more arenas of their lives, than they could in the 1960s and 1970s.

Juchitecos exercised such voice and accountability in their participation in ritual and artistic activity and their relatively unproblematic assertion of their cultural identity, in comparison to other indigenous and minority groups. They exercised voice and accountability in their capacity to pressure agrarian agencies and labor courts for fair treatment, their ability to solve local problems by local means, their freedom to bring their own language to official offices, their access to complex networks of information, and their influence in municipal governments that repeatedly secured funding from the central state during periods of national economic crisis.

7

Ambiguity and Contradiction in COCEI

"Who Are We? What Is Our Name?" [1]

In discussing leftist movements in Mexico and Latin America today, scholars and activists often criticize Leninist strategies and praise the less hierarchical, more identity-based politics of recent social movements. At the same time, observers of social movements often wonder whether such decentralized, autonomous, and plural efforts can forge successful challenges to broad structures of domination (Calderón, Piscitelli, and Reyna 1992, 27). For example, in contrast to expectations of broadening alliance and increasing political clout on the part of Colombian social movements a decade ago (Fals Borda 1986), observers painted a bleak picture of the Colombian left in the early 1990s. Marc Chernick and Michael Jiménez document the simultaneous failures of Colombian guerrilla movements, characterized by "unambiguous vanguardism" and an unarmed left weakened by fragile mobilization and violent repression (1993, 73–74). In another context, Amrita Basu contrasts the weaknesses of radically democratic grassroots organizing in the Indian state of Maharashtra with those of the Leninist politics of the Communist Party of India (Marxist), which governed the state of West Bengal. After promising beginnings for each form of opposition, grassroots organizing in Maharashtra could not sustain itself and splintered over issues of gender and political strategy, while the communists in West Bengal promoted only very limited reforms. As a result, Basu argues that "if a political strategy is to be radical, it must maintain a creative tension between 'guided spontaneity' and organizational discipline" (1992, 237).

COCEI's success in mounting continuous challenges to local and national authorities in the face of violence has occurred in large part because Juchitecos created a new and hybrid political culture in the course of recurring daily activities. In analyzing COCEI's internal characteristics,

I will argue that this political culture exhibited the sort of "creative tension" Basu described and that the source of this creativity lay in the numerous axes of ambiguity and contradiction within the movement itself. Indeed, the success of COCEI's activism shows that the process of "unsettl[ing] dominant cultural meanings" through collective action (Alvarez, Dagnino, and Escobar n.d.) is simultaneously one of constructing and reconstructing unstable meanings within movements. Consequently, rather than portraying a social movement as an internally coherent set of beliefs and practices, I make use of my experiences of daily life among COCEI supporters to focus on "the blurred zones in between" what were once seen as "the crystalline patterns of a whole culture" (Rosaldo 1989, 209). These blurred zones within COCEI include ambiguity with regard to social and political forms (such as violence, democracy, and gender) and contradictions concerning people's claims about their own and others' experiences (such as between the accounts of COCEI leaders and ordinary Juchitecos, and between those of men and women). Both of these phenomena illustrate the ongoing presence within COCEI of different and at times opposing forms of discourse and practice. In addition, COCEI's experiences demonstrate that a politics based on vanguard leadership, dogmatic Marxist analysis, and often confrontational stances can be successful and also contain spaces for the production of meaning by ordinary people, for alliance and accommodation, and for internal contestation over representation and mobilization.

Analysis of the patterns of ambiguity and contradiction among COCEI's practices illuminates the "submerged networks" (Melucci 1988b, 248) out of which visible collective action emerges. Such networks are shaped by ordinary Juchitecos as they reappropriate spaces and transform meanings "by means of a multitude of 'tactics' articulated in the details of everyday life" (de Certeau 1984, xiv). Furthermore, what de Certeau calls "tactics" and "strategies" (xix) coexist in COCEI, so that the improvised, "tactical" manipulations that people perform in their daily lives can challenge, through COCEI's own actions, the more coordinated, "strategic" power of the regime. In this process, ordinary Juchitecos experience impositions from their own movement. This occurs as a result of the hierarchical process through which COCEI determines its strategies, and derives from what Néstor García Canclini calls "deductivist" economism and "inductivist" folklore (1988). COCEI leaders and intellectuals assume both homogeneous class interests (that Juchiteco peasants and workers share a

207

common class position and corresponding material interests) and inherent Zapotec identity (that all Juchitecos are and know themselves to be members of an indigenous culture whose attributes remain fixed through time). García Canclini argues that the prevalence of such essentialist assumptions explains "why so many popular projects for transformation do not manage to alter the social structure" (1988, 484). However, COCEI's experiences indicate that García Canclini overemphasizes the extent to which essentialist discourses necessarily constrain collective action and social transformation.[2]

Indeed, COCEI's successes demonstrate that the transformative potential of collective action lies in its balancing of different sorts of internal practices, rather than in the prevalence of one or another set of relatively homogeneous ones. The ambiguities and contradictions within COCEI show how characteristics praised by new-social-movement theorists, such as internal democracy, nonviolence, and participation by women, appear in complex interaction with other, less obviously praiseworthy attributes.[3] In the case of COCEI, these include "threads of violence" in imagery and action, militant and hostile stances toward a variety of "others," and the relative absence of internal democracy. In addition, many of COCEI's historical claims contradict the experiences of ordinary Juchitecos, and, despite COCEI's extensive promotion of images of women's activism, women are excluded from positions of political leadership and artistic innovation in the movement.

My understanding of COCEI and the sorts of contradictions to which I am most sensitive grew out of my own location between COCEI leaders and supporters during my fieldwork. While COCEI leaders treated me cordially, for the most part, and tacitly accepted my presence in Juchitán, they refused interviews, except during my two visits to Juchitán with reporters, before the initiation of my fieldwork. My fieldwork, in contrast, consisted primarily of participation in daily activities and rituals, along with much discussion and questioning, in extended-family courtyards in Juchitán's poor neighborhoods, as well as in the central market. From this position, it was apparent that COCEI's internal characteristics differed from those of conventional portraits of leftist grassroots movements, including many of COCEI itself. Such conventional descriptions, which emphasize congruence between the claims of leaders and the experiences of supporters, are captured in straightforward representations of COCEI leaders and COCEI itself as children of the pueblo fighting against oppression. In contrast, COCEI in its daily functioning and Juchitecos in their lives exhibit multiple and conflicting representations and strategies with regard to violence, militancy, internal democracy, economic change, disorganization, gender, and culture.[4]

Leaders As Children of the Pueblo

One of the primary sources of COCEI's power has been the way in which COCEI leaders and the movement itself consistently have been viewed, across classes, as having grown from within the pueblo. Representations of this relationship as straightforward appear repeatedly in the speeches and writings of COCEI leaders, in journalistic and scholarly accounts, and in the responses of COCEI supporters to questions about the movement. Writers in *El Satélite* made such claims throughout the 1970s: "Thus the combative and nonconformist spirit of the Juchitecos has awakened in the Coalition." And it was the children of the pueblo who led this process, beginning at "the moment when its youth break the silence to raise the banner of total liberation." So that despite the loss of militants in acts of repression, "thousands and thousands of revolutionaries . . . are being shaped in the heart of the pueblo" (*ES* 27 Oct. 1974, 9 May 1976, 12 Feb. 1978).

In addition to arising from within the pueblo, COCEI consistently has been perceived as paying close attention to what people needed and acting strictly in the interests of the poor. This has occurred through COCEI's actions on behalf of individuals, as well as through its efforts to articulate and seek redress for grievances of a collective nature. COCEI activist Leopoldo de Gyves Pineda described this characteristic during his imprisonment for protest against electoral fraud: ". . . the triumph of the COCEI is the result of the total identification of this organization with the problems and needs of the most numerous, oppressed, and marginalized sectors of the pueblo Juchiteco . . . The demands championed by COCEI . . . captured the confidence, sympathy, support and solidarity of the masses . . ." (*Por Esto!* 16 July 1981, 50).

COCEI has achieved this position by consistently combining radical goals with practical short-term objectives, and by interweaving processes of consciousness raising and mobilization. While asserting that problems could be resolved for the benefit of the popular classes only when policymaking was the responsibility of exclusively those classes, COCEI leaders have stated that, in the meanwhile, "we can advance by extracting from the state partial solutions to our problems" through "widespread popular mobilization" (COCEI 1983, 7).

These descriptions of the origins and practice of radical politics, which are similar to many portraits of popular movements in Latin America, suggest a one-dimensional notion of mobilization: poor people rally in support of a radical movement with which they identify, and which fights to rectify commonly perceived oppressions and injustices. Much of this book, in its analysis of the complexity of Juchitán's regional history and the multiple influences of that history on radical political action, demonstrates why this view of politics oversimplifies the connections between past and present. The discussions of violence, militancy, nondemocracy, gender, and ethnicity that follow will similarly complicate and modify the notion of unified, self-sustaining mobilization as a response to oppression. However, the explanations presented above by political leaders and observers correspond to the ways in which most poor Juchitecos have described their relationship to COCEI. While it may not be the whole story, this vision—of people who identify themselves as poor uniting with leaders whom they characterize as children of the pueblo to fight individuals and groups they view as oppressive—clearly has been a key element of the success of COCEI. Along with many other things, poor Juchitecos understood and experienced politics in this way, and as a result acted to transform the world around them.

Regime Violence and the Threat of Indigenous Explosiveness

Violent repression contributed directly to the development of class consciousness and the rootedness of COCEI in people's daily lives, as ordinary Juchitecos experienced and recounted instances of harassment, shootings, and massacres of their family members and neighbors. COCEI made explicit this connection in its public images and speeches, as well as its neighborhood fiestas and meetings, and writers in *El Satélite* observed the connection between violence and mobilization as well: "In this city, with the direct or indirect intervention of authorities imposed by the PRI, they have assassinated many of our fellow Juchitecos"; "All that has awakened thousands of our countrymen, and they are fighting to have new leaders for the future" (*ES* 13 May 1979, 23 Oct. 1977).

In this context, the manipulation of boundaries between violence and nonviolence constituted a key element in COCEI's own (predominantly nonviolent) political strategy. A national PRI official in Juchitán, interviewed by reporters in August 1983, used the phrase "threads of violence" to characterize what he saw as COCEI's quasi-savage nature. In virtually all of its mobilization activities, COCEI made explicit use of such "threads of violence"—forms of Zapotec language perceived as violent or inciting of violence, explicit threats of violence, the selective use of violence, and references to an inherent potential for violence on the part of Juchitecos. Indeed, it was only by appearing to threaten the existing order that the movement was able to pressure authorities to grant concessions.

When it formed in 1973, COCEI explicitly rejected guerrilla tactics, which had been employed by opposition movements in other southern regions of Mexico since the 1960s. By the time of COCEI's mobilizations, these guerrilla movements had for the most part been destroyed by counterinsurgency programs. COCEI's mass activities, in contrast, operated in the area of the illegal but politically tolerated, and at the margins of nonviolence. In practice, this meant impassioned, angry demonstrations, occupations of buildings, sequestering of buses, painting of slogans on walls, and occasional looting, in addition to strictly legal activities through official channels.

While COCEI never made use of the sort of murderous brutality and harassment practiced by elites and the regime, COCEI supporters praised their leaders for such actions as beating up a corrupt peasant boss who attacked a poor peasant (Campbell 1990b, 311) and threatening to burn Coca-Cola trucks during a strike. Forms of limited violence practiced by COCEI supporters, as well as the creation and repetition of images of violence, included an attack on Oaxaca governor Jiménez Ruíz by a group of Zapotec market women and the looting of stores around the central plaza when police fired at a protest demonstration (Campbell 1990b, 323, 320). COCEI supporters repeated with relish the rumor of women fish vendors, who were known for their quick tongues and sharp knives, cornering a young priísta in an alley and castrating him. COCEI leaders chose passionate and threatening forms of speech—forms that indeed existed in a language that had been used to rebel in the past—

because those forms inspired listeners to gather in the streets and risk their lives in protest. COCEI projected the image not of a restrained, calm, nonviolent movement, but rather of a noisy, unruly force that appeared at times to be on the verge of getting out of control.

Threatening the existing order meant not only pressing the borders of nonviolence, but doing so in a way that made use of images and beliefs about the dangerous character of Indians. When COCEI supporters occupied public buildings or blocked a highway they were not just poor Mexicans, but fierce Indians whose tempers could not wholly be trusted to respond to the unwritten rules and language of secular Mexican politics. COCEI leaders fostered this image of indigenous violence in the newspaper, as well as in their mobilizations and speeches, offering "our warmest welcome to the violence of the humble campesino" (*ES* 26 Dec. 1976) and predicting that "after exhausting all parliamentary means . . . [the pueblo] will finally respond to aggression in the same language [of violence]" (*ES* 30 Nov. 1975). While COCEI leaders made these remarks in written Spanish in the newspaper, they inspired Juchitecos to chant slogans and raise their fists in the air in a language (Isthmus Zapotec) that state and national officials, as well as some prominent local businesspeople, could not understand.

Even politically moderate members of Juchitán's middle and upper classes, most of whom could understand this language, feared the violence to which COCEI leaders referred. They insisted that it led to chaos and the end of family stability, and they observed that some COCEI supporters chose language that was "out of the ordinary" (*ES* 10 Mar. 1974). In seeking to keep COCEI in the realm of the acceptable, moderates counseled the movement to avoid extremes and proceed with care in a dangerous world: "You are battling in the middle of a lagoon where there are thousands of poisonous animals that can jump out at any moment and you won't know from where. Use your intelligence and don't go crazy. Because the extremes are disastrous" (*ES* 10 Mar. 1974). COCEI's ability to manipulate its stances just inside or outside the cultural border between "the ordinary" and "disastrous extremes" enabled the movement alternately to gain support from moderates and threaten them. COCEI's manipulation of violence thus made use of complex emotions on the part of both supporters and opponents. In the face of elite perception of the proximity and danger of extremes, it was precisely COCEI's threats and threads of violence, including its real ability to bring together angry crowds, that complemented COCEI's character as the legitimate children and champions of the pueblo. The fears and angers that made possible such a politics, furthermore, were not simply turned on or off as a political tactic. Rather, the very unruliness and complexity of emotion that empowered radical politics, and that originated in large part outside COCEI, were consistently central to the nature of the movement itself and the context in which it operated. In describing the practice of liberation theology in Nicaragua, Roger Lancaster observed that ordinary people's visions of radical politics are "tormented by demons and motivated by dreams," and that "the Jehovah of the Poor . . . is the wrath of the people incarnate" (1988, xxi). COCEI's discourse of violence, along with its practices of militancy and hostility, indicate that such demons and wrath were an integral part of mass mobilization in Juchitán.

Militancy

Along with its "threads of violence," COCEI adopted a militant public posture that engendered considerable criticism on the part of some middle-class and elite sympathizers as well as opponents of all classes. Despite instances of flexibility in their private negotiations with regime officials, in public COCEI leaders consistently employed radical Marxist rhetoric, derogated leftist political parties, expressed extreme hostility to outsiders, and dealt with local opponents in confrontational rather than conciliatory ways.[5] In several of these areas, the public positions and private beliefs of leaders differed from the language and experiences of COCEI's peasant and worker supporters. This did not elicit comment or criticism from most of these supporters, however, as different conceptions of politics and daily life appear to have coexisted easily and fluidly. Rather than weakening the movement, COCEI's militancy, like its manipulation of violent action and imagery, strengthened the movement's ability to rally supporters and challenge the Mexican regime.

Political Ideology and Political Parties

COCEI leaders explained international relations, Mexican politics, and regional economic development in parsimonious Marxist terms, though with an explicit cultural component: U.S. imperialism dominated Latin

American economies and politics; the PRI ruled Mexico in the interest of the Mexican economic oligarchy and international capital; and the state promoted economic development in the Isthmus in order to achieve large-scale, capitalist production and marginalize or destroy indigenous culture. In the words of COCEI leader Daniel López Nelio, "The Zapotec race is oppressed by a whole economic system, the same as the working class," and "the Benito Juárez dam was meant to systematically destroy Zapotec culture" (1993, 235, 233).[6] Furthermore, these forms of domination were opposed by the inevitable and growing strength of "the people"; state repression in Juchitán was "the political response of those who see their privileges threatened by the irrepressible advance of the masses" (*ES* 12 Feb. 1978).

In defending Zapotec culture, COCEI leaders opposed political parties throughout the 1970s, characterizing them as corrupt and dedicated to their own institutional needs (*ES* 6 Oct. 1974). In COCEI leaders' view, direct mobilization of the people in acts of protest was always the central and most important activity of an opposition movement. Participation in elections was useful only if it furthered the more important goals of developing consciousness and support (*Punto Crítico* 1977; Martínez López 1985).

In a series of interviews during the Ayuntamiento Popular, COCEI leaders emphasized these themes, contrasting their beliefs and tactics to those of the PCM and PSUM (Waterhouse 1983, 87–92). COCEI leaders asserted, as they had throughout the previous decade, that COCEI was not an electoral organization, that there could be no viable alternative for opposition through parliamentary means, and that their goals necessitated demonstrations and popular mobilizations, including illegal acts, such as the takeover of stolen land and the seizure of private property. Even as COCEI gained local office through alliance with the PCM, municipal president Leopoldo de Gyves proclaimed COCEI the head of the revolution, the Communist Party its tail. COCEI opposed the national electoral strategies of the PCM and PSUM, as well as those parties' criticisms of COCEI for its lack of internal democratic procedures and the absence of separations between COCEI as a political movement and COCEI in office. According to Campbell, COCEI leaders responded to his questions about "downplaying ethnicity and regionalism in order to forge larger political alliances" with mention of local accomplishments, along with the question "Why shouldn't the national left conform to our way of doing things?" (1990b, 350).

Outsiders

COCEI's militancy included ongoing hostility to most outsiders, a category that in practice applied to people who had not been raised in Juchitán. This hostility was not uniform, and where it existed it often had numerous origins in the behaviors of the outsiders themselves (de la Cruz 1993). However, in contrast to a stance of openness on the part of many grassroots movements elsewhere, COCEI chose a public and private position of hostility and harassment toward even sympathetic outsiders that paralleled its ongoing public condemnation of political parties.

COCEI's stance toward the Juchiteco middle class and elite is another, and probably the most consequential, example of the movement's confrontational political style. Despite the presence of a discernible moderate discourse in support of COCEI, and commonly held beliefs that many moderate priístas, fed up with corrupt government, had voted for COCEI in the 1980 and 1981 elections, Juchitecos who did not identify with COCEI felt themselves to be harassed and mistreated throughout the Ayuntamiento Popular. They complained vehemently about patronage practices on the part of the COCEI municipal government and harassment of non-COCEI supporters in the streets.[7] In addition, they protested the transformation of the city's central plazas into focal points of radical political culture, including revolutionary music, protest banners, and solidarity with popular struggles in Nicaragua and Chile.[8] In addition, both businesspeople and Communist Party members who claimed to be supportive of COCEI complained of the organization's refusal to seek accords with the private sector. This does not mean that critics would have supported COCEI if the movement had pursued its radical demands in conciliatory language or through democratic procedures. Rather, it demonstrates that COCEI leaders repeatedly chose to present a dogmatic political ideology and to maintain hostile public and private stances toward leftist political parties, outsiders, and local priístas. Such a practice contrasts with the more tolerant and open stance attributed to contemporary popular movements generally and indeed exhibited by some.

215

Militancy and Ordinary Juchitecos

COCEI's militant stance also contrasts in a number of ways with the political language and approach of ordinary Juchitecos. Little of the dogmatic analysis used by the leadership appeared in popular discussion, which was much more grounded in description of local experience. COCEI supporters identified themselves as the poor people and identified those who exploited them as merchants, landowners, government agencies, and political officials. They were more likely, however, to speak in terms of *los pobres* and *los ricos,* and of the PRI-*gobierno,* than to use words such as "capitalism" or "class." In addition, COCEI supporters generally did not advocate a return to subsistence agriculture or speak nostalgically about a past (and present) of unpaved roads and oxen, despite the praise with which a variety of COCEI leaders, intellectuals, and professionals described these matters (López Nelio 1993). Most poor Juchiteco peasants valued some forms of agricultural technology, credit, and insurance, as well as urban jobs, and they strove to acquire household amenities, such as televisions, refrigerators, and concrete floors, rather than to maintain or return to a more rustic past.

COCEI's militancy toward the local middle class and elites also differed from the attitudes and behavior of ordinary Juchitecos. In part, there was common ground—COCEI supporters rallied behind COCEI attacks on local landowners and businesses and generally approved of the harassment and biased treatment about which priístas complained. On the other hand, COCEI supporters were members of family networks that generally included some priístas, poor or not so poor, and ritual events tended to bring COCEI and PRI activists into the same courtyards. Both groups found ways to bridge the political hostility and establish cordial and even respectful relations, at least in some contexts. In one striking event, some of COCEI's highest leaders attended an All Saints' vigil in honor of a deceased young woman, an ardent COCEI supporter and a relative of one of them, whose elderly father was a distinguished local PRI politician.

Some families made banter and disagreements about politics a form of daily interaction and pleasure. The members of one COCEI family, for example, gleefully provoked their Tía Ramona nightly for her allegiance to the PRI, and she responded, in stereotypical Juchiteca fashion, with robust tales of her zealous activity in support of her party. In the midst of heated argument, they nevertheless all agreed that "people join together with those they like to hang around with," and that "one is at home in one's party." In another case, Elena's family of PRI-supporting moderates expressed interest in and respect for the way in which COCEI had won over their schoolteacher aunt through union activities. COCEI-supporting young people in one family hid their mother's voting card when she told them she would vote for a PRI politician; she related the incident with amusement. Doña Mariana, an elderly midwife, attended equally to the births and health of PRI and COCEI women in Juchitán, despite her overt skepticism of COCEI's intentions and competence. Revealingly, it took a year and a half of a relatively close relationship for Doña Mariana to reveal to my wife and me that she had come to see value, late in life, in a habit she had roundly criticized to us often—the habit on the part of many poor Juchitecos of eating with their hands. In a similar fashion, I suspect that Doña Mariana may also have had some understanding of and sympathy for the political behaviors she criticized.

These examples indicate that Juchitecos, through their complex and close-knit personal interactions, developed understandings and relationships considerably more nuanced than those expressed in the public stances of their leaders toward a variety of "others": foreign political groups, Mexican political parties, outside visitors, and local PRI supporters. COCEI's strength derived not only from its ability to evoke emotions of anger and fear, acting politically at the margins of violence, but also from its leaders' successes in fostering hostile and militant actions that were at odds with key aspects of Juchitecos' daily experience.

Democracy

In the minds of both COCEI leaders and supporters, the advance of peasant and worker interests did not require procedural democracy. Rather, it required the kind of attentiveness and trustworthiness that was demonstrated repeatedly in the direct-action campaigns of the 1970s. While COCEI participated in a variety of elections, pressing for adherence to formal procedures and seeking to gain control of local associations and government through votes, the ideology of the organization did not favor democratic procedure over other forms of organization and decision making. Furthermore, moderates writing in *El Satélite* in the

1970s shared this view, though their plans for change differed from those of COCEI.

COCEI activist Carlos Sánchez offered a view of democracy in keeping with Leninist and Maoist practices of democratic centralism: the leadership of COCEI didn't change by way of democratic elections, but through incorporation of new leaders from among those who participated. This was, according to Sánchez, a democratic process not because of elections, but because it produced a vanguard to lead the struggle of the pueblo. Through COCEI, "the pueblo is choosing its leaders organically"; "the leaders gain their position in the course of the struggle" (interview, Aug. 1983). Macario Matus, director of the Casa de la Cultura and COCEI supporter, defined democracy this way: "that the base is taken into account. That decisions aren't arbitrary" (interview, Aug. 1983).

COCEI supporters understood democracy to mean participation and responsiveness, with electoral procedures contributing one useful means of participation among several. Families in Juchitán's poor neighborhoods emphasized repeatedly that COCEI leaders knew them, listened to them, helped them, and acted faithfully in their interest. People expected to participate in COCEI's political activities in a variety of ways, to make their opinions known and to argue for their viewpoints, but they did not necessarily expect this to occur through any sort of democratic procedures, such as elections or representative committees.

Jonathan Fox suggests that internal democracy be measured by degrees of responsiveness and accountability in the relationship between leaders and supporters of grassroots movements. He argues that high levels of democracy of this sort are likely to arise through changing combinations of electoral procedures and other forms of meeting, discussion, and organization. Consequently, determinations about the democratic character of grassroots movements are best made by evaluating the pathways by which people become leaders and the relationships between leaders and members over time (1992).

From this perspective, COCEI can be characterized as exhibiting a significant but limited degree of internal democracy. COCEI leaders and supporters did not value electoral procedures within the movement, and such procedures appear to have occurred only infrequently. On the other hand, COCEI leaders were responsive to the needs and interests of poor Juchitecos, and the extensive comments in the course of my fieldwork on the part of peasants and workers regarding this responsiveness is testimony to its depth and endurance. In practice, there appears to have been little serious disagreement between the felt needs of poor Juchitecos and the goals and strategies of COCEI leaders. However, in terms of allowing and promoting expression, recognizing difference, establishing spaces and procedures for autonomy and debate, and indeed incorporating voices and suggestions, my observations and interviews in Juchitán suggest that COCEI leaders, despite their responsiveness, and despite instances of accountability, exhibited considerable disregard for internal democracy in theory and practice.[9]

At the same time, electoral procedures constituted an important component of COCEI's activity over two decades, and the place of electoral competition for public office in the ideology and practice of COCEI was both ambiguous and changing. In the 1970s, it was illegal for COCEI to participate in elections without allying with a political party, and there was no legal leftist party in Mexico. In this context, COCEI attacked all parties and rejected national elections, but argued for popular sovereignty at the municipal level and participated as an independent group in municipal elections. COCEI also undertook electoral activity in the Communal Land Commission and the Livestock Association, winning majority support in each of these local organizations. However, in its internal debate over participation in national elections, most COCEI leaders ignored the movement's immersion in regional electoral activity and argued that radical politics could occur only "at the margins of elections" (*ES* 22 July 1979).

In the 1980s, COCEI moved further in the direction of electoral politics. As the movement participated in elections, governed, opposed military occupation and repression, and governed again, it relied on the rules of democratic procedure in advancing its claims. In so doing, COCEI constructed what Evelina Dagnino characterizes as new and broad forms of citizenship, including "the invention/creation of *new* rights" (n.d., 10 in ms.). In the course of the 1980s, Juchitecos gained rights to speak out in government agencies, solve local problems collectively, bring their own language to official proceedings, gain access to complex networks of information, and maintain their own ritual practices and standards of beauty. However, COCEI leaders did not describe these capabilities in terms of citizenship. Rather, like activists in the Organization of Black

Communities of the Pacific Coast of Colombia, they "emphasiz[ed] cultural autonomy and the right to be who we are and have our own life project" (Escobar 1995, 212).[10]

COCEI's lack of internal democracy, its changing participation in elections, and the multifaceted rights it achieved for Juchitecos demonstrate that powerful electoral and nonelectoral political practices coexisted in the movement, with neither COCEI leaders nor supporters appearing to find the situation problematic. Like the coexistence of divergent approaches to Marxist ideology, to outsiders, and to local priístas on the part of COCEI's leaders and supporters, as well as the movement's changing mix of nonviolence and violence, the issues of democracy and citizenship illustrate COCEI's multiple and even contradictory political understandings and approaches. Furthermore, the convergence between the views of COCEI leaders and moderates within the PRI about the limited value of procedural democracy suggests that COCEI's nondemocratic beliefs and practices did not arise primarily from democratic centralist convictions, as critics often claimed, but rather from the history of beliefs and practices about democracy in Juchitán. In the course of this history, procedural democracy was one strand among many political forms that safeguarded or endangered different people's interests and goals.

Economic Change and Political Activism

Juchitecos' clear sense of themselves as exploited, together with the absence of descriptions of economic threats to their physical survival, suggests that the relationships between processes of economic transformation, the development of consciousness, and the formation of a radical political opposition were less direct than COCEI leaders and outside observers suggested. This is another, and perhaps the most striking, example of the coexistence within COCEI of contradictory understandings about the experiences of Juchitecos. It is also an example of the uses made by COCEI leaders—and, in this case, academic researchers—of a militant and dogmatic posture, rather than a representation of recent history based more directly on people's local experiences. COCEI leaders claimed that COCEI formed in response to a direct threat to peasant survival, a result of the construction of the Benito Juárez Dam and accompanying irrigation district. Scholars and COCEI leaders alike characterized this threat as the result not only of land monopolization, but of an oil-led, dual economy and of the untrammeled expansion of capitalism and the economic arm of the central state (Binford 1983; Campbell 1990b; COCEI 1983; Prevôt-Schapira and Rivière D'Arc 1986).[11] The living and working conditions of peasants and workers were "relegated to secondary importance" with new agricultural and industrial projects "signifying new and fiercer forms of oppression" (López Monjardin 1983b, 76). In this situation, faced with losing their land, their income, and their way of life in the 1960s and 1970s, peasants rebelled.

One of the most interesting and perplexing aspects of my fieldwork in Juchitán was the fact that a wide range of ardent COCEI supporters did not describe their families' economic histories in the 1960s and 1970s in terms compatible with those of the researchers. They spoke, rather, of gradual changes and piecemeal adaptation, of changes in family economies rather than threats to survival. Juchitecos told of selling land, if asked specifically about that, in response to particular personal situations. They told of not having access to credit in the past as a simple statement of fact, in relation to knowing about it and having it now, and they never mentioned lack of access to water. This includes politically active and committed COCEI supporters who were quite astute at describing instances of economic exploitation and evaluating the political interaction between regime and opposition.

While it may be the case that people did not perceive the whole picture, as described by leaders and researchers, Juchitecos' descriptions of their family histories and current situations indicate that matters were considerably more heterogeneous than observers claimed and that economic transformation was not a uniform or life-threatening process. People continued to have land twenty years after the construction of the dam, just less of it, and jobs were available in the urban economy to make up for lost agricultural income. Furthermore, while COCEI spokesmen presented peasant life in the mid-1980s as a uniform continuation of past oppressions, COCEI supporters often expressed satisfaction with aspects of their present economic lives, at the same time as they fought against what they identified as exploitative economic and political relations.

In 1985, for example, Antonio Rodríguez and Ana María Díaz, two articulate and committed COCEI activists, commented with satisfaction on the recent sorghum harvest and the prices for the crop, as well as on the sugar crop and the functioning of the nearby, state-run sugar mill. In contrast, COCEI was at that time particularly critical of pressures on peasants to grow alternative crops such as sorghum and sugar, as well as of the exploitative and inefficient functioning of the sugar mill. Similarly, Ta Mauricio, another poor peasant and ardent COCEI supporter, lived humbly but relatively securely by farming three hectares of irrigated land. Ta Mauricio's understanding of the past differed from that of COCEI; despite COCEI's large-scale mobilizations in support of a 1964 ejido decree (which was canceled), Ta Mauricio did not seem to know about the ejido efforts, stated that land in Juchitán had always been private property, and observed that the balance between rich and poor had stayed the same over time in the city and that poor people had benefited from irrigation. Contrary to COCEI's claims about the present, furthermore, Ta Mauricio grew corn, received the water to which he was entitled through irrigation, and had access to credit, though he declined to use it.

In the eyes of Ta Juan, another strong COCEI supporter, the banks helped peasants by providing them with insurance when they lost a harvest and, again, the land had always been private property, except that the rich had taken all the unowned land when the dam was constructed, before poor people realized what was happening. According to a woman who sold orange juice in the central market, people lived a little better in the present than in the past. Na Maricela, a fruit and vegetable vendor, said that it was good when the irrigation came, there were bigger harvests; she didn't remember any land conflict. According to Aníbal, a young COCEI-supporting peasant, credit provided useful help in getting machinery and insurance, and it was readily available. Aníbal said he didn't get credit before 1982 because his father hadn't wanted to; he didn't mention COCEI's securing of credit for peasants as a key turning point. In addition, though he grew corn at the time, Aníbal said that friends had been trying to convince him to plant sugarcane, and that this sounded like a reasonable choice to him. In this discussion of his experience, Aníbal mentioned neither COCEI's role in securing credit for peasants nor the organization's critique of the sugar mill. Finally, in another sort of example, Victoria and her husband Angel spoke of the new availability of drainage in their outlying neighborhood of Juchitán, and of the contributions they made to be hooked up to the system, which they found to be reasonable. Though they were both sympathetic to COCEI, and their children were strong COCEI supporters, their observations differed sharply from COCEI's insistence, at just that time, that the PRI municipal government was investing money only in showy projects in the center of town, and completely ignoring needs for drainage and potable water.

How can these apparent discrepancies be explained? For one thing, it is likely that poor peasants and workers were relatively satisfied with aspects of their economic lives in 1985 precisely because COCEI had fought so successfully to defend and support local family economies. In addition, it is not necessarily contradictory to express satisfaction *and* identify exploitation; Juchitecos may well have been pleased, in a context of extreme exploitation, to be doing as well as they were. However, there still appears to be a contradiction between the above views and the explicit and militant claims of COCEI leaders and intellectuals, as well as of outside observers. The Juchitecos I have quoted actively supported one of the strongest and most radical grassroots movements in Mexico, and they had done this, at the time of my discussions with them, over the course of thirteen years. However, these same Juchitecos did not remember the ejido land conflict on which many of COCEI's early mobilizations, and most of COCEI leaders' claims to early legitimacy and success, were based. These Juchitecos did not speak of their survival as having been threatened by economic transformation in the 1960s and 1970s, they expressed some satisfaction in the 1980s with the agricultural institutions that COCEI harshly and uniformly condemned, and they did not qualify their satisfaction by observing that these institutions dealt with them fairly *because* of COCEI's mobilizations.

These contradictions, like those regarding violence, militancy, and recent economic changes, demonstrate that COCEI leaders and intellectuals made use of, and perhaps held, a militant and uniform understanding of local political and economic history that was at odds with many of the understandings and experiences of COCEI's peasant and worker supporters. COCEI's success in confronting the Mexican regime suggests that this militancy in analysis and action was an extraordinarily powerful means of threatening the regime, withstanding repression, and achieving sustained negotiation for twenty years. Furthermore, COCEI's success in maintaining steadfast mass support among poor Juchitecos—and the absence of comment or criticism regarding the apparent discrepancies between their own and their leaders' representations of recent economic experiences—suggest that ordinary Juchitecos do not find these discrepancies troubling. This may be because they understood that their leaders' beliefs and claims were meant to serve as effective tactics in public politics, and in fact did so extraordinarily well. It may also be the case that Juchitecos *agreed* with the statements of COCEI leaders, even when those statements contradicted some of the details of people's daily lives.

Thus, COCEI's claims that ejido land was stolen from Juchiteco peasants, that Juchiteco's survival was threatened by economic transformation, that local elites and state agricultural agencies consistently exploited them, and that PRI municipal governments did nothing for them may well have been seen by ordinary Juchitecos as a reasonable representation of their experiences, even though these statements were not what the same Juchitecos said when they spoke in their own words about their lives. In contrast, the economic experiences of COCEI supporters indicated not only that exploitation was uneven and contradictory, but that the multiple discrepancies between the discourse of COCEI leaders regarding economic change, the experiences of ordinary Juchitecos, and the ways in which Juchitecos speak of these experiences—like similar contradictions regarding the movement's violence, militancy, and democratic practices—were not minor aberrations, but rather constitute a prominent characteristic of radical political mobilization in Juchitán.

Disorganization and Backward Vision

In addition to its use of images of violence, its militant stance, and multiple discrepancies between the views of leaders and supporters, another prominent characteristic of COCEI was its lack of institutionalization. COCEI was very well organized in the sense that it had identifiable leaders and supporters, participated in elections, negotiated with regime officials, and carried out numerous local projects, such as the creation of health centers, squatter settlements, and markets. In addition, one of COCEI's most important strengths was its ability to coordinate the massing of thousands of people from diverse neighborhoods and towns in political mobilizations.

Yet there was a disorganized side to COCEI. For example, many COCEI supporters didn't vote, even at the height of important electoral campaigns. Voting had multiple meanings, and COCEI leaders made only uneven efforts to shape these meanings in the direction of widespread participation. The young women in one family spent hours getting dressed up to vote and then voted more than once. Voting in this case was at once an important social activity and a strategic effort to combat fraud with fraud. In other families, in contrast, COCEI supporters commented that they lacked voting identification cards or would not vote. They usually attributed this abstention to confusion or obstruction in the registration process, to other commitments, to pressure from employers or co-workers against voting for COCEI, or to convictions that voting did not matter all that much.

In another example of disorganization, COCEI supporters in one town who began campaigning for a local health center knew little of COCEI's successful efforts to establish a health center in another town several years before. Sympathetic critics in Juchitán argued that COCEI had not set up processes of discussion and learning that could have kept COCEI supporters informed and active in all arenas of the movement's activity. However, the lack of such initiatives, together with the relative absence of criticism on the subject, suggests that such disorganization was at least in part a deliberate strategy. Some leftist critics also related COCEI's disorganization to something they saw as an even more significant flaw in COCEI's approach: the absence of what they called a forward-looking plan for regional economic development (Zermeño 1987, 79–88). These critics compared COCEI unfavorably to grassroots organizations of producers, such as coffee-growing peasants in Oaxaca and Guerrero, who organized cooperative ventures with the goal of carving out a niche in the evolving international economy. Instead of developing such efforts, COCEI rhetorically praised the subsistence maize economy, took steps to assure the survival of small-scale production through credit and insurance, and acted to defend peasant and worker claims within existing economic arrangements. While COCEI leaders frequently alluded to a future of alternative economic development for the benefit of the producers, they never presented detailed proposals or sponsored the establishment of new enterprises.

COCEI leaders appear to have chosen a flexible style of mobilization, promoting centers of activity without necessarily coordinating them, so long as there was a system by which to get out information and assemble people in large gatherings. Such flexibility depended on forms of disorganization. COCEI leaders chose to let the movement follow ebbs and flows of political intensity, to accept that sometimes radical politics would "disappear," while at other times it was everywhere, in people's

225

greetings, words, and daily affairs. Alberto Melucci describes grassroots organizing in this fashion when he states that collective action "assumes the form of networks submerged in everyday life . . . The 'movements' emerge only in limited areas, for limited phases and by means of moments of mobilization . . ." (Melucci 1988b, 248). Such an understanding of collective action coincided with the ways in which ordinary people were willing to become involved in politics, with COCEI leaders learning this aspect of grassroots mobilization in part from Juchitecos themselves.

In their study of poor people's movements in the United States, Frances Fox Piven and Richard Cloward (1977) argue that it was precisely when such movements appeared to be disorganized and explosive that state authorities felt pressured to enact significant reforms. With respect to oft-repeated urgings for grassroots movements to institutionalize themselves, by establishing membership lists and committees and by developing political and economic programs, Piven and Cloward found that such activities tended to lead to demobilization and ineffectiveness (xxi–xxii). In contrast, COCEI's "disorganized" strategy indeed functioned to "escalate the momentum and impact of disruptive protest at each stage in its emergence and evolution" (Piven and Cloward 1977, 37).[12] This included many of the practices described above, such as flexibility and lack of extensive organizational structure, use of images and acts of violence, militant stances, and lack of emphasis on internal democracy. In addition, COCEI's rootedness in Zapotec history, art, and daily life fueled the disorganized and insurgent aspects of the movement. Thus, COCEI was strong because it indeed responded directly to the needs people felt, to the language they spoke and the humor and puns with which they spoke it, and to the varying rhythms of their lives. In its strategic battles, COCEI was able to draw on fierce tempers, on the unpredictability and changing locations of political passions, on the quick movement and militancy allowed by the absence of internal democracy, and on the fear of insurgency that could be elicited by images of indigenous violence.

Furthermore, COCEI's "disorganization amidst organization," in the way it respected people's own preferences and the changing demands of their lives, provided a protection from the dangers to grassroots endurance posed by people's exhaustion. It made possible what Melucci characterizes as "experimentation with and direct practice of alternative frameworks of meaning . . . on which the networks [of collective action] themselves are founded and live from day to day" (1988b, 248). Rather than impose a set of demands and an ideology, COCEI's looser relationship with individual Juchitecos enabled people to live in partial autonomy from formal politics, an autonomy from which people could be rallied, or could rally others, time and again in the course of twenty years.

Thus, despite discrepancies between public ideology and local belief, COCEI was strong precisely because it indeed took popular experience and popular culture seriously. Instead of promoting a particular economic project, COCEI responded repeatedly to people's economic lives as they existed. Instead of sponsoring campaigns for cleanliness, as did reformist members of the PRI, COCEI celebrated local cultural practices. COCEI did not challenge people's commitment to their work as small agricultural producers, market vendors, artisans, fisherman, or midwives. Nor did the movement challenge people's potential ability to be individually successful in these activities. At the same time, in defending the rights of peasants and workers to the guarantees provided them by the Mexican constitution and Mexican law, COCEI indeed undertook the radical act of constructing new forms of citizenship.

Manuel López Mateos, an early COCEI activist and for many years a professor of mathematics in Mexico City, responded to criticism of COCEI's "backward-looking" economic and cultural perspective by suggesting that fair economic relations could arise from within local cultural discourses:

. . . the defense of our culture is not a "salvage operation" (we are not flora and fauna becoming extinct), nor does it represent a return to primitivism. The defense of our culture signifies the defense of a way of organizing social relations. This defense is based on the recovery and joint exploitation of our communal resources, on fair interchange of the products of labor, and on control of the negotiating instruments to make the decisions which affect us. (1993, 259)

Ethnicity, Gender, and COCEI's Cultural Project

COCEI's self-conscious acceptance of and embeddedness in Zapotec history, identity, and cultural forms have provided the movement with the intimate connection to ordinary Juchitecos that animated radical politics. At the same time, both leaders and supporters have developed a mutually constitutive (Comaroff 1987, 313) relationship with Zapotec culture, recreating and manipulating ethnic beliefs and practices even as they themselves are shaped and defined by those very practices. Ethnic identity and cultural production, furthermore, like the characteristics of COCEI described in previous sections, have involved multiple discrepancies and ambiguities, between men and women and between the statements of COCEI leaders, artists, and intellectuals and the beliefs and historical experiences of ordinary Juchitecos.

Ethnic Practices and Radical Organizing

From its inception, COCEI conducted its activities in Zapotec, speaking to people in their courtyards and addressing meetings, demonstrations, and marches in the local language. The extensive use of Zapotec in public forums, in particular, differentiated the language of the opposition from that of the official party. During the years of the Ayuntamiento Popular, Zapotec was spoken with greater frequency in schools and government offices (Campbell 1990b, 358). According to COCEI intellectual Víctor de la Cruz, "The young [COCEI] administrators begin to feel that the presence of Zapotec is much stronger when they have municipal power. Up in City Hall, they yell, tell jokes, collect taxes, and administer justice in Zapotec" (1984, 23, cited in Campbell 1990b, 356). Humor was an important aspect of the Zapotec character of COCEI speech, and one of the ways in which COCEI leaders established intimate forms of communication with supporters. Miguel Covarrubias, a Mexican painter and writer who visited Juchitán in the 1940s, observed that Isthmus Zapotecs "cultivate language with an unusual intensity" (1986 [1946], 310, cited in Campbell 1990b, 203), and Campbell underscored Juchitecos' attention to "skills at verbal banter and double-entendre" (1990b, 435).

Also from the beginning, COCEI carried out its public activities with the customs and adornments of Zapotec ritual. These ceremonial practices involved the active participation of women, who attended demonstrations in the embroidered blouses and long skirts reserved for fiestas and distributed food and gifts much the way this was done in ritual celebrations. Oxcarts brought to COCEI events were adorned with branches and flowers, filled with children, and paraded through the streets of the city. At demonstrations, women formed the first large band of supporters surrounding the speakers' platform, filling the scene with red ribbons, floral prints, and embroidery and raising their fists in the air in militant opposition to the government.

In addition to its role in public events, ethnic identity contributed to the content of popular thinking about economics and politics and provided specific pathways of language and social life through which people could respond to the ideas and activities of COCEI. Juchitecos brought to their politics shared memories of the succession of nineteenth- and early-twentieth-century rebellions in the city. They referred frequently to the nineteenth-century battle against the French, in which a Juchiteco battalion routed the occupiers in a decisive encounter, and to the Che Melendrez, Che Gómez, and 1932 rebellions against political and economic impositions by the state government. COCEI leaders made frequent references to this rebellious past in speeches and writing, and local artists and intellectuals researched and depicted the popular uprisings throughout the years of COCEI's activism. In this context, women and men in Juchitán's family courtyards and neighborhoods began to connect the present to the rebellions past in new ways. They not only characterized themselves as poor, but identified the individuals, private enterprises, and state agencies that exploited them and denounced the political impositions that denied them local self-government. These discussions, conducted almost uniformly in Zapotec, occurred in market stalls, local bars, and family courtyards, the physical and social locations that had been constructed by, and in turn contributed to the reelaboration of, local cultural beliefs and practices.

Family courtyards were particularly important places for discussion and mobilization, and their gender and class characteristics provided fertile ground for rethinking politics and getting people out into the streets. Such courtyards generally included several branches of the same extended family, each living in its own one- or several-room house around one or more central areas. As a result of the economic changes of the previous twenty years, the members of these families frequently did different types of work, and consequently the various families had different levels and kinds of economic resources. In contrast to many other urban environments in Mexico, however, an increase in family economic resources in Juchitán did not generally mean either leaving the family courtyard or abandoning Zapotec identity and ritual. For this reason, a variety of families worked, conversed, raised children, relaxed, and celebrated in a common space and with a common language. In this space,

229

COCEI's attention to the needs of any one occupational group, in the context of its championing of Zapotec identity and political sovereignty, was generally seen as support for all.

Gender and Radical Organizing

Through their control of family courtyards, the central market, and neighborhood marketing networks, Juchiteca women played a key role in the development of political consciousness and grassroots mobilization. This often began in the market in early morning, where news of the previous day would be disseminated, and continued through the preparation and selling of a variety of foods and goods in the central market, in the streets, and in family courtyards. In the central market, women from all of the city's neighborhoods sat side by side, so that information and events from one part of one neighborhood would travel through the market and then radiate outward to all parts of the city in the course of a day. The market itself was a crowded, expanding, "disorderly" place. Though its central, two-story structure occupied an enormous city block, vendors also crowded into surrounding streets, and women with their wares in baskets or on blankets found places in front of or between the larger stalls or circulated through the market on foot. In addition to providing multiple and mobile public spaces, the market offered the fully visible, but less public, spaces behind the tables on which products were displayed. This was the space where the vendors stood or sat as they sold their wares, talked with each other or with family members when business lagged, and ate meals. In my own work, I was introduced to the difference between the spaces in front of and behind the market stalls in dramatic ways. In front of the stalls, I engaged in banter about prices and gossip, as well as caught up on the events of the day. Six months later, after my foreignness was rhetorically noted and challenged, I was invited to sit on the vendors' side of the stall and permitted to ask detailed questions about the women's family histories and their involvement with COCEI.

The circulation of information in Juchitán also occurred through communal planning and preparations for fiesta activities, which brought women and their families across the city from one neighborhood to another. Juchitán's urban character ensured that this communication occurred within dense personal and occupational networks that employed not only gossip, but local and national newspapers, magazines, and radio as well, many of which repudiated official government positions. Juchitecas used this information and their convictions about the events of the day literally to get their families out into the streets—to attend neighborhood meetings, gather together before proceeding to demonstrations in the center of the city, and register and vote.

Men and women played distinctly different roles in perpetuating the vibrant Zapotec culture that was arguably the single factor most responsible for COCEI's power. Men monopolized formal artistic culture in Juchitán—painting, poetry, and songwriting—along with certain forms of artisanal production and the less formal singing and philosophizing that occurred in local cantinas. Campbell has shown these activities to be essential components of COCEI's elaboration of culture and dissemination of ideas (1994, 179–89). However, the success of COCEI's radical political efforts hinged as much or more on the production of an engaged, creative culture of daily life—in courtyard, neighborhood, and market—by women.[13] The activities of women in Juchitán have been more involved with shaping and contesting aspects of life in these daily domains, while men have been more involved in establishing a formal narrative of that life. In this sense, men's cultural activities are closer to the ideological, militant stances that characterize COCEI's public politics—and that have been developed and practiced by COCEI's young male leaders—while women's cultural activities are more directly related to the daily experiences that contradict or modify those public stances.

Shoshana Sokoloff's research on the relationship between midwives and doctors in Juchitán supports this observation (1993). Sokoloff notes that male COCEI leaders, in accord with their essentialist representations of Zapotec culture, portrayed midwives as native to Juchitán's poor neighborhoods, practicing an art that had been passed down for generations. In contrast, Sokoloff found a variety of birthplaces, linguistic abilities, and forms of training among midwives. Doña Mariana, for example, who was known throughout Juchitán as "the mother of us all," was born of Spanish parents in another part of the state, had been trained to deliver babies (to spite her mother!) by her brother-in-law, a Japanese doctor, and spoke only rudimentary Zapotec.

In addition, contrary to the image of midwives as folk figures set apart from Western medicine, Sokoloff found that midwives interacted routinely with doctors, referring patients for tests and evaluations or for deliveries in risky situations, as well as borrowing techniques of which they could make practical use. In contrast to most Third World encounters between midwives and Western doctors, Sokoloff found that Juchitán's midwives had not been replaced by the outside, but had interacted with it on very much their own terms, preserving their own prestigious social and economic positions in the process. While the male narratives about midwifery reinforced COCEI's cultural project and militant stance, it was the daily activities of women, as mothers and midwives, that performed the practical work of keeping Zapotec cultural practice alive and strong by achieving a trustworthy, *Zapotec* way of delivering babies in an urban setting.

Like their romantic view of local midwives, COCEI's male leaders claimed a feminism that was at odds with women's actual social and political roles. COCEI leaders spoke repeatedly about Juchitán's egalitarian gender relations and about the equal participation of women in the movement. In political events and in widely disseminated photographs, COCEI featured proud-looking women in festive Zapotec attire, and COCEI artists and writers highlighted the strength and exoticism of local female sexuality. However, despite women's central role in the work of cultural adaptation, as well as in developing political consciousness and mobilizing family members, women did not hold positions of leadership within COCEI and generally did not participate in the artistic and literary activities that were central to the movement's cultural project. Furthermore, Juchitecas suffered enduring forms of exploitation and subordination on a day-to-day basis, including sexual double standards, limited educational opportunities, responsibilities for both household and money-earning activities, and domestic violence.

Zapotec culture in Juchitán exhibited forms of difference and ambiguity regarding male gender roles that were also absent from COCEI's artistic and political narratives. Men publicly identified in both Zapotec and Spanish by the Zapotec word *muxe* played a prominent role, distinct from those of both women and other males, in economic and ritual activity. Boys often took up this identity in adolescence and went on to perform economic roles associated with women, such as food preparation and marketing, to reside in their mothers' houses, and to dress in ways that were partly, though not entirely, associated with women. Muxe also played particular public roles in the division of labor at fiestas, where they also sat among women and danced as women, while exhibiting body forms, dress, and adornment that mixed common "male" and "female" characteristics. At the same time, prominent men rumored to be homosexual who did not adopt the muxe identity were spoken of pejoratively, and there was strong public sentiment against either men or women living together as couples.

The public prominence of an alternative male gender role illustrates in yet another way the richness and innovativeness of the culture that supports political radicalism in Juchitán, along with the prominence of ambiguity within that culture. It also underscores the fact that in its depictions of women and sexuality, as in its militancy, claims about the origins of political activism, and "disorganization," COCEI promotes representations of local life that correspond to some aspects of the worldviews of Juchitecos and arouse their passions, while at the same time the movement coexists with, and relies on, quite different, less homogeneous, and far more contested daily practices. Despite the harms and costs of its misrepresentations—such as the continuing exclusion of women from positions of political power, the lack of attention to women's domestic and occupational subordination, the exclusion from political discourse of a prominent form of male social life and marked muxe support for the PRI—COCEI achieves its ongoing strength, including gains valued by women and muxe, through its ability to balance (mis)representation and respect for the autonomy of daily practice.

COCEI's Cultural Project

In the course of its twenty-year history, COCEI has developed a unique and far-reaching cultural project. This has included an influential role in the activities of the government-funded Casa de la Cultura (Cultural Center), the promotion of painting, music, poetry, and Zapotec language among young Juchitecos from all classes, and the fostering of a prominent group of young, male artists. These artists brought their talents to COCEI mobilizations and began to make names for themselves on the state and national art scene. In addition, they formed the nucleus of what Campbell describes as an active local bohemian subculture (1990b, 377–85). As a result of these efforts,

large numbers of Juchitecos began to compose ballads and poems in honor of COCEI martyrs, revive disappearing arts and crafts, collect oral histories, write their memoirs, photograph local sites, and improve their ability to speak Zapotec. Additionally, Juchitán became a town where 19 year old indigenous youths discussed political philosophy and new trends in the art world as well as the fine points of their own historical and cultural traditions. (Campbell 1990b, 389)

COCEI's cultural project involved the elaboration of a narrative of Juchitán's history in political speeches and newspapers. This discourse also developed through the production of literary texts and artistic representations, historical and political analyses, and posters and T-shirts. Since 1975, COCEI intellectuals have published a sophisticated literary magazine, *Guchachi' Reza* (Zapotec for "sliced-open iguana"). The magazine has featured work by some of Mexico's foremost writers and artists, including sexually explicit illustrations that Juchiteco peasants had difficulty explaining to the organization's opponents. The magazine's title evokes Juchitecos' sense of identity and difference: "Now, what is our concern? That our children know how to speak Zapotec and play in Zapotec. This is our concern. Why? For the continuity of our history and so that in one hundred years or three centuries, we can continue eating iguana . . ." (López Nelio 1993, 235). COCEI's cultural project has bridged cultural and class distances with fluidity and eclecticism, at the same time that its public stances have reinforced class divisions and sought to keep various outsides out. COCEI has thus maintained control of its cultural borders by combining essentialist representations with boundary-crossing practices. COCEI not only revived and recreated a Juchiteco Zapotec identity and history, but did this in a way that connected young people in poor neighborhoods to a local cultural institution, to the imagery and practice of radical politics, and to national artists and intellectuals. These connections have encouraged Juchitecos to look outward, much as the midwives looked outward, not to embrace the foreign as better, but to make use of that which came from outside in elaborating the local. Juchitán's artistic connections to the outside have also attracted outsiders in, reinforcing Juchitecos' own sense of autonomy and importance, as well as bringing allies and protections at the national level.[14]

COCEI's cultural project, like other aspects of COCEI ideology and political practice, has been based in numerous discrepancies between pasts claimed and pasts experienced: "The coceísta intelligentsia recast Juchiteco history as a lineal trajectory culminating in the COCEI, and framed contemporary political events in terms of 'parallel' events in

Juchitán's past . . . its discourse about Zapotec culture, gender, and ethnic relations obscures social tensions and contradictions within the movement and Isthmus society in general" (Campbell 1990b, 494).

These tensions and contradictions related to characteristics of Juchitán's history ignored or denied in COCEI's cultural account, such as the subordinate position of women in Juchitán, mistreatment of surrounding ethnic minorities, long periods of coexistence with outside authorities, critiques of local power relations from within the PRI, and hidden meetings through which COCEI negotiated some of the terms of its existence with state and national authorities. COCEI's cultural representations have also ignored the ambitions of poor Juchitecos to advance economically and participate in the national consumer culture around them, as well as the continuing presence in Juchitán of some peasants and workers who supported the official party rather than COCEI.

Yet COCEI's strategic essentialism has enabled the movement to wrest control over public cultural display and experimentation from local elites and make use of its own sources of energy and talent to establish a new artistic arena and historical narrative. COCEI's cultural project has thus involved more than making use of existing historical memories and ethnic mechanisms for the purposes of political mobilization. COCEI has succeeded in developing a powerful regional presence and keeping the Mexican regime at bay in part by claiming cultural activities for a poor people's movement and making use of them not only to represent and define, but to empower and give pleasure. Such an explicit cultural project is without parallel in contemporary Mexico. It is a rare affirmation not only of the value of indigenous life and culture, but of that culture's ability to sustain and reinvent itself and to appropriate the outside from a position of equality and power.

Heterogeneity and Empowerment

COCEI has exhibited ambiguity with regard to violence, political division within families, electoral practices, levels of organization, and gender roles. Similarly, the claims of its political and intellectual leaders have contradicted those of ordinary Juchitecos, with regard to outsiders, past and present economic experiences, and the social experiences of women. Together, these ambiguities and contradictions suggest that it is the coex-

235

istence of multiple forms of difference that animates a radical social movement. This coexistence of difference has significant negative consequences, such as continuing violence toward and exclusions of women, rejection of political moderates, inability on the part of COCEI leaders to speak the language of groups outside Juchitán and thereby make alliances, and the absence of internal democracy. However, the coexistence of difference also provides new spaces for the production of meanings (Escobar 1992a, 82) that mobilize, impassion, and threaten, and thereby create new political forces and transform formal politics and daily life.

This understanding of radical politics calls into question portrayals of leftist movements as consisting of, or moving toward, unified and homogeneous class consciousness and action. It supports Mary Louise Pratt's call for ways of theorizing heterogeneity, as well as for recognizing that what looks like fragmentation to those in dominant positions can be both integrating and empowering to subordinate actors in social movements. Indeed, COCEI's internal characteristics and the multifacetedness of democracy in Juchitán in the 1990s suggests, as does Pratt herself, that democratic processes *produce* heterogeneity (Pratt 1996).

The ambiguity and contradiction within COCEI challenges claims about the presence of internal democracy, gender equality, and other praiseworthy characteristics in grassroots movements. In his work on Nicaragua, Roger Lancaster argues that popular religion played a central role in the radical consciousness of Sandinista supporters. The contradictions Lancaster identifies within popular religion and the distances between religion and the formal aspects of Sandinista politics parallel the discrepancies in Juchitán between practices of daily life and COCEI's public positions. In Lancaster's analysis, radical consciousness in Nicaragua is in significant part a place of hidden spaces and semiprivate discourses absent from the official voices of Sandinismo and liberation theology (1988, 143–44, 162). Power, in this context, "is an ongoing negotiation between macro- and micro-discourses, between official narratives and private rumors" (162), much as COCEI's power results from negotiations between Juchitecos' own understandings of their experiences and COCEI's public claims, and between women's reshaping of daily procedures and men's formal artistic narratives. The resulting social movement "can successfully reproduce itself, not only *despite*, but *because of*, the pervasiveness of complaint and conflict" (162–63, italics in original).

COCEI illustrates a radical politics characterized by flexible and changing mixtures of Leninist and new-social-movement political practices. COCEI's leaders chose over the course of twenty years to maintain and elaborate the distances between the discourses of the political movement and those of its supporters because the resulting political strategies were extraordinarily efficacious in wresting concessions from the state and maintaining organizational cohesion. Similarly, ordinary Juchitecos' tactics for describing and adapting the practices of daily life were effective in fostering survival and pleasure in workplace and courtyard, as well as in the more formal locations of radical politics. In its mixture of these two sets of activities, COCEI has maintained multiple locations of "complaint and conflict" and indeed reproduced itself in the face of formidable opposing powers.

COCEI's striking success in fostering cultural autonomy and political voice for indigenous people suggests that class-based and essentialist discourses, when combined in ambiguous ways with other forms of belief and action, can simultaneously reflect people's experiences and be of considerable strategic use. It is precisely within such spaces of ambiguity, the distances between militant confrontation and neighborhood accommodation, between Marxist analysis of development and daily work experience, between nonviolence and looting, that ordinary people act as "agent[s] of culture in process" (Fiske 1990, 86), reforming and adapting their own practices and beliefs with those invented by others. This is where ordinary Juchitecos as well as their leaders—at times in tension with one another—perform "an 'art of making' that proceeds by manipulating imposed knowledges and symbols at propitious moments" (Escobar 1992a, 74, drawing on de Certeau). In family courtyards, neighborhood committee meetings, cantinas, and schools, as well as in the many activities of the city's Casa de la Cultura, Juchitecos forge justifications of and limits to violence, reinterpret the meaning of their labor, cajole and defy political opponents, and reinvent ritual and art through a discourse of political opposition. In this way they give life to a political movement that can challenge existing relations of power.

8

Culture and Regional Politics in Mexico

Decentering the Regime

The complexity of regional history and the ambiguity and contradiction within COCEI show clearly that democratization in Juchitán can be understood only in part as the result of interaction between a centralized state and a unified grassroots opposition. Tropes of barbarism, contested domains of sovereignty, fragmented narratives, and multifaceted spaces of voice and accountability are also key ingredients in the construction of political meaning and the shaping of institutional change. Chapter 1 critiqued the state-centered model of Mexican politics, proposing in its stead the regional and cultural approach employed in subsequent chapters to analyze Juchitán's history and COCEI's mobilizations. This chapter will show that such decentered approaches are equally relevant to other Mexican regions and to analysis of Mexican politics generally. To do so, it will look first at alternative interpretations of the nineteenth century and the Cárdenas period. It will then focus on Mexico since the 1930s, examining, in addition to Juchitán, the states of Puebla, Guerrero, San Luis Potosí, Nayarit, and Sonora and the cities of Naranja and Namiquipa.[1]

Empirical evidence from these studies demonstrates that Mexican states and regions were not ruled in any direct sense by national authorities or even by political bosses themselves between the 1930s and the 1950s. Rather, as in Juchitán regional structures of power grew out of changing interactions between past local histories, contemporary local cultures and economies, and the needs and projects of an internally complex central state. Subsequently, the deaths of caciques in the 1950s and 1960s precipitated some of the central political dilemmas of recent decades—how to create functioning political parties and satisfactory arrangements of participation and representation. As a result of dramatic conflict over these issues, new regional forms of political voice and negotiation, as well as new forms of domination, were constructed throughout Mexico in the 1980s.

These new arrangements were shaped not only by the regional events immediately preceding them, but by the cultural practices and political conflicts of the cacique years as well. In analyzing these oftentimes circuitous historical relationships, I challenge the very notions of a national account and a circumscribed understanding of politics. I do this by showing how cultural practices of religion, ethnicity, political ideology, and gender played pivotal roles in shaping both regional and national forms of power. In the process, politics was understood, debated, and acted upon in routine and extraordinary ways by ordinary Mexicans. It was their actions, often at the regional level and in arenas outside of formal politics, that shaped and challenged the policies of state actors, providing vetoes, new languages, changing cultural and political forces, and alternative institutional arrangements.

While the argument in this chapter proceeds in two stages, focusing first on regional politics and then on regional cultures, its goal is to move beyond these distinctions. Detailed material from across Mexico reinforces the lessons of Juchitán: that politics is embedded in cultural meaning and practice and that what we traditionally label "national" occurs in and through what we call "regional." In this decentered view, culture is neither exclusively national nor regional. Rather, it refers to interrelated beliefs and practices that are as present in the policymaking of the central state (in its embrace of economic liberalization or its negotiation with armed Indians) as in municipal discourses of decency and citizenship (which shape electoral contestations) and elaborations of indigenous ritual (which interpret nationalism and negotiate state policies).

The Nineteenth Century and the Cárdenas Period

Revisionist work on the colonial period and the nineteenth century has illuminated the kinds of partial sovereignties and contested hegemonies that have been absent from analysis of postrevolutionary Mexico. Historians John Tutino (1986), Paul Vanderwood (1981), Alan Knight (1986), and Florencia Mallon (1995), for example, have demonstrated the regional rootedness of national events, the ongoing interaction between region and central state, and the incomplete presence of the central state in the nineteenth century.[2] Ernest Gruening (1934) and Alicia Hernández (1979) have addressed similar issues for the 1920s and 1930s, respectively, the former focusing on the endurance of regional power structures before Cárdenas and the latter identifying the mechanisms by which such forms of power persisted through the Cárdenas administration. The contributors to *Everyday Forms of State Formation* (Joseph and Nugent 1994) provide compelling illustrations of the varied cultural and political forms through which postrevolutionary hegemony was constructed.

By examining the course of the Hidalgo revolt in the Bajío region of central Mexico, Tutino explains why it gained support in some regions, but was opposed in others, as well as how the reasons for support or opposition differed from one region to the next. While Tutino focuses more on socioeconomic phenomena than on culture and politics, his analysis explains an event of national significance by looking closely at regional events and variation. It lays the groundwork for tracing regional changes and conflicts throughout the nineteenth century and then understanding the revolution as a product of these different regional events, as well as the result of actions of the central state under Díaz. This form of analysis is also employed by Alan Knight (1986) in his study of the revolution, in which he examines in detail the many different regional patterns and conflicts that occurred in its course. The absence of this focus on regions and ongoing rebellion led earlier historians to divide the nineteenth century too neatly, identifying a national-level progression from failed rebellion to unsuccessful centralization to political consolidation under Díaz, and then to revolution.

Paul Vanderwood's work on the Mexican *rurales* (rural police) during the Porfiriato complements Tutino's study of rebellions by demonstrating the incomplete and uneven nature of the state's presence under Porfirio Díaz, as well as the role of ideology and symbol in creating the myth of Díaz's all-powerful rule—among Díaz's contemporaries as well as later historians. "The pax Porfiriano," Vanderwood writes, "was more imagined than real, invented by those who stood to profit from such an impression." Vanderwood's research on what was actually going on among Díaz's rural police discredits many of the assertions that had been made on the basis of relative regime stability at the national level. In so doing, Vanderwood makes arguments similar to those I will make below about postrevolutionary regions and the national regime. For example, he finds the rurales to have had sizable roles in the creation and recreation of regional "orders and disorders." They were arbiters of local justice and had their own ambitions for economic and political power: "as frequently as *rurales* did the bidding of local strongmen, they refused to be hand-maidens to such authorities . . . the relationship between the *rurales* and a jéfe político . . . raised the question, Who is in charge?" (1981, 127).

Vanderwood also finds a coexistence of regional identities and power structures and the Porfirian state, and, relatedly, notes the very partial physical presence of the rurales in the territory of the country: "Regional-ism did not just evaporate under the impact of dictatorship and develop-ment. It took until 1892 to foist Porfirian governors on Michoacán and Chihuahua . . . And, unlike the dictator, governors frequently faced substantial opposition to their reelection" (1981, 85). Vanderwood de-scribes how hard Díaz worked to keep up the myth of the all-powerful and everywhere-present police, particularly among those for whom the rurales were not a day-to-day presence: "The president systematically created pomp and circumstances to feed imaginations" (135).

In the middle third of the twentieth century, regional bosses were perhaps the key element in this linking of the local and the national. Ernest Gruening and Alicia Hernández show clearly where twentieth-century bosses came from, and how and why their power was reinforced by the newly powerful central state. In a detailed discussion of fourteen states, Gruening describes the growing strength of the federal govern-ment, the high degree of conflict within that government (1934, 397), and the wide range of maneuverings by which that government coexisted with different regional forces in all of the states. Gruening catalogs, on the one hand, successful impositions of elected authorities by existing state governments and by the governments of adjacent states, and, on the other, successful oppositions to existing state governments and to such impositions.[3] His descriptions of state politics in the 1920s suggest sev-eral characteristics of Mexican politics that Hernández shows to have been present during the Cárdenas period and that bear some striking similarities to post-1968 contestation as well: the interweaving of state and national political power and policymaking; the combining of elec-toral and nonelectoral forms of political battle and maneuvering; the mobilization of civic coalitions for honest public administration and clean elections, and the endurance of regional political factions and ideologies. In addition, critiques of these political arrangements and pressures for reform have also been enduring characteristics of Mexican politics. Opposition to Díaz in the years after he was granted unlimited succession rights shared language and goals with reformist oppositions during and after the years of boss rule, in Juchitán and elsewhere, and with many of those who argue for procedural democracy today: "Within two years, reformists were campaigning for press freedom and judicial independence, for cutting fat from the army budget, and for broadening the electoral process" (Vanderwood 1981, 87).

In his discussion, Gruening never loses sight of the chieftains. Alicia Hernández explains the ways in which these revolutionary military leaders became political bosses, developing and elaborating forms of regional economic and political power even as the military as a whole became subservient to civilian authority (1979, 77–78). In her discussion of "la mecánica Cardenista," the mechanisms by which Cárdenas transformed the central state, Hernández documents the costs of overcoming these regional power bases. This is how her analysis differs from other studies of the Cárdenas period. Like other scholars (Hamilton 1982; Cornelius 1973), Hernández documents the political skill with which Cárdenas transferred and outmaneuvered politicians and military leaders. At the same time, however, Hernández shows how the regional locus of power persisted through the formation of the official party in 1929 and its subsequent reformulations, as well as through Cárdenas's political maneuverings and impositions at the state level in the early years of his term.

The National Revolutionary Party (PNR) was formed originally as a federation of regional parties, with its membership and power resting on the political power that regional groups and families had acquired. In 1933, these parties were dissolved and their members reincorporated individually into the PNR, "but this measure did not wipe out the force held by the local politicians nor eliminate the internal divisions in the party that these groups caused" (Hernández 1979, 27). The permanence and rootedness of these groups, in turn, derived from the fact that "each of their members, while ascending the political ladder, had been cultivating contacts and influence in the agrarian leagues, the unions, and other groups that made up the political life of each state" (27). Finally, the ability of these groups to organize state politics was essential for effective national public administration, "because in the decade of the 1920s the federal government still lacked centralized institutional mechanisms, and it was by way of these local groups that it obtained the effective regional control that it needed" (27).

Hernández shows that the very method by which Cárdenas outmaneuvered some power blocs in the states reinforced the strength of others. While he transformed the national institutional landscape, Cárdenas did not transform the human occupants of those institutions at the state level:

In 1936 he had restructured his second cabinet with people whom he thought believed in his idea of government, *while in the states he returned to power those political groups who had been displaced by Obregonismo and then by Callismo.* (1979, 74, italics mine)

These individuals and groups were willing to support Cárdenas's policies in the short term in exchange for access to power.[4] However, since the newly empowered leaders were not chosen because they shared Cárdenas's vision of Mexican politics, they were generally willing to support subsequent presidents in limiting or undoing the widespread reforms that had been achieved during Cárdenas's presidency.

Part of Nora Hamilton's pathbreaking analysis of Cardenismo mirrors Hernández's findings about regional power: Despite the dominance of new, progressive groups at the national level during the first half of Cárdenas's term, "the previously dominant coalition . . . did not disappear. Moreover, certain groups within this alliance . . . continued to be strengthened during this period, in part through state initiatives favoring private accumulation" (Hamilton 1982, 276). However, in focusing on the central state, and on the national class structure, Hamilton sees the events of the Cárdenas period as resulting in one predominant, national transformation: "Within the next fifteen years, a powerful governing group—the Sonoran dynasty—emerged and achieved the centralization of state power, eliminating regional military and political power bases . . ." (272). "The state has been limited as an arena for class conflict; in general it functions to repress mobilized groups it cannot coopt" (280). In contrast to these conclusions, the work of Gruening and Hernández, and the regional histories presented below, indicate that the state of Mexico was not a limited arena for conflicts. Even as centralized, potentially authoritarian mechanisms of control and mediation were constructed at the national level, other forms of control and mediation, perhaps equally likely to be repressive and authoritarian, but often in different ways and in conflict with the central government, were reinforced at the state and local level.

Mexican Regions since the 1930s

In the cities of Juchitán, Naranja, and Namiquipa and the states of Puebla, Guerrero, Nayarit, San Luis Potosí, and Sonora, the new postrevolutionary state coexisted with powerful regional bosses. These bosses and their political allies maintained power from the 1930s until the late 1950s or early 1960s, steering a course between accommodation and autonomy. While the 1930–60 framework corresponds roughly to the periodization of the state-centered analysis, the regional histories suggest a different understanding of that period and connect its key political events and conflicts more directly to what came before and after. The autonomies secured by the caciques responded to claims for which regional groups had long been fighting, often since the middle of the nineteenth century. The politics of caciquismo itself engendered ongoing political opposition to both its procedures and substance, oppositions linking discourses of clean government and administrative efficiency to claims about religion, ethnicity, social justice, and democracy. In addition, the immense difficulties of forging a public politics following the deaths of the bosses fostered a turbulent process of political contestation in the 1960s and subsequent decades; the task of forming a political party was complex and urgent, and the result uneven and contested. The dynamics of this contestation were shaped profoundly by the events of the cacique years, in interaction with initiatives of the central state. In turn, the conflicts and alliances that emerged in the 1960s and 1970s, which differed from region to region, established the framework for negotiations over electoral competition, economic restructuring, the autonomy of popular movements, and the meaning of citizenship in the 1980s and 1990s.

In Juchitán, as previous chapters have shown, regional political arrangements during General Charis's rule, which began with negotiations with President Cárdenas, succeeded in garnering regional support for the new national state precisely because they left the Isthmus alone, guaranteeing for Juchitecos, at least initially, the sort of economic and political autonomy for which they had repeatedly rebelled. In addition, the multi-class alliance that supported Charis shared in the elaboration of Zapotec language and ritual practices, an activity that was reinforced by the central state's use of narratives of Indianness in shaping and legitimizing its rule. The PRI barely existed in the Isthmus between 1930 and 1960, with political activists calling themselves Charistas even as they supported the new national system, and with mass organizations forming later and far more unevenly than accounts of national politics suggest. In addition, Charis was challenged almost immediately by local and state-level reformers, with his tenure as regional boss marked not only by intrigue, murder, and a mixture of protection and exploitation of peasants, but by stormy, public political battles—often centered around elections—between two opposing elite camps with conflicting visions of present and future political life.

These tensions came to a head in Juchitán in the 1960s and early 1970s, years that were marked by dramatic, public conflicts over private property, electoral procedures, and the place of the PRI. The politics of the Charis period had produced neither a political party nor any other accepted mechanisms for distributing and exercising local political authority. The construction of schools, hospitals, highways, and, finally, a dam—the fruits of the regional-national alliance and of national economic development plans—had begun a process of urban commercialization and agricultural change that transformed daily life and public discourse. In the name of the pueblo, elites actively mobilized peasants and workers behind two major projects, both of which were successful: in the mid-1960s, the repeal of the presidential decree that would have turned most of the Juchitán irrigation district into an ejido; and, in the early 1970s, the election of the reformist Tarú government in opposition to the PRI.

Thus, in Juchitán it was elites in the 1960s—not grassroots radicals in the 1970s—who first promoted mass mobilizations and widespread electoral participation as political strategies and who first articulated thoroughgoing critiques of failed economic development, widespread poverty, and political corruption. Throughout this and subsequent conflicts over political competition and social life, the very meaning of citizenship was debated and reshaped in Juchitán. The promotion of elections in the 1960s and early 1970s, as in subsequent years, did not signify an overriding desire for electoral democracy on the part of Juchitecos so much as an

245

ongoing weighing of the importance of elections as compared to other pressing matters, such as the internal character of the PRI, the value of a ruling party, and the path of economic development.

In the wake of the failure of the 1971–73 Tarú government, radical students in Juchitán formed COCEI, gathering consistent support among Juchitecos by drawing on and reshaping ethnic language, customs, art, and historical knowledge. As the preceding two chapters have shown, COCEI fought for rural land and agricultural opportunities, urban wages and benefits, and municipal sovereignty, withstanding violent repression in the process. In the early years of Mexico's reforma política, the radical movement pressured the regime to annul fraudulent elections and recognize its victory in the subsequent contest. During its 1989–92 and 1992–95 administrations, the COCEI government participated in the Salinas administration's concertación social program, thereby securing considerable development funds for the city. Along with only a small number of other indigenous and leftist groups, COCEI is recognized by the Mexican government as a legitimate and autonomous political force.

The presence of COCEI not only provided a powerful force for radicalism and democracy, but prompted considerable change within the PRI as well. The perceived threat of militant opposition increased the clout of reformists within the official party. While reformist groups had played pivotal roles in regional politics throughout the century—in opposition to Charis in the 1940s and 1950s, in support of internal primaries in the 1960s, and in opposition to the PRI in the early 1970s—they had consistently lost their bids for control of the party, with a new version of the old-style boss gaining the upper hand in the early 1980s. COCEI's presence, however, and its success in winning elections, fortified the alliance between the central government and the reformers within the PRI. By the late 1980s, the Salinas government faced two substantial regional forces in the Isthmus that had not existed a decade earlier: a radical opposition committed to negotiation and some forms of economic development, and a moderate wing of the elite and the official party committed to some degree of electoral competition, administrative openness, and social well-being.

At the state level, reform efforts in Oaxaca made explicit the ongoing and complex nature of regional, state, and national relations. Federal reform attempts in the 1940s and 1950s provided limited but significant support and access to office for the modernizing, reform coalition in Juchitán, the Front for Democratic Renovation. The rapid failure of federal efforts, however, contributed to the Front's inability to successfully challenge General Charis. The Isthmus land-reform effort of the 1960s, sponsored by Oaxaca governor Brena Torres and President López Mateos, also failed to challenge existing power relations, serving instead to unify multiclass opposition to outside intervention and give new life to the pueblo-versus-outside politics that had predominated during the years of rebellion and of Charis's cacicazgo.

In the 1960s, the Benito Juárez Dam in the Isthmus, and accompanying agricultural projects, promoted new forms of economic development. These projects affected the interaction between region, state, and nation in two related ways. On the one hand, they inaugurated the process of economic transformation and disruption that would play a central role in the development of COCEI. On the other hand, the development projects promoted the growth of entrepreneurial groups with which the federal government could ally in seeking political reform and economic growth in the state of Oaxaca. Thus, federal investment promoted two oppositions to established political elites: COCEI and the modernizing economic sector. The regime's strategy in the 1980s, in the face of escalating class conflict in the Isthmus, was to make use of *both* of these oppositions to bring about political and economic activity more in keeping with national goals than had previously existed in the state. Thus, the regime's reformist project of replacing the elites who ascended to or consolidated power after the Mexican Revolution with new groups more open to political competition and state-led economic development—and at times more willing to tolerate a role for leftist popular movements— was a forty-year process in Oaxaca.

In Puebla and Guerrero, the breakdown of state-level cacicazgos took different forms, and led to different political scenarios in the 1980s and 1990s.[5] In Puebla, the university was the arena for conflict over the Avila Camacho cacicazgo. As Wil Pansters demonstrates, this conflict was shaped and polarized by a discourse of anticommunism. Promoted by state-level elites who linked drugs, pornography, crime, the progressive church, leftist guerrillas, and homosexuality, this discourse pitted leftist students, workers, and peasants against the coalition of bourgeoisie, church, and private sector upon which the Avila Camacho cacicazgo had been based. Grassroots mobilizations within and outside the university, together with this "moral panic" (Pansters 1990, 131), eventually produced two new political forces, a result in part similar to that which occurred in Juchitán. Both new political groups in Puebla consisted primarily of younger people, a left wing linked to the old university and to poor people's struggles, and a right wing, with its own new university, linked to the private sector, opposed to statism, and partially allied with the conservative PAN party. In addition, as in Juchitán, the combination of discursive conflict, mobilization, and political maneuvering shaped the nature of citizenship and beliefs about politics in Puebla in enduring ways.[6]

In Puebla, as in Juchitán, polarized conflict provided a pathway for reformist federal intervention, though with differing results. In Puebla, Echeverría initially supported the leftist student and grassroots groups, much as he sided with the radical COCEI in Juchitán. However, as COCEI moved beyond his control, the regime responded with violence and military intervention from the 1970s to the mid-1980s. When reformist accommodations occurred later in that decade, they centered around the participation of a powerful left. In Puebla, in contrast, the regime in the 1960s and 1970s acted as an arbiter between left and right. The left in Puebla did not emerge from the radicalism of the 1970s with a coherent political movement, while the new right used the preexisting heritage of conservative ideology, the presence of the PAN, and the emphasis on elections to influence the official party and emerge as a powerful political force.

In Guerrero, what Armando Bartra (1991) calls an *"agrarista* cacicazgo" was established under Cárdenas. The governor of Guerrero promoted agrarian reform in the 1930s, renewing radicalism of the 1920s, which had been defeated, and including former guerrillas in the implementation of the reform. Radical organizations and leaders thus survived the formation of new state institutions, though, in Bartra's analysis, they were fully controlled within the corporatist framework.[7] In the 1950s, new organizations sought unsuccessfully to survive outside of the PRI. As in Puebla, full-blown conflict occurred in the 1960s, in this case, as in Juchitán, escaping regime control, though here leading to an armed guerrilla struggle. As in Puebla and Juchitán in the same years, opposition in Guerrero first occurred within the system and included contestation about the meaning of citizenship. Protest against electoral fraud in the town of Atoyac in the early 1960s, however, brought escalating conflicts between civilians and soldiers, as well as an ongoing military presence and accompanying abuses.

Led by schoolteachers Genaro Vásquez and Lucio Cabañas in successive mobilizations, the guerrillas in Guerrero survived for at least nine years. This armed battle, in Bartra's view, separated antiregime struggle from the daily lives of the nonguerrilla population, where efforts for change had been rooted since the 1950s. In contrast to Juchitán, it thus put a stop to processes of radicalization and grassroots opposition. Guerrilla leaders in Guerrero, in Bartra's view, did not see the possibility of the sort of nonviolent social movement that indeed emerged in subsequent years in other parts of Mexico. Like Pansters in his discussion of anticommunism in Puebla, Bartra combines political economy and attention to political discourse in explaining the course of regional political crises, attributing the strategic choices of the left in Guerrero in significant part to the evolving worldview of its leaders. These choices and their consequences, in turn, elicited particular regime responses. In Guerrero, the regime responded to the guerrilla conflict with agricultural reform. Grassroots movements that formed in the 1980s then positioned themselves against the state and its agrarian agencies and policies, rather than primarily against regional caciques and elites as in Puebla and Juchitán. This opposition, in turn, fostered new forms of engagement, with the result that some of the strongest grassroots movements in Guerrero in the late 1980s and the 1990s were producer cooperatives. These groups were more willing to negotiate with the state over economic issues, and more willing to pursue innovative economic relations with the outside, than the leftist movements in Puebla and Juchitán.

In both Puebla and Guerrero, as in Juchitán, oppositions to boss rule in the 1950s, which failed to overturn existing power relations, were followed by more far-reaching and disruptive challenges in the 1960s. As in Juchitán, these challenges began around issues of elections, accountability, and moderate reform, and concluded with militant, class-based pressures for economic, political, and cultural transformations. These arguments were fierce and public, and they were carried on largely outside of and in explicit critique of official, national politics. What these studies of Juchitán, Puebla, and Guerrero demonstrate is that key political phenomena of the 1980s—the formation of a leftist movement and its participation in concertación social in Juchitán; the strengthening of the

PAN and the development of new forms of political influence on the part of business groups in Puebla; and the establishment of agricultural cooperatives in Guerrero—originated in Mexican regions in the 1960s and 1970s.

In his analysis of political conflict in San Luis Potosí, in central Mexico, Enrique Márquez (1987) emphasizes the importance of regional cultural history and structures of power in explaining the phenomenon of Navismo, a political movement that first challenged state-level caciquismo between 1958 and 1961, and then reappeared in 1981 to challenge Governor Carlos Jonquitud Barrios, also head of the corrupt national teachers' union. Dr. Salvador Nava Martínez's opposition to boss rule shared several characteristics with the reform movements in Juchitán and Puebla. The Potosí Civic Union, like Juchitán's Front for Democratic Renovation, which opposed Charis, was a coalition of "good government" supporters who sought to end the "fierce, greedy cacicazgo of Gonzalo N. Santos" (Márquez 1987, 112). Presidential candidate López Mateos supported the Union, declaring during a campaign visit that "cacicazgos persist only where the people tolerate them" (113). Following a statewide Navista strike before and after municipal elections, which Nava won with more than 90 percent of the vote, the central government recognized the opposition victory and oversaw the transfer of municipal power to Nava. However, when Nava sought the governorship in 1961, he was rejected by the PRI, and his independent candidacy resulted in military occupation of the state and his own arrest. A similar pattern occurred in the 1980s, when initial support on the part of the de la Madrid administration for Nava in municipal elections gave way in the face of Governor Jonquitud Barrios's hostility to the reformer.

In contrast to Juchitán, Puebla, and Guerrero, where conflict came to assume a class-based character after initial multiclass reform efforts, Navismo recurred in the 1980s with much the same multiclass membership and middle-class ideology it had assumed in the 1950s. Despite this difference, Navismo reinforces the picture of Mexican politics derived from the preceding discussion of other states. While the PRI indeed existed in San Luis Potosí, it took a backseat to Gonzalo Santos until 1958 and functioned largely as a set of impositions from Mexico City thereafter. The locus of political belief and activism in the 1950s and in the 1980s was outside of the PRI, and, as in Juchitán, Puebla, and Guerrero, the reformers' inability to gain a place in the official party greatly complicated the task of forging political mechanisms to mediate interests and generate consent.

Márquez explains this process in much the way I have interpreted accounts of post-cacique politics in other states, as a politics structured by caciquismo rather than corporatism. In his analysis, attention to national electoral processes and state policies failed to take into account the extent to which "the dynamics of regional power and the presence of local traditions of political culture and ideology help explain the progress as well as the absence of political parties" (1987, 111). The creation of new forms of interest mediation, partially successful between 1967 and 1979, and associated with the "modernized" politics favored by central-state reformers, was limited by rural social structures and caciquismo. Where a new consensus did arise, "it did so primarily in the capital, and even then only among businessmen" (121). The politics and cultural life of San Luis Potosí, like those of Juchitán and Puebla, thus had a distinctly local identity and history and can be understood as part of a local, in contrast to a national, project, which Márquez calls the "Potosí style" (121–23).

The growth and national prominence of Navismo in the 1950s provides another example of the high level of conflict in the period of supposed corporatist peace. It also demonstrates that in San Luis Potosí, as in Juchitán, cacique politics and opposition to it—and, subsequently, the very construction of a political party—were the central political characteristics of the postrevolutionary decades. In addition, Navismo's 1980s incarnation brought considerable prominence to the PAN, with which it was allied. In this way, the regional history that engendered the appearance and reappearance of Navismo was significant in shaping national negotiations surrounding both elections and business-government relations.

This pathway of resurgence for the PAN in San Luis Potosí shows that it is not simply or primarily the homogeneous strength of the center, or of center-business alliances, that has set the underpinnings for neoliberal reform in Mexico. Rather, the hegemony that permits economic restructuring results from ongoing contestation and reformulation. This can be seen clearly in the northern state of Sonora, where business interests have played a prominent role in politics in recent years.[8] In Sonora, politics in the 1920s and 1930s involved confrontation and negotiation, often centered around elections, between regional bosses, as well as between civil and military leaders. Supporters of General Calles generally prevailed, controlling access to power and running the state branch of the national party, until they were ousted by the combined efforts of religious groups, peasants demanding land, and leftist politicians when Cárdenas won out in his national power struggle with Calles. Here, as in the quite different southern state of Guerrero and central states of Michoacán and Nayarit, leftist forces active before and during the revolution achieved a role in the political arrangements overseen by Cárdenas. In Sonora, peasant and worker organizations sought and partially gained influence in state politics in the 1930s and 1940s, culminating in the activities of the General Union of Mexican Workers and Peasants (UGOCM) under Jacinto López. These activities parallel in some ways the challenges of the Front for Democratic Renovation in Juchitán and the Potosí Civic Union, though popular movements in Sonora during this time represented an explicit class challenge in a way the other organizations did not. The successful exclusion of these challenges from Sonoran politics in the 1950s was followed by new forms of organization and opposition within the official party after 1958 and a series of reform movements in the 1960s. When reform negotiations failed, broad popular movements mobilized around gubernatorial elections.

The Echeverría administration responded to the radical challenge posed by 1975 land invasions in Sonora with federal intervention and land expropriation. Land recipients went on to form the Coalition of collective Ejidos of the Yaqui and Mayo Valleys (CECVYM), an enduring rural organization of collective agricultural enterprises that negotiated successfully with state agencies and addressed economic and social needs of its members. Business groups responded to their weakened position first by transforming the PAN into a strong opposition in the 1980s, and then, in 1985, by conducting preelection negotiations with the PRI candidate for governor and supporting him in the elections (Guadarrama S. 1977, 104–5). This pattern of events closely resembles that in Juchitán— a region quite different economically and culturally from Sonora—with reform movements within the PRI giving way to class-based challenge, regime intervention, and, in the 1980s, the coexistence of an enduring peasant movement and a strengthened position for pro-business reformers within the PRI. In this light, it can be seen that new forms of business-state relations, a central component of Salinas's economic liberalization, have developed in close interaction with radical grassroots mobilizations.

In the center-western state of Nayarit, an *agrarista* cacicazgo broadly similar to that in Guerrero engendered not only a moderate reformist movement, centered on schoolteachers and their newspaper, but prompted the rise of a famous local bandit, El Caso, to the status of regional peasant leader. El Caso, who championed peasant causes, formed the Congress of Tuxpán in 1956, initiating a new, large-scale grassroots movement that expanded in the course of the 1960s and achieved significant gains between 1966 and 1970. As in Juchitán and Guerrero, furthermore, one sort of opposition in the 1960s contributed to the formation of a more innovative and potentially radical one in the 1970s, in Nayarit a coalition of ejidos, the Union de Ejidos Lázaro Cárdenas (UELC) (Hernández 1990).[9] The survival of this movement through the 1980s provided a model of a producer organization that, along with the CECVYM in Sonora, influenced the formation of producer cooperatives in Guerrero and Oaxaca in the late 1980s and also played a role in negotiations with the central state over agricultural economics as part of a national coalition of producer organizations, UNORCA.

These accounts demonstrate that twentieth-century Mexican politics has been significantly shaped by the formation and decline of regional cacicazgos, as well as by the conflicts over authority that succeeded them. They suggest both a common pattern of political crises (different from those put forth by the state-centered analysis) and a panoply of contexts in which these crises occurred, with the result that political beliefs and power relations varied widely across states and regions in the 1980s, much as they had in preceding decades. While on some level such a conclusion is obvious—the political, economic, and cultural landscape of Mexico has always been characterized as diverse—the claim here is that such variation directly contradicts the relative homogeneity of political process and outcome postulated by the state-centered approach.

Culture and Daily Life

One of the reasons such alternatives occur is the disjunction between the fabric and substance of regional life and the identity and projects of the central state. This disjunction was underlined above by Márquez's description of Potosinidad, with its historical roots and cultural identity separate from national Mexicanness, itself a complex category (R. Bartra 1992; Lomnitz-Adler 1992). Pansters and (Armando) Bartra, in contrast, each assumed that caciquismo and corporatism in Puebla and Guerrero were compatible until the explosive civic conflicts of the 1960s. I will question this compatibility by examining local political and cultural practices in three locations, one northern, one central, and one southern. The power relations of local life in these places were distinct from those promoted by the central state, and they obstructed state projects. In addition, the forms of alternative belief and practice constructed in each of them—including historically rooted regional identities and political cultures—influenced regional and national politics in key ways.

In his study of regional politics in Michoacán from the 1930s to the 1960s, *The Princes of Naranja* (1986), Paul Friedrich details the political and cultural life of a regional cacique and his political clan. Jenny Purnell's work (1993) on nineteenth-century Michoacán and the counterrevolutionary Cristero wars of the 1920s forms a useful complement to Friedrich's analysis, in that she demonstrates the striking variation not only between region and central state, but within the state of Michoacán, where some towns pursued militant organizing for land reform and took up arms to defend the postrevolutionary government, while others violently opposed the policies of that government in the name of Catholicism and private property. Purnell locates the origins of this conflict, which had considerable impact on national politics, in the evolution of nineteenth-century patterns of landholding and political rule, on the one hand, and, on the other, in the ways in which beliefs about religion, ethnic authority, and community life were articulated in an increasingly politicized environment in the decades preceding the Cristero Rebellion. In this way, Purnell does for an earlier period what Pansters did for the 1960s in Puebla, and what Bartra suggested for the 1970s in Guerrero— she shows that cultural discourses directly influenced the form and course of major political conflicts.

Friedrich's work, situated in one of the two divergent pathways Purnell described, further emphasizes the distance between regional and national power relations by showing that even those towns that supported the postrevolutionary government did so by way of formal political arrangements and daily cultural practices that severely limited the reach of central authorities. In Juchitán and Naranja, it is more appropriate to speak of "Charistas" or "Caso politics" (the Casos were the ruling political clan in Naranja) than of the official party. In each place, the boss supported by Cárdenas had considerable local support in the 1920s, but was denied entry to local and, especially, state-level politics until Cárdenas arranged a deal between the boss, his popular supporters, and regional elites. While such a deal nominally entailed the formation of local branches of national mass organizations, the National Peasant Confederation (CNC) did not become a means of central-government control in either place; in Juchitán it barely existed, and in Naranja it existed as a result of local agrarian mobilizations and remained largely under the control of the boss's allies. For example, when the boss's political group expropriated the ejido land of a rival faction, they could convince and/or buy off the representatives of the central government to support their claim. When President Avila Camacho opposed their policies, they disregarded national directives: "The delegate read them the order. Ezequiel said they were going to disobey" (Friedrich 1986, 23).

In Naranja, as in Juchitán, the ability to gain and achieve the status of boss depended on the capacity, repeatedly attributed to Charis, to *traer gente*, to demonstrate and mobilize a following. In Michoacán, according to Friedrich, "Local mounted militias were a key factor in the struggle for power in the village, the region, and even the state and national arenas . . . candidates who could bring a few thousand such men into the state capital stood a better chance of getting elected" (1986, 8).

In both Juchitán and Naranja, wordplay in the indigenous language was a central component of local political speech (Friedrich 1986, 16), and the regional boss gained his hearing in state and national political arenas through a combination of political and military connections and claims to representation of Indian identities and interests (30–31, 174). In each place, the authoritarian aspects of the boss's control were complemented by the relative autonomy he achieved for the region.

The administration of justice in Naranja was distinctly local. Camilo Caso, a "grassroots judge and lawyer," arranged settlements among people who brought their disagreements to him, "usually in the form of a payment of damages that entails a rather complicated network of obligations." For cases that went outside of Naranja, "he or Scarface (Elías Caso) often make informal judgments of some sort that are transmitted to the forces of federal justice in the county seat." The Casos' decisions combined impulses toward equal justice for all with "the size of the bribes and the respective political affiliations of the parties—two factors that remain important at the county level . . ." The politics of local justice, furthermore, like cacique politics generally, functioned in key ways to keep the outside out: "Camilo tries to judge in accordance with local mores, to distribute compensations and punishments over as wide a field as possible, and to protect fellow villagers from state and national law . . ." (Friedrich 1986, 37).

Friedrich's work demonstrates considerable disjunction between regional experiences and national projects. In both Juchitán and Naranja, local life exhibits qualities of intensity, self-awareness, and self-definition at odds with the notion of a territory penetrated by state-centered ideological, economic, and mobilizational mechanisms.[10] Corporatism, as it has been used to describe Mexican politics, implies state structuring of political interests and institutions, just as or even before those interests emerge in public form. An all-encompassing state, similarly, implies centralized regulation of social and political life. Cacique politics, in contrast, is much more caught up in local conceptions of the world and local structures of power. Caciques allow, in paternalistic and authoritarian ways, not only for people's survival, but also for aspects of shared community life whose dynamics differ considerably from those of national projects. The accounts presented above demonstrate that in Juchitán and Naranja, from the 1930s to the 1960s, local cultural forms acted simultaneously to challenge the directives and projects of the central state and to shelter and recreate forms of local autonomy, including the distribution of ejido land, the use of indigenous language, the administration of local justice, and the manipulation of electoral activity.

In the northern Mexican town of Namiquipa, anthropologists Daniel Nugent (1989), and Ana Alonso (1988a, 1988b) found a clearly discernible, historically rooted local life distinct from and often opposed to the institutions and policies of the central state. Nugent and Alonso traced the twentieth-century culture of Namiquipans to the origins of the town as a land-grant, military settlement at the end of the eighteenth century. Alonso (1988a) examines the notions of civilization, male honor, female reproduction, and sexuality that were constructed during and after the period of vanguard civilizing that continued through most of the nineteenth century, when the settlers acted with the full support of what central state existed. After the conclusion of the Apache wars around

1880, a succession of landlords and capitalists, with the support of the Porfirian state, attacked just the autonomy that had served preceding states so well in their tasks of pacification (Nugent 1989, 220). As a result, the supposed "Porfirian peace" consisted in Namiquipa of a succession of middle-class and peasant rebellions and confrontations with the federal army, the national rural police, and U.S. mercenaries over control of land and exercise of economic power. Alonso shows the ways in which the discourses of gender and sexuality developed during the earlier period fostered opposition to the newer state policies; the commercialization of land, for example, was experienced and opposed as an attack on male honor (1988a, 19–22).

During the Mexican Revolution, Namiquipans sided first with Villa, in his militant, armed defense of local interest. Then, when the United States occupied the area in opposition to Villa, they abruptly shifted their stance. In 1916, Namiquipans formed local militias that cooperated with the United States in opposing the by-then nationalist and anti-imperialist Villa. In explaining this perhaps surprising shift—a Mexican pueblo actively collaborating with the North Americans—Alonso focuses on the disjunction between the local identity and needs of the Namiquipans and the nationalist consciousness that scholars tend to assume was present in all locations (1988b).

Nugent's description of the subsequent period of coexistence between the Namiquipans, now *ejidatarios*, and the central state resembles the situation in Juchitán and Naranja during the same years, as well as the coexistence of region and nation described by Vanderwood with regard to the Porfiriato. While Namiquipa, because of its enormous ejido, constituted "an image the State hoped to perpetuate throughout the country" of a community where agrarian conflict had been successfully resolved (Nugent 1989, 225), Nugent observed that local institutions, such as the municipal government, the ejidal commissariat, and the municipal and state police, were "nominally connected to the State and to the Party," but that "power was in fact being exercised by the leaders of the successful faction to emerge from the Revolution" (1989, 225). As a result, Nugent argues that the actual organization of relations of power and production within the community and especially within the ejido remained largely in the hands of the Namiquipans. Alonso (1992) and Nugent (1992) also discern pathways of difference and opposition between region and central state in the construction of music, work, and technologies of beauty in Namiquipa. In daily practices central to their identities and family economies, men and women borrowed selectively and creatively from cultural forms north of the border, using them to elaborate the *norteño* identity that had long opposed the cultural and political claims of the center, and that has become central to north-south divides in Mexican politics today.

Nugent explains that the myth of the centralized state could take hold in both political and academic discourse because, from the outside, the local scene looked like a miniature version of the supposed national peace. The same was true for Juchitán and Naranja. Resistance and opposition were local during these years. The cacique, while presiding over intensely local politics and culture quite different from those promoted by the state, could at the same time be imagined to be an extension of the state. However, in carrying out the functions assigned him during these years—the maintenance of order, the administration of justice, and the establishment of official organizations and agencies—the boss presided over regional identities and politics—in Juchitán and Naranja, as in Puebla and San Luis Potosí—that had direct impacts on national politics.

Regional power structures were not simply obstructions to national arrangements, but rather active forces in shaping local people's daily experiences and defining the arenas and possibilities of central-state action. In Juchitán, for example, the elaboration of Zapotec culture in a city during the years of Charis's rule—the ability to resist the hegemony of the national urban culture, while actively borrowing from that culture—provided resources of which COCEI made extensive and creative use several decades later in its militant, class-based mobilizations. The endurance of Zapotec ethnicity in Juchitán resulted both from local phenomena—the boss's protections and the peripheral but relatively strong nature of the economy—and from the ways in which the national project in the 1930s and 1940s provided tools and pathways for the survival of local ethnicity, even as it attacked ethnic identities generally. COCEI's enduring strength, in turn, along with the successes of other regional grassroots organizations, pressed Mexican politics in such a way that concertación social—the coexistence of established grassroots oppositions and technocratic, market-oriented PRI officials in Mexico City—could be imagined and implemented in the 1990s, as could turbulent and conflictual local democracy in Juchitán. In addition, in Chiapas, government officials, as well as the Zapatistas themselves, could view the 1994 uprising in part through the lens of this coexistence and democracy, and thereby envision, albeit in conflicting ways, negotiated resolutions to the conflict.

General Charis's support for Zapotec ethnic practices was complemented and enabled by his resistance to the CNC and CTM, the national peasant and worker organizations, and his attention to local land and livestock associations. This stance, by helping to keep out the state, contributed to the fostering of spaces for discussion and resistance in the 1960s, in local organizations, in the newly forming PRI, and in the local newspaper. The church, the opposition movement within the teachers' union, the central market, and local information and media networks further expanded spaces for voice and autonomy outside the domain of state authority and electoral politics in subsequent decades. Myths and practices of women's economic and cultural prominence, furthermore, constituted one of the most important of such spaces, in part because women played a key role in incorporating foreign influences while maintaining the prestige of Zapotec language and daily customs. As a result of this women's activity, which was closely related to predominant male control over violence, artistic production, and formal political narrative, Zapotec culture could simultaneously galvanize political solidarity and negotiate the tasks of daily life in practical ways. In its public elaboration of an alternative male gender role, furthermore, Zapotec culture demonstrated its capacity for complex forms of cultural experimentation and autonomy.

In these ways—the selective creation and adaptation of formal political procedures, the elaboration of genres of ethnic practice, and a particular linking of gender, sexuality, and cultural production—the boss and the system of power that he represented set the stage for a politics of conflict and innovation. In this politics, the central state was one actor—neither all-encompassing nor unchanging—among several. The enduring self-government that resulted has been one prominent component of the struggle for democracy in Mexico. A focus on the pathways of the hegemony that joined region and center in Juchitán in the 1930s and how that hegemony changed over time—on cacique power structures and the re-signification of ethnic identity—is thus essential for understanding both the uneven phenomenon of democratization at the national level and the meaning of democracy in the daily lives of Juchitecos.

In Naranja, the power of the Casos, together with the battle against and reservoir of resentment toward their cacicazgo, was the most salient characteristic of regional politics, and, as in Juchitán, this sort of power made central-state penetration and control very problematic. It meant that the nature of local rule was in some ways personal and arbitrary, was contested by numerous local individuals and groups, and did not directly represent or implement the beliefs and policies of the central state. It meant that the state couldn't carry out its policies at the regional level—Avila Camacho's efforts to settle an ejido dispute were successfully resisted by Scarface and the other "princes," and later outside efforts to support local oppositions to the Casos were overturned through alliances between the local princes and other outside allies. The state thus faced limits in using the people and political organizations of this region in a politics aimed alternately at implementing regional economic changes, establishing new political procedures, and combating class-based oppositions.

Cuauhtémoc Cárdenas's enormous success in Michoacán in the 1988 presidential elections can be seen as an event comparable to the mobilizations of COCEI in Juchitán in the 1970s and 1980s or the growing political clout of the PAN in Puebla or Sonora in the early 1980s, in terms of demonstrating the national implications of the kinds of regional conflicts and practices outlined above. In Michoacán, the organizations that were supposedly the local organs of the national PRI "suddenly" exercised a completely different politics, and the national and state PRI responded with considerable violence, electoral fraud, and social-welfare funding. The local nature of identity and politics demonstrated in Friedrich's work on the 1930–1960 period explains the context in which such political shifts could occur, while the more recent work of Rob Aitken (1994) uncovers the dynamics of recent changes. Aitken shows that support for Cárdenas was by no means a straightforward transfer of the loyalty of local political clans, the descendants of *agrarista* caciques like the Casos, from the PRI to Cárdenas. Rather, Cárdenas's support grew out of challenges to established cacique power on the part of *ejidatarios* and indigenous people who had begun to resist cacique control by competing for local offices and organizing independent indigenous and peasant movements (20–23). Massive opposition politics in Michoacán was thus facilitated by people's roots in past Cardenismo *and* their opposition to it. Furthermore, the regional and cultural divisions in Michoacán made support for the PRD an intensely local and varied matter, rooted in the partial autonomy of the local branches of national mass organizations and the persistence of ethnic identities and practices amenable to new forms of party politics. Here, as in Juchitán, the key to understanding the regional politics of the 1980s and its dramatic impacts on national politics lies in unraveling cultural and political histories that preceded the state formation of the 1930s and developed in partial autonomy from corporatist organizations.

In sum, the work of Friedrich, Aitken, Nugent, and Alonso, and my own on Juchitán, suggest a definition of politics considerably broader than that employed in standard accounts of Mexican politics, one that includes the way people define various aspects of their collective social life: religion, violence, gender, kinship, land cultivation, and positions of public economic and political authority. The successes of COCEI in Oaxaca, Cuauhtémoc Cárdenas in Michoacán, and the PAN in the center and north stem directly from these arenas. State officials today negotiate with independent grassroots oppositions and worry about democratic political competition in significant part because ethnicity was preserved and recreated and the PRI and its mass organizations kept at a distance in Juchitán, because the Casos joked in Tarascan, controlled local politics, and oversaw land distribution and agricultural practice, and because anti-communist discourses in Puebla could survive regime hostility, link up with a redefined PAN, and connect social and religious commitments to a neoliberal economic agenda. Similarly, the successes and failures of the Salinas administration in implementing its National Solidarity Program, as well as the short- and long-term effects that program will have, depend on distinct interactions, rooted in particular histories, with regional popular movements (Haber 1994; Fox and Moguel 1993), indigenous organizations (Fox 1994b), urban social forces (Contreras and Bennett 1994), and, as in Chiapas, cacique-based power structures (Harvey 1994). Region as a political location and culture as a political force are central to Mexican politics because they are the places where life is experienced and characterized, where national initiatives are mediated and become practice, and where repositories of habitual, accommodating, alternative, and challenging political discourses are perpetually recast. Seen in this light, the numerous cultural phenomena described in this section are as much the shapers of power in Mexico as the central state privileged by most theorists or the regional configurations of power outlined in the first half of this chapter.[11]

Rethinking Regimes

What then are we to make of regime and state, as political rules and centralized entity of administration and coercion? Analysis of Mexican regions and cultures suggests the need for several kinds of rethinking of social-science approaches to politics and power in Mexico. It remains true that there is a state, though not a unified one, as well as discernible political rules, if informal and unstable. However, the regional histories discussed above have shown, first, that the presence of that state and the implementation of those rules are far less complete, in terms of geography, as well as domains of social life, than the model of the all-encompassing or corporatist state asserts. Second, the discussion above has shown that the local or regional, as distinct from the national, not only accommodates or resists national procedures and projects, but, in interaction with the national, creates or shapes new political forms. These new configurations of power, in turn, become the terrain on which the center acts, as well as a primary source of the knowledge with which that action is imagined and implemented.

Third, analysis of regional power has demonstrated the centrality of cultural discourses and practices to the formation of even narrowly political phenomena, such as parties, elections, policymaking, and social movements. Fourth, the contrasting economies, cultures, and political identities and alliances of the regions described above demonstrate that there is no one system of Mexican politics. While regime and state may assume particular (if partial and changing) forms at the national level, the functioning of power in Mexico—the configurations of knowledge and action within which leaders, organizations, economies, and ordinary people exist and act—differs across geographic and cultural locations. For the study of politics, state and regime are pieces in a network of relations that reaches in multiple directions. To study Mexican politics, or Latin American politics, then, should be to discern these networks, within and across borders.

The juxtaposition of my own work on Juchitán with that of Mary Roldán (1992) on Antioquia, Colombia, before and during the period of La Violencia provides an example of the direction such work might take. As I do for Juchitán, and Alonso and Nugent do for Namiquipa, Roldán distinguishes politics in Antioquia from claims about national politics, detailing the construction of beliefs about decency and order that shape

and maintain Antioqueño society. In addition, she contrasts this hegemonic discourse with the economic and cultural practices of frontier
regions in the state. She then uses this cultural and subregional analysis
to explain the different courses taken by violence in the two different
arenas: limited violence within the diffuse bounds of Liberal Party–
Conservative Party conflict, and enduring guerrilla opposition.

A comparison of Roldán's work and the Mexican examples above suggests the possibility of making regions or forms of cultural life the unit of
analysis. From this perspective, it makes more sense for those studying
power to describe and compare Puebla and Antioquia, or gender relations
in the Antioqueño frontier and Namiquipa, or discourses of decency and
anticommunism in Medellín and San Luis Potosí, than to study "Mexican"
or "Colombian" politics or regimes. By focusing on the building blocks
out of which hegemonies are constructed, this approach makes it possible to understand the complexity of formations of power and the varied
ways they change over time. It illuminates the "dense web" of power
relations of which regimes and states are the "institutional crystallization"
(Foucault 1990 [1976], 96, 93). This, in turn, makes it difficult to describe
regime rules and state formations in parsimonious ways or to provide
step-by-step connections between region and nation or between culture
and politics. At the same time, such an approach reveals previously un-
discerned similarities and differences among regimes themselves. For example, Roldán's work on Antioquia and my own on Juchitán suggest
considerably more similarity between the Colombian and Mexican regimes, in terms of the unevenness of state presence, the impact of urban
discourses of civility, and the complexity of ideological transmission
between center and region than predominant political-science models
indicate.

This form of analysis, based on subnational comparison across borders,
contributes to new ways of talking about phenomena that consist of
multiple locations, such as regimes or states. In this regard, the approach I
have taken for analyzing COCEI's internal dynamics is useful. Within
COCEI, experiences of violence, democracy, gender, historical narrative,
and cultural elaboration involve leaders and supporters, men and women,
middle class and poor in crosscutting ways, while at the same time a
coherent political force powerfully challenges central government authority. In order to understand how this coherence occurs, it is essential to
examine the movement's complex history, its situatedness in region and

nation, and the conflictual cultural locations within it. A regime or state may similarly be seen as a political form that consists of multiple and shifting constructions of meaning and experience—of multiple and shifting hegemonies—and at the same time acts with apparent coherence in assembling and enforcing public policies. Indeed, contrary to the assumptions about power inherent in the corporatist-state analysis of Mexico, incompleteness, instability, and domination are intimately connected.

Conclusion

At both the beginning and end of the twentieth century, when the nature of sovereignty in Mexico has been dramatically contested, Zapatistas[1] and other opposition movements have spoken powerfully for a rethinking of the identity of the nation and a renegotiation of the role of Indians in its culture and economy. If regimes are decentered and political movements animated by ambiguity and contradiction, as previous chapters have shown, then democratization must be reconceptualized to take account of the politics and cultures of such oppositions and of the contested and changing nature of hegemony itself. The histories of Juchitán and other Mexican regions illustrate the distinct and often circuitous pathways by which forms of political voice, economic well-being, and cultural autonomy can be established amidst persistently unequal power relations. As Partha Chatterjee suggested for the regions of India, these Mexican histories "[contain] in the divergences in their trajectories and rhythms the possibility of a different imagining of nationhood" (1993, 114). Consequently, they also recommend a different imagining of the processes and outcomes of democratization.

COCEI's battle with the Mexican regime was animated and shaped by Juchitán's past and present of such different imaginings, along with the alternative forms of development they engendered. The path from violence in the 1970s to leftist municipal government in the 1990s involved how the nation was envisioned and negotiated, from Juchitán and from Mexico City, and how it was made the basis for the exercise of rule. Indeed, the place of region and ethnicity in the nation is precisely what was fought over and reconfigured in Juchitán since the rebellions of the nineteenth century. The establishment of successive political arrangements has gone hand in hand with reworkings of class, culture, gender, and economy, in the course of which borders between "inside" and "outside" have repeatedly shifted. In this context, the possibility and pathway of democratization in Juchitán involved such matters as the forging of a Zapotec domain of sovereignty within the Mexican nation, the cultivation of capacities for violence and disruption, the articulation of a moderate discourse of development and reform, the building of artistic and literary connections between Juchitán and Mexico City, and the creation of myths and practices of Zapotec women's autonomy. These phenomena interacted with more explicitly "political" forces in the 1970s and 1980s, such as national political openings, international geopolitical pressures, and militant grassroots mobilization. The "art of making" (Escobar 1992a, 74) at the heart of democratization in Juchitán thus involved interrelated processes linking past and present, region and regime, in the articulation of local discourses of Western democracy and the forging of alternative development practices.

Region, Ethnicity, and Nation in Juchitán

In the second half of the nineteenth century in Juchitán, Zapotec ethnicity defined a multiclass pueblo at odds with the outside, making repeated use of violent and nonviolent forms of resistance to evade the economic claims and political impositions of elites in the state capital. After the Mexican Revolution, in contrast, the Zapotec pueblo coexisted with the outside, accepting a position within the nation rather than defining itself as separate and hostile. General Charis and the Isthmus gained considerable autonomy—a "domain of sovereignty"—in exchange for recognizing the authority of the postrevolutionary state. Charis, in turn, based his regional authority on having secured for Juchitecos many of the economic and political prerogatives for which they had repeatedly fought in the nineteenth- and early-twentieth-century rebellions. Paradoxically, accepting a place within the nation—now a nation that based its legitimacy on recognition of its Indian past—brought benefits that had previously been sought by constructing Indianness in opposition to Oaxacan and Mexican identities.

The viability of this arrangement depended on Charis's ability to negotiate his "Indianness" successfully among both his constituents in the Isthmus and generals and politicians in Mexico City. Indianness itself was recast in the process. Ethnic activity in Juchitán focused less on acts and representations of rebellion writ large and more on elaborating the art, music, and daily rituals that accompanied the coexistence of national and local economies. At the same time, the tropes of barbarism used by outsiders during the years of rebellion became part of the "inside," as artists, musicians, storytellers, and politicians made use of this imagery to characterize Zapotec culture and history.

The domain of sovereignty in Juchitán signified a configuration of region and nation in which cacique politics could resist outside political forces and shape regional politics in its own fashion. This arrangement involved a particular construction of Zapotec leadership' that enabled Zapotec elites to be recognized by ordinary Juchitecos as legitimate political authorities and arbiters of Zapotec style, even as they made successful forays into regional and national economic and artistic activities. Zapotec elites during this period were Indians *and* Mexicans, a flexible identity made possible by the dual dynamics of Zapotec social life and Mexican nationalism. The domain of sovereignty also meant that economic endeavors in Juchitán remained predominantly, though not exclusively, small-scale and local and that ordinary people could perform daily activities of speech, ritual, and work in ways that distinguished these activities from national Mexican ones. The resulting social and economic relations were not egalitarian, but they were distinctly different in character and internal meaning from the politics and culture of the center.

During this period of coexistence, Juchiteco artists began to make a name for themselves on the national cultural scene. The crossing of borders between regional, ethnic art and national "high" culture—as between Zapotec and Mexican elites—could occur because representations of Indianness coincided with the nationalist identity and political project constructed by the postrevolutionary state. Artistic border-crossing was also a gendered activity. Men produced formal art and through that art represented Zapotec identity to Juchitecos and to the outside. Male artists spoke with recognized public authority. They developed their narratives and visions in cantinas and workshops, and they portrayed Zapotec culture as consisting of traditions that had existed locally "from time immemorial" and that were exclusively indigenous. In this way, male Juchiteco artists acted to keep the outside out of Zapotec historical and cultural narratives.

In contrast, Juchiteca women brought in, modified, and made use of economic and cultural practices from outside the city. They ensured that

267

Zapotec culture itself was desirable and worth defending—and continued to provide margins of maneuver for women—by making it serve practical needs on a day-to-day basis. Furthermore, before the construction of the dam and irrigation district in the Isthmus in the 1960s, much of this women's activity of appropriation and reconfiguration occurred in the absence of men, who left for months at a time to find work or, earlier, to fight in nineteenth-century rebellions and in the revolution. Women thus acted with authority in daily life in a gendered domain of sovereignty within the geographic and cultural one, developing local practices in courtyards and markets. Women's authority was fortified by myths of Juchitecas' power and sexuality. This discourse, produced by nineteenth-century male European travelers and twentieth-century Mexican artists and journalists, many of them female, was reinforced by Juchiteco men and women in local art, ritual practices, and daily banter. These representations of women's power responded to and in turn fortified the various ways in which women had unusual room for maneuver in Juchitán. They also hid from view many processes of violence and exclusion that Juchitecas shared with women elsewhere in Mexico and themselves experienced in powerful and enduring forms.

In the 1960s in Juchitán, the domain of sovereignty was both continued and reshaped, as it intersected in new ways with the national economy and state and as Juchitecos confronted, with the death of the boss, the need for new regional political forms. Government agencies acted to bring outside economic practices into the Isthmus through the construction of the irrigation district and various agro-industrial projects, which were generally welcomed by Juchiteco businesspeople and commentators. As they experienced the interaction of the Zapotec domain of sovereignty and national economic changes, Zapotec elites themselves acted to bring more of the national economy and culture into Juchitán as well, pressing for further industrialization and for urban forms of architecture, communication, commerce, and education. Yet Zapotec elites also sought to maintain for themselves legitimate leadership status. They wanted to rework the domain of sovereignty—its interrelations of economy, ethnicity, and nation—on their own terms, including considerable borrowing from discourses of Western democracy. Elites mobilized Juchitecos politically to do this around issues of private property and clean government.

But Zapotec culture had by this time also changed in response to outside influence, particularly the critical student and intellectual perspectives of the 1960s. As a result, the local artistic culture infused art and representation with new social and political content related to class and a critical stance toward the regime. The tropes of barbarism and difference with which Juchitán had long been represented took on new, explicitly political content at the same time that the cultural and political domain of sovereignty was experiencing new strains and ordinary people faced economic dislocation and change. In this context, as students and intellectuals politicized Zapotec art in new ways, moderates among Juchitán's educated elite and middle class produced a powerful critique of the state's development policies and political practices. They did so simultaneously as insiders and outsiders. Juchiteco moderates fiercely denounced the corruption and inefficiency of state agencies and the absence of democracy within the PRI, even as they argued for a better, reformed PRI that could lead the city to clean government and economic prosperity. Moderates defended the integrity and needs of the Zapotec pueblo, to which they belonged, even as they joined outside planners at times in decrying local cultural practices as incompatible with development.

Despite its ambivalence, the vehemence of this indigenous critique of outside economic policies aptly characterized the combination of mobilization and exclusion experienced by Juchiteco students, peasants, and workers in the 1960s. The confluence of politicized artistic culture, economic critique, and changing daily experience contributed to the formation and strength of COCEI in the 1970s and 1980s. During these years, Zapotec men's artistic representations were effective in bringing outside political support, as well as scaring authorities with images of Indian fierceness. COCEI made use of the myths of matriarchy in Juchitán to construct an easily identifiable, alluring, and frightening iconography to represent the radical political movement to the outside. In this way, outsiders' romanticizations of Juchiteca women were used to challenge and restrain the outside, and also to empower and limit women in daily social relations. These representations also became, for many women activists and scholars and for ordinary Juchitecas, the image of women in COCEI. At the same time, Juchitecas themselves, through cultural practices quite distinct from those that the male artists and political leaders described, fostered the daily cultural richness and flexibility that could sustain radical politics over time, in the face of fierce repression and steep familial conflicts and losses.

269

The construction of gender and sexuality that took shape in the domain of sovereignty functioned both to reinforce and to resist structures of power. The alternative male gender role, muxe, was largely invisible in COCEI's artistic representations, and many muxe allied with the PRI in the 1980s, thereby linking prominent Zapotec cultural practices to PRI political authority. But muxe identity also embodied the kinds of cultural difference, experimentation, and display that have both sustained Zapotec culture and empowered COCEI's radical politics. Similarly, women's identity and sexuality—women's physical bodies, verbal boldness, self-confidence, and margins of sexual freedom—have both upheld and challenged dominant power relations. Juchiteca identity provided a vocabulary of forthrightness and militancy that directly facilitated radical mobilization. But the characteristics attributed to Juchitecas also lent an eroticism and allure to social life as it existed, thereby enhancing both the usefulness and seductiveness of the regime's political authority.

Democratization in Juchitán

The separateness and internal complexity of the regional, Zapotec activities that constituted the domain of sovereignty in Juchitán thus provided the terrain on which oppositional activities would be shaped—and strengthened and limited—during the fierce, class-based battles of the 1970s and 1980s. These battles produced a new set of relationships among ethnic tropes, regional class relations, and nation. In the 1970s, as COCEI organized a class-based opposition, the pueblo again defined itself in opposition to outside authority, as it had in the nineteenth century, but this time in opposition to the Zapotec elite as well. This new relationship between the Zapotec pueblo and the outside brought military occupation and shootings in the streets in the 1970s and municipal democracy at the end of the 1980s. Since then, Juchitán has become a striking example of an enduring and multifaceted democratic space within a system of domination. In contested and changing ways, the path from polarization to transformation brought fair elections, opposition government, new opportunities for alternative linguistic and cultural elaboration, spaces for dissent and democracy in labor unions and community associations, and protection for small-scale agriculture.

In achieving these spaces for autonomy, voice, and well-being, the workings of democracy in Juchitán have been tempestuous. Investors feel well treated one moment, then betrayed when COCEI blocks the Pan-American Highway to protest unfair labor practices. Peasants feel represented when COCEI secures credit or insurance for them, but angered when the organization welcomes reform-minded members of the official party into its municipal government. Some COCEI leaders feel justified, in light of their achievements, in making decisions unilaterally, while other COCEI activists insist that internal procedures need to be more democratic. In this context, COCEI today faces numerous dilemmas. In power for its third term, the movement risks in the long run becoming a moderate supporter of the status quo and an aging organization insulated from ordinary people's needs. Avoiding this result depends in large part on COCEI's ability to make space for new leaders and continue the delicate balancing of internal ambiguities and contradictions that generated creative and threatening political force in the past. At the same time, as much of southern Mexico becomes increasingly militarized, COCEI's more disruptive mobilizations may upset networks of support within Juchitán and elicit economic and military repression from a besieged regime. Avoiding this outcome means continuing to steer a viable path between disruption and accommodation in rapidly changing national and international circumstances.

This politics is explosive and exclusionary, even as it is competitive and open-ended. Indeed, multifaceted democracy was secured in Juchitán through the combination of locally mediated discourses of Western democracy and ongoing mobilization at the borders of violence. In Juchitán, the economic and social complexity of a rural city, the strategic importance of a development zone, and the domestic politics of an unevenly liberalizing regime intersected. Enduring militancy resulted in significant part from COCEI's ability to claim control of the meanings, practices, and pleasures of Zapotec ethnicity for a poor people's movement in such a location. Through its flexible and changing mixture of Leninist and new-social-movement practices, COCEI sustained activism and forged innovative opposition practices, including leftist participation in elections and an extensive Zapotec cultural project. What COCEI achieved was not a new inclusion of Indians in the nation (as has begun to occur since the Zapatista rebellion in Chiapas), but rather the opportunity for poor Juchitecos to be ignored as Indians but included within the quasi-democratic maneuverings of the Mexican regime. In the 1980s, a new form of entry into the nation and a corresponding expansion of the benefits of citizenship could occur through the discourses and practices of electoral competition. By virtue of being frightening and "unknown" Indians, Juchitecos achieved a new version of the domain of sovereignty *and* a new level of involvement with Western democracy. At this juncture of democracy and difference new power relations were forged.

As a result of their Zapotec past and their experiences with Mexico's turbulent student movements, COCEI leaders not only spoke Zapotec with humor and skill, but they spoke the language of the regime as well. COCEI survived because its leaders consistently took advantage of the ambivalence and conflict within the regime regarding reform or repression as political strategies. Furthermore, key moments in the shift from repression to democratization in Juchitán occurred during the Mexican oil boom, which was also a time when violence in Central America—just down the coast from Juchitán—was expanding. This put conflicting pressures on the already divided Mexican government: not to let "the next domino" happen in Mexico, but also not to use violent repression in a way that would promote more explosive conflict or discredit Mexico internationally. In this context, COCEI leaders knew when and how to provoke, retreat, and negotiate.

They did so, much as Charis had, by being both Zapotec and Mexican and manipulating these identities successfully at home and in Mexico City. Charis had mediated between region and nation at midcentury as a general who had traveled the country fighting for the Mexican Revolution. The Zapotec ethnicity within which he maneuvered had been defined by rebellion and was just beginning to find a workable place within the new Mexican nationalism. In the 1960s and 1970s, COCEI leaders gained their skills and worldview in Marxist student movements seeking a class-based transformation of postrevolutionary Mexico. Their Zapotec ethnicity had accommodated to the regime in preceding decades and had been newly politicized by national and international cultural trends. In each case, a space for Indianness, sovereignty, and/or democracy within the nation was secured by simultaneously mobilizing ethnicity and difference *and* speaking the language of the regime.

The vocal and influential group of political moderates in Juchitán consistently recognized the reasonableness of many of COCEI's claims. This moderate political discourse, which gained prominence and popular support in campaigns against PRI corruption in the 1960s and early

1970s, was itself an outgrowth of challenges to cacique rule in the 1940s and 1950s. Moderates spoke in a language of open political competition, civil rights, and economic development (though their commitments to these goals varied and they had little success in achieving them). By being willing to question the system in fundamental and increasingly radical ways and to speak in defense of the Zapotec pueblo, moderates themselves outlined much of COCEI's later agenda. In the 1970s, when COCEI faced regime intransigence and violence, moderates defended the integrity of the Zapotec movement and the justness of its claims. However, when COCEI governed Juchitán in the early 1980s and pursued the radical goals it had previously championed, moderates opposed the leftist movement, charging that it fostered violence and anarchy. When COCEI was removed from power, moderates made use of the political views they had articulated in preceding decades to ally with the regime in support of democracy in Juchitán and reform of the local PRI, a strategy they believed would bring a reinvigorated official party to power through fair elections. In this way, a culture of politics that emerged in the 1940s, simultaneously within the Zapotec domain of sovereignty and in opposition to its boss politics, and that developed a vehement Zapotec critique of state policies in the 1960s, provided an essential ally for the state and ingredient for democratization in the 1980s. Two local cultures of politics thus interacted in Juchitán in the process of democratization, both with dual origins in the midcentury domain of sovereignty and in Mexican politics. Moderate reformists sought to educate the barbarous Zapotec pueblo for "development" and clean civic government, while COCEI linked Zapotec rebelliousness to class-based revolution. These two cultures of politics came together in the 1980s in Juchitán around questions of Western procedural democracy.

The Ayuntamiento Popular, the COCEI government of the early 1980s, galvanized peasant and worker support for COCEI at the same time that it alienated middle-class Juchitecos and businesspeople, some of whom had voted for the movement (or abstained in municipal elections) and might have been willing to continue supporting it in office. The Ayuntamiento Popular fostered militant class conflict and governed in favor of COCEI supporters, treating others with hostility and arbitrariness. It also defended and celebrated the popular culture of the poor, including those aspects of Zapotec daily life that middle classes and elites rejected as obstacles to "decency" and development. In contrast, COCEI's stance during the 1986 coalition government and the subsequent, democratically elected COCEI administrations was more conciliatory in these areas.

Such a shift underscores the usefulness of moderation in democratic politics. However, the trajectory of conflict and democratic accommodation in Juchitán suggests as well that militancy and hostility were important steps in the path to leftist government. This history also suggests that multifaceted and enduring democracy was achieved in Juchitán because the establishment of Western democratic norms was only one of a variety of goals for moderates and COCEI alike. Discourses and practices of Western democracy emerged among different Juchitecos in different decades, embedded in local meanings and local methods of disruption. Moderates debated the meaning of democracy and weighed it against the notion of an official party during campaigns for internal PRI primaries in the 1960s. COCEI forged democratic electoral practices on the ground since its inception, even as it rejected them in theory and refused them internally. It was thus Juchitán's own complex discourse of democracy, combined with mobilization and government at the borders of violence, that impassioned supporters, frightened opponents, and brought democratic transformation. Disruption may be equally crucial to the vitality of democracy itself. As its leaders age and its administrations balance mobilization and conciliation, COCEI's own past poses a key question for leftist government in systems of unequal power relations: where can spaces be forged, in or out of elected government, for the militancy and disruption that may be necessary to reinforce and deepen democratic politics?

Democracy and Difference

In Juchitán, militancy and disruption were facilitated by difference. Democracy occurred not because Western cultural and economic practices proceeded apace, but because the outside was kept out in significant ways and the normalization characteristic of Western development was avoided. Juchitán's domain of sovereignty, like those described by Chatterjee in India, served "to resist the sway of the modern institutions of disciplinary power" (Chatterjee 1993, 75). As a result, the intersection of Zapotec and Mexican cultures and economies produced a hybrid form of modernity (García Canclini 1989) unusually open to innovation. The links between hybridity, difference, and innovation are evident in Juchitán not only in the physical and ritual panorama of the city, but in the stunning alternatives of gender, sexuality, and language there. In Stuart Hall's words, "this notion of hybridity is very different from the old internationalist grand narrative, from the superficiality of old style pluralism where no boundaries are crossed" (1993, 362). In Juchitán, boundaries are crossed in the strength and size and forthrightness of women and the myths describing them, in midwives who make use of doctors to maintain their own prestige and wealth, and in the unabashed mixture of typically male and female clothing, bodily appearance, and demeanor among muxe males in public places. In Juchitán, women are not harassed in the streets, babies are born at home or in midwives' courtyards, and males in women's dress dance with other males in women's dress at public fiestas. In all of these locations, furthermore, and in businesses and government as well, Juchitecos' rich and playful use of a "barbarous" indigenous language establishes yet another border with the rest of urban Mexico.

Juxtapositions of "unruliness" and discipline, of "nature" and technology in Juchitán are the results not only or primarily of poverty, but of preference and sensibility and identity. In choosing and perpetuating an urban panorama that startles and offends outsiders, Juchitecos suggest what change in the twentieth century might have looked like if the encounter between Western and indigenous cultures and economies had occurred on less unequal terms. It would have been a twentieth century not necessarily of "appropriate" technology and "sustainable" development, but indeed one where the uses, values, and paths of economic and social change were more grounded in local needs and commitments. Thus, Juchitecos pursue forthrightly, and indeed celebrate, the habits that modernizers decry. COCEI's experiences in the last two decades demonstrate the possibility of being radical and taking on the regime, of governing and managing budgets, and simultaneously of resisting the language of economic development and cultural normalization. Yet neither Juchitecos nor COCEI unilaterally reject the benefits or pleasures of new technologies or the possibility of profit. Juchitecos disagree vehemently among themselves about how much of the outside to embrace and on what terms, and through these disagreements Zapotec culture is shaped and elaborated. Juchitecos' forthrightness with strangers and engagement with multiple economies and cultures bring not only satisfaction and autonomy, furthermore, but an ability to stand up to and even ridicule and dismiss Western assumptions. As a result, modernity in Juchitán can be open-ended.

Juchitán does not provide a recipe for democratization. Rather, it demonstrates the embeddedness of democracy in particular cultural and historical forms at the regional level. At the end of the twentieth century, Juchitán offers the paradoxical lesson that the persistence and elaboration of difference can foster the establishment of multifaceted democracy. Difference does not make democracy happen or necessarily pave its way. But in Juchitán the intersection of an open-ended modernity with Western democratic discourse has indeed produced unprecedented democratic innovation. To approach the analysis of democracy this way—through the place of region in the nation and through alternative pathways of development—is thus not to ignore democratic procedures. Rather, it is to recognize that much of the inequality and violence that democratic procedures obscure—and that have come increasingly to characterize situations of democratic transition in Latin America—can be seen and negotiated in these other arenas. Over time, the voice and autonomy of Zapotec ethnicity has been articulated in contestation with Mexican nationalism, and the economic survival and relative prosperity of Juchitecos in contestation with Western development. Western democratic discourse has been essential for democratization in Juchitán not as a "universal" political theory, imposed or imported from without, but always "insist[ing] on specificity, on conjuncture" (Hall 1988, 46). The negotiated position of region in nation and the boundary-crossing hybridity of development have given Juchitecos considerable margins for maneuver in their encounters with Western modernity. Through the Zapotec modernity and democratic discourses they constructed, Juchitecos formed and empowered COCEI and achieved democratization.

Notes

Introduction

1 In viewing Juchitán as a site of alternative forms of development, I am indebted to Arturo Escobar for his critique of the Western discourse of development and his suggestions for reimagining encounters between Western and "Third World" locations and cultures (1995).

2 The Popular Defense Committee of Durango (CDP) achieved such recognition at approximately the same time as COCEI, early in the Salinas administration (Haber 1993). The armed Zapatista movement in Chiapas seems to have gained a similar status, though its survival continues to be threatened by military occupation, paramilitary violence, and government intransigence.

3 The evolution of the scholarly literature on Mexican politics is set out in detail in chapter 1.

4 The vast majority of Juchitecos are bilingual, and I conducted these interviews in Spanish. While living in Juchitán, I also learned basic Zapotec, which I spoke in social situations.

1 Theorizing Power and Regimes

1 Before recent transitions to democracy, this was seen to occur in an "authoritarian" and "corporatist" fashion (Collier 1979; Malloy 1977a; O'Donnell 1977; Schmitter 1974; Stepan 1978). The more recent literature on transitions to democracy in Latin America has continued to focus on the center and on narrowly political negotiations and conflicts (Karl 1990; O'Donnell and Schmitter 1986; Schmitter and Karl 1993). While it illuminates the nuances of elite bargaining and acknowledges some of the limits of existing democracies, this literature nevertheless tends to evaluate democracy in terms of national political processes and explicitly political actors.

2 The current regime has been in place for more than sixty years, longer than the vast majority of Third World and European regimes.

3 By "center," I refer simultaneously to a place (Mexico City), an institutional apparatus of power and decision making, and a set of "national" cultural discourses.

Notes

4 Eric Van Young (1992) suggests that "it is social embeddedness and the dimension of time . . . that define regions" (7), which "are to be seen less as rarefied entities, with discernible boundaries . . . than as processual spaces whose internal architecture and direction are subject to constant negotiation by actors both within and without" (27). Generally, I use "region" and "regional" to refer to roughly drawn geographic spaces of this sort that are larger than a town or city, but smaller than a state. I use the term "local" somewhat more flexibly, depending on context, to refer to more clearly defined and smaller entities, such as cities, towns, neighborhoods, and workplaces.

5 A *cacique* is a political boss who maintains power through clientelistic relationships and generally makes use of electoral fraud and violence. *Caciquismo* refers to this form of politics, which is similar to old-style machine politics in the U.S. *Cacicazgo* refers to the political structure itself, akin to the U.S. political "machine."

6 Collier and Collier separate the incorporation project into two phrases: mobilization and reform under Cárdenas and conservative reaction and retrenchment between 1940 and 1952 (1991, 407–20).

7 When applied to Latin America, the term "corporatism" implies state corporatism, as opposed to societal corporatism, following Philippe Schmitter's distinction. In state corporatism, "singular, noncompetitive, hierarchically ordered representative 'corporations' . . . were created by and kept as auxiliary and dependent organs of the state . . ." (Schmitter 1974, 102). In addition, the theorists of corporatism cited below distinguish their use of the term as a form of institutional arrangement from the cultural meaning that others, most prominently Howard Wiarda (1974), attribute to corporatism.

8 For a more historical and less homogeneous view of the Mexican regime, see Whitehead 1981.

9 Some accounts of authoritarianism emphasized the presence of at least "limited pluralism" (Linz 1970), and others a considerable degree of diversity and exchange (Anderson and Cockcroft 1972 [1966]; Collier and Collier 1991), but all accounts placed such competition within a context of centralized control and continuity.

10 As described by Fagen and Tuohy, the city of Jalapa experienced little political contestation in the 1960s, and elections had no importance beyond straightforward symbolism. Emphasizing elite control and mass quiescence across classes, they found that "the local agenda is single-mindedly focused on economic and service deficiencies to the almost complete exclusion of structural and political problems. It is an agenda of people who live in a well managed political environment" (1972, 74).

11 Earlier theorists did not discern Cárdenas's pivotal state-building role. Needler, for example, characterized Cárdenas as "another strong personality and military figure," and suggested that "with Cárdenas' successor, the task of institutionalization was resumed" (1971, 6).

12 By formal political organizations and actors, I mean those who are explicitly part of public bodies of administration and coercion, such as officials of all sorts and the national, state, and local governmental bodies of which they are a part; those who compete in elections and other processes for the designation of officeholders, such as politicians, parties, and political bosses; and others, such as unions, business associations, media, and grassroots movements insofar as they seek explicitly to influence public policy and competition for office.

13 The rebellion that began in Chiapas in January 1994 makes this clear in the Mexican context, with the emergence of armed opposition from within ostensibly PRI-supporting indigenous villages and with the dramatic changes in national discourse and policymaking prompted by the rebellion. Seen through this lens, President Salinas was able to carry out a transformative economic project—and faced limits in doing so—because a complex and changing state was able to negotiate separate pathways among part-distinct, part-interrelated regions and cultures.

2 Continuity and Disjunction in Zapotec Ethnicity

1 Rivera Cabrera and Gómez n.d.-b., 3.

2 Quotes from the weekly Juchitán newspaper *El Satélite* will be cited in the text by date of publication, preceded when necessary by the initials *ES*.

3 Colección Porfirio Díaz, Libro 41, Caja 7.16, documento 339, p. 154, 5 Sept. 1889.

4 For this account, I have drawn primarily on de la Cruz 1983a and Tutino 1980 and 1993. For brief descriptions of other nineteenth-century rebellions in Juchitán, see de la Cruz 1983b and Henestrosa de Webster 1985, 61–87.

5 In addition to the rebellions cited above, Hart documents a prolonged period of rebellion in the early eighteenth century, as well as a peasant war across the Mexican southwest in the 1840s (1987, 3–4, 34–37). Juchitecos also point to rebellions in 1870 and 1882, as well as a short-lived 1932 rebellion in support of General Charis, which will be discussed in the following chapter.

6 "Lies," or a ritualized form of storytelling.

7 Campbell (1990b) observed that some elite families began to move away from this ethnic identification in the 1960s. The ethnic claims of COCEI may well have prompted renewed emphasis on ethnic practices among these families in the 1970s and 1980s. On the ethnic character of the bourgeoisie, see Royce 1975.

3 Cacique Rule and the Zapotec Domain of Sovereignty, 1930–1960

1 Cecilio de la Cruz, during his successful campaign for federal deputy for the PRI (*ES* 8 July 1973).

2 In uncovering a complex history of resistance during a period when, according to previous scholars, "nothing happened," I was guided by the work of Jeffrey Gould (1990) on the rich history of peasant organizing in Nicaragua.

3 Charis himself, perhaps with this outcome in mind, initially encouraged the doctors, but in the end did not back their armed rebellion (de la Cruz 1983c, 71).

4 Interviews with Luis Pineda and Victoriano López Toledo, summer 1986.

5 Interviews, summer 1986.

6 Interviews, 1985 and 1986. There are also a number of short books and oral histories concerning Charis: Altamirano Conde 1985, de la Cruz 1989, Escuela Secundaria Federal 1978, López Marín 1985.

7 Juchiteco intellectual Víctor de la Cruz sees this story as representative and revealing, but questions its accuracy. De la Cruz disputes the fact that Avila Camacho visited Juchitán as presidential candidate.

8 Claudio Lomnitz-Adler's description of Huasteca cacique Gonzalo Santos makes similar points about the boss's embeddedness in local culture, as well as the complexity of his role as an interlocutor with the outside (1992, 301–2).

9 Many businesses in Juchitán are owned and run by women, so this term is more appropriate than "businessmen."

10 I use "reformist" and "modernizing" interchangeably in this sense to describe projects focused on improving the economic and social prospects of middle classes and elites. At times, a modernizing perspective of this sort explicitly recognized the problems of poverty and marginalization as well, but assumed that a combination of good administration, education, and economic growth was the necessary and sufficient means for bringing about more generalized well-being.

11 Interview with Victoriano López Toledo, summer 1986.

12 Interviews with Luis Pineda and Serafina Pineda, summer 1986.

13 The Zapotec *Ta* and *Na* frequently precede adult first names as terms of respect in direct address and third-person reference. In most cases, when full names or last names are given (usually for politicians or prominent public figures) they are people's real names, while first names preceded by Ta or Na are pseudonyms.

14 There were several small ejidos near Juchitán, such as those in Santiago Laollaga and in La Venta, which resulted from land redistribution. However, in La Venta, where I did extensive interviewing, the CNC never established a strong or exclusive presence.

15 A local branch of the CTM was officially inaugurated in the early 1960s, with Fidel Velásquez, the CTM's national leader, coming to Juchitán for the occasion. However, the local organization never expanded significantly beyond its initial base among the *cargadores*, the men who transported goods by hand-drawn carts.

16 López Toledo himself claims more enduring success for the Front for Democratic Renovation than I was able to corroborate by other accounts. In his own words, "I destroyed Charismo here."

4 The Politics of Reform, 1960–1973

1 *ES* 6 Aug. 1972.

2 I have found it difficult to establish accurate population figures. Campbell (1994, 83) attributes the above figures to a SEDUE report development plan and a National University of Mexico study (Ministry of Urban Development and Ecology [SEDUE], "Plan de desarrollo urbano de centro de población de Juchitán de Zaragoza, Oaxaca," Mexico City, 1988; and Ignazio Félix Díaz, "El Area Urbano-Regional del Estado de Oaxaca en el Istmo de Tehuantepec," in *El Puerto Industrial de Salina Cruz*, Mexico City: Instituto de Geografía, UNAM, 1984). Jhabvala, citing census data, presents the following population figures: 16,811 in 1950, 23,870 in 1960, and 37,686 in 1970 (1982, 50). The 1980 census itself gives the population as 45,011.

3 Jhabvala defines secondary-sector activities as "manufacturing, construction, electricity, oil, petrochemicals, etc." In the Isthmus, these included manufacture of limestone bricks, production of railroad ties, construction, oil refining and transport, and other activities related to transport and communication. Jhabvala attributes the higher value added per capita in the Isthmus to the higher level of secondary-sector activities there.

4 While health-care resources in the Isthmus were strikingly inferior to national averages (Jhabvala 1982, 112), Juchitán had a lower infant mortality rate (83 per 1000), lower mortality rates between ages 5 and 10, and higher life expectancies for men and women (52 years) than virtually all other Oaxaca cities and towns except the capital (Corona 1979).

5 The proportion of manufacturing in the national economy increased from 19.2 to 22.8 percent, while in the Isthmus it decreased from 21.3 to 17.7 percent. The gross product per capita in the Isthmus decreased by an average of .39 percent per year (Jhabvala 1982, 20, 39, 43).

6 Such conflicts occurred, for example, in the southern state of Guerrero, the central states of Puebla and San Luis Potosí, and the northern state of Sonora. These events will be discussed in detail in chapter 8.

7 Binford's article presents a fascinating account of the history and political effects of the land-tenure conflict.

8 The ejido events in Juchitán also demonstrate the inconsistencies and errors with which the central state acted to make and implement policies. Binford emphasizes the confusion and ineptitude involved in every stage of the effort, from the failure to exclude some landholdings from the ejido decree, as had been promised, to the selection of rice for cultivation in the irrigation district (1985).

9 Sesame, a cash crop in the region, was harmed by a fungus caused by the moisture from the irrigation, and native corn was not aided by additional water in years of normal rainfall. Neither rice nor cotton, two of the products promoted in the region, grew successfully in the presence of the fierce Isthmus winds, and cane

did not grow nearly as well in the Oaxaca Isthmus as it did in the nearby state of Veracruz (Campbell 1990b, 228, 230–32, 236).

10 Except where otherwise noted, information on political events during this period comes from interviews carried out in Juchitán in 1985 and 1986.

11 The tactic of withholding budget money, which also characterized the PRI's response to COCEI government in 1981, was aided by a new tax system. Instead of the *municipio* collecting its taxes directly, funds went directly to state and national coffers, to be returned in part afterward (*ES* 25 Mar., 17 June 1973).

12 These percentages are informed guesses, based on interviews. The difficulties of interpreting voting statistics and of determining the precise degree of support for COCEI in Juchitán will be discussed in the following chapter.

13 This approach was presented in articles by Daniel López Nelio and Efigenio de la Cruz M., the first writing from Juchitán and the second from Mexico City.

5 Mobilization and Repression in the 1970s

1 Leopoldo de Gyves de la Cruz, interviewed in *Por Esto!* 16 July 1981, 44.

2 "Didxazá," in de la Cruz 1983a, 68. English translation by Nathaniel Tarn, in Campbell et al. 1993.

3 *Por Esto!* 23 July 1981.

4 This observation came from a Juchiteco student who went on to establish a professional career in Mexico City.

5 The House for Isthmus Students became a residence and political center for COCEI students in Mexico City throughout the 1970s and 1980s. It thus served as an important link between the national political center, Juchiteco student experiences in that arena, and COCEI activities in Juchitán. National protest activities in support of COCEI, for example, could be coordinated from the House.

6 On this process generally in Mexico, see Bennett 1993. On Juchitán, see Prevôt-Schapira and Rivière D'Arc 1984, 14.

7 The organization went through several name changes before settling on COCEI, first including just students and peasants in Juchitán, then including workers, and then claiming a wider geographical area by replacing "Juchitán" with "Isthmus." It became COCEI in 1975. For clarity I will use the name COCEI throughout.

8 On the growth of COCEI in the 1970s, see Gutiérrez 1981, López Monjardin 1983, Martínez López 1985, Ornelas Esquinca 1983b, and Prevôt-Schapira and Rivière D'Arc 1984.

9 According to the Mexico City professional quoted above.

10 Paul Haber (1993) describes the strategies of the CDP of Durango similarly, with the striking exception of electoral participation, which the CDP rejected in the 1970s. Also, there was no explicit ethnic or cultural component in the CDP, though there were efforts to initiate a cultural project (Cruz et al. 1986, 40–42).

11 The following issues of *El Satélite* provided information on 1974 events: 6 Jan., 17 Feb., 10 Mar., 12 May, 21 July, 18, 25 Aug., 8 Sept., 13 Oct., 10 Nov. Also, see chronologies in Gutiérrez 1981, 253–55, and Ornelas Esquinca 1983, 122–27.

12 It is useful to think of Juchitán as a rural city, since it includes both an active urban center and a periphery of agricultural land. The economic and social character of Juchitán's elite, when compared to that of elites in the northern Isthmus (part of the state of Veracruz), matches that of the north's rural elite far more closely than that of its urban elite (Münch 1980, 27–29).

13 These proportions are approximate. The data presented in several sources differ slightly, but there are no big discrepancies (Campbell 1990b, 227; Jhabvala 1982, 71, 74, 77; Rueda Jiménez 1976, 151).

14 Interview, summer 1986.

15 From 17 to 24 percent lacking meat, eggs, and fish to 10 to 15 percent lacking those items. From 50 to 25 percent lacking milk (Jhabvala 1982, 107–9).

16 The 1970 data for houses that have water is 61, 44.3, and 34.7 percent in Mexico, the Isthmus, and the state of Oaxaca, respectively, and for electricity, 58.9, 39.6, and 27.4 percent (Jhabvala 1982, 102–3).

17 The regional office of the Ministry of Agriculture (SARH) for the irrigation district has only the most recent listing of landholdings, and sorting out the use of *prestanombres*, the names of family members and friends used to disguise large holdings, would be an enormously complicated and politically sensitive matter. Binford found that average landholdings range from 2 to 10 hectares, with variation between municipalities (1985, 13, cited in Campbell 1990a, 264n 30). According to Campbell, an upper-level official in the Ministry of Agriculture suggested an average of 4.5 hectares per landholder (1990a, 264n 30). Overall, land was less concentrated in Juchitán than elsewhere in Mexico. Binford found that in Juchitán, 20 percent of sugarcane producers controlled 40 percent of the land under cane cultivation, while in Mexico as a whole the comparable figures would be 6 percent controlling 40 percent (1983, 209).

18 COCEI leaders, wealthy priístas, and officials of the Ministry of Agriculture all observed that there are many large landholdings in the region. Binford states that there were holdings ranging from 100 to 500-plus hectares in the vicinity of Juchitán, but offers no numbers (cited in Campbell 1990a, 264n 30). In 1972, Warman found 10 holdings of 50 to 100 hectares and 4 holdings greater than 100 hectares (cited in Campbell 1990a, 265n 34). In 1976, topographers from the Agrarian Affairs Department (DAAC, at that time) characterized 262 landholders as monopolists, meaning that they held more than the legal limit, which was approximately 30 hectares (Binford 1985, 199).

19 This was clear from interviews I carried out during my fieldwork, which include land histories of individual families.

20 In reflecting on the process of organizing against landowners and the government, peasants in Alvaro Obregón have also spoken about the difficulties of the battles for the land, lamenting the sacrifices they were asked to make by COCEI

even as they praised the movement's integrity and success (Campbell 1990b, 311–12). The appearance of this limited questioning of the strategies of the movement's leaders is unusual among accounts of COCEI activities, and it is perhaps significant that this discussion occurred in a town outside of Juchitán. Viewed alongside the seamless evocations of solidarity and consciousness described in the quotes above, it evokes an as yet unspoken and unexamined side (from the perspective of researchers) of Juchitecos' political experiences in the 1970s.

21 All of the quotes in the remainder of this section are from my fieldwork in Juchitán.

22 Leopoldo de Gyves de la Cruz, the son of Leopoldo de Gyves Pineda.

23 This is what Juchiteco elites say as well, when they discuss COCEI's successes.

24 While some peasants I talked with during my fieldwork knew little of the CNC, the National Peasant Confederation, others, such as the peasants in La Venta, where there was ejido land, either knew of the organization or belonged to it. However, contrary to the usual picture of the CNC enforcing support for the PRI, CNC members could support COCEI, and sometimes the local branch of the CNC did so as well.

25 Dario Ruíz Aquino, of the COCEI-affiliated Asociación de Ganaderos Mayoritarios de Juchitán y sus Anexos, presented the history of the Livestock Association conflict in *ES* 4, 11 Mar. 1979. Also see Ornelas Esquinca 1983, 127–28.

26 Whether or not this actually occurred, and to what degree it was controlled by the commission or the municipal government, is not clear. Binford suggests that a number of different ways of claiming land, all independent of the commission, coexisted in the years before the construction of the dam (1985, 184–85).

27 Dario Ruíz Aquino, from COCEI, on the Communal Land Commission conflict, *ES* 25 Mar. 1979. Additional sources on the Land Commission are *ES* 3, 17, 24 Feb., 10, 17 Mar., 15 Sept. 1974, 13, 27 July 1975, 16 July, 6 Aug. 1978; also articles by COCEI leaders on Land Commission elections: Dario Ruíz Aquino, *ES* 18 Feb., 25 Mar. 1979, and Arturo López, *ES* 18 Mar. 1979. Also see Ornelas Esquinca 1983, 114.

28 For coverage of land-related events generally, see Ornelas Esquinca 1983, 130–39, and Gutiérrez 1981. On negotiations with Echeverría, see interview with Hector Sánchez in *ES* 22 Mar. 1977.

29 One hundred thousand hectares were expropriated, including forty thousand hectares of irrigated land belonging to prominent families (Baird and McCaughan 1979, 57).

30 On Gómez Sandoval's openness, see Yescas Martínez 1980 and Zafra 1980.

31 For example, the Tierra y Libertad movement of urban squatters in Monterrey opposed electoral participation in the 1970s and 1980s. So did the Comité de Defensa Popular de Durango (Haber 1993). In the 1980s, the Coordinadora Nacional de Movimientos Urbanos Populares (CONAMUP) left decisions on electoral participation up to its individual member groups, while the national organization clearly favored other forms of political action (Hernández S. 1987).

32 See debates about elections from *El Satélite,* 1979, below. Also see Bennett 1993.

33 This occurred in the elections and subsequent rebellions of 1911 and 1932, the elections of 1934, the 1940s and 1950s challenges on the part of the Front for Democratic Renovation, and the 1968 and 1971 challenges posed by the Juchitán Democratic Front and the PPS.

34 Abel Toledo, in *ES* 5, 12 Dec. 1975; interview with COCEI leader Desiderio de Gyves, Nov. 1983.

35 Election results appeared in *ES* 22 Aug. 1976. The estimate of the size of the electorate comes from Bere Lele, *ES* 28 Dec. 1974.

36 Ornelas Esquinca 1983, 125–27; interview with Desiderio de Gyves, Nov. 1983.

37 Juchitán is divided into eight geographic areas, called *secciones,* or sections. On the formation of the Ayuntamiento and the section committees, see Ornelas Esquinca 1983, 111, and *ES* 4, 18 Dec. 1977, 15 Jan. 1978.

38 The views of the Mexican Communist Party in the 1970s, which parallel those of López Morales, are presented in Carr 1985.

39 Martínez López 1985, 62.

40 Sources on repression include the chronology in Ornelas Esquinca 1983, 103–38, which is drawn from COCEI sources for 1974 to 1977 and from *Punto Crítico* and *Información Sistemática* for 1977 to 1979. Also, *El Satélite* for all those years.

41 Interviews with PRI moderates in Juchitán.

42 Much of the information below on specific meetings comes from an interview with a regional PRI politician conducted in Mexico City in January 1985.

43 See Fox's discussion of the Mexican state and the policy currents within it. Fox argues that "past waves of social mobilization embedded a recurrent reformist presence within the state," and that "reformists' capacity to overcome powerful opposition in both state and society depended on their efforts to reach out to their counterparts in civil society" (1993, 40).

44 According to Campbell, *El Satélite* (21 Dec. 1975) reported meetings in Cancún and in Mexico City with President Echeverría to discuss the land problem (1990b, 311).

6 Leftist Government in the 1980s and 1990s

1 De la Cruz 1984, 23, cited in Campbell 1990b, 356.

2 For analysis of the political reform, an effort to channel the independent grassroots activity of the decade into formal political competition, see Middlebrook 1986. For an argument for leftist participation in electoral competition, see González Casanova 1979.

3 The best discussion of the conflicts within the PRI appears in Martínez López

Notes

1985. For reporting on municipal corruption, see the issues of the local newspaper *El Satélite* throughout 1978 and 1979.

4 Evidence of middle- and upper-class sentiment in favor of allowing COCEI to govern comes from extensive interviewing. Little can be determined about multi-class voting for COCEI from neighborhood-level election results, which were unreliable. In interviews, priístas indicated that in some elections they declined to support the PRI publicly and did not strongly oppose the decision on the part of outside authorities to allow COCEI to govern.

5 It is difficult to determine exactly what proportion of Juchitán's population supported COCEI. COCEI supporters, as well as some members of the business and professional wing of the PRI, asserted that COCEI had a clear majority in the city. Official election results gave COCEI 52, 46, and 44 percent of the votes in the 1981, 1983, and 1986 elections, respectively. Since there was ample evidence of fraud in these elections, and it was in the interest of the officials who controlled the electoral process to minimize COCEI's strength, it seems reasonable to conclude that COCEI did have the support of at least a simple electoral majority. Other indicators of support for COCEI include the large size of its political rallies, in comparison to those of the PRI, and the common expressions of support for COCEI I heard in my fieldwork in Juchitán's poor neighborhoods. From these indicators I concluded that COCEI had a clear majority, which I would place at 60 percent or above.

6 Thorough coverage of these events can be found in the Oaxaca newspaper *Hora Cero*, 1981–82.

7 Interview with Gobernación official, Jan. 1985.

8 COCEI's labor- and land-related mobilizations were generally concerned with securing for Juchitecos material benefits or procedural guarantees to which they were legally entitled. Accounts of the activities of the Ayuntamiento Popular can be found in *Hora Cero*, 1981–83, Ornelas Esquinca 1983, Taller de Investigación Sociológica 1984, and Matloff 1982.

9 I do not have detailed information about these payments. COCEI opponents insisted that they were forced. However, while peasants may have felt that they had no choice but to contribute, I did not hear any complaints about this procedure from contributors themselves. The significance of this silence is unclear, however. While peasants may have seen such practices as entirely reasonable, they may have withheld complaints from an outsider.

10 The PSUM was a direct descendant of the Mexican Communist Party, with which COCEI had first allied.

11 Interviews in Juchitán, 1985.

12 On national right-wing responses to the COCEI government, see Bailón Corres 1985, 11–13. See also COPARMEX 1983. For discussion of the increasing role of business groups in political affairs at this time, see Maxfield and Anzaldúa Montoya 1987.

13 By "middle class" I mean an economic group with no unified political ideology. By "political moderates" I refer to a particular subset of the middle class and elite in Juchitán that favored political and economic reform. I use the term "reformers" interchangeably with "moderates."

14 Interviews in Juchitán, 1985–86. Supporters of the business and professional group within the PRI use the term *preparado* to describe those who they believe are fit to govern.

15 In an apparent repeat of this 1980s effort, President Zedillo unveiled an "Isthmus Megaproject" in July 1996 that would include a railway line, superhighway, and two electricity plants (Mexpaz 1996).

16 The violence, in the course of which two priístas were killed, occurred during the simultaneous final campaign rallies of the PRI and COCEI. It is not clear who initiated the violence, although COCEI was blamed on national television. COCEI claimed that the PRI orchestrated the incident in order to initiate a process of ousting the COCEI government that had already been planned.

17 Interviews in Juchitán, 1985–86.

18 This section is based primarily on my field research in Juchitán and includes information gathered through interviews, participant observation, and newspaper research in 1985 and 1986.

19 COCEI remained the electoral ally of succeeding incarnations of the PSUM, following its merger with other leftist parties in the Mexican Socialist Party (PMS) and the Socialist Party's subsequent joining with the backers of Cuauhtémoc Cárdenas to form the Party of the Democratic Revolution (PRD). During the 1988 presidential campaign, COCEI organized its largest public demonstrations since 1983 in support of Socialist Party candidate Heberto Castillo and then in support of Cárdenas, in whose favor Castillo withdrew from the race. However, COCEI's relations with the PRD have been marked by hostility and discord since COCEI's decision to participate in President Salinas's social-welfare program, PRONOSOL.

20 Official results gave the PRI slightly more than 50 percent in 1980, 48 percent in the subsequent 1981 contest, and 54 percent in 1983.

21 Legally, such proportional representation was the proper outcome; national electoral reform authorized proportional representation in cities with populations of at least three hundred thousand, and this was lowered in Oaxaca to one hundred thousand, with Juchitán included in this category, although census results suggested a somewhat lower population. However, few people expected that proportional representation could or would be implemented in Juchitán.

22 For discussion of concertación on the part of the Durango CDP, see Haber 1993.

23 These observations are based on field research in November 1993.

24 On the difficulties of relationships between the PRD and popular movements, see Bruhn 1994. On the Oaxaca PRD's opposition to COCEI, see Vásquez López 1993.

Notes

25 Interviews with Father Nicolás Bichido and other local priests, 1985.
26 Macario Matus, who was director of the Casa de la Cultura during the 1980s, acted explicitly to maintain this separation, even as he encouraged the Casa's use as a center for COCEI support and activity.
27 The concepts of "spaces" and "islands" of democratization come from Jonathan Fox, in his comments at the conference on rural democratization he organized at MIT (Page and Purnell 1989). These concepts are explored in a variety of ways in the editor's introduction and the other, country-based studies in the book that came out of the conference (Fox 1990a).

7 Ambiguity and Contradiction in COCEI

1 From the poem "Who Are We? What Is Our Name?" by Víctor de la Cruz (Campbell et al. 1993, 117–18).
2 For other examples of the importance of strategic essentialism in grassroots mobilization, see Grueso, Rosero, and Escobar n.d., on the Organization of Black Communities of the Pacific Coast of Colombia, and Warren n.d., on the Pan-Mayan movement. For mobilizations more committed to an antiessentialist politics, see Gomes da Cunha n.d., on black movements in Rio de Janeiro. For a theoretical defense of strategic essentialism and a bibliography on the subject, see Krishna 1993.
3 New-social-movement theorists in the 1980s tended to see the praiseworthy, "new" characteristics as predominant in emerging social movements (Fals Borda 1986; Slater 1985). In contrast, more recent writers have emphasized the coexistence of opposing, "old" and "new" forms (Lancaster 1992; Starn 1992).
4 I should say at the outset that I take up issues of complexity and ambiguity in only some of the many ways they might fruitfully be explored. While focusing on the above-mentioned categories, for example, this chapter will not examine differences and tensions among different groups of poor Juchitecos. Thus, I will make use of broad categories of "ordinary Juchitecos" or "Juchiteca women" that in themselves embody the sort of essentialism of which I am otherwise critical. These overgeneralized categories enable me to identify areas of ambiguity and contradiction, while at the same time suggesting the need to explore differences considerably further.
5 COCEI leaders began to modify this stance in 1986, when they agreed to join the coalition municipal government arranged by Governor Heladio Ramírez.
6 COCEI's cultural focus, in which "actors recognize the stakes in terms of a cultural project," provides a Latin American illustration of the control of historicity that Touraine locates at the center of European social movements (Escobar 1992b, 404; Touraine 1988).
7 These critics acknowledged or ignored, but did not deny, that similar patronage and harassment had generally been practiced by the PRI.

8 Like many other Latin American social movements, COCEI sought "the appropriation of the city by the urban poor not only as an economic but as a cultural space" (Escobar 1992a, 80).

9 There have been recent pressures within COCEI to change this approach and institute democratic procedures for leadership selection and decision making (interviews, 1993). For a broadly similar analysis of the absence of internal democracy in a successful grassroots movement, see Haber's comments on the Comité de Defensa Popular de Durango (1992).

10 The quote is from Libia Grueso, Leyla Arroyo, and Carlos Rosero. Veronica Schild (n.d.) also cautions against defining social-movement goals in terms of citizenship, pointing to the negative effects of neoliberal discourses of citizenship in Chile.

11 One analysis of the regional economy details the process by which state agencies controlled the distribution of credit and water, diverting water from subsistence maize producers to PEMEX oil facilities or to those who grew products promoted by the state, such as sugarcane (Prevôt-Schapira and Rivière D'Arc 1986, 140).

12 Since 1986, and especially since COCEI's participation in concertación social under Salinas, COCEI has also been moving in a direction that might be characterized as demobilizing by Piven and Cloward, that of accepting and depending on elite resources (1977, xxii). While COCEI has negotiated with elites and accepted elite resources throughout its history, the concertación agreements represented unprecedented levels of financial resources, along with unprecedented recognition of and cooperation with the regime. Some of COCEI's critics have praised COCEI for putting aside its militancy, governing impartially for all Juchitecos, and making good, long-term use of newly acquired economic resources. Others fear a weakening of COCEI's oppositional stance.

13 Most commentary on Juchitecas, dating at least from nineteenth-century European travelers, exaggerated their power and erroneously portrayed them as the powerholders in a matriarchal society. Nonetheless, in comparison to women of other indigenous groups, it was the margin of economic, social, and sexual autonomy that Juchitecas indeed possessed that both motivated and enabled them to maintain Zapotec culture and their own position within it.

14 During and after the Ayuntamiento Popular, when COCEI faced military occupation and repression, events in Juchitán were reported, and COCEI was defended, in Mexico's most prestigious intellectual, artistic, and journalistic circles.

8 Culture and Regional Politics in Mexico

1 In selecting these cities and states, I have included locations that exhibit a considerable range of geographic, ethnic, and economic characteristics. Thus, my argument does not rest on exceptional cases.

2 Tutino, Vanderwood, Knight, and Mallon draw on previous work in regional

analysis of the nineteenth century, exemplified by González y González 1972. Wasserman (1984) has made points similar to Vanderwood's for the Porfiriato. In contrast, an earlier generation of scholars had established a tradition of "top-down" and national histories of nineteenth-century Mexican politics and ideology (Reyes Heroles 1988 [1961]; Hale 1968). The works of Inga Clendinnen (1987) and Serge Gruzinski (1993) on the colonial period link issues of culture and representation to the dynamics of colonial domination.

3 See Gruening 1934, 397–98, for a summary of political conflicts and arrangements in the states, and 399–467 for a detailed analysis of each state.

4 See Pansters 1990, 74, for an example of Cárdenas's maneuvering in Puebla.

5 The following discussions of Puebla and Guerrero draw on Pansters 1990 and Bartra 1991, respectively.

6 As Teresa Caldeira (1994) demonstrates in her discussion of debates about the death penalty and human rights for prisoners in Brazil, beliefs about democracy— in the Brazilian case, concerning the protections from violence afforded human bodies—derive as much from the sorts of social issues Pansters identifies in Puebla as from experiences of elections, parties, and government.

7 I question Bartra's conclusion about corporatism during this period in Guerrero, as well as Pansters's claims about its significance in Puebla. Pansters argues that personalism and institutionalism were fused to produce a new form of political organization (1990, 74–75). In so doing, he revises the corporatist analysis, but leaves intact the notion of one predominant political location and form. I believe that more information would make it possible to further modify the corporatist framework and link 1930–1960 events in these states to preceding and subsequent historical processes in a different manner.

8 This discussion of Sonora is drawn primarily from Guadarrama 1977.

9 The historical information on Nayarit, before the formation of the UELC, is covered in Hernández's manuscript, but does not appear in the published version.

10 For broader discussions of Michoacán that support this characterization, see Purnell 1993, on the nineteenth century and the Cristero Rebellion, and Aitken 1994, on the postrevolutionary period.

11 For more examples of the complexity of everyday cultural practices and their relationship to the construction of regional and national hegemonies, see Alonso 1992 and Nugent 1992, on Namiquipa; Aitken 1994, Becker 1994, 1993, and Purnell 1993, on Michoacán; and Campbell 1994, 1990b and Rubin 1991, on Juchitán. For new work of this sort on Mexico generally, see Beezley, Martin, and French 1994, Joseph and Nugent 1994, García Canclini 1989, and Lomnitz-Adler 1992.

Conclusion

1 I refer here to the Zapatistas in Morelos during the Mexican Revolution and the Zapatistas in Chiapas in the 1990s.

Bibliography

Aitken, Rob. 1994. "Political Culture and Local Identities in Michoacán." Paper presented at the conference "Political Culture in Mexico." Utrecht.

Alfaro Sánchez, Carlos Javier. 1984. "El Contexto Económico, Político, y Cultural de los Medios de Comunicación: El Caso de XEAP, Radio Ayuntamiento Popular de Juchitán, Oaxaca." Licenciatura, UNAM, Facultad de Ciencias Polítcas y Sociales.

Almond, Gabriel A., and Sidney Verba. 1963. *The Civic Culture*. Princeton: Princeton UP.

Alonso, Ana María. 1988a. " 'Progress' as Disorder and Dishonor: Discourses of Serrano Resistance." *Critique of Anthropology* 8 (1): 13–33.

——. 1988b. "U.S. Military Intervention, Revolutionary Mobilization, and Popular Ideology in the Chihuahuan Sierra, 1916–17." In *Rural Revolt on Mexico and U.S. Intervention*. Edited by D. Nugent. La Jolla: Center for U.S.-Mexican Studies. 129–228.

——. 1992. "Work and Gusto: Gender and Re-Creation in a North Mexican Pueblo." In *Workers' Expressions*. Edited by J. Calagione, D. Francis, and D. Nugent. Albany: State U of New York P. 164–85.

Altamirano Conde, Guillermo. 1985. *Anecdotas: El Famoso General Charis*. Mexico City: Portada.

Alvarez, Sonia E., Evelina Dagnino, and Arturo Escobar. n.d. "The Cultural and the Political in Latin American Social Movements." Introduction to *Cultures of Politics/Politics of Cultures: Revisioning Latin American Social Movements*. Edited by S. E. Alvarez, E. Dagnino, and A. Escobar. Boulder: Westview.

Amnesty International. 1986. *Mexico: Human Rights in Rural Areas*. London: Amnesty International.

Anderson, Bo, and James D. Cockcroft. 1972 [1966]. "Control and Co-optation in Mexican Politics." In *Dependence and Underdevelopment: Latin America's Political Economy*. Edited by J. D. Cockcroft, A. G. Frank, and D. L. Johnson. Garden City, NY: Anchor. 219–24.

Anonymous. 1983. *Juchitán: ¡Un Pueblo Que Clama Justicia!* Juchitán.

Aziz Nassif, Alberto. 1989. "Regional Dimensions of Democratization." In *Mexico's Alternative Political Futures*. Edited by W. Cornelius, J. Gentleman, and P. Smith. La Jolla: Center for U.S.-Mexican Studies. 87–108.

Bibliography

Bailón Corres, Moisés. 1985. "El Desconocimiento del Ayuntamiento de la COCEI." *Guchachi' Reza* 23.

———. 1987. "Coyote Atrapa a Conejo: Poder Regional y Lucha Popular—El Desconocimiento del Ayuntamiento de Juchitán en 1983." In *Juchitán: Limites de Experiencia Democrática*. Edited by M. J. Bailón Corres and S. Zermeño. Mexico City: Instituto de Investigaciones Sociales, UNAM. 7–64.

Baird, Peter, and Ed McCaughan. 1979. *Beyond the Border: Mexico and the U.S. Today.* New York: NACLA.

Bartra, Armando. 1991. "La Ardua Construcción del Ciudadano: Movimiento Cívido y Lucha Gremial en la Costa Grande de Guerrero." Unpublished manuscript.

Bartra, Roger. 1992. *The Cage of Melancholy.* New Brunswick: Rutgers UP.

Basu, Amrita. 1992. *Two Faces of Protest: Contrasting Modes of Women's Activism in India.* Berkeley: U of California P.

Becker, Marjorie. 1995. *Setting the Virgin on Fire: Lázaro Cárdenas, Michoacán Peasants, and the Redemption of the Mexican Revolution.* Berkeley: U of California P.

———. 1994. "Torching La Purísima, Dancing at the Altar: The Construction of Revolutionary Hegemony in Michoacán, 1934–1940." In *Everyday Forms of State Formation: Revolution and the Negotiation of Rule in Modern Mexico.* Edited by G. M. Joseph and D. Nugent. Durham: Duke UP. 247–64.

Bennett, Tony, et al., ed. 1981. *Culture, Ideology and Social Process.* London: Batsford.

Bennett, Vivienne. 1993. "The Origins of Mexican Urban Popular Movements: Political Thought and Clandestine Political Organizing of the 1960s and 1970s." Unpublished manuscript.

Bennett, Vivienne, and Jeffrey Rubin. 1988. "How Popular Movements Shape the State: Radical Oppositions in Juchitán and Monterrey, Mexico, 1973–1987." Fourteenth International Congress of the Latin American Studies Association. New Orleans.

Berry, Charles R. 1981. *The Reform in Oaxaca, 1856–76: A Microhistory of the Liberal Revolution.* Lincoln: U of Nebraska P.

Beezley, William H., Cheryl E. Martin, and William E. French. 1994. *Rituals of Rule, Rituals of Resistance: Public Celebrations and Popular Culture in Mexico.* Wilmington: Scholarly Resources.

Bichido, Nicolás. 1983. "La Iglesia Social." *El Buscón* 1 (6): 68–73.

Binford, Leigh. 1983. "Agricultural Crises, State Intervention, and the Development of Classes in the Isthmus of Tehuantepec, Oaxaca, Mexico." Ph.D. diss., U of Connecticut.

———. 1985. "Political Conflict and Land Tenure in the Mexican Isthmus of Tehuantepec." *Journal of Latin American Studies* 17: 179–200.

Bizberg, Ilan. 1982. *La acción obrera en Las Truchas.* Mexico City: El Colegio de México.

Booth, John. 1985. *The End and the Beginning.* Boulder: Westview.

Bourdieu, Pierre. 1977. *Outline of a Theory of Practice.* Cambridge: Cambridge UP.

Bourdieu, Pierre, and Loic J. D. Wacquant. 1992. *An Invitation to Reflexive Sociology.* Chicago: U of Chicago P.

Brasseur, Charles. 1981 [1861]. *Viaje por el Istmo de Tehuantepec, 1859–1860.* Mexico City: Fondo de Cultura Económica.

Bruhn, Kate. 1994. "The Seven Year Itch: Neoliberal Politics, Popular Movements, and the Left in Mexico." Eighteenth International Congress of the Latin American Studies Association. Atlanta.

Burdick, John. 1992. "Rethinking the Study of Social Movements: The Case of Christian Base Communities in Urban Brazil." In *The Making of Social Movements in Latin America: Identity, Strategy, and Democracy.* Edited by A. Escobar and S. E. Alvarez. Boulder: Westview. 171–84.

Burguete, Araceli. 1985. Interview. Jan.

Caldeira, Teresa. 1994. "Violence, the Unbounded Body, and the Disregard for Rights: Limits of Democratization in Brazilian Society." Paper presented at the Eighteenth International Congress of the Latin American Studies Association, Atlanta.

Calderón, Fernando, Alejandro Piscitelli, and José Luis Reyna. 1992. "Social Movements: Actors, Theories, Expectations." In *The Making of Social Movements in Latin America: Identity, Strategy, and Democracy.* Edited by A. Escobar and S. E. Alvarez. Boulder: Westview. 19–36.

Campbell, Howard. 1989. "The COCEI: Culture, Class, and Politicized Ethnicity in the Isthmus of Tehuantepec." *Ethnic Studies Report* 7 (2).

——. 1990a. "Juchitán: The Politics of Cultural Revivalism in an Isthmus Zapotec Community." *Latin American Anthropology Review* 2 (1).

——. 1990b. "Zapotec Ethnic Politics and the Politics of Culture in Juchitán, Oaxaca (1350–1990)." Ph.D. diss., U of Wisconsin, Madison.

——. 1994. *Zapotec Renaissance: Ethnic Politics and Cultural Revivalism in Southern Mexico.* Albuquerque: U of New Mexico P.

Campbell, Howard, et al., eds. 1993. *Zapotec Struggles: Histories, Politics, and Representations from Juchitán, Oaxaca.* Washington, D.C.: Smithsonian Inst.

Campbell, Howard, and Susanne Green. 1993. "A History of Representations of Isthmus Zapotec Women." Thirteenth International Congress of Anthropological and Ethnological Sciences. Mexico City.

Canel, Eduardo. 1992. "Democratization and the Decline of Urban Social Movements in Uruguay: A Political-Institutional Account." In *The Making of Social Movements in Latin America: Identity, Strategy, and Democracy.* Edited by A. Escobar and S. E. Alvarez. Boulder: Westview. 276–90.

Cardoso, Ruth Correa Leite. 1992. "Popular Movements in the Context of the Consolidation of Democracy in Brazil." In *The Making of Social Movements in Latin America: Identity, Strategy, and Democracy.* Edited by A. Escobar and S. E. Alvarez. Boulder: Westview. 291–302.

Carr, Barry. 1985. "Mexican Communism 1968–81: Eurocommunism in the Americas?" *Journal of Latin American Studies* 17: 201–88.

Bibliography

Carr, Barry, and Ricardo Anzaldúa Montoya, eds. 1986. *The Mexican Left, the Popular Movements, and the Politics of Austerity.* Monograph Series, vol. 18. La Jolla: Center for U.S.-Mexican Studies.

Centeno, Miguel. 1994. *Democracy within Reason: Technocratic Revolution in Mexico.* University Park: Pennsylvania State UP.

Chalmers, Douglas. 1977. "The Politicized State in Latin America." In *Authoritarianism and Corporatism in Latin America.* Edited by J. M. Malloy. Pittsburgh: U of Pittsburgh P. 23–45.

Charis, Heliodoro. 1982 [1920]. "Plan de San Vicente." *Guchachi' Reza* 11, 34–35.

Chatterjee, Partha. 1993. *The Nation and Its Fragments: Colonial and Postcolonial Histories.* Princeton: Princeton UP.

Chernick, Marc W., and Michael F. Jiménez. 1993. "Popular Liberalism, Radical Democracy, and Marxism: Leftist Politics in Contemporary Colombia, 1974–1991." In *The Latin American Left: From the Fall of Allende to Perestroika.* Edited by B. Carr and S. Ellner. Boulder: Westview. 61–81.

Chiñas, Beverly López. 1983. *The Isthmus Zapotecs: Women's Roles in Cultural Context.* Prospect Heights, Ill. Waveland.

Clendinnen, Inga. 1987. *Ambivalent Conquests: Maya and Spaniard in Yucatan, 1517–1570.* Cambridge: Cambridge UP.

Cline, Howard F. 1963. *Mexico: Revolution to Evolution: 1940–1960.* New York: Oxford UP.

COCEI. 1983. "La Tenencia de la Tierra y el Movimiento Campesino en el Istmo de Tehuantepec." Paper presented at the Primer congreso Sobre Problemas Agrarios, in Chilpancingo, Guerrero, 1982. In *COCEI: alternativa de organización y lucha para los pueblos del istmo.* Edited by COCEI. Juchitán: COCEI. 2–7.

Cockcroft, James D. 1983. *Mexico: Class Formation, Capital Accumulation, and the State.* New York: Monthly Review Press.

Collier, David. 1979. *The New Authoritarianism in Latin America.* Princeton: Princeton UP.

Collier, Ruth Berins. 1982. "Popular Sector Incorporation and Political Supremacy: Regime Evolution in Brazil and Mexico." In *Brazil and Mexico: Patterns in Late Development.* Edited by S. A. Hewlett and R. S. Weinert. Inter-American Politics Series, vol. 3. Philadelphia: Institute for the Study of Human Issues. 57–109.

Collier, Ruth Berins, and David Collier. 1979. "Inducements versus Constraints: Disaggregating 'Corporatism.'" *American Political Science Review* 73: 967–86.

——. 1991. *Shaping the Political Arena.* Princeton: Princeton UP.

Comaroff, Jean. 1985. *Body of Power, Spirit of Resistance: The Culture and History of a South African People.* Chicago: U of Chicago P.

Comaroff, John L. 1987. "Of Totemism and Ethnicity: Consciousness, Practice, and the Signs of Inequality." *Ethnos* 52: 301–23.

Contreras, Oscar F., and Vivienne Bennett. 1994. "National Solidarity in the Northern Borderlands: Social Participation and Community Leadership." In

Transforming State-Society Relations in Mexico: The National Solidarity Strategy. Edited by W. A. Cornelius, A. L. Craig, and J. Fox. La Jolla: Center for U.S.-Mexican Studies. 281–305.

Cook, Maria Lorena. 1990. "Organizing Opposition in the Teachers' Movement in Oaxaca." In *Popular Movements and Political Change in Mexico.* Edited by J. Foweraker and A. Craig. Boulder: Rienner. 199–212.

COPARMEX. 1983. "Juchitán, Algo Mas que una Presidencia Municipal." *Hechos de la Semana* 36 (2–8 Aug.).

Cornelius, Wayne A. 1973. "Nation Building, Participation, and Distribution: The Politics of Social Reform under Cárdenas." In *Crisis, Choice, and Change: Historical Studies of Political Development.* Edited by G. A. Almond, S. C. Flanagan, and R. J. Mundt. Boston: Little. 392–498.

———. 1975. *Politics and the Migrant Poor in Mexico City.* Stanford: Stanford UP.

———. 1995. "Designing Social Policy for Mexico's Liberalized Economy: From Social Services and Infrastructure to Job Creation." In *The Challenge of Institutional Reform in Mexico.* Edited by R. Roett. Boulder: Rienner. 139–54.

Cornelius, Wayne A., Ann L. Craig, and Jonathan Fox, eds. 1994. *Transforming State-Society Relations in Mexico: The National Solidarity Strategy.* La Jolla: Center for U.S.-Mexican Studies.

Cornelius, Wayne A., Judith Gentleman, and Peter H. Smith, eds. 1989. *Mexico's Alternative Political Futures.* Monograph Series, vol. 30. La Jolla: Center for U.S.-Mexican Studies.

Corona, Rodolfo. 1979. *Cuantificación del Nivel de la Mortalidad en Oaxaca, 1970.* Oaxaca: Centro de Sociología de la UABJO.

Covarrubias, Miguel. 1986 [1946]. *Mexico South: The Isthmus of Tehuantepec.* London: KPI.

Cruz, Marcos, et al. 1986. *Llego la Hora de Ser Gobierno: Durango, Testimonios de la lucha del Comité de Defensa Popular, General Francisco Villa.* Mexico City: Equipo Pueblo.

Cruz, Oscar. 1991. "Juchitán: La Lucha por un Ayuntamiento Popular." In *Municipio y Democracia: Participación de las Organizaciones de la Sociedad Civil en la Política Municipal.* Edited by D. Paas et al. Mexico City: Fundación Friedrich Naumann.

Cumberland, Charles. 1968. *Mexico: The Struggle for Modernity.* London: Oxford UP.

Dagnino, Evelina. n.d. "Culture and Politics: Changing Approaches in the Left." In *Cultures of Politics/Politics of Cultures: Revisioning Latin American Social Movements.* Edited by S. E. Alvarez, E. Dagnino, and A. Escobar. Boulder: Westview.

Davis, Diane E. 1989. "Divided over Democracy: The Embeddedness of State and Class Conflicts in Contemporary Mexico." *Politics and Society* 17 (3): 247–79.

———. 1992. "Mexico's New Politics: Changing Perspectives on Free Trade." *World Policy Journal* 9 (4): 655–71.

de Certeau, Michel. 1984. *The Practice of Everyday Life.* Berkeley: U of California P.

de la Cruz, Víctor. 1983a. *La Flor de La Palabra.* Mexico City: Premiá.

———. 1983b. *La Rebelión de Che Gorio Melendre.* Juchitán: H. Ayuntamiento Popular de Juchitán.

———. 1983c. "Rebeliones Indígenas en el Istmo de Tehuantepec." *Cuadernos Políticos* 38: 55–71.

———. 1984. "Hermanos o ciudadanos: dos lenguas, dos proyectos políticos en el Istmo." *Guchachi' Reza* 21: 18–24.

———. 1989. *Relatos sobre el General Charis.* Mexico City: Dirección General de Culturas Populares.

———. 1992. "El General Charis y la educación." *Cuadernos del Sur* 1 (1): 61–70.

———. 1993. "Social Scientists Confronted with Juchitán: Incidents of an Unequal Relationship." In *Zapotec Struggles: Histories, Politics, and Representations from Juchitán, Oaxaca.* Edited by H. Campbell et al. Washington, D.C.: Smithsonian Inst. 143–46.

del Conde, Octavio, and José Piedra. n.d. "Problematica del Distrito de Riego No. 19." Tehuantepec, Oaxaca (manuscript).

Drake, Paul, and Eduardo Silva. 1986. *Elections and Democratization in Latin America, 1980–1985.* La Jolla: Center for Iberian and Latin American Studies.

Dresser, Denise. 1991. *Neopopulist Solutions to Neoliberal Problems.* Center for U.S.-Mexican Studies, La Jolla. Current Issue Brief.

Eckstein, Susan. 1977a. *The Poverty of Revolution: The State and the Urban Poor in Mexico.* Princeton: Princeton UP.

———. 1977b. "The State and the Urban Poor." In *Authoritarianism in Mexico.* Edited by J. L. Reyna and R. S. Weinert. Inter-American Politics Series, vol. 2. Philadelphia: Institute for the Study of Human Issues. 23–46.

Erickson, Kenneth P. 1977. *The Brazilian Corporative State and Working Class Politics.* Berkeley: U of California P.

Escobar, Arturo. 1992a. "Culture, Economics, and Politics in Latin American Social Movements Theory and Research." In *The Making of Social Movements in Latin America: Identity, Strategy, and Democracy.* Edited by A. Escobar and S. E. Alvarez. Boulder: Westview. 62–85.

———. 1992b. "Culture, Practice, and Politics: Anthropology and the Study of Social Movements." *Critique of Anthropology* 12 (4): 395–432.

———. 1995. *Encountering Development: The Making and Unmaking of the Third World.* Princeton: Princeton UP.

Escobar, Arturo, and Sonia E. Alvarez, eds. 1992a. *The Making of Social Movements in Latin America: Identity, Strategy, and Democracy.* Boulder: Westview.

———. 1992b. "Theory and Protest in Latin America Today." Introduction to *The Making of Social Movements in Latin America: Identity, Strategy, and Democracy.* Edited by A. Escobar and S. E. Alvarez. Boulder: Westview. 1–15.

Escuela Secundaria Federal, Juchitán Oaxaca. 1978. *Homenaje al General Heliodoro Charis Castro.* Juchitán.

Esteva, Gustavo. 1983. *The Battle for Rural Mexico.* South Hadley, Mass.: Bergin.

Fagen, Richard R., and William S. Tuohy. 1972. *Politics and Privilege in a Mexican City.* Stanford: Stanford UP.

Fals Borda, Orlando. 1986. "El Nuevo Despertar de los Movimientos Sociales." *Revista Foro* 1: 76–83.

Fauvergue, Sylvie. 1982. "Cambios en el Istmo de Tehuantepec: El Ejemplo de Salina Cruz." In *Impactos Regionales de la Polítical Petrolera en México.* Edited by L. Allub and M. A. Michel. Mexico City: CIIS.

Fiske, John. 1990. "Ethnosemiotics: Some Personal and Theoretical Reflections." *Cultural Studies* 4 (1): 85–99.

Foucault, Michel. 1979 [1975]. *Discipline and Punish: The Birth of the Prison.* New York: Vintage.

——. 1990 [1976]. *The History of Sexuality, Volume I.* New York: Vintage.

Foweraker, Joe. 1990. "Popular Movements and Political Change in Mexico." In *Popular Movements and Political Change in Mexico.* Edited by J. Foweraker and A. L. Craig. Boulder: Rienner. 3–20.

——. 1993. *Popular Mobilization in Mexico: The Teachers' Movement, 1977–87.* Cambridge: Cambridge UP.

Foweraker, Joe, and Ann L. Craig, eds. 1990. *Popular Movements and Political Change in Mexico.* Boulder: Rienner.

Fox, Jonathan. 1990a. Personal conversation.

——, ed. 1990b. *The Challenge of Rural Democratisation: Perspectives from Latin America and the Philippines.* London: Cass.

——. 1990c. Editor's introduction. In *The Challenge of Rural Democratisation: Perspectives from Latin America and the Philippines.* Edited by J. Fox. London: Cass. 1–18.

——. 1992. "Democratic Rural Development: Leadership Accountability in Regional Peasant Organizations." *Development and Change* 23 (2): 1–36.

——. 1993. *The Politics of Food in Mexico: State Power and Social Mobilization.* Ithaca: Cornell UP.

——. 1994a. "The Difficult Transition from Clientelism to Citizenship: Lessons from Mexico." *World Politics* 46 (2): 151–84.

——. 1994b. "Targeting the Poorest: The Role of the National Indigenous Institute in Mexico's Solidarity Program." In *Transforming State-Society Relations in Mexico: The National Solidarity Strategy.* Edited by W. A. Cornelius, A. L. Craig, and J. Fox. La Jolla: Center for U.S.-Mexican Studies. 179–216.

Fox, Jonathan, and Gustavo Gordillo. 1989. "Between State and Market: The Prospects for Autonomous Grassroots Development in Rural Mexico." In *Mexico's Alternative Political Futures.* Edited by W. A. Cornelius, J. Gentleman, and P. H. Smith. La Jolla: Center for U.S.-Mexican Studies. 131–72.

Fox, Jonathan, and Julio Moguel. 1993. "Pluralism and Anti-Poverty Policy: Mexico's National Solidarity Program and Left Opposition Municipalities." In *Opposition Government in Mexico: Past Experiences and Future Opportunities.* Edited by V. Rodríguez and P. Ward. Albuquerque: U of New Mexico P. 189–204.

Bibliography

Friedrich, Paul. 1986. *The Princes of Naranja*. Princeton: Princeton UP.

Fuentes Valdivieso, Javier. 1985. "Primer Informe Anual, 3 Febrero, 1985." *Pulso* 1–9 Feb.

García Canclini, Néstor. 1988. "Culture and Power: The State of Research." *Media, Culture, and Society* 10: 467–97.

———. 1989. *Cultural híbridas: Estrategias para entrar y salir de la modernidad*. Mexico City: Grijalbo.

Gomes da Cunha, Olívia Maria. n.d. "Depois de Festa: movimentos negros, culturas e 'políticas de identidade.'" In *Cultures of Politics/Politics of Cultures: Revisioning Latin American Social Movements*. Edited by S. E. Alvarez, E. Dagnino, and A. Escobar. Boulder: Westview.

Gómez Tagle, Silvia. 1980. *Insurgencia y democracia en los sindicatos electricistas*. Mexico City: El Colegio de México.

González Casanova, Pablo. 1970 [1965]. *Democracy in Mexico*. Oxford: Oxford UP.

———. 1979. "The Political Reform in Mexico." *LARU Studies* 3 (1): 27–42.

González Obregón, Luis. 1907. *Las Sublevaciones de Indios en el Siglo XVII*. Mexico City: Museo Nacional.

González y González, Luis. 1972. *Pueblo en Vilo: Microhistoria de San José de Gracia*. Mexico City: El Colegio de México.

Gould, Jeffrey. 1990. *To Lead as Equals: Rural Protest and Political Consciousness in Chinandega, Nicaragua, 1912–1979*. Chapel Hill: U of North Carolina P.

Gramsci, Antonio. 1971. *Selections from the Prison Notebooks*. New York: International.

Grindle, Merilee. 1977. *Bureaucrats, Politicians, and Peasants in Mexico*. Berkeley: U of California P.

———. 1986. *State and Countryside*. Baltimore: Johns Hopkins UP.

Gruening, Ernest. 1934. *Mexico and Its Heritage*. New York: Appleton.

Grueso, Libia, Carlos Rosero, and Arturo Escobar. n.d. "El Proceso Organizativo de Comunidades Negras En el Pacífico Sur Colombiano." In *Cultures of Politics/Politics of Cultures: Revisioning Latin American Social Movements*. Edited by S. E. Alvarez, E. Dagnino, and A. Escobar. Boulder: Westview.

Gruzinski, Serge. 1993. *The Conquest of Mexico*. Cambridge: Polity.

Guadarrama, Rocío. 1987. "Elections in Sonora." In *Electoral Patterns and Perspectives in Mexico*. Edited by A. Alvarado. La Jolla: Center for U.S.-Mexican Studies. 43–80.

Guadarrama S., Graciela. 1987. "Entrepreneurs and Politics: Businessmen in Electoral Contests in Sonora and Nuevo León, July, 1985." In *Electoral Patterns and Perspectives in Mexico*. Edited by A. Alvarado. La Jolla: Center for U.S.-Mexican Studies. 81–110.

Guha, Ranajit. 1988. *An Indian Historiography of India: A Nineteenth-Century Agenda and Its Implications*. Calcutta: Bagchi.

Gurrión, Adolfo. 1937. "La Mujer en la Historia de Juchitán." *Neza* 3 (1).

Gutiérrez, Roberto J. "Juchitán, Municipio Comunista." A: Análysis Histórico y Sociedad Mexicana 2 (4): 251–80.

Haber, Paul. 1993. "Cárdenas, Salinas, and the Urban Popular Movement." In Mexico: Dilemmas of Transition. Edited by N. Harvey. London: British Academic Press. 218–48.

——. 1994. "Political Change in Durango: The Role of National Solidarity." In Transforming State-Society Relations in Mexico: The National Solidarity Strategy. Edited by W. A. Cornelius, A. L. Craig, and J. Fox. La Jolla: Center for U.S.-Mexican Studies. 217–32.

——. 1992. "Collective Dissent in Mexico: The Politics of Contemporary Urban Popular Movements." Ph.D. diss., Columbia U.

Hale, Charles. 1968. Mexican Liberalism in the Age of Mora, 1821–1853. New Haven: Yale UP.

Hall, Stuart. 1988. "New Ethnicities." In Black Film, British Cinema. Edited by K. Mercer. BFI/ICA Documents 7. 27–31.

——. 1993. "Culture, Community, Nation." Cultural Studies 7 (3): 349–63.

Hamilton, Nora. 1982. The Limits of State Autonomy. Princeton: Princeton UP.

Hansen, Roger. 1971. The Politics of Mexican Development. Baltimore: Johns Hopkins UP.

Hart, John Mason. 1987. Revolutionary Mexico: The Coming and Process of the Mexican Revolution. Berkeley: U of California P.

Harvey, David. 1993. "From Space to Place and Back Again: Reflections on the Condition of Postmodernity." In Mapping the Futures: Local Cultures, Global Change. Edited by J. Bird et al. London: Routledge. 3–29.

Harvey, Neil. 1990. "Peasant Strategies and Corporatism in Chiapas." In Popular Movements and Political Change in Mexico. Edited by J. Foweraker and A. L. Craig. Boulder: Rienner. 183–98.

——. 1994. Rebellion in Chiapas. Center for U.S.-Mexican Studies, La Jolla. Transformation of Rural Mexico series.

Heclo, High. 1974. Modern Social Politics in Britain and Sweden. New Haven: Yale UP.

Hellman, Judith Adler. 1983 [1978]. Mexico in Crisis. New York: Holmes.

Henderson, Peter V. N. 1981. Félix Díaz, the Porfirians, and the Mexican Revolution. Lincoln: U of Nebraska P.

——. 1983. "Un Gobernador Maderista: Benito Juárez Maza y la Revolución en Oaxaca." Guchachi' Reza 16: 3–9.

Henestrosa, Andrés. 1993 [1929]. "The Foundation of Juchitán." In Zapotec Struggles: Histories, Politics, and Representations from Juchitán, Oaxaca. Edited by H. Campbell et al. Washington, D.C.: Smithsonian Inst. 39–40.

Henestrosa de Webster, Cibeles. 1985. Juchitán: Un Pueblo Singular. Mexico City: Alcaraván.

Hernández Chavez, Alicia. 1979. La Mecánica Cardenista. Mexico City: El Colegio de México.

Bibliography

Hernández, Luis. 1990. "Autonomía y Liderazgo en una Organización Campesina Regional." *Cuadernos Desarrollo de Base* 1.

——. 1994. "The Chiapas Uprising." Center for U.S.-Mexican Studies, La Jolla. Transformation of Rural Mexico series.

Hernández López, Odilón. 1972. "José F. Gomez: Interview with His Daughters." *El Satélite* 12 Nov.

Hernández S., Ricardo. 1987. *La Coordinadora Nacional de Movimiento Urbano Popular: CONAMUP, Su historia 1980–1986.* Mexico City: Equipo Pueblo.

Hirschman, Albert O. 1973. *Journeys toward Progress.* New York: Norton.

Huntington, Samuel. 1968. *Political Order in Changing Societies.* New Haven: Yale UP.

Instituto Nacional de Estadística, Geografía e Informática (INEGI). 1984. *X Censo General de Población y Vivienda, 1980.* Mexico City: INEGI.

Iturbide, Graciela, and Elena Poniatowska. 1989. *Juchitán de las Mujeres.* Mexico City: Toledo.

Jhabvala, Firdaus. 1982. *Plan Integral del Istmo de Tehuantepec, Documento Central.* Oaxaca: Gobierno del Estado de Oaxaca, Instituto Tecnológico de Oaxaca, Centro de Graduados e Investigación.

Joseph, Gilbert M., and Daniel Nugent, eds. 1994. *Everyday Forms of State Formation: Revolution and the Negotiation of Rule in Modern Mexico.* Durham: Duke UP.

Juárez, Benito. 1993 [1850]. "The Juchitecos As Seen by Benito Juárez." In *Zapotec Struggles: Histories, Politics, and Representations from Juchitán, Oaxaca.* Edited by H. Campbell et al. Washington, D.C.: Smithsonian Inst. 123–24.

Karl, Terry. 1986. "Mexico, Venezuela, and the Contadora Initiative." In *Confronting Revolution.* Edited by M. J. Blachman, W. M. Leogrande, and K. Sharpe. New York: Pantheon. 273–77.

——. 1990. "Dilemmas of Democratization in Latin America." *Comparative Politics* 23 (Oct.): 1–21.

Knight, Alan. 1986. *The Mexican Revolution, Volume 1: Porfirians, Liberals, and Peasants.* Lincoln: U of Nebraska P.

Krishna, Sankaran. 1993. "The Importance of Being Ironic: A Postcolonial View on Critical International Relations Theory." *Alternatives* 18: 385–417.

Laclau, Ernesto, and Chantal Mouffe. 1985. *Hegemony and Socialist Strategy: Towards a Radical Democratic Politics.* London: Verso.

Lancaster, Roger. 1988. *Thanks to God and the Revolution: Popular Religion and Class Consciousness in the New Nicaragua.* New York: Columbia UP.

——. 1992. *Life Is Hard: Machismo, Danger, and the Intimacy of Power in Nicaragua.* Berkeley: U of California P.

Linz, Juan. 1970. "An Authoritarian Regime: Spain." In *Mass Politics.* Edited by E. Allardt and S. Rokkan. New York: Free. 251–83.

Lomnitz-Adler, Claudio. 1991. "Concepts for the Study of Regional Culture." *American Ethnologist* 18 (2): 195–215.

——. 1992. *Exits from the Labyrinth: Culture and Ideology in the Mexican National Space.* Berkeley: U of California P.

López Gurrión, Ricardo. 1982. *Efemérides Istmeñas.* Mexico City.

López Marín, Galindo. 1985. *Vida y Hazaña del General de División Heliodoro Charis Castro.* Mexico City.

López Mateos, Manuel. 1993. "When Radio Became the Voice of the People." In *Zapotec Struggles: Histories, Politics, and Representations from Juchitán, Oaxaca.* Edited by H. Campbell et al. Washington, D.C.: Smithsonian Inst. 259–62.

López Monjardin, Adriana. 1983a. "COCEI: ¿Una Etnia Redefinida?" Mesa redonda sobre la cuestión étnica. Juchitán.

——. 1983b. "Juchitán, las historias de la discordia." *Cuadernos Políticos* 38: 72–80.

——. 1986a. Personal conversation.

——. 1986b. "Oaxaca: Una Historia y 20 Años de Lucha Popular." *Punto Crítico* 150.

López Morales, Alberto. 1981. "El PCM Ante el Primer Informe del Ayuntamiento Popular de Juchitán." *Hora Cero* 23 Aug. 1981.

López Nelio, Daniel. 1983. "Los Difíciles Pasos de la Autonomía Municipal: Una Conversación con el Padre Nicolás Bichido." *El Buscón* 1 (6): 74–79.

——. 1993. "Interview with Daniel López Nelio." In *Zapotec Struggles: Histories, Politics, and Representations from Juchitán, Oaxaca.* Edited by H. Campbell et al. Washington, D.C.: Smithsonian Inst. 233–35.

López Nelio, Ruperto. n.d.-a. "Sobre Gui' xhi' ro' y Charis." Recorded and translated from the Zapotec by Macario Matus. *Guchachi' Reza* 7.

——. n.d.-b. "Sobre Valentín Carrasco y Roque Robles." *Guchachi' Reza* 6: 7–12.

López Rui Marín, Máxima Eraclia, and Toribio Salinas. 1980. *Dos Testimonios Sobre la Revolución de 1911.* Translated by Macario Matus. Juchitán: Ediciones del Patronato de la Casa de la Cultura del Istmo.

Lustig, Nora. 1992. *Mexico: The Remaking of an Economy.* Washington, D.C.: Brookings Inst.

Mallon, Florencia. 1995. *Peasant and Nation: The Making of Postcolonial Mexico and Peru.* Princeton: Princeton UP.

Malloy, James M., ed. 1977a. *Authoritarianism and Corporatism in Latin America.* Pittsburgh: U of Pittsburgh P.

——. 1977b. "Authoritarianism and Corporatism in Latin America: The Modal Pattern." In *Authoritarianism and Corporatism in Latin America.* Edited by J. M. Malloy. Pittsburgh: U of Pittsburgh P. 3–19.

Manso de Contreras, Cristobal. 1987, 1661. *La Rebelión de Tehuantepec.* Juchitán: H. Ayuntamiento Popular de Juchitán, Oaxaca.

Márquez, Enrique. 1987. "Political Anachronisms: The Navista Movement and Political Processes in San Luis Potosí, 1958–1985." In *Electoral Patterns and Perspectives in Mexico.* Edited by A. Alvarado. La Jolla: Center for U.S.-Mexican Studies. 111–25.

Bibliography

Martínez, Anastasia. 1985. "Recuerdos de Anastasia Martinez." Compiled and translated by Macario Matus. *Guchachi' Reza* 23: 19–21.

Martínez López, Felipe. 1985. *El Crepusculo del Poder: Juchitán, Oaxaca 1980–1982.* Oaxaca: UABJO: IIS.

Matloff, Judith. 1982. "Mexico's Juchitán: A Popular Challenge to the PRI." *NACLA* 16 (6): 41–43.

Maxfield, Sylvia. 1990. *Governing Capital: International Finance and Mexican Politics.* Ithaca: Cornell UP.

Maxfield, Sylvia, and Ricardo Anzaldúa Montoya, eds. 1987. *Government and Private Sector in Contemporary Mexico.* La Jolla: Center for U.S.-Mexican Studies.

Melucci, Alberto. 1988a. "Getting Involved: Identity and Mobilization in Social Movements." In *International Social Movement Research: From Structure to Action—Comparing Social Movements Research across Cultures.* Vol. 1, edited by H. Kriesi, S. Tarrow, and B. Klandermans. London: JAL. 329–48.

——. 1988b. "Social Movements and the Democratization of Everyday Life." In *Civil Society and the State: New European Perspectives.* Edited by J. Deane. London: Verso. 245–61.

Mexpaz. 1996. "Heartbeat of Mexico." 1 Aug.

Middlebrook, Kevin. 1986. "Political Liberalization in an Authoritarian Regime: The Case of Mexico." In *Transitions from Authoritarian Rule: Latin America.* Edited by G. O'Donnell, P. Schmitter, and L. Whitehead. Baltimore: Johns Hopkins UP. 123–47.

Migdal, Joel S. 1988. *Strong Societies and Weak States.* Princeton: Princeton UP.

Münch, Guido. 1980. "Aspectos del Istmo de Tehuantepec." In *El Sur de México, Datos Sobre la Problematica Indígena.* Serie Antropológica, vol. 29. Edited by G. Münch et al. Mexico City: Instituto de Investigaciones Antropológicas, UNAM.

Munck, Gerardo. 1990. "Identity and Ambiguity in Democratic Struggles." In *Popular Movements and Political Change in Mexico.* Edited by J. Foweraker and A. L. Craig. Boulder: Rienner. 23–42.

Nash, June. 1979. *We Eat the Mines and the Mines Eat Us.* New York: Columbia UP.

Needler, Martin. 1971. *Politics and Society in Mexico.* Albuquerque: U of New Mexico P.

Nugent, Daniel. 1989. "Are We Not [Civilized] Men? The Formation and De-volution of Community in Northern Mexico." *Journal of Historical Sociology* (Sept.): 206–39.

——. 1992. "Popular Musical Culture in Rural Chichuahua: Accommodation or Resistance?" In *Workers' Expressions: Beyond Accommodation and Resistance.* Edited by J. Calagione, D. Francis, and D. Nugent. Albany: State U of New York P. 29–47.

——. 1994. *Spent Cartridges of Revolution.* Chicago: U of Chicago P.

Nuñez Ríos, Herón. 1969. *Apuntes Biográficos de José F. Gómez y Gregorio Melendre.* Mexico City.

O'Donnell, Guillermo. 1977. "Corporatism and the Question of the State." In *Authoritarianism and Corporatism in Latin America*. Edited by J. M. Malloy. Pittsburgh: U of Pittsburgh P. 47–97.

——. 1988. "Challenges to Democratization in Brazil." *World Policy Journal* 5 (2).

O'Donnell, Guillermo, and Philippe Schmitter. 1986. *Tentative Conclusions about Uncertain Democracies*. Baltimore: Johns Hopkins UP.

O'Donnell, Guillermo, Philippe Schmitter, and Laurence Whitehead, eds. 1986. *Transitions from Authoritarian Rule: Latin America*. Baltimore: Johns Hopkins UP.

Ong, Aiwa. 1987. *Spirits of Resistance and Capitalist Discipline: Factory Women in Malaysia*. Albany: State U of New York P.

Ornelas Esquinca, Marco Antonio. 1983. "Juchitán, Ayuntamiento Popular." Licenciatura (B.A. thesis), Instituto Tecnológico Autónomo de México.

Ortiz Wadgymer, Arturo. 1971. *Aspectos de la Economía del Istmo de Tehuantepec*. Mexico City: UNAM.

Ortner, Sherry B. 1989. *High Religion: A Cultural and Political History of Sherpa Buddhism*. Princeton: Princeton UP.

Padgett, Vincent. 1976 [1966]. *The Mexican Political System*. Boston: Houghton.

Page, Stephen, and Jenny Purnell. 1989. "CIS Workshop Summary Report: The Challenge of Rural Democratization in Developing Countries." MIT Center for International Studies, Cambridge. Working paper.

Pansters, Wil. 1990. *Politics and Power in Puebla*. CEDLA Latin America Studies, vol. 57. Amsterdam: CEDLA.

Pérez Güemas, Efraín, and Alma Rosa Garza del Toro. 1984. "El Movimiento de Posesionarios en Monterrey, 1970–1983." Seminario Sobre Movimientos Sociales en Mexico, Región Noreste. Monterrey, Mexico.

Piven, Frances Fox, and Richard Cloward. 1977. *Poor People's Movements: Why They Succeed, How They Fail*. New York: Vintage.

"Plan de San Vicente." 1920. *Mercurio* 29 May: 2.

Pratt, Mary Louise. 1994. "La heterogeneidad y el pánico de la teoría." *Revista de Crítica Literaria Latinoamericana*.

——. 1996. Paper presented at conference, Cultures of Politics/Politics of Cultures: Revisioning Latin American Social Movements. Saõ Paolo.

Pred, Allan, and Michael John Watts. 1992. *Reworking Modernity: Capitalisms and Symbolic Discontent*. New Brunswick: Rutgers UP.

Prevôt-Schapira, Marie-France, and Hélène Rivière D'Arc. 1983. *Les Investissements Publics et la Région: l'Isthme d'Oaxaca*. CREDAL. Documents de Recherche.

——. 1984. "Los Zapotecos, el PRI, y la COCEI, Enfrentamientos Alrededor de las Intervenciones del Estado en el Istmo de Tehuantepec." *Guchachi' Reza* 19: 11–26.

——. 1986. "Poder y Contrapoder en el Istmo de Tehuantepec." In *Poder Local, Poder Regional*. Edited by J. Pádua N. and A. Vaneph. Mexico City: El Colegio de México. 137–43.

Punto Crítico. 1977. No. 83 (15 Nov.).

Purcell, Susan Kaufman. 1973. "Decision-Making in an Authoritarian Regime: Theoretical Implications from a Mexican Case Study." *World Politics* 26 (1): 28–54.

Purnell, Jenny. 1993. "The Politics of Identity: The Cristeros and Agraristas of Revolutionary Michoacán." Ph.D. diss., MIT.

Quijano, Aníbal. 1988. *Modernidad, Identidad y Utopia en América Latina.* Lima: Sociedad y Política.

Ramírez Saiz, Juan Manuel. 1990. "Urban Struggles and Their Political Consequences." In *Popular Movements and Political Change in Mexico.* Edited by J. Foweraker and A. L. Craig. Boulder: Rienner. 234–46.

Rappaport, Joanne. 1994. *Cumbe Reborn: An Andean Ethnography of History.* Chicago: U of Chicago P.

Reding, Andrew. 1988. "The Crumbling of the Perfect Dictatorship." *World Policy Journal* 7 (2).

———. 1994. "Chiapas Is Mexico: The Imperative of Political Reform." *World Policy Journal* 11 (1): 11–25.

Reina Aoyama, Leticia. 1992. "Las Dos Caras de la Modernidad." *Guchachi' Reza* 34: 20–28.

———. 1993. "Los Pueblos Indios del Istmo de Tehuantepec. Readecuación Económica y Mercado Regional." In *Indio, Nación y Comunidad en el México del Siglo XIX.* Edited by A. Escobar O. Mexico City: Centro de Estudios Mexicanos y Centroamericanos. 137–51.

Reyes Heroles, Jesus. 1988 [1961]. *El liberalismo mexicano.* Mexico City: Fundo de Cultura Económica.

Reyna, José Luis. 1977. "Redefining the Authoritarian Regime." In *Authoritarianism in Mexico.* Edited by J. L. Reyna and R. S. Weinert. Inter-American Politics Series, vol. 2. Philadelphia: Institute for the Study of Human Issues. 155–71.

Reyna, José Luis, and Richard S. Weinert, eds. 1977. *Authoritarianism in Mexico.* Inter-American Politics Series, vol. 2. Philadelphia: Institute for the Study of Human Issues.

Rivera Cabrera, Crisóforo, and José F. Gómez. n.d.-a. "Del Diario de los Debates del Congreso Constituyente de 1917." *Guchachi' Reza* 5: 13–17.

———. n.d.-b. "Del Diario de los Debates del Congreso Constituyente de 1917." *Guchachi' Reza* 6: 3–6.

Rivera Cusicanqui, Silvia. 1987. *Oppressed but Not Defeated.* Geneva: UNRISD.

———. 1990. "Liberal Democracy and Ayllu Democracy in Bolivia: The Case of Northern Potosí." In *The Challenge of Rural Democratisation: Perspectives from Latin America and the Philippines.* Edited by J. Fox. London: Cass. 97–121.

Rojas, Basilio. 1962. *Efemerides Oaxaqueñas 1911.* Mexico City.

Roldán, Mary. 1992. "Genesis and Evolution of La Violencia in Antioquia, Colombia (1900–1953)." Ph.D. diss., Harvard U.

Rosaldo, Renato. 1989. *Culture and Truth: The Remaking of Social Analysis.* Boston: Beacon.

Roxborough, Ian. 1984. *Unions and Politics in Mexico: The Case of the Automobile Industry.* Cambridge: Cambridge UP.

Royce, Anya Peterson. 1975. *Prestigio y Afiliación en una Comunidad Urbana: Juchitán, Oaxaca.* Mexico City: Instituto Nacional Indigenista.

Rubin, Jeffrey W. 1991. "Rethinking Post-Revolutionary Mexico: Regional History, Cultural Identity, and Radical Politics in Juchitán, Mexico." Ph.D. diss., Harvard U.

———. 1994. "Indigenous Autonomy and Power in Chiapas: Lessons from Mobilization in Juchitán." Center for U.S.-Mexican Studies, La Jolla. Transformation of Rural Mexico series.

———. 1996. "Decentering the Regime: Culture and Regional Politics in Mexico." *Latin American Research Review* 31 (3): 85–126.

Rueda Jiménez, María Magdalena. 1976. "Estudio Geográfico Económico del Municipio de Juchitán, Oaxaca." Tesis Profesional, Facultad de Filosofía y Letras, Colegio de Geografía, UNAM.

Ruiz Campbell, Obdulia. 1993. "Representations of Isthmus Women: A Zapotec Woman's Point of View." In *Zapotec Struggles: Histories, Politics, and Representations from Juchitán, Oaxaca.* Edited by H. Campbell et al. Washington, D.C.: Smithsonian Inst. 137–42.

Rus, Jan. 1994. "The 'Comunidad Revolucionaria Institucional': The Subversion of Native Government in Highland Chiapas, 1936–1968." In *Everyday Forms of State Formation: Revolution and the Negotiation of Rule in Modern Mexico.* Edited by G. M. Joseph and D. Nugent. Durham: Duke UP. 265–300.

Sanderson, Steven E. 1981. *Agrarian Populism and the Mexican State: The Struggle for Land in Sonora.* Berkeley: U of California P.

SARH. n.d. *General Plan of Irrigation District #19.* Tehuantepec: SARH (Ministry of Agriculture).

Santibañez Orozco, Porfirio. 1980. "Oaxaca: La Crisis de 1977." In *Sociedad y Política en Oaxaca 1980: 15 estudios de caso.* Edited by R. Benitez Zenteno. Oaxaca: Instituto de Investigacciones Sociológicas. 309–29.

Schild, Veronica. n.d. "New Subjects of Rights? Women's Movements and the Construction of Citizenship in the 'New Democracies.'" In *Cultures of Politics/Politics of Cultures: Revisioning Latin American Social Movements.* Edited by S. E. Alvarez, E. Dagnino, and A. Escobar. Boulder: Westview.

Schirmer, Jennifer. 1988. "Rule of Law or Law of Rule? Guatemalan Military Attitudes toward Law, National Security, and Human Rights." Unpublished manuscript.

Schmitter, Philippe. 1974. "Still the Century of Corporatism?" In *The New Corporatism.* Edited by F. B. Pike and T. Stritch. Notre Dame: U of Notre Dame P. 85–131.

Schmitter, Philippe, and Terry Karl. 1993. "What Democracy Is . . . and Is Not." In *The Global Resurgence of Democracy.* Edited by L. Diamond and M. Plattner. Baltimore: Johns Hopkins UP.

Scott, James C. 1990. *Domination and the Arts of Resistance.* New Haven: Yale UP.

Semo, Enrique. 1986. "The Mexican Left and the Economic Crisis." In *The Mexican Left, the Popular Movements, and the Politics of Austerity*. Edited by B. Carr and R. Anzaldúa Montoya. La Jolla: Center for U.S.-Mexican Studies. 19–32.

Slater, David, ed. 1985. *New Social Movements and the State in Latin America*. Amsterdam: CEDLA.

Smith, Gavin. 1989. *Livelihood and Resistance*. Berkeley: U of California P.

Sokoloff, Shoshana. 1993. "The Proud Midwives of Juchitán." In *Zapotec Struggles: Histories, Politics, and Representations from Juchitán, Oaxaca*. Edited by H. Campbell et al. Washington, D.C.: Smithsonian Inst. 267–77.

Starn, Orin. 1992. "'I Dreamed of Foxes and Hawks': Reflections on Peasant Protest, New Social Movements, and the Rondas." In *The Making of Social Movements in Latin America: Identity, Strategy, and Democracy*. Edited by A. Escobar and S. E. Alvarez. Boulder: Westview. 89–111.

Stepan, Alfred. 1978. *The State and Society: Peru in Comparative Perspective*. Princeton: Princeton UP.

Stephen, Lynn. 1990a. Personal conversation. Jan.

——. 1990b. "The Politics of Ritual: The Mexican State and Zapotec Autonomy, 1926–1989." In *Class, Politics, and Popular Religion in Mexico and Central America*. Edited by L. Stephen and J. Dow. Washington, D.C.: American Anthropological Assn. 43–60.

——. 1991. *Zapotec Women*. Austin: U of Texas P.

Taller de Investigación Sociológica, UNAM. 1984. "Juchitán: El Fin de la Ilusión." In *Oaxaca Una Lucha Reciente: 1960–83*. Edited by R. Bustamante V. Mexico City: Nueva Sociología. 306–451.

Thompson, E. P. 1966. *The Making of the English Working Class*. New York: Vintage.

Touraine, Alain. 1988. *Return of the Actor: Social Theory in Postindustrial Society*. Minneapolis: U of Minnesota P.

Tsing, Anna Lowenhaupt. 1993. *In the Realm of the Diamond Queen: Marginality in an Out-of-the-Way Place*. Princeton: Princeton UP.

Tutino, John. 1980. "Rebelión Indígena en Tehuantepec." *Cuadernos Políticos* 24: 89–101.

——. 1986. *From Insurrection to Revolution: Social Bases of Agrarian Violence, 1750–1940*. Princeton: Princeton UP.

——. 1993. "Ethnic Resistance: Juchitán in Mexican History." In *Zapotec Struggles: Histories, Politics, and Representations from Juchitán, Oaxaca*. Edited by H. Campbell et al. Washington, D.C.: Smithsonian Inst. 41–62.

Vanderwood, Paul. 1981. *Disorder and Progress: Bandits, Police, and Mexican Development*. Lincoln: U of Nebraska P.

Van Young, Eric. 1992. "Are Regions Good to Think?" Introduction to *Mexico's Regions: Comparative History and Development*. Edited by E. Van Young. La Jolla: Center for U.S.-Mexican Studies. 1–36.

Vázquez López, Eloí. 1993. *Por Un Nuevo Pacto de Fundación del PRD en Oaxaca*. Oaxaca: PRD.

Von Tempsky, G. F. 1993 [1858]. "A German Traveler's Observations in Juchitán." In *Zapotec Struggles: Histories, Politics, and Representations from Juchitán, Oaxaca*. Edited by H. Campbell et al. Washington, D.C.: Smithsonian Inst. 119–22.

Warman, Arturo. 1972. *Los Campesinos, Hijos Predilectos del Régimen*. Mexico City: Editorial Nuestro Tempo.

Warren, Kay. n.d. "Indigenous Movements As a Challenge to a Unified Social Movement Paradigm for Guatemala." In *Cultures of Politics/Politics of Cultures: Revisioning Latin American Social Movements*. Edited by S. E. Alvarez, E. Dagnino, and A. Escobar. Boulder: Westview.

Wasserman, Mark. 1984. *Capitalists, Caciques, and Revolution*. Chapel Hill: U of North Carolina P.

Waterhouse, Isabelle. 1983. "Co-optation and Control: The Case of the Mexican Communist Party." M. Phil. thesis, Oxford U.

White, Stephen K. 1991. *Political Theory and Postmodernism*. Cambridge: Cambridge UP.

Whitehead, Laurence. 1981. "On 'Governability' in Mexico." *Bulletin of Latin American Research* 1 (1).

Wiarda, Howard J. 1974. "Corporatism and Development in the Iberic-Latin World: Persistent Strains and New Variations." In *The New Corporatism: Social Political Structures in the Iberian World*. Edited by Frederick B. Pike and Thomas Stritch. Notre Dame: U of Notre Dame P.

Wickham-Crowley, Timothy P. 1989. "Winners, Losers, and Also-Rans: Toward a Comparative Sociology of Latin American Guerrilla Movements." In *Power and Popular Protest*. Edited by S. Eckstein. Berkeley: U of California P. 132–81.

Williams, Raymond. 1977. *Marxism and Literature*. Oxford: Oxford UP.

Winn, Peter. 1986. *Weavers of Revolution: The Yarur Workers and Chile's Road to Socialism*. Oxford: Oxford UP.

Womack, John, Jr. 1968. *Zapata and the Mexican Revolution*. New York: Random.

Yescas Martínez, Isidoro. 1980. "La Coalición Obrero-Campesino-Estudiantil de Oaxaca: 1972–1974." In *Sociedad y Política en Oaxaca 1980*. Edited by R. Benítez Zenteno. Oaxaca: Instituto de Investigaciones Sociológicos. 289–308.

Zafra, Gloria. 1980. "Problemática Agraria en Oaxaca: 1971–75." In *Sociedad y Política en Oaxaca 1980*. Edited by R. Benítez Zenteno. Oaxaca: Instituto de Investigaciones Sociológicas. 331–49.

Zermeño, Sergio. 1978. *México: una democracia utópica, el movimiento estudiantil del 68*. Mexico City: Siglo XXI.

——. 1987. "Juchitán, la Cólera del Régimen." In *Juchitan: Límites de una Experiencia Democrática*. Edited by M. J. Bailón Corres and S. Zermeño. Mexico City: Instituto de Investigaciones Sociales, UNAM. 65–97.

Index

Index

Jeffrey W. Rubin is a Member in the School of Social Science at the Institute for Advanced Study in Princeton, New Jersey.